Evolutionary Computation and Optimization Algorithms in Software Engineering:
Applications and Techniques

Monica Chiş
Siemens IT Solutions and Services PSE, Romania

INFORMATION SCIENCE REFERENCE

Hershey · New York

Director of Editorial Content:	Kristin Klinger
Director of Book Publications:	Julia Mosemann
Acquisitions Editor:	Lindsay Johnston
Development Editor:	Joel Gamon
Publishing Assistant:	Deanna Zombro
Typesetter:	Michael Brehm
Production Editor:	Jamie Snavely
Cover Design:	Lisa Tosheff
Printed at:	Yurchak Printing Inc.

Published in the United States of America by
Information Science Reference (an imprint of IGI Global)
701 E. Chocolate Avenue
Hershey PA 17033
Tel: 717-533-8845
Fax: 717-533-8661
E-mail: cust@igi-global.com
Web site: http://www.igi-global.com/reference

Library of Congress Cataloging-in-Publication Data

Evolutionary computation and optimization algorithms in software engineering : applications and techniques / Monica Chis, editor.
       p. cm.
  Includes bibliographical references and index.
  Summary: "This book presents applications of evolutionary computation in the software enginnering field, including how evolutionary algorithms are used to solve different search and optimization problems in the area of software engineering"--Provided by publisher.
  ISBN 978-1-61520-809-8 (hardcover) -- ISBN 978-1-61520-810-4 (ebook) 1. Software engineering. 2. Evolutionary computation. 3. Genetic algorithms.
I. Chis, Monica, 1972-
  QA76.758.E984 2010
  005.1--dc22
                          2009047892

British Cataloguing in Publication Data
A Cataloguing in Publication record for this book is available from the British Library.

All work contributed to this book is new, previously-unpublished material. The views expressed in this book are those of the authors, but not necessarily of the publisher.

Table of Contents

Detailed Table of Contents

Chapter 1

Monica Chiş, Siemens IT Solutions and Services PSE, Romania

This chapter aims to present a part of the computer science literature in which the evolutionary computation techniques are used to solve different search and optimization problems in the area of software engineering.

Chapter 2

Filomena Ferrucci, University of Salerno, Italy
Carmine Gravino, University of Salerno, Italy
Rocco Oliveto, University of Salerno, Italy
Federica Sarro, University of Salerno, Italy

Software development effort estimation is a critical activity for the competitiveness of a software company; it is crucial for planning and monitoring project development and for delivering the product on time and within budget. In the last years, some attempts have been made to apply search-based approaches to estimate software development effort. In particular, some genetic algorithms have been defined and some empirical studies have been performed with the aim of assessing the effectiveness of the proposed approaches for estimating software development effort. The results reported in those studies seem to be promising. The objective of this chapter is to present a state of the art in the field by reporting on the most significant empirical studies undertaken so far. Furthermore, some suggestions for future research directions are also provided.

Chapter 3

The evaluation of software reliability depends on a) The definition of an adequate measure of correctness and b) A practical tool that allows such measurement. Once the proper metric has been defined it is needed to estimate whether a given software system reaches its optimum value or how far away this software is from it. Typically, the choice of a given metric is limited by the ability to optimize it: mathematical considerations traditionally curtail such choice. However, modern optimization techniques (such as Genetic Algorithms [GAs]) do not exhibit the limitations of classical methods and, therefore, do not limit such choice. In this work we describe GAs, the typical limitations for measurement of software reliability (MSR) and the way GAs may help to overcome them.

Chapter 4

One of the biggest challenges for the developer of object-oriented software is the modeling and developing of the objects themselves, so that they are easily reusable in complex systems. The final quality of the software depends mostly on the quality of the modeling developed for it. Modeling and specification of software are fundamental steps for making the software development an activity of engineering. Design is the activity in which software behavior and structure are elaborated. During this phase many models are developed anticipating several views of the final product and making software evaluation possible even before the software is implemented. Consequently, the synthesis of a software model can be seen as a problem of optimization, where the attempt to find a better configuration among the elements chosen through the object-oriented paradigm, such as classes, methods and attributes that meet quality design criteria. This work studies a possibility to synthesize higher quality modelings through the evolution of Genetic Algorithms, a technique that has proved to be efficient in dealing with problems involving large search spaces. The work was divided in three main stages: a study of object-oriented software engineering; the definition of a model using genetic algorithms; and co-evolution of species for the synthesis of object-oriented software modeling, aiming at quality improvement; and at the implementation of a model for case study. The study of object-oriented software engineering involved the establishment of software development phases and the characterization of the representation used in modeling phase and, in particular, the characterization of class diagrams based on UML. The study also investigated software quality metrics such as Reutilization, Flexibility, Understandability, Functionality, Extensibility and Effectiveness. The specification of genetic algorithm consisted in the definition of the structure of the chromosome that could provide a good representation of modeling diagram and a function of evaluation of the design that could take the software quality metrics in to consideration. As a result, the chromosomes represent metadata of a simplified UML diagram of classes, which may later be used as an entry of a CASE (Computer Aided Software Engineering) Tool that can create the implementation code in the chosen pattern. The evaluation function was defined focusing at the synthesis of a higher quality object-oriented software modeling. In order to observe the use of more than one objective at the same time the Pareto technique for multi objective problems was used. The construction of a co-evolutionary model consisted in defining distinct species so that each one would represent part of the problem to be evolved, thus enabling a more efficient representation of the model. The co-evolutionary model allowed the evolution of more complex structures, which would not be possible in a simple Genetic Algorithm. The chromosomes related to each species codify metadata and that is why the solution assembly (design) makes use of a decoder. A case study was done to synthesize the modeling of an elevator controller. The results achieved in this section were compared to the modelings produced by specialists, and the characteristics of these results were analyzed. The GA performance in the optimization process was compared to that of a random search and, in every case, the results achieved by the model were always better.

Chapter 5

Cagatay Catal, Information Technologies Institute, Turkey
Soumya Banerjee, Birla Institute of Technology, International Center, Mauritius

Artificial Immune Systems, a biologically inspired computing paradigm such as Artificial Neural Networks, Genetic Algorithms, and Swarm Intelligence, embody the principles and advantages of vertebrate immune systems. It has been applied to solve several complex problems in different areas such as data mining, computer security, robotics, aircraft control, scheduling, optimization, and pattern recognition. There is an increasing interest in the use of this paradigm and they are widely used in conjunction with other methods such as Artificial Neural Networks, Swarm Intelligence and Fuzzy Logic. In this chapter, we demonstrate the procedure for applying this paradigm and bio-inspired algorithm for developing software fault prediction models. The fault prediction unit is to identify the modules, which are likely to contain the faults at the next release in a large software system. Software metrics and fault data belonging to a previous software version are used to build the model. Fault-prone modules of the next release are predicted by using this model and current software metrics. From machine learning perspective, this type of modeling approach is called supervised learning. A sample fault dataset is used to show the elaborated approach of working of Artificial Immune Recognition Systems (AIRS).

Chapter 6

Wasif Afzal, Blekinge Institute of Technology, Sweden
Richard Torkar, Blekinge Institute of Technology, Sweden
Robert Feldt, Blekinge Institute of Technology, Sweden
Tony Gorschek, Blekinge Institute of Technology, Sweden

Software fault prediction can play an important role in ensuring software quality through efficient resource allocation. This could, in turn, reduce the potentially high consequential costs due to faults. Predicting faults might be even more important with the emergence of short-timed and multiple software releases aimed at quick delivery of functionality. Previous research in software fault prediction has indicated that there is a need i) to improve the validity of results by having comparisons among number of data sets from a variety of software, ii) to use appropriate model evaluation measures and iii) to use statistical testing procedures. Moreover, cross-release prediction of faults has not yet achieved sufficient attention in the literature. In an attempt to address these concerns, this paper compares the quantitative and qualitative attributes of 7 traditional and machine-learning techniques for modeling the cross-release prediction of fault count data. The comparison is done using extensive data sets gathered from a total of 7 multi-release open-source and industrial software projects. These software projects together have several years of development and are from diverse application areas, ranging from a web browser to robotic controller software. Our quantitative analysis suggests that genetic programming (GP) tends to have better consistency in terms of goodness of fit and accuracy across majority of data sets. It also has comparatively less model bias. Qualitatively, ease of configuration and complexity are less strong points for GP even though it shows generality and gives transparent models. Artificial neural networks did not perform as well as expected while linear regression gave average predictions in terms of goodness of fit and accuracy. Support vector machine regression and traditional software reliability growth models performed below average on most of the quantitative evaluation criteria while remained on average for most of the qualitative measures.

Chapter 7

    Hakima Mellah, Research Centre in Scientific and Technical Information - CERIST, Algeria
    Soumya Banerjee, Birla Institute of Technology, International Center, Mauritius
    Salima Hassas, University of Lyon, France
    Habiba Drias, USTHB, Algeria

The chapter presents a Multi Agent System (MAS) approach, for service discovery process to consider the user in the service discovery process involving his interactions under constraints. The service discovery has become an emerging phenomenon in software engineering and process engineering as well. The proposed MAS have demonstrated significant self organizing potential. This feature is very crucial for assuring a correct service delivery, to avoid failures or mal-function for the service discovery environment. The requirements for self organizing choreographed services have been well realized, in case of operational, functional and behavioral faults. Self organization within the MAS is adopted by the recourse to a self organizing protocol conceived from bacteria colony and evolutionary computation paradigm.

Chapter 8

    Pandian Vasant, University Technology Petronas, Malaysia

Many engineering, science, information technology and management optimization problems can be considered as non linear programming real world problems where the all or some of the parameters and variables involved are uncertain in nature. These can only be quantified using intelligent computational techniques such as evolutionary computation and fuzzy logic. The main objective of this research chapter is to solve non linear fuzzy optimization problem where the technological coefficient in the constraints involved are fuzzy numbers which was represented by logistic membership functions by using hybrid evolutionary optimization approach. To explore the applicability of the present study a numerical example is considered to determine the production planning for the decision variables and profit of the company.

Software testing is a key part of software development life cycle. Due to time, cost and other circumstances, exhaustive testing is not feasible, that's why there is need to automate the testing process. Generation of the automated and effective test suit is a very difficult task in the software testing process. Effective test suite can decrease the overall cost of testing as well as increase the probability of finding defects in software systems. Testing effectiveness can be achieved by the State Transition Testing which is commonly used in, real time, embedded and web-based kind of software system. State transition testing focuses upon the testing of transitions from one state of an object to other states. The tester's main job is to test all the possible transitions in the system. This chapter proposed an Ant Colony Optimization technique for automated and fully coverage state-transitions in the system. Through proposed algorithm all the transitions are easily traversed at least once in the test-sequence.

Chapter 10

Testing is a difficult and costly activity in the development of object-oriented programs. The challenge is to come up with a sufficient set of test scenarios, out of the typically huge volume of possible test cases, to demonstrate correct behavior and acceptable quality of the software. This can be reformulated as a search problem to be solved by sophisticated heuristic search techniques such as evolutionary algorithms. The goal is to find an optimal set of test cases to achieve a given test coverage criterion. This chapter introduces and evaluates genetic programming as a heuristic search algorithm which is suitable to evolve object-oriented test programs automatically to achieve high coverage of a class. It outlines why the object paradigm is different to the procedural paradigm with respect to testing, and why a genetic programming approach might be better suited than the genetic algorithms typically used for testing procedural code. The evaluation of our implementation of a genetic programming approach, augmented with program analysis techniques for better performance, indicates that object-oriented software testing with genetic programming is feasible in principle. However, having many adjustable parameters, evolutionary search heuristics have to be fined-tuned to the optimization problem at hand for optimal performance, and, therefore, represent a difficult optimization problem in their own right.

Chapter 11

Software Quality Assurance consists of monitoring the software engineering processes and ensuring the highest quality. But, the software quality attributes that we deal with are not explicit in the outset and cannot be easily measured. The same attribute has multiple significance and importance in multiple contexts. The user, the developer and the manager of a software product may have different stands regarding the significance of a quality attribute. A software quality engineer, while measuring the total software quality should provide appropriate weight to each of the decision makers. This chapter proposes a fuzzy multi-criteria approach to measure the total software quality and to identify the best alternative from a set of software products.

Chapter 12

The chapter describes the validation of the attributes of linked list using modified pheromone biased model (of Ant colony) under complex application environment mainly for kernel configuration and device driver operations. The proposed approach incorporates the idea of pheromone exploration strategy with small learning parameter associated while traversing a linked list. This process of local propagation on loop and learning on traversal is not available with the conventional validation mechanism of data structure using predicate logic. It has also been observed from simulation that the proposed ant colony algorithm with different pheromone value produces better convergence on linked list.

Foreword

The importance of using evolutionary computation and optimization algorithms in software engineering domain is evident by the great number of books and papers dedicated to this subject. Executing any software project requires skills in two key dimensions— engineering and project management. While engineering deals with issues of architecture, design, coding, testing etc., project management deals with planning, monitoring, risk management etc. Consequently, this book - Evolutionary Computation and Optimization Algorithms in Software Engineering: Applications and Techniques - focus on these two dimensions, and has presented some new evolutionary techniques in these directions.

The present book is one which presented some interesting idea of applying evolutionary techniques in software engineering domain.

From my point of view, the book can be useful for those who study software engineering because they can optimize the existing information and processing and both for people which work on the evolutionary computation and optimization field because they can discover new directions for their research.

The 12 chapters of the book have been written by a number of researcher and practitioners in software engineering and evolutionary computation and optimization from all over the word.

The book starts with a short introduction in some applications of evolutionary and bio-inspired techniques in the software engineering. This step was important because have been tried to identify the key points of this subject and to point the importance of the subject. The readers can start using this book as preliminary information in order to study more other subjects. This step is essential because it the contact with the general subject. Another very important chapter is the usage of evolutionary approaches in the software development effort estimation. A very interesting a state of the art in the field by reporting on the most significant empirical studies is presented in the first chapter. Another interesting topic discussed in this book is the application of Genetic Algorithms to the evaluation of software reliability. It is very interesting the way in which Genetic Algorithms are used for optimization.

One of the biggest provocations for the developer of object-oriented software is modeling and developing of the objects themselves, so that they are easily reusable in complex systems. The final quality of the software depends mostly on the quality of the modeling developed for it. Modeling and specification of software are fundamental steps for making the software development an activity of engineering. Design is the activity in which software behavior and structure are elaborated. During this phase many models are developed anticipating several views of the final product and making software evaluation possible even before the software is implemented. The work studies a possibility to synthesize higher quality modeling through the evolution of Genetic Algorithms, a technique that has proved to be efficient in dealing with problems involving large search spaces. The study of object-oriented software engineering involved the establishment of software development phases and the characterization of the representation used in modeling phase and, in particular, the characterization of class diagrams based on UML. The study also investigated software quality metrics such as Reutilization, Flexibility, Understandability, Functionality, Extensibility and Effectiveness.

Fault prediction is one of the key important issues in software development. The idea of applying Artificial Immune Systems Paradigm for Developing Software Fault Prediction Models it is another very important topic of the book.

In this context the idea of using Genetic Programming (GP) for cross-release fault count predictions in large and complex software projects presented in this book is very useful for application in software development.

Software fault prediction can play an important role in ensuring software quality through efficient resource allocation. This could, in turn, reduce the potentially high consequential costs due to faults. Predicting faults might be even more important with the emergence of short-timed and multiple software releases aimed at quick delivery of functionality. Previous research in software fault prediction has indicated that there is a need: i) to improve the validity of results by having comparisons among number of data sets from a variety of software; ii) to use appropriate model evaluation measures and iii) to use statistical testing procedures. Moreover, cross-release prediction of faults has not yet achieved sufficient attention in the literature. In an attempt to address these concerns, this paper compares the quantitative and qualitative attributes of 7 traditional and machine-learning techniques for modeling the cross-release prediction of fault count data. The comparison is done using extensive data sets gathered from a total of 7 multi-release open-source and industrial software projects. These software projects together have several years of development and are from diverse application areas, ranging from a web browser to robotic controller software. Our quantitative analysis suggests that Genetic Programming tends to have better consistency in terms of goodness of fit and accuracy across majority of data sets. It also has comparatively less model bias. Qualitatively, ease of configuration and complexity are fewer strong points for GP even though it shows generality and gives transparent models. Artificial Neural Networks did not perform as well as expected while linear regression gave average predictions in terms of goodness of fit and accuracy. Support Vector Machine regression and traditional software reliability growth models performed below average on most of the quantitative evaluation criteria while remained on average for most of the qualitative measures.

An interesting topic presented in this book was Multi Agent System (MAS) approach, for service discovery process to consider the user in the service discovery process involving his interactions under constraints. Self organization within the MAS is adopted by the recourse to a self organizing protocol conceived from bacteria colony and evolutionary computation paradigm.

Another interesting chapter refers to innovative hybrid genetic algorithms and line search method for industrial production management which can be very useful in software engineering.

Software testing is a key part of software development life cycle. The book contains a chapter on Ant Colony Optimization technique for automated and fully coverage state-transitions in the system is presented. This is a very useful theme for the practitioners and researchers.

Testing is a difficult and costly activity in the development of object-oriented programs. Very useful chapters in which has been evaluated genetic programming as a heuristic search algorithm which is suitable to evolve object-oriented test programs automatically to achieve high coverage of a class have been included in the present book.

Software Quality Assurance consists of monitoring the software engineering processes and ensuring the highest quality. A fuzzy multi-criteria approach to measure the total software quality and to identify the best alternative from a set of software products have been presented in the book. This is a very interesting topic for companies which work for software quality assurance. The fact that there are new techniques which can be applied is very useful.

The book does not cover the entire topic in the software engineering. Parts of some interesting subject are presented together and can be useful for the topics selected for presentation in the university curricula. Also it can be useful for the people involved in software engineering in the companies because can offer another interesting approaches for software development.

It is clear that this book is valuable and useful to all practitioners and researchers working on different fields in software engineering, evolutionary computation or optimization. Therefore it is recommended to anyone who has interest in new techniques in software engineering. It is hoped that others will follow the example and the topics presented in this book and present more studies in this field.

Consider that the book can be useful.

Crina Groşan
Babeş Bolyai University Cluj-Napoca
Romania

Crina Groşan *received her MS degree in Mathematics and PhD degree in Computer Science from Babes-Bolyai University, ClujNapoca, Romania in 2005. She is a Lecturer of Artificial Intelligence at Babes-Bolyai University. Her research focuses on different global optimization techniques and applications. She has been researching such topics as multiobjective optimization, global optimization, operations research, numerical analysis, computational intelligence and swarm intelligence. She has published over 100 research articles in peer reviewed international journals, book chapters and conference proceedings. She is co-author of two books on programming languages and is also a co-editor of four volumes titled Stigmergic Optimization, Swarm Intelligence in Data Mining, Hybrid Evolutionary Algorithms and Engineering Evolutionary Intelligent Systems, published by Springer Verlag, Germany. She guest edited a special issue on Soft Computing for Modeling and Simulation for the International Journal of Simulation Systems, Science & Technology, published by the UK Simulation Society. She is the managing editor of International Journal of Computational Intelligence Research and also serves the editorial board of few other Journals. She co-founded the Evolutionary Multiobjective Optimization: Design and Applications (EMODA) International workshop series in 2005.*

Preface

The idea of this book was conceived a long time ago when I started to research activities in the field of software engineering and I tried to apply evolutionary computation techniques. In that moment, I realized that there is a lot of research in this field and it would be better to put together some research in this field. Of course it is impossible to keep in a single book all the topics in this field.

The book "Evolutionary Computation and Optimization Algorithms in Software Engineering: Applications and Techniques" is a collection of techniques and applications which try to solve software engineering problems by using evolutionary computation and optimization techniques.

THE MOTIVATION OF SOFTWARE ENGINEERING AND EVOLUTIONARY COMPUTATION

According to the Software Engineering Body of Knowledge (SWEBOK), Software engineering is the application of a systematic, disciplined, quantifiable approach to the development, operation, and maintenance of software, and the study of these approaches. Software engineering means the application of engineering to software. Software Engineering is related to the disciplines of computer science, project management and systems engineering. It is considered to be a subfield of Computer science. The building of a software system is usually considered a project and the management of it borrows many principles from the field of Project management. A lot of problems from complexity of large systems knowledge are applied to many software engineering problems.

Evolutionary Computation (EC) is the general term for several computational techniques which are based to some degree on the evolution of biological life in the natural world. Evolutionary Computation methods have been successfully extended to solve multi-objective optimization tasks. Several evolutionary computational models have been developed, including evolutionary algorithms, genetic algorithms, the evolution strategy, evolutionary programming.

The importance of using evolutionary computation and optimization algorithms in software engineering domain is evident by the great number of books and paper dedicated to this subject. Executing any software project requires skills in two key dimensions— engineering and project management. While engineering deals with issues of architecture, design, coding, testing etc., project management deals with planning, monitoring, risk management etc. Consequently, this book focuses on these two dimensions, and has presented some new evolutionary techniques in these directions.

The present book is one which presents some interesting ideas for applying evolutionary techniques in some problems from software engineering.

For my point of view can be useful for those who study software engineering because they can optimize the existing information and processing and both for people which work on the evolutionary computation and optimization field because they can discover new directions form their research.

A GUIDED TOUR OF THE CHAPTERS

The book is composed of 11 chapters, plus an introduction chapter which is a short survey of some research activities in the field of the application of evolutionary computation in software engineering. The chapters are authored by different groups of researchers and practitioners in software engineering and evolutionary computation and optimization from all over the word.

The book starts with a short introduction in some application of evolutionary and bio-inspired techniques in the software engineering. The introduction chapter has the role to identify the key points of this subject and to point the importance of the subject. The readers can start use this as a preliminary information in order to study more about the applications of evolutionary computation and optimization techniques into the software engineering problems.

In Chapter 1, **Introduction: A Survey of the Evolutionary Computation Techniques for Software Engineering**, *Monica Chiş* aims to present a part of the computer science literature in which the evolutionary computation techniques are used to solve different search and optimization problems in the area of software engineering.

Software development effort estimation is a critical activity for the competitiveness of a software company. Effort estimation is one of the most important parts of the project development for planning and monitoring project development and for delivering the product on time and within budget. In Chapter 2, **Using Evolutionary Based Approaches to Estimate Software Development Effort**, *Filomena Ferrucci, Carmine Gravino, Rocco Oliveto, Federica Sarrohave* present a state-of-the-art in the field of using evolutionary computation techniques for effort estimation. Some suggestions for future research directions are also provided.

Chapter 3, **The Application of Genetic Algorithms to the Evaluation of Software Reliability** is written by *Angel Fernando Kuri-Morales*. The author shown that evolutionary computation (illustrated in this chapter with genetic algorithms) is a tool enabling the designer to tackle the software reliability problem by solving the complex optimization involved in evaluating the status of the systems and taking the appropriate decisions in line with the development of the system.

The possibility to synthesize higher quality modeling through the evolution of Genetic Algorithms was presented in Chapter 4, **Synthesis of Object-Oriented Software Structural Models Using Quality Metrics And Co-Evolutionary Genetic Algorithms.** The authors *Dilza Szwarcman, Thiago S. M. Guimarães, André Vargas Abs da Cruz and Marco Aurélio C. Pacheco* elaborated and evaluated a model able to combine the technique of the Co-evolutionary Genetic Algorithm to the object oriented software engineering and to the metrics proposed in the QMOOD model (Quality Models for Object-Oriented Modeling), in order to synthesize software modeling with better quality. The research evaluated the performance of the model before the random search by its application, in order to optimize the different quality attributes in simple and more complex modeling problems.

Artificial Immune Systems, a biologically inspired computing paradigm such as Artificial Neural Networks, Genetic Algorithms, and Swarm Intelligence, embody the principles and advantages of vertebrate immune systems. It has been applied to solve several complex problems in different areas such as data mining, computer security, robotics, aircraft control, scheduling, optimization, and pattern recognition. An interesting and very useful work was presented in Chapter 5 **Application of Artificial Immune Systems Paradigm for Developing Software Fault Prediction Models.** The authors, *Cagatay Catal and Soumya Banerjee,* have showed that the Artificial Immune Systems (AISR) is an emerging computational intelligence technique that provides promising results for many problems. They have investigated the use of Artificial Immune Systems paradigm for software fault prediction problem during the research implementation. The study showed the elaborated working steps fur such algorithm with a software engineering dataset.

Software fault prediction can play an important role in ensuring software quality through efficient resource allocation. Chapter 6, **Genetic Programming for Cross-Release Fault Count Predictions in Large and Complex Software Projects**, written by *Wasif Afzal, Richard Torkar, Robert Feldt, Tony Gorschek* have used the genetic programming for fault prediction.

The paper evaluates genetic programming (GP) for cross-release prediction of fault counts on data set from large real world projects. The authors evaluate the created models on fault data from several large and real world software projects, some from open-source and some from industrial software systems. Some very useful part of this work is the part in which multiple different fault count modeling techniques, both traditional and several machine learning approaches are compared.

The service discovery has become an emerging phenomenon in software engineering and process engineering as well. In Chapter 7, **Exploring a Self Organizing Multi Agents Approach for Service Discovery,** the authors, *Hakima Mellah, Soumya Banerjee, Salima Hassas, Habiba Drias*, have been presented the service discovery referring bio-inspired and evolutionary agents. The emphasis has been initiated a model for service failure detection and recovery in distributed environment with the help of the proposed self organized Multi Agent. The positioning of the self organized agents and its protocol has been elaborated in the chapter with a brief service case model. The relevance and potential applications of self organized agents in service discovery paradigm is an emerging field of research in different flavors of software engineering and recommender system. The information of this chapter can be use very useful for different area of work. Collective intelligence from nature has already been envisaged effectively in the service response and failure coverage; hence service discovery through self organized agents could be treated as major mile stone of software engineering research.

Another useful chapter for the software engineering domain is the Chapter 8, **Innovative Hybrid Genetic Algorithms and Line Search Method for Industrial Production Management,** written by *Pandian Vasant*. In this chapter a hybrid optimization approach was presented. The hybrid genetic algorithm with line search approach has improved the fitness value obtained by genetic algorithms alone. This technique is a robust and excellent efficient method for non-liniar industrial production planning problems. in particular this is a very useful techniques for planning in software engineering problems. The author strongly believes that there should be another hybrid approach such as particle swarm optimization, ant colony optimization, artificial immune system, neural network, fuzzy logic, tabu search and evolutionary computation (Genetic programming, Evolutionary strategy & Genetic algorithms) to improve the solution for the decision variables in real world situation. The hybrid optimization techniques of meta-heuristic approaches with classical optimization approaches will be great added advantages for solving production management problems in a fuzzy environment.

Chapter 9, **Automatic Test Sequence Generation for State Transition Testing via Ant Colony Optimization**, written by *Praveen Ranjan Srivastava and Baby* have proposed an Ant Colony Optimization technique for automated and fully coverage state-transitions in the system. Through proposed algorithm all the transitions are easily traversed at least once in the test-sequence.

According to the *Arjan Seesing and Hans-Gerhard Gross* Testing is a difficult and costly activity in the development of object-oriented programs. The challenge is to come up with a sufficient set of test scenarios, out of the typically huge volume of possible test cases, to demonstrate correct behavior and acceptable quality of the software. For this they have presented in Chapter 10, **Object Oriented Software Testing with Genetic Programming and Program Analysis**, genetic programming as a heuristic search algorithm which is suitable to evolve object-oriented test programs automatically to achieve high coverage of a class. The chapter introduced a method for generating test cases automatically according to a coverage criterion for object-oriented software, based on the application of genetic programming. The authors have considered the genetic programming as a likely more suitable technique for the generation of test operation invocation sequences, in contrast to applying genetic algorithms. They have presented the principles of Genetic Programming-based test case generation and shown how it can be improved with program analysis techniques and a two-stage execution.

Chapter 11, **Assessment of Software Quality: A Fuzzy Multi-Criteria Approach** is written by *Praveen Ranjan Srivastava, Ajit Pratap Singh and Vageesh K.V.* The authors have proposed a fuzzy multi-criteria approach to quantify the abstract software quality attributes. This approach gives a method to identify the best software product from a set of products by accommodating the perspectives of a manager, user and developer involved with the product. The model can be further enhanced by increasing the number of quality attributes, and linguistic variables for example by increasing the degrees of importance to eleven linguistic values.

Chapter 12, **Verification of Attributes in Linked Lists Using Ant Colony Metaphor,** describes the validation of the attributes of linked list using modified pheromone biased model (of Ant Colony) under complex application environment mainly for kernel configuration and device driver operations. The authors *Soumya Banerjee and P.K. Mahanti* incorporates into the presented work the idea of pheromone exploration strategy with small learning parameter associated while traversing a linked list. This process of local propagation on loop and learning on traversal is not available with the conventional validation mechanism of data structure using predicate logic.

We consider that the book can be very useful for researchers and teachers in the field of evolutionary computation and optimization techniques for software engineering.

I wanted to thank again to all the people who contribute to this project in order to develop and to put together different researches. The fact that the book presents different applications and techniques it is very important for us to contribute to the development of new applications. The presented book chapters can represent some important information for the future works in software engineering in which the evolutionary computation techniques have to be applied.

Acknowledgment

The editor wants to express their gratitude to all those colleagues who supported, in many different ways, the pleasant effort for editing this book. First and foremost, the authors that contributed to the writing of the book's chapters; they are the actual creators of the qualified research that is described in the book, and they must be especially thanked for the patience exhibited in the editing process. Special thanks to all the authors that help in the editing process. Special thanks to all the reviewers which help me in the editorial activities. Speaking of patience, I need not to overlook the contribution of the IGI Globals's publishing editor, Joel Gamon, altogether with all the very efficient staff at IGI Global. Joel Gamon helps me in every step of the editorial process and I dedicated many thanks for this. A final word of thanks is dedicated to my whole family and all my friends who support me in editing work without even knowing it.

Monica Chiş
Editor

Chapter 1

Introduction:
A Survey of the Evolutionary Computation Techniques for Software Engineering

Monica Chiş
Siemens IT Solutions and Services PSE, Romania

ABSTRACT

This chapter aims to present a part of the computer science literature in which the evolutionary computation techniques, optimization techniques and other bio-inspired techniques are used to solve different search and optimization problems in the area of software engineering.

MOTIVATION

Evolutionary algorithms are methods, which imitate the natural evolution process. An artificial evolution process evaluates fitness of each individual, which are solution candidates. The next population of candidate solutions is formed by using the good properties of the current population by applying different mutation and crossover operations.

Different kinds of evolutionary algorithm applications related to software engineering were searched in the literature. Because the entire book presents some interesting information chapter of some evolutionary computation techniques applied into the software engineering we consider necessary to present into this chapter a short survey of

some techniques which are very useful in the future research of this field.

The majority of evolutionary algorithm applications related to software engineering were about software design or testing.

Software Engineering is the application of a systematic, disciplined, quantifiable approach to the development, operation, and maintenance of software, and the study of these approaches; that is, the application of engineering to software (Abran and Moore, 2004).

The purpose of this book is to open a door in order to find out the optimization problems in different software engineering problems. The idea of putting together the application of evolutionary computation and evolutionary optimization techniques in software engineering problems provided to the researchers the possibility to study some existing

DOI: 10.4018/978-1-61520-809-8.ch001

works in this fields and to found approaches and methodologies that will combine advances in computational methods to model and analyze complex problems with powerful optimization techniques based on evolutionary principles in order to create more general, robust, accurate and computationally methods for evolutionary computation applications.

Software Engineering

Software engineering describes the collection of techniques that apply an engineering approach to the construction and support of software products. Software engineering activities include managing, costing, planning, modeling, analyzing, specifying, designing, implementing, testing and maintaining software products. Whereas computer science provides the theoretical foundations for building software, software engineering focuses on implementing software in a controlled and scientific way (Fenton et al. 1997).

Measurement is the process by which numbers or symbols are assigned to attributes of entities in the real world in such a way as to describe them according to clearly defined rules.

An entity is an object or an event in the real world. An attribute is a feature or property of an entity. We measure attributes of entities. Rules are used to determined the values for an attribute in order to made the process repeatable not subjective. It is very important to consider the representation form of each attributes (measurement unit).

Measurement is considered to be fundamental to any engineering principle. Software projects well managed have to be measured first. There are a lot of applications of evolutionary computation and optimization in the field of software engineering problems.

Defining the project estimated cost, duration and maintenance effort early in the development life cycle is a valuable goal to be achieved for software projects. There are a lot of researches in this which have used evolutionary computation in the applications of software engineering.

Evolutionary Computation

Evolutionary computation is emerging as a new engineering computational paradigm, which may significantly change the present structural design practice. A great number of evolutionary computational models have been developed, including evolutionary algorithms, genetic algorithms, the evolution strategy, evolutionary programming.

Evolutionary Algorithm (EA) incorporates aspects of natural selection or survival of the fittest. An evolutionary algorithm maintains a population of structures (initially randomly generated) that evolves according to rules of selection, recombination, mutation and survival, referred to as genetic operators. EAs are useful for optimization when other techniques such as gradient descent or direct, analytical discovery unsuccessful.

The background on various implementations of evolutionary algorithms is provided in Fonseca and Fleming (1995), Bäck (1996), Coello (1999), and Van Veldhuizen and Lamont (2000).

Genetic Programming creates computer programs in the scheme computer languages as the solution. A genetic algorithm creates a string of numbers that represent the solution.

Genetic programming consists of the following four steps:

1. Generate an initial population of random compositions of the functions and terminals of the problem (computer programs).
2. Execute each program in the population and assign it a fitness value according to how well it solves the problem.
3. Create a new population of computer programs.
4. The best computer program that appeared in any generation, is selected as the result of genetic programming (Koza 1992; Benzhaf, Nordin, Keller and Francone, 1998).

Genetic programming is distinguished from other evolutionary algorithms in that it uses a tree (hierarchical) representation of variable size rather than of linear strings of fixed length. The flexible representation scheme is important because it allows the underlying structure of the data to be discovered automatically.

Application of Evolutionary Computation and Optimization Techniques in Software Engineering

Applying evolutionary computation and optimization techniques in software engineering problems can help authors to obtained very good results with a lot of applications. Evolutionary computation is considered to be an interesting application into the field of software engineering. In this section, the applications of evolutionary computation techniques for groups of problems from software engineering area are presented.

The estimation of developing software project cost is one of the more daunting tasks confronted by the software manager at the beginning of the projects. The methods used for making estimates are varied, ranging from expert judgment, classical regression, neural networks, fuzzy logic, case-based reasoning and, lately, genetic programming and other computational intelligence techniques.

Cost and effort estimation for a software development involved a lot of variables and some parameters which are very difficult to control. Larger number of variables affects the total cost of software. Many computational intelligence methods have been applied to estimate cost of software project development.

Dolado (1999) have presented some results related to the use of classical regression, Neural Networks (NN) and Genetic Programming (GP) for software cost estimation. The results presented the idea that the estimates of classical regression can be improved by Neural Networks and Genetic Programming.

In Dolado (2000) was reported the results of the validation of the component-based method for software sizing. In order to do this, the author was done the analysis of 46 projects involving more than 100,000 Lines of Code (LOC) of a fourth-generation language. Several conclusions concerning the predictive capabilities of the method were presented.

In Dolado (2001) the research about of finding a function for software cost estimation has been made by using the technique of Genetic Programming (GP) for exploring the possible cost functions. Both standard regression analysis and Genetic Programming have been applied and compared on several data sets. The basic size–effort relationship does not show satisfactory results, from the predictive point of view, across all data sets.

Aguilar-Ruiz, Ramos, Riguilme and Toro (2001) have used dynamic models and simulation environments in connection with software projects for simulating the behavior of the projects. They have presented a new approach based on the combination of a Software Project Simulator (SPS) and Evolutionary Computation. The purpose was to provide accurate decision rules in order to help the project manager to take decisions at any time in the development process. The SPS generates a database from the software project, which is provided as input to the Evolutionary Algorithm for producing the set of management rules. These management rules had the role to help the project manager to keep the project within the cost, quality and duration targets.

Lefley and Shepperd (2003) have investigated the use of various techniques including Genetic Programming, with public data sets, to attempt to model and hence estimate software project effort. Experiments are reported, designed to assess the accuracy of estimates made using data within and beyond a specific company. The research has given an overview of the performance of Genetic Programming (GP) into the fields of effort estimation. The authors have showed that for the data set that are using Genetic Programming performs consistently well, but is harder to configure and produces more complex models. The evidence here agrees with other researchers that companies would do well to base estimates on in house data rather than incorporating public data sets. The complexity of the GP must be weighed against the small increases in accuracy to decide whether to use it as part of any effort prediction estimation.

In (Sheta, 2006) two model structures considered modeling software effort as a function of the developed line of code (DLOC) were presented. This function helps project managers to accurately allocate the available resources for the project. They concentrated on the presentation on two new model structures to estimate the effort required for the development of software projects using Genetic Algorithms (GAs). A modified version of the COCOMO (Constructive Cost Model) model provided to explore the effect of the software development adopted methodology in effort computation was presented. The performances of the developed models were tested on NASA software project dataset. The developed models were able to provide good estimation capabilities. Genetic Algorithms were used to estimate the COCOMO (Boehm, 1981) model parameters.

In (Uysal, 2008) a multivariate interpolation model was developed to estimate the effort component of the software projects. A COCOMO model was used to represent the effort function. The data set that was used consists of two independent variables: Lines of Code (LOC) and Methodology (ME) and one dependent variable Effort (CE). Data set is taken from NASA projects and the results that are obtained in this work are compared with the compared with the results of Sheta (Sheta, 2006) who is produced a similar model for estimating the effort component of software projects.

In (Satyananda Reddy and Raju, 2009) the role of cost drivers in improving the precision of effort estimation using Constructive Cost Model (COCOMO) was investigated. Cost drivers have significant influence on the COCOMO. Fuzzy logic has been applied to the COCOMO using the Symmetrical Triangles and Trapezoidal Membership Functions (TMF) to represent the cost drivers. The authors are using the Gaussian Membership Function (GMF) for the cost drivers for studying the behavior of COCOMO cost drivers. Gaussian function is performing better than the trapezoidal function.

Other important application of some evolutionary computation techniques in the software engineering problems is in the part of software failures.

Software failures occur after some implementation tasks have already been completed. It is very important to manage the software failures problems in the software development process and to find the failures in the early phases of development.

In the development process of the software products should be identified parts in which some special reliability techniques have to be used.

Software reliability was defined as the probability that software will not cause a failure of a system for a specified time under specified conditions is one of the most important manifestations of quality. Most of the software reliability models those were designed to quantify the likelihood of software failure are based on software failure observations made during test or operation (Lyu, 1995).

In (Yongqiang and Huashan, 2006) Genetic Programming (GP) evolution algorithm to establishing software reliability model based on mean time between failures' (MTBF) time series was presented. The evolution model of GP is then analyzed and appraised according to five characteristic criteria for some common-used software testing cases. Some traditional probability models and the neural network model are selected to compare with the new GP model separately.

Evett, Khoshgoftar, Chien and Allen (1998) have described a model based on Genetic Programming, which can be used to find modules with high probability of failure and should be implemented with improvements of reliability techniques. The Genetic Programming system has been used to predict a number of faults the module is likely to produce. Number of faults was used to rank the modules. The final evaluation of quality was based on ordinal criteria rather than number of failures.

In the research field of software failure can be found a software quality data from software development projects. Data set has attributes for unique and total number of operators and operands, lines of source code, lines of executable code, and two values for cyclomatic complexity (McCabe's cyclomatic complexity and extended cyclomatic complexity), number of linearly-independent paths through a program (McCabe and Butler, 1994). Modules are classified as fault-prone and not fault-prone (Evett, Khoshgoftar, Chien, and Allen, 1998). The data was split to training and validation data sets. The Genetic Programming system was trained by using training data. For every run, the best program was returned as the result.

The ability of the trained program to generalize the data was measured by using the result program to predict faults also for validation set. Best-of-run programs were ordered accordingly. The usefulness of the model is evaluated by its ability to approximately order modules from the most fault-prone to the least fault-prone. The order was compared to random order of modules. The result which explained that the random order results were really different than GP results (Evett et al., 1998). According to Pareto's Law, 20% modules have 80% of total number of failures (in this case, over 70% of modules has near zero failures) and developers should be interested in those top 20% of modules in order.

In (Baisch and Liedtke, 1998), Genetic Algorithms are used to assist human experts to define rule-base for classification. Every individual into population represents one fuzzy expert system

encoded as a binary string. Fitness function was based on the contingency-table like weighting according to false and correct classification data. Modules were classified to two different classes: modules with fault amount of 0 to 5 and more than 20 faults. Data was divided in training and test sets. The authors have shown that extracted expert system was able to classify correctly 87.8% of training data (409 modules) and 82.4% of test data (301 modules). System was also tested with real-world application.

Liu and Khoshgoftaar (2001) have used Genetic Programming to classify software modules. They have used real world datasets from large software written in C++. The used dataset was about 807 software modules classified as fault-prone or not fault-prone. Dataset has attributes for a number of times the source code was inspected, number of Lines of Code for different production phases and final number of commented code. Data was divided into two sets (training and validation). The fitness function was calculated from number of hits and raw fitness. Hits and raw fitness come from pre-defined cost of misclassification values. Genetic Programming model tries to predict number of faults for each module and then it classifies modules. They have demonstrated that the Genetic Programming has a very good accuracy (Liu and Khoshgoftaar, 2001).

Bouktif, Kegl and Sahraoui (2002) have proposed the use of existing models as independent experts. They have combined decision trees into one final classifier system with Genetic Algorithms. When the input vector was given to the system, decision making starts from the root of the tree and corresponding edges are followed.

Chromosome representation of trees was made with set of boxes with sides parallel to the axes. Fitness was calculated by using the average correctness per attribute.

According to Bouktif et al. (2002) the system was tested by predicting the stability of classes written in Java. They have selected for attributes 22 structural software metrics about coupling, cohesion, inheritance, and complexity. Data was randomly split into 10 datasets with equal size and then the classifier is trained with 9 sets. The last one dataset was used as test data. This was repeated with all 10 possible combinations. After test experiments, it was concluded, that resulting meta-expert model can perform significantly better than individual models.

Genetic Algorithm has used to train Artificial Neural Network to predict software quality in (Hochmann, Khoshgoftaar, Allen, Hudepohl, 1996) and (Hochmann, Khoshgoftaar, Allen, Hudepohl, 1997).

Rammana, Peters and Ahn (2002) and Evett, Khoshgoftaar and Allen (1999) have used genetic programming to determine software quality.

During early phases of a software development project, developers usually do not have an exact awareness about the problem, which should be solved using the software. One way to avoid increased development cost is to collect more knowledge about the problem to be solved with the software.

In (Feldt, 1999) was presented the idea about using genetic programming to explore the difficulty from input data. The term software problem exploration using genetic programming (SPE-GP) is proposed to solve this approach. The target system is software, which controls arresting of landing aircraft on a runway. This is commonly used in military aircraft carriers, where the length of the runway is limited.

Reliability is one of the most important aspects of software systems of any kind (embedded systems, information systems, intelligent systems, etc.). The size and complexity of software is growing dramatically during last decades and especially during last few years. Various methods can be used to achieve the software reliability i.e. software reliability engineering, fault tolerance, testing strategies, fault tree techniques, simulation, machine learning and software metrics.

In the area of testing using evolutionary computation there are a lot of researches in the last years. One of this is considered to be evolutionary testing.

Evolutionary testing (ET) is a technique by which test data can be generated automatically through the use of optimizing search techniques. The search space is the input domain of the software under test. Evolutionary testing has been shown to be successful for generating test data for many forms of testing, namely specification testing (Arcuri and Yao, 2007), extreme execution time testing (Montana, 1993) and structural testing (Wappler and Wegener, 2006).

In the field of evolutionary testing there are some interesting papers in the research literature.

There are two levels which can be considered for evolutionary testing: one source code and second byte-source code.

Ribeiro, Rela and de Vega (2007) have presented evolutionary testing as an emerging methodology for automatically generating high quality test data. They have presented an approach for generating test cases for the unit-testing of object-oriented programs, with basis on the information provided by the structural analysis and interpretation of Java bytecode and on the dynamic execution of the instrumented test object. The explanation for working at the bytecode level was that even when the source code is unavailable, insight can still be obtained and used to guide the search-based test case generation process. Test cases are represented using the Strongly Typed Genetic Programming paradigm, which mimics the polymorphic relationships, inheritance dependences and method argument constraints of object-oriented programs.

McMinn and Holcombe (2003) have introduced the state problem for evolutionary testing. State variables can hinder or render impossible the search for test data and can be dependent on the input history to the test object, as well as just the current input. They do not form part of the input domain to the test object, and therefore cannot be optimized by the ET search process. The use of ant colony algorithms was proposed as a means of heuristic search and evaluation of sequences of transitional statements, in order to find one that makes the current test goal possible.

McMinn (2004) have made a review of meta-heuristic techniques that have been used in software test data generation, namely Hill Climbing, Simulated Annealing and Evolutionary Algorithms. He has summarized automating test data generation in the areas of structural testing, functional testing, and grey-box testing.

In Tonella (2004) a genetic algorithm was exploited to automatically produce test cases for the unit testing of classes in a generic usage scenario. Test cases are described by chromosomes, which include information on which objects to create, which methods to invoke and which values to use as inputs. The proposed algorithm mutates them with the aim of maximizing a given coverage measure. The implementation of the algorithm and its

In (Müller, Lembeck and Kuchen, 2004), the layout of a symbolic Java virtual machine (SJVM), which discovers test cases using a definable structural coverage criterion with basis on static analysis techniques, was described. Java bytecode is executed symbolically, and the decision whether to enter a branch or throw an exception is based on the earlier constraints, a constraint solver and current testing criterion. The SJVM has been implemented in a test tool called GlassTT.

Mantere and Alander (Mantere and Alander, 2005) have presented an in-depth index of the work developed in the area of evolutionary testing, focused on genetic algorithms applied to coverage testing, test data generation, testing program dynamics, black-box testing and software quality.

In (Wappler and Lammermann, 2005) a method for the automatic generation of test programs for object-oriented unit testing was presented. The method has focusing on the usage of Universal Evolutionary Algorithms. An encoding was proposed that represented object oriented test programs as basic type value structures, allowing for the application of various search-based optimization techniques such as Hill Climbing or Simulated Annealing. The generated test programs could be transformed into test classes according to popular testing frameworks.

In (Wappler and Wegener, 2006) Strongly-Typed Genetic Programming (STGP) methodology have been used for encoded, with method call sequences being represented by method call trees. These trees are able to express the call dependences of the methods that are relevant for a given test object. To account for polymorphic relationships which exist due to inheritance relations, the STGP types used by the function set are specified in correspondence to the type hierarchy of the test cluster classes. The emphasis of this work is on sequence feasibility. The fitness function does need, however, to incorporate a penalty mechanism for test cases which include method call sequences that generate runtime exceptions.

In (Wappler and Schieferdecker, 2007) an improvement of automated search-based test generation approach was presented. The objective functions were extended by an additional component that accounts for encapsulation. The authors have proposed a modification of the search space which increases the efficiency of the approach. They have demonstrated the value of the improvement in terms of achieved code coverage is demonstrated by a case study with seven real-world test objects. In contrast to other approaches which break encapsulation in order to test non-public methods, the tests generated by this approach inherently guarantee that class invariants are not violated.

Particle swarm optimization (PSO) is an alternative search technique, often outperformed GAs when applied to various problems. In (Windisch, Wappler, and Wegener, 2007), the authors have tried to explain how PSO competes with GAs in the context of evolutionary structural testing. They have performed experiments with 25 small artificial test objects and 13 more complex industrial test objects taken from various development projects. The results show that PSO outperforms

GAs for most code elements to be covered in terms of effectiveness and efficiency.

There are some evolutionary approaches to the unit-testing of object-oriented software that employ dynamic bytecode analysis to derive structural testing criteria. In this case there are some works in the literature which we can present here in this chapter. The application of evolutionary algorithms and bytecode analysis for test automation was studied in (Cheon, Kim and Perumendla, 2005) an attempt to automate unit testing of object-oriented programs is described. A black-box approach for investigating the use of genetic algorithms for test data generation is employed, and program specifications written in JML are used for test result determination. The JML compiler was extended to make Java bytecode produce test coverage information.

In (Lefticaru and Ipate, 2007) an approach for automatic generation of test data, using state diagrams and genetic algorithms was presented. The strategy is simple; the derivation of the fitness function is straightforward and so could be easily adopted in industrial software development. Furthermore, experimental evidence show that the test data obtained can cover difficult paths in the machine and a slightly different design of the fitness function can be used for specification conformance testing. Future work concerns the possibility of extending the strategy presented for multi-class testing and the derivation of the fitness function from hierarchical and concurrent state machine diagrams.

Many papers in the field of software engineering present different aspects of state-based testing, like: generation of test cases for finite state machine (FSMs).

Lefticaru and Ipate (2008) investigates the use of search-based techniques for functional testing, having the specification in form of a state machine. They have generated input data for chosen paths in a state machine, so that the parameter values provided to the methods satisfy the corresponding guards and trigger the desired transitions. A general form of a fitness function for an individual path was presented and this approach is empirically evaluated using three search techniques: simulated annealing, genetic algorithms and particle swarm optimization.

Ant Colony Optimization (ACO) algorithm is a probabilistic technique for solving computational problems which can be reduced to finding good paths through graphs.

Recently, Ant Colony Optimization (ACO) was successfully applied in software testing. Doerner and Gutjahr (2003) described an approach involving ACO and a Markov Software Usage model for deriving a set of test paths for a software system, and McMinn and Holcombe (2003) reported on the application of ACO as a supplementary optimization stage for finding sequences of transitional statements in generating test data for evolutionary testing. However, the results obtained so far are preliminary and none of the reported results directly addresses specification-based software testing.

Li and Lam (2005) have proposed an Ant Colony Optimization approach to test data generation for the state-based software testing. They have used UML State chart diagrams and ACO for test data generation. The advantages of the that approach are: directly using of the standard UML artifacts created in software design processes, the automatically generated test sequence is always feasible, non-redundant and achieves the all state coverage criterion.

This introduction chapter made only a short survey of a lot of research papers which presents the application of different evolutionary computation and optimization techniques in the field of software engineering.

Differential Evolution (DE) is a simple evolutionary algorithm that creates new candidate solutions by combining the parent individual and several other individuals of the same population. The DE algorithm was introduced by Storn and Price (Storn and Price, 1995) as a heuristic, inspired by simplex methods, able to efficiently solve difficult optimization problems on continuous domains. Its particularity consists in the search operator based on an internal perturbation scheme not on an external one as is usual in classical mutation operators.

A candidate replaces the parent only if it has better fitness. This is a rather greedy selection scheme that often outperforms traditional EAs.

Testing is the primary way used in practice to verify the correctness of software. Becerra, Sagarna and Yao (2009) have presented a test data generator employing Differential Evolution (DE) to solve each of the constrained optimizations problems, and empirically evaluate its performance for several Differential Evolution models. They have extended the experiments to the Breeder Genetic Algorithm and face it to Differential Evolution, and compare different test data generators in the literature with the Differential Evolution approach. The results present Differential Evolution as a promising solution technique for this real-world problem.

In this short survey we have presented only a part of the research results in the field of applying evolutionary computation techniques in software engineering problems. We consider that this overview of the literature in this domain is a good start

This paper has surveyed a wide range of applications of the evolutionary computation and bio-inspired and optimization techniques in software engineering problems This knowledge will be applied maybe for future research in this field. The survey provides information about only a part of the literature in the domain and I think will be very useful for future research. The paper has briefly enumerated the applications and we think can be a good start for the researchers which want to learn more about solving software engineering problems.

The applications of bio-inspired techniques in solving software engineering problems will be extend in the future with a lot of interesting research.

REFERENCES

Abran, A., & Moore, J. W. (2004). Guide to the Software Engineering Body of Knowledge. Pierre Bourque and Robert Dupuis (Eds.). Washington, DC: IEEE Computer Society.

Aguilar-Ruiz, J. S., Ramos, I., Riquelme, J. C., & Toro, M. (2001). An evolutionary approach to estimating software development projects. *Information and Software Technology*, *14*(43), 875–882. doi:10.1016/S0950-5849(01)00193-8

Alander, J. T., & Lampinen, J. (1997). Cam shape optimization by genetic algorithm. In Poloni, C., & Quagliarella, D. (Eds.), *Genetic Algorithms and Evolution Strategies in Engineering and Computer Science, Trieste, Italy, Nov 1997* (pp. 153–174). New York: John Wiley & Sons.

Arcuri, A., & Yao, X. (2007). *Search based testing of containers for object-oriented software.* Technical Report CSR-07-3.

Bäck, T. (1996). *Evolutionary Algorithms in Theory and Practice*. New York: Oxford University Press.

Baisch, E., & Liedtke, T. (1998). Automated knowledge acquisition and application for software development projects. In *Automated Software Engineering, Proceedings. 13th IEEE International Conference*, Honolulu, USA, (pp. 306–309).

Becerra, L., Sagarna, R., & Yao, X. (2009). An evaluation of Differential Evolution in Software Test Data Generation. In *CEC'09, Proceedings of the Eleventh Conference on Congress on Evolutionary Computation*, (pp. 2850-2857).

Benzhaf, W., Nordin, P., Keller, R. E., & Francone, F. D. (1998). *Genetic Programming: An Introduction*. San Francisco: Morgan Kaufmann.

Boehm, B. (1981). *Software engineering economics*. Englewood Cliffs, NJ: Prentice-Hall.

Bouktif, S., Kegl, B., & Sahraoui, H. (2002). Combining software quality predictive models: an evolutionary approach. *International Conference on Software Maintenance*, (pp. 1063–6773).

Burgess, C. J., & Lefley, M. (2001). Can genetic programming improve software effort estimation - a comparative evaluation? *Information and Software Technology, 43*(14), 863–873. doi:10.1016/S0950-5849(01)00192-6

Cheon, Y., Kim, M., & Perumendla, A. (2005). A complete automation of unit testing for Java programs. In *International Conference on Software Engineering Research and Practice*, Las Vegas, Nevada, (pp. 290–295).

Coello, C. A. C. (1999). A comprehensive survey of evolutionary-based multiobjective optimization techniques. *Knowledge and Information Systems, 1*(3), 269–308.

Doerner, K., & Gutjahr, W. J. (2003). *Extracting Test Sequences from a Markov Software Usage Model by ACO. LNCS 2724* (pp. 2465–2476). Berlin: Springer Verlag.

Dolado, J. J. (1999). Limits to the methods in software cost estimation. In Ryan C. and Buckley J. (Eds.), *Proceedings of the 1st International Workshop on Soft Computing Applied to Software Engineering*, University of Limerick, Ireland, 12-14 April 1999, (pp. 63–68). Limerick, Ireland: Limerick University Press.

Dolado, J. J. (2000). A validation of the component-based method for software size estimation. *IEEE Transactions on Software Engineering, 26*(10), 1006–1021. doi:10.1109/32.879821

Dolado, J. J. (2001). On the problem of the software cost function. *Information and Software Technology, 43*(1), 61–72. doi:10.1016/S0950-5849(00)00137-3

Eiben, A. E., & Bäck, T. (1997). Empirical investigation of multiparent recombination operators in evolution strategies. *Computational Intelligence, 5*(3), 347–365.

Evett, M., Khoshgoftar, T., Chien, P., & Allen, E. (1998). GP-based software quality prediction. In J. R. Koza, W. Banzhaf, K. Chellapilla, K. Deb, M. Dorigo, D. B. Fogel, et al (eds.), *Genetic Programming 1998: Proceedings of the Third Annual Conference*, University of Wisconsin, Madison, WI, (pp. 60–65). San Francisco: Morgan Kaufmann.

Evett, P., Khoshgoftaar, T., & Allen, E. (1999). Using genetic programming to determine software quality. In A. N. Kumar, & I. Russell, (Eds.), *Proceedings of the Twelfth International Florida Artificial Intelligence Research Society Conference*, Orlando, USA, May 1999, (pp. 113–117). Cambridge, MA: AAAI Press.

Feldt, R. (1999). Genetic programming as an explorative tool in early software development phases. In C. Ryan & J. Buckley, (Eds.), *Proceedings of the 1st International Workshop on Soft Computing Applied to Software Engineering*, University of Limerick, Ireland, April 12-14, 1999, (pp. 11–20). Limerick, Ireland: Limerick University Press.

Fonseca, C. M., & Fleming, P. J. (1995). An overview of evolutionary algorithms in multiobjective optimization. *Evolutionary Computation, 3*(1), 1–16. doi:10.1162/evco.1995.3.1.1

Hochmann, R., Khoshgoftaar, T., Allen, E., & Hudepohl, J. (1996). Using the genetic algorithm to build optimal neural networks for fault-prone module detection. In *Proceedings of the Seventh International Symposium on Software Reliability Engineering*, White Plains, Nov 1996, (pp. 152–162). Washington, DC: IEEE Computer Society Press.

Hochmann, R., Khoshgoftaar, T., Allen, E., & Hudepohl, J. (1997). Evolutionary neural networks: a robust approach to software reliability problems. In *Proceedings of the Eight International Symposium on Software Reliability Engineering*, Albuquerque, NM, (pp. 13–26). Washington, DC: IEEE Computer Society Press.

IEEE. (1990). *IEEE standard glossary of software engineering terminology*. Technical Report 610.12-1990, IEEE, New York.

Koza, J. R. (1992). *Genetic Programming: On the Programming of Computers by Means of Natural Selection*. Cambridge, MA: MIT Press.

Koza, J. R. (1994). *Genetic Programming II: Automatic Discovery of Reusable Programs*. Cambridge, MA: MIT Press.

Lefley, M., & Shepperd, M. J. (2003). Using Genetic Programming to Improve Software Effort Estimation Based on General Data Sets. In Cantú Paz, E. (Eds.), *GECCO 2003, LNCS 2724* (pp. 2477–2487).

Lefticaru, R., & Ipate, F. (2007). Automatic State-Based Test Generation Using Genetic Algorithms. In V. Negru, T. Jebeleanu, D. Petcu, & D. Zaharaie (Eds.), *Proceedings of the Ninth International Symposium on Symbolic and Numeric Algorithms for Scientific Computing*, SYNASC 2007, Timisoara, Romania, September 26-29, 2007, (pp. 188-195). Washington, DC: IEEE Computer Society.

Lefticaru, R., & Ipate, F. (2008). Functional Search-based Testing from State Machines. In *First International Conference on Software Testing, Verification, and Validation, ICST 2008*, Lillehammer, Norway, April 9-11, (pp. 525-528). Washington, DC: IEEE Computer Society.

Li, H., & Lam, C. (2005). Software Test Data Generation using Ant Colony Optimization. In Proceedings of World Academy of Science, Engineering and Technology, (1), 1-4.

Liu, Y., & Khoshgoftaar, T. (2001). Genetic programming model for software quality classification. In *Sixth IEEE International Symposium on High Assurance Systems Engineering*, (pp. 127–136).

Lyu, M. R. (1995). *Handbook of Software Reliability Engineering*. New York: McGraw-Hill.

Mantere, T., & Alander, J. T. (2005). Evolutionary software engineering, a review. *Applied Soft Computing*, *5*(3), 315–331. doi:10.1016/j.asoc.2004.08.004

McCabe, T. J., & Butler, C. W. (1994). Software complexity. *Crosstalk. Journal of Defense Software Engineering*, *7*(12), 5–9.

McMinn, P. (2004). Search-Based Software Test Data Generation: A Survey. Software Testing. *Verification and Reliability*, *14*(2), 105–156. doi:10.1002/stvr.294

McMinn, P., & Holcombe, M. (2003). The State Problem for Evolutionary Testing. In GECCO 2003, (LNCS Vol. 2724, pp. 2488-2500). Berlin: Springer Verlag.

Montana, D. J. (1993). Strongly typed genetic programming. Technical Report #7866, Cambridge, MA, 02138.

Müller, R., Lembeck, C., & Kuchen, H. (2004). A symbolic Java virtual machine for test-case generation. In *Proceedings IASTED Conference on Software Engineering*, (pp. 365—371).

Musa, J. D., Iannino, A., & Okumoto, K. (1987). *Software Reliability: Measurement, Prediction, Applications*. New York: McGraw-Hill.

Ramanna, S., Peters, J., & Ahn, T. (2002). Software quality knowledge discovery: a rough set approach. In *Proceedings 26th Annual International Computer Software and Applications*, (pp. 1140–1145). Los Alamitos, CA: IEEE Computer Soc.

Ribeiro, J. C. B., Rela, M. Z., & de Vega, F. F. (2007). *An Evolutionary Approach for Performing Structural Unit-Testing on Third-Party Object-Oriented Java Software* (pp. 379–388). NICSO.

Satyananda Reddy, C., & Raju, K. V. S. V. N. (2009). An Improved Fuzzy Approach for CO-COMO's Effort Estimation Using Gaussian Membership Function. *Journal of Software*, *4*(5), 452–459.

Seesing, A., & Gross, H. G. (2006). A genetic programming approach to automated test generation for object-oriented software. *ITSSA*, *1*(2), 127–134.

Sheta, A. F. (2006). Estimation of the COCOMO Model Parameters Using Genetic Algorithms for NASA Software Project. *Journal of Computer Science*, *2*(2), 118–123. doi:10.3844/jcssp.2006.118.123

Storn, R., & Price, K. (1995). *Differential evolution - a simple and efficient adaptive scheme for global optimization over continuous spaces. Technical report*. Berkley, CA: International Computer Science Institute.

Storn, R., & Price, K. (1997). Differential evolution a simple and efficient heuristic for global optimisation over continuous spaces. *Journal of Global Optimization*, *11*, 341–359. doi:10.1023/A:1008202821328

Tonella, P. (2004). Evolutionary testing of classes. In *International Symposium on Software Testing and Analysis (ISSTA)*, (pp. 119–128).

Uysal, M. (2008). Estimation of the Effort Component of the Software Projects Using Simulated Annealing Algorithm. In *Proceedings of World Academy of Science* (pp. 258–261). Buenos Aires, Argentina: Engineering and Technology.

Van Veldhuizen, D. A., & Lamont, G. B. (2000). Multiobjective Evolutionary Algorithms: Analyzing the State-of-the-Art. *Evolutionary Computation*, *8*(2), 125–147. doi:10.1162/106365600568158

Wappler, S., & Lammermman, F. (2005). Using evolutionary algorithms for the unit testing of object-oriented software. In *Proceedings of the 2005 Conference on Genetic and Evolutionary Computation*, (pp. 1053-1060).

Wappler, S., & Schieferdecker, I. (2007). *Improving evolutionary class testing in the presence of non-public methods* (pp. 381–384). ASE.

Wappler, S., & Wegener, J. (2006). Evolutionary unit testing of object-oriented software using strongly-typed genetic programming. In *GECCO '06: Proceedings of the 8th annual conference on Genetic and evolutionary computation*, (pp. 1925–1932). New York: ACM Press.

Windisch, A., Wappler, S., & Wegener, J. (2007). *Applying particle swarm optimization to software testing* (pp. 1121–1128). GECCO.

Yongqiang, Z., & Huashan, C. (2006). Predicting for MTBF Failure Data Series of Software Reliability by Genetic Programming Algorithm. In *Intelligent Systems Design and Applications, 2006. ISDA '06. Sixth International Conference on*, (pp. 666-670).

Chapter 2
Using Evolutionary Based Approaches to Estimate Software Development Effort

Filomena Ferrucci
University of Salerno, Italy

Carmine Gravino
University of Salerno, Italy

Rocco Oliveto
University of Salerno, Italy

Federica Sarro
University of Salerno, Italy

ABSTRACT

Software development effort estimation is a critical activity for the competitiveness of a software company; it is crucial for planning and monitoring project development and for delivering the product on time and within budget. In the last years, some attempts have been made to apply search-based approaches to estimate software development effort. In particular, some genetic algorithms have been defined and some empirical studies have been performed with the aim of assessing the effectiveness of the proposed approaches for estimating software development effort. The results reported in those studies seem to be promising. The objective of this chapter is to present a state of the art in the field by reporting on the most significant empirical studies undertaken so far. Furthermore, some suggestions for future research directions are also provided.

INTRODUCTION

Several factors characterise the costs of the software development (such as general costs, hardware, human resources, etc.). Nevertheless, it is widely recognised that the main factor is the "effort", meant as the amount of time spent to complete the project, expressed in terms of person-hours or man-months. So, the competitiveness of a software company heavily depends on the ability of its project managers to accurately predict in advance the effort required

DOI: 10.4018/978-1-61520-809-8.ch002

to develop software systems. Indeed, significant over or under-estimates can be very expensive for a company. Moreover, effort estimation is a critical basic activity for planning and monitoring software project development and for delivering the product on time and within budget.

Several methods have been proposed in order to estimate software development effort. Many of them determine the prediction exploiting some relevant factors of the software project, named cost drivers. These methods, named data-driven, exploit data from past projects, consisting of both factor values that are related to effort and the actual effort to develop the projects, in order to estimate the effort for a new project under development (Briand, Emam, Surmann, Wiekzorek, and Maxwell, 1999; Briand, Langley, and Wiekzorek, 2000; Shepperd and Schofield, 2000). In this class, we can find some widely used techniques, such as Linear and Stepwise Regression, Classification and Regression Tree, and Case-Based Reasoning (Briand and Wieczorek, 2002).

In the last years, some attempts have been made to apply search-based approaches to estimate software development effort. In particular, genetic algorithms (Goldberg, 1989) have been defined and assessed by some empirical studies (Burgess and Lefley, 2001; Chiu and Huang, 2007; Conte, Dunsmore, and Shen, 1986; Dolado, 2000; Lefley and Shepperd, 2003; Shan, Mckay, Lokan, and Essam, 2002; Shukla, 2000). The results reported in those studies seem to be promising.

Goal of the Chapter

The objective of this chapter is to report on the most significant empirical studies undertaken so far with the aim of assessing the effectiveness of search-based approaches for estimating software development effort. Furthermore, we provide some suggestions for future research directions.

Organization of the Chapter

The rest of the chapter is organised as follows. Section 2 introduces the problem of estimating development effort and briefly presents the widely employed estimation techniques as well as the validation methods and evaluation criteria used to assess an estimation technique. Section 3 provides a description of evolutionary based approaches for estimating development effort and reports on case studies performed to assess their effectiveness. Future research directions are instead described in Section 4.

BACKGROUND: ESTIMATING SOFTWARE DEVELOPMENT EFFORT

The prediction of software development effort plays a crucial role for the competitiveness of a software company and it is very important not only for the company that produces the software but also for its customers. Several benefits can be derived from an accurate estimate of software project development effort. Among them (Briand and Wieczorek, 2002):

- The possibility of defining the appropriate software costs, thus obtaining the contracts for the development of the software projects;
- The possibility of suitably planning/monitoring the project and allocate resources adequately, thus ensuring time to market and adequate software quality.

Software development effort can be influenced by several factors, among them the size of the software is the main factor. Other factors are the skill and the experience of the subjects involved in the projects, the complexity of the software, the non functional requirements, the adopted software development process, etc. In the last decades, several approaches have been defined, which combine, in different ways, these factors by employing modelling techniques. A widely accepted taxonomy of estimation methods classified them in Non-Model Based and Model Methods (Briand and Wieczorek, 2002). While Non-Model Based Methods mainly take into account expert judgments (thus obtaining highly subjective evaluations), Model Based Methods involve the application of some algorithms to a number of factors to produce an effort estimation. These approaches use data from past projects, characterised by attributes that are related to effort (e.g. the size), and the actual effort to develop the projects, in order to construct a model that is used to estimate the effort for a new project under development.

Widely employed Model Based estimation methods are Linear Regression (LR), Case-Based Reasoning (CBR), and Classification And Regression Tree (CART) (Briand *et al.*, 1999; Briand *et al.*, 2000; Briand and Wieczorek, 2002; Shepperd and Schofield, 2000). Other novel approaches have been proposed in the literature. Any new approach must be validated by some empirical studies in order to verify its effectiveness, i.e., whether or not the predicted efforts are useful estimations of the actual development efforts. To this aim historical datasets are employed. In order to ensure strength to the validation process, it is recommended that data coming from the industrial world are employed. They can come from a single company or from several companies (cross-company datasets), such as the publicly available repository of the International Software Benchmarking Standards Group (ISBSG) that contains data from a great number of projects developed by companies around the world (ISBSG, 2009). A technique that is widely employed to validate an estimation approach is *cross-validation*. One round of cross-validation involves partitioning

the dataset into two randomly complementary sets: the *training set* for model building and the *test set* (or *validation set*) for model evaluation (Briand and Wieczorek, 2002). To reduce variability, multiple rounds of cross-validation are performed using different partitions. The prediction accuracies are then averaged over the rounds. Several strategies have been proposed to obtain training and test sets. The *k-fold cross validation* suggests to partition the initial dataset of N observations in k randomly test sets of equal size, and then for each test set we have to consider the remaining observations as training set in order to build the estimation model. The *leave-one-out cross-validation* is widely used in the literature when dealing with small datasets, e.g. (Briand *et al.*, 1999). To apply the cross-validation, the original dataset of N observations is divided into N different subsets of training and validation sets, where each validation set has one project. Then, N steps are performed to get the predictions for the N validation sets.

Another technique that is often exploited is the *hold-out validation*, where a subset of observations is chosen randomly from the initial dataset to form the training set, and the remaining observations from the test set. Usually, about a third of the initial dataset is used as validation set.

To assess the acceptability of the derived estimations some evaluation criteria are proposed in the literature. Among them several summary measures, like *MMRE*, *MdMRE*, and *Pred(25)* (Conte, Dunsmore, and Shen, 1986), are widely employed and considered *de facto* standard evaluation criteria. They are based on the evaluation of the residuals, i.e., the difference between the actual and estimated efforts. In the following, we will report the definitions of these summary measures taking into account a validation set of n elements.

In order to take into account the error with respect to the actual effort, the *Magnitude of Relative Error* (Conte, Dunsmore, and Shen, 1986) is defined as:

$$MRE = \frac{\left| EF_{real} - EF_{pred} \right|}{EF_{real}}$$

$$AMSE = \sum_{i=1}^{n} \frac{\left| EF_{real_i} - EF_{pred_i} \right|^2}{EF_{real_i} EF_{pred_i}}$$

where EF_{real} and EF_{pred} are the actual and the predicted efforts, respectively. *MRE* has to be calculated for each observation in the validation dataset. All the MRE values are aggregated across all the observations using the mean and the median, giving rise to the *Mean of MRE* (*MMRE*), and the *Median MRE* (*MdMRE*), where the latter is less sensitive to extreme values.

The *Prediction at level l* (Conte, Dunsmore, and Shen, 1986) is defined as:

$$Pred(l) = \frac{k}{n}$$

where k is the number of observations whose *MRE* is less than or equal to l, and n is the total number of observations in the validation set. Generally, a value of 25 for the level l is chosen. In other words, *Pred*(25) is a quantification of the predictions whose error is less than 25%. According to Conte *et al.* (1986), a good effort prediction model should have a *MMRE* ≤ 0.25 and *Pred*(25) ≥ 0.75, meaning that at least 75% of the predicted values should fall within 25% of their actual values. Other summary measures sporadically used are the *Balanced MMRE* (*BMMRE*), the *Mean Squared Error* (*MSE*) (Conte, Dunsmore, and Shen, 1986) and the *Adjusted Mean Square Error* (*AMSE*) (Burgess and Lefley, 2001). They are defined as follows:

$$BMMRE = \sum_{i=1}^{n} \left(\frac{\left| EF_{real_i} - EF_{pred_i} \right|}{min \left(EF_{real_i}, EF_{pred_i} \right)} \right) \frac{100}{n}$$

$$MSE = \frac{1}{n} \sum_{i=1}^{n} (EF_{real} - EF_{pred})^2$$

where EF_{real_i} and EF_{pred_i} are the actual and the estimated efforts of the ith observation of the validation set and n is the number of observations in the validation set.

Finally, in order to have an insight on the usefulness of a new method, its estimation accuracy is compared with the ones of other techniques. Several different benchmark methods are exploited to carry out such a comparison taking into account the above evaluation criteria. It is worth to noting that in the last years it has been widely recognized that the summary measures should be complemented by the analysis of boxplot of residuals and the comparisons among estimation techniques should be carried out by testing also the statistical significance of the absolute residuals. Such tests should be used to verify the following null hypothesis: "the considered populations of absolute residuals have identical distributions", thus allowing us to assess if the differences exist due to chance alone or due to the fact that the samples are from different populations (Kitchenham, Pickard, MacDonell, and Shepperd, 2001).

EVOLUTIONARY BASED APPROACHES FOR EFFORT ESTIMATION

On the basis of the observations in the previous section, it is clear that the problem of identifying an estimation method on the basis of historical data can be seen as the problem of finding an estimation method that minimise the residual values, i.e. the difference between the actual and predicted efforts. Thus, it can be seen as an optimisation problem and evolutionary based approaches could be exploited to address it. As a matter of fact, in the last years genetic algorithms

(GAs), which are based on the evolutionary ideas of natural selection (Goldberg, 1989), have been defined to estimate software development effort, e.g., (Burgess and Lefley, 2001; Dolado, 2000; Lefley and Shepperd, 2003; Shan *et al.*, 2002). At the same time, some other approaches have been proposed aiming to improve some existing Model Based techniques by suitably combining them with genetic algorithms, e.g., (Braga, Oliveira, and Meira, 2008; Chiu and Huang, 2007; Koch and Mitlöhner, 2009; Shukla, 2000).

In this section, we first describe the genetic approaches proposed in the literature and report on the most relevant empirical studies conducted to assess their effectiveness in estimating software development effort. Then, we summarise some studies that investigated whether the use of evolutionary based approaches can improve estimation accuracy of other techniques.

Genetic Algorithms

Basically a Genetic Algorithm (GA) simulates the evolution of natural systems, emphasising the principles of survival of the strongest, first set by Charles Darwin. As such they represent an intelligent exploitation of a random search within a defined search space to solve a problem. GAs were first pioneered by John Holland in the 1960s (Holland, 1975). Then they have been extensively studied, experimented, and applied in many fields in the world of science and practice. It is important to note that GA not only provides an alternative method to solving problems, but, in several cases, it consistently outperforms other traditional methods (Goldberg, 1989; Harman and Jones, 2001).

In the computer implementation of a genetic algorithm, a crucial role is played by the solution representation. In general a solution for the problem being solved is represented by a fixed length binary string, which is called chromosome (in analogy with the biological equivalent). Each solution is evaluated using a fitness function that gives an indication of its goodness.

Despite of a number of variations, the elementary process of the genetic algorithm is the follows: (i) first a random initial population, i.e., a family of chromosome, is generated; (ii) then, a new population (i.e., generation) is created starting from the previous one by applying genetic operators (e.g., crossover, mutation) to the best chromosomes (according to the fitness value); (iii) the second step is repeated until either the fitness of the best solution has converged or a certain number of generations have been made. The chromosome that gives the best solution in the final population is taken in order to define the best approximation to the optimum for the problem under investigation.

The analysis of the process suggests that there are several key parameters that have to be determined for the application of GAs to any given optimisation problem (Goldberg, 1989; Harman and Jones, 2001). In particular, the following issues have to be addressed:

1. Defining the way for encoding a solution and the number of solutions (i.e. population size).
2. Choosing the fitness function, to measure the goodness of a solution;
3. Defining the combination of genetic operators, to explore the search space;
4. Defining the stopping criteria.

In the context of effort estimation, a solution consists of an estimation model described by an equation that combines several factors, i.e.,

$$Effort = c_1 \ op_1 \ f_1 \ op_2 ... \ op_{2n-2} \ c_n \ op_{2n-1} \ f_n \ op_{2n} \ C \quad (1)$$

where f_i represents the value of the ith factor and c_i is its coefficient, C represents a constant, while $op_i \in \{+, -, \cdot\}$ represents the ith operators of the model.

Table 1. The settings of the genetic algorithms defined for effort estimation

Reference	Fitness function	Genetic operators	Size of population	Number of evolutions
(Burgess and Lefley, 2001)	MMRE	Basic crossover, mutation, and selection	1000	500
(Dolado, 2000)	MSE	Basic crossover, mutation, and selection	25	3,4,5
(Lefley and Shepperd, 2003)	MMRE	Basic crossover, mutation, and selection	1000	500
(Shan *et al.*, 2002)	MSE	Basic crossover, mutation	1000	200

As for its encoding this equation can be implemented in several ways, e.g. by a fixed binary string or a binary tree. Regarding the fitness function, the fitness value of a solution can be determined by using summary measures, usually employed to evaluate the goodness of obtained effort estimates (Briand *et al.*, 1999; Briand *et al.*, 2000; Briand and Wieczorek, 2002; Finnie, Wittig, and Desharnais, 1997; Kitchenham *et al.*, 2001; Shepperd and Schofield, 2000), such as MMRE, Pred(25), and MSE (Conte, Dunsmore, and Shen, 1986). Finally, selection, crossover, and mutation are the genetic operators widely employed to explore the search space in order to find good solutions.

Empirical Studies That Investigated Evolutionary Approaches to Estimate Software Development Effort

Table 1 reports on the settings of the genetic algorithms proposed in the literature to estimate software development effort highlighting the main GAs control parameters, such as the employed fitness functions, the population size, the genetic operators, and the maximum number of evolutions. As we can observe, to evaluate the goodness of a solution three proposals employed MSE (Dolado, 2000) as fitness function and two used MMRE. Moreover, all the proposals exploited the genetic operators originally defined by Holland (1975), namely crossover, mutation and selection operator, except for (Shan *et al.*, 2002) that did not use the selection operator. As

for the population size and the evolutions number, almost all settings employed a population of 1000 chromosomes and a number of evolutions ranging from 200 to 500. Only one setting (Shukla, 2000) exploited very small values for these control parameters.

Table 2 summaries the main aspects of the empirical studies carried out to assess the proposed genetic algorithms, e.g. the employed dataset, validation method, evaluation criteria, benchmark method, and the number of runs of the genetic algorithms (i.e. the number of test performed for each validation round to ensure reliability of the results). It is worth noting that all the case studies performed a hold-out validation on industrial datasets except for one (Dolado, 2000) that employed a dataset which contains academic projects. All the industrial datasets has been widely used in effort estimation case studies; they come from a single company, e.g., the Desharnais dataset (Desharnais, 1989; Finnie *et al.*, 1997) or from multiple companies, e.g., Finnish (Burgess and Lefley, 2001) and ISBSG (ISBSG, 2009) datasets. The criteria used to evaluate the accuracy of the obtained estimates are all based on summary measures; in particular MMRE and Pred(25) are employed in all case studies, while fewer studies exploited MSE, AMSE, BMMRE, and Pred(50). In order to assess reliability of accuracy of the obtained estimates for each case study at least five test runs are performed. Finally, in order to assess the effectiveness of GAs for effort estimation, in each case study the proposed genetic-based approaches are compared with other benchmark

Table 2. Summary of the empirical studies that assessed genetic algorithms for effort estimation

Reference	Case study dataset	Validation method	Evaluation criteria	Benchmark methods	Number of test runs
(Burgess and Lefley, 2001)	Finnish Dataset (Burgess and Lefley, 2001)	hold-out validation training set: 149 test set: 15	AMSE MMRE BMMRE Pred(25)	Artificial Neural Networks Linear Regression CBR (2 Nearest Neighbours) CBR (5 Nearest Neighbours)	10
(Dolado, 2000)	46 academic projects (Conte, Dunsmore, and Shen, 1986)	hold-out validation training set: 30 test set: 16	MMRE Pred(25)	Linear Regression Artificial Neural Networks	>15
(Lefley and Shepperd, 2003)	Desharnais (Desharnais, 1989; Finnie et al., 1997)	hold-out validation training set: 63 test set: 18	AMSE MMRE BMMRE Pred(25)	Artificial Neural Networks Linear Regression CBR (2 Nearest neighbours) CBR (5 Nearest neighbours)	10
(Shan *et al.*, 2002)	423 projects from the ISBSG dataset (ISBSG, 2009)	hold-out validation: training test: 211 test set: 212	MMRE Pred(25) Pred(50) MSE	Linear Regression	5

methods, such as Linear Regression, Case-Based Reasoning, and Artificial Neural Networks.

In the following, we provide more details for each proposal, highlighting the validation results. Dolado (2000) was the first to employ an evolutionary approach in order to automatically derive equations alternative to multiple linear regression. The aim was to compare the linear equations with those obtained automatically. The proposed algorithm was run a minimum of 15 times and each run had an initial population of 25 equations. Even if in each run the number of generation varied, the best results were obtained with three to five generations (as reported in the literature, usually more generations are used) and by using MSE as fitness function. As dataset, 46 projects developed by academic students (using Informix-4GL) were exploited through a hold-out validation. It is worth noting that the main goal of Dolado work was not the assessment of evolutionary algorithms but the validation of the component-based method for software sizing. However, he observed that the investigated algorithm provided similar or better values than regression equations.

Burgess and Lefley (2001) performed a case study using the Desharnais dataset (Desharnais,

1989) to compare the use of GA for estimating software development effort with other techniques, such as LR, CBR, and ANN (Artificial Neural Networks). The comparison was carried out with respect three dimensions, namely estimation accuracy, transparency, and ease of configuration. The settings they used for the employed genetic algorithm were: an initial population of 1000, 500 generations, 10 executions, and a fitness function designed to minimise MMRE. They compared the accuracy of the analysed estimation techniques by taking into account summary statistics based on MRE, namely MMRE, Pred(25), BMMRE, and AMSE. Even if GA did not outperform the other techniques the results were promising and Burgess and Lefley suggested that a better set up of the evolutionary algorithm could improve the accuracy of the estimations. In particular they highlighted that the use of a fitness function specifically tied to optimise one particular measure could degrade the other evaluation measures. As a matter of fact GA obtained the best estimates in terms of MMRE and the worst in terms of the other summary measures AMSE, Pred(25), BMMRE.

As for the transparency of the solution, the authors highlighted that widely used techniques such as LR and CBR allowed the user to have a deep insight on the problem making explicit any information about the contribution of each variables in the prediction model and the degree of similarity to the target project respectively. GAs also produced transparent solution because the solution is an algebraic expression, while neural networks did not make explicit any information. As for the ease of configuration, i.e. the effort required to build the prediction system, LR and CBR were easy to use because are widely used method often well supported by tool (Shepperd and Schofield, 2000). Neural networks and GA approaches required instead some effort to choose appropriate values for control parameters because different settings may be lead to different results.

Successively, Shepperd and Lefley (2003) also assessed the effectiveness of an evolutionary approach and compared it with several estimation techniques such as LR, ANN, and CBR. As for genetic algorithm setting, they applied the same choice of Burgess and Lefley (2001), while a different dataset was exploited. This dataset is refereed as "Finnish Dataset" and included 407 observations and 90 features, obtained from many organisations. After a data analysis, a training set of 149 observations and a test set of 15 observations were used for a hold-out validation. Even if the results revealed that there was not a method that provided better estimations than the others, the evolutionary approach performed consistently well. In particular the proposed approach applied on general company wide data obtained the best results in terms of AMSE, MMRE and Pred(25), while on the company specific dataset the best results were achieved only in terms of MMRE and BMMRE. However, the authors again observed that the algorithm was quite hard to configure and companies have to weigh the complexity of the algorithm against the small increases in accuracy to decide whether to use it to estimate development effort (Lefley and Shepperd, 2003).

An evolutionary computation method, named Grammar Guided Genetic Programming (GGGP),

was proposed in (Shan *et al.*, 2002) to overcome some limitations of GAs, with the aim of improving the estimation of the software development effort. Indeed they proposed to use grammars in order to impose syntactical constraints and incorporate background knowledge aiming to guide the evolutionary process in finding optimal or near-optimal results. Data of software projects from the ISBSG (ISBSG, 2009) dataset was used to build the estimation models using GGGP and LR. The fitness function was designed to minimise MSE, an initial population of 1000 was chosen, the maximum number of generations was 200, and the number of executions was 5. The models were built and validated performing a hold-out validation with training and test sets of the same size. The results revealed that GPPP performed better than Linear Regression on all the exploited evaluation criteria, not just on the MSE, the criterion that was used as fitness function.

Empirical Studies That Investigated the Use of Evolutionary Based Approaches to Improve the Effectiveness of Some Existing Estimation Techniques

Some efforts have been made to improve the estimation performance of existing estimation techniques combining them with genetic algorithms. These are summarised in Table 3. As we can observe, three of the six proposed approaches combines GA with CBR, the other ones combine GA with less frequently used techniques, such as Artificial Neural Networks (ANN), Support Vector Regression (SVR) and Gray Relational Analysis (GRA). Concerning the GAs settings all the empirical studied exploited basic crossover, mutation and selection operators except for some settings (Braga *et al.*, 2008; Shukla, 2000) that employed a multi-point crossover. To evaluate the goodness of a solution two settings exploited a combination of MMRE and Pred(25) as fitness function and three settings used a fitness function based only

Table 3. Combinations of genetic algorithms with other estimation techniques

Reference	Employed technique	Fitness function	Genetic operators	Number of evolutions	Size of population
(Braga et al., 2008)	GA + SVR	(100 − PRED(25)) + MMRE	Two-point crossover, mutation, and selection	25	500
(Chiu and Huang, 2007)	GA + CBR	(MMRE - Pred(25))	Basic crossover, mutation, and selection	1000*number of Variables	10* number of Variables
(Huang et al., 2008).	GA + GRA	MMRE	Basic crossover, mutation, and selection	1000*number of Variables	10* number of Variables
(Koch and Mitlöhner, 2009)	GA + CBR	MMRE	Basic crossover, mutation, and selection	1000	2000
(Li et al., 2009)	GA + CBR	MMRE	Basic crossover, mutation, and selection	1000*number of Variables	10* number of Variables
(Shukla, 2000)	GA + NN	MSE	Special MRX multi-point crossover, mutation, and selection	100	400

on MMRE. Only one setting used MSE values as fitness function. Concerning population size and evolutions number, Chiu and Huang (2007) and Huang et al. (2008) exploited a population composed by 10*V chromosomes, where V is the number of variables to be explored for GA. Moreover they proposed to stop the generation process not only after the execution of a fixed number of generations (e.g., 1000*V trials) but also if the solution does not change after a fixed number of generations (e.g. 100*V trials). The case study proposed in (Li, Xie, and Goh, 2009) followed this guidelines, while other case studies (Braga et al., 2007; Koch and Mitlöhner, 2009; Shukla, 2000) employed instead a fixed number of evolutions and a population composed by 400, 500 and 2000 chromosomes, respectively.

Table 4 summarizes the main aspects of the empirical studies carried out to assess the above proposals. All the case studies employed industrial dataset and several validation methods were applied, such as k-fold cross-validation (Chiu and Huang, 2007; Huang et al., 2008; Shukla, 2000), leave-one-out cross-validation (Braga et al., 2007; Koch and Mitlöhner, 2009), and hold-out validation (Li et al., 2009). Almost case studies employed the summary measures MMRE,

MdMRE, and Pred(25) to evaluate the accuracy of the obtained estimates. Only one case study used a statistical significance test to evaluate the residuals, i.e. the difference between actual and predicted effort. Several estimation methods are employed as benchmark in each case study, ranging from widely used techniques, such as Constructive Cost Model (COCOMO), Case-Based Reasoning (CBR), Classification and Regression Trees (CART), and (Linear Regression) LR, to less frequently used techniques, e.g. Grey Relational Analysis (GRA), Step-wise Regression (SWR), Artificial Neural Network (ANN) and its variants. In the following we provide a brief description for each proposal.

The first attempt to combine evolutionary approaches with an existing effort estimation technique was made by Shukla (2000) applying genetic algorithms to Neural Networks (NN) predictor (namely, neuro-genetic approach, GANN) in order to improve its estimation capability. In particular, in the proposed approach the role played by NN was learning the correlation that exists between project features and actual effort and also learning any existing correlations among the predictor variables, while the GA had to minimise MSE values. The proposed case study exploited

Table 4. Summary of the empirical studies that assessed the use of estimation techniques in combination with genetic algorithms

Reference	Employed techniques	Case study dataset	Validation method	Evaluation criteria	Benchmark methods	Number of test runs
(Braga *et al.*, 2008)	GA + SVR	Desharnais (Deshar-nais, 1989; Finnie et al., 1997) and NASA (Oliveira, 2006; Shin and Goel, 2000)	leave-one-out cross-validation	MMRE Pred(25)	Support Vector Regression and its variants	10
(Chiu and Huang, 2007)	GA + CBR	Canadian Financial (Abran and Robillard, 1996) and IBM DP service (Matson, Barrett, and Mellichamp, 1994)	3-fold cross-validation	MMRE MdMRE Pred(25)	Ordinary Least Square Regres-sion Artificial Neural Networks CART	-
(Huang et al., 2008)	GA + GRA	Albrecht (Albrecht and Gaffney, 1983) and COCOMO (Abran and Robillard, 1996; Boehm, 1981)	3-fold cross-validation	MMRE Pred(25)	CBR Artificial Neural Networks CART	-
(Koch and Mitlöhner, 2009)	GA + CBR + social choice	Albrecht (Albrecht and Gaffney, 1983), ERP (Bernroider and Koch, 2001), and COCOMO (Boehm, 1981)	leave-one-out cross-validation	MMRE MdMRE Pred(25)	COCOMO Basic Model Neural Networks Linear Regression Grey Relational Analysis CBR CART	-
(Li et al., 2009).	GA + CBR	Desharnais (Deshar-nais, 1989; Finnie et al., 1997), Albrecht (Albrecht and Gaffney, 1983), and two artificial datasets (Li et al., 2009)	hold-out valida-tion training set and test set of the same size	MMRE MdMRE Pred(25)	CBR Support Vector Regression Artificial Neural Networks CART	-
(Shukla, 2000)	GA + NN	78 software projects from (Boehm, 1981) and (Kemerer, 1987)	10-fold cross validation training sets: 63 test sets: 15	Student's t-test	Regression Tree based NN (Srinivasan and Fisher, 1995), Back-Propagation trained NN (Rumelhart *et al.*, 1988), Quick Propagation trained NN (Parlos et al., 1994)	10

as dataset information from 78 software projects, obtained from the combination of the COCOMO (Boehm, 1981) and the Kemerer (1987) datasets and a statistical significance test was employed to assess whether the neuro-genetic approach provided significant improvement respect of com-mon used AI-oriented methods (Parlos, Fernandez, Atyla, Muthusami, and Tsai, 1994; Rumelhart, Hinton, Williams, 1988; Srinivasan and Fisher,

1995). In particular the employed Student's t-test revealed that the mean prediction error for GANN is less to that for CARTX and less to that for Quick Propagation trained NN (Parlos *et al.*, 1994). These results showed that GANN obtained significantly better prediction than CARTX and QPNN. It is worth to nothing that the authors highlighted that the employed chromosome encoding played a crucial role in the NN predictor system and that a number of experiments were needed to determine a suitable choose.

Recently, Chiu and Huang (2007) applied GA to another AI-based method such Case-Base Reasoning obtaining interesting results. In particular, GA was adopted to adjust the reused effort obtained by considering similarity distances between pairs of software projects. As for the application of CBR, three similarity distances were considered, Euclidean, Minkowski, and Manhattan distances, and a linear equation was used to adjust the reused effort. As for the application of GA, the population included 10*V chromosomes and the generation was stopped after 1000*V trials, or when the best results did not change after 100*V trials, where V is the number of variables that GA explored. The performed case study exploited two industrial datasets (Abran and Robillard, 1996; Matson *et al.*, 1994) of 23 and 21 observations respectively and the results based on the MMRE, Pred(25) and MdMRE evaluation criteria revealed that the adjustment of the reused effort obtained by applying GA improved the estimations of CBR even if the achieved accuracy did not satisfy threshold proposed by Conte et *al.* (1986). As a matter of fact applying the proposed approach on the IBM DP service (Matson *et al.*, 1994) dataset an improvement of 58% and 126% is reached in terms of MMRE and Pred(25) respectively, but the obtained values were far enough from the proposed threshold (i.e. MMRE=0.52, Pred(25)=0.43).

Furthermore, the proposed approaches was also comparable with the models obtained by applying traditional techniques such as ordinary least square regression (OLS), CART and ANN, on both the exploited datasets.

In (Li *et al.*, 2009) it was also proposed a combination of evolutionary approach with CBR aiming at exploiting genetic algorithms to simultaneously optimize the selection of the feature weights and projects. The proposed GA worked on a population of $10*V$ chromosomes and explored the solution space to minimize MMRE value by considering $1000*V$ evolutions, where V is the

number of variables. As for CBR method the authors exploited several combinations of similarity measures, K value, and solution functions. The performed case study employed a hold-out validation on two industrial datasets (Albrecht and Gaffney, 1983; Desharnais, 1989) and two artificial datasets. The obtained estimates were compared with those achieved by applying only CBR and the results showed that the use of GA can provide significantly better estimations even if there was no clear conclusion about the influence of similarity and solution functions on the method performance. It is worth to nothing that on the Desharnais (Desharnais, 1989; Finnie *et al.*, 1997) and Albrecht (Albrecht and Gaffney, 1983) dataset the accuracies of the obtained estimates did not satisfy the threshold proposed by Conte et *al.* (1986), while this was true for the results obtained applying the proposed approach on the two artificial datasets.

The GA method was also used to improve the accuracy of an effort estimation model built by combining social choice and analogy-based approaches (Koch and Mitlöhner, 2009). In particular, voting rules were used to rank projects determining similar projects and GA method was employed to find suitable weights to be associated to the project attributes. To this end, a weight between 0 and 99 was assigned to each attribute and GA started with a population of 2000 random weight vectors. By exploiting error based on summary measures, the proposed GA searched through 1000 generations an optimal assignment for the weights. The validation of the obtained weighted model was performed with a leave-one-out approach by considering as dataset those used in (Albrecht and Gaffney, 1983; Bernroider and Koch, 2001; Boehm, 1981). The accuracy of the proposed model was compared with that obtained by applying other estimation techniques, such as LR, ANN, CART, COCOMO, and GRA. The results revealed that the proposed approach provided the best value for Pred(25) but the worst MMRE value with respect to the other techniques.

Finally, we report on two case studies carried out to investigate the combination of GA with techniques not frequently employed for effort estimation. Braga *et al.* (2008) exploited the use of GAs with Support Vector Regression (SVR) (Cortes and Vapnik, 1995), a machine learning techniques based on statistical learning theory, building a regression model employed to predict effort of novel projects on the basis of historical data. In particular they exploited a GA previously used to solve classification problems (Huang and Wang, 2006) to address the problems of feature selection and SVR (Cortes and Vapnik, 1995) parameters optimisation aiming to obtain better software effort estimations. The proposed GA started with a population of 500 chromosomes and used roulette wheel selection, two-point crossover, mutation, and elitism replacement to create 25 generations. A combination of MMRE and Pred(25) is used as fitness function. To evaluate the proposed method they used two datasets, namely Desharnais (Desharnais, 1989) and NASA (Oliveira, 2006; Shin and Goel, 2000), and performed 10 runs for each dataset. The results showed that the proposed GA-based approach was able to improve the performance of SVR and outperformed some recent results reported in the literature (Braga, Oliveira, and Meira, 2007-a; Braga, Oliveira, Ribeiro, and Meira, 2007-b; Oliveira, 2006; Shin and Goel, 2000). It is worth nothing to note that the results obtained applying the proposed approach on NASA dataset satisfied the threshold proposed by Conte *et al.* (1986). On the other hand applying the same method on Desharnais dataset the obtained MMRE value is not less than 0.25, while the Pred(25) is greater than 0.75.

Chiu and Huang (2007) integrated a genetic algorithm to the Grey Relational Analysis (GRA) (Deng, 1989) method to build a formal software estimation method. Since GRA is a problem-solving method that is used to deal with similarity measures of complex relations, the GA method was adopted in the GRA learning process to find the best fit of weights for each software effort

driver in the similarity measures. To this end the weights of each effort driver were encoded in a chromosome and the MMRE was the value to be optimized. A case study was performed by exploiting the COCOMO (Boehm, 1981) and the Albrecht datasets (Albrecht and Gaffney, 1983) and the experimental results showed that when GA was applied to the former dataset the accuracies of the obtained estimates outperformed those obtained using CBR, CART, and ANN, while on Albrecht dataset all the exploited methods achieved a comparable accuracy. In both cases the accuracy obtained applying the proposed approach did not satisfy the thresholds proposed by Conte *et al.* (1986).

FUTURE RESEARCH DIRECTIONS

The results so far obtained using genetic algorithms for effort estimation are comparable with those provided by other widely used estimation techniques, in terms of the summary measures adopted for the comparison (such as MMRE and Pred(25)). The analysis of the case studies reported in the previous sections has also highlighted that genetic algorithms can be suitably combined with existing techniques to improve their estimation accuracy. Thus, further investigations deserve to be carried out to analyze the usefulness of genetic algorithms in the context of effort estimation. In particular, as highlighted also by (Burgess and Lefley, 2001; Lefley and Shepperd, 2003; Li *et al.*, 2009; Shukla, 2000) specific empirical studies should be performed to understand the role played by different configurations of the evolutionary based approaches to improve the obtained estimates. These configurations could be based on:

- Several fitness functions possibly not employed in the previous works. Indeed, the choice of fitness function could influence the achieved results (Harman, 2007), particularly when the measure used by the algorithm to optimise the estimates is the same used to evaluate the accuracy of them (Burgess and Lefley, 2001). An example of novel fitness function might be a combination of Pred(25) and MMRE. Such a combination can be achieved maximising the ration between these two metrics.

- Aggregated fitness or Pareto optimality to consider a multi-objective optimisation (Harman, 2007);
- An interactive optimisation approach where users can influence the evaluation of fitness (Harman, 2007).
- Other combinations of genetic operators, to better explore the solution space.

It is important to stress that future investigations should use statistical significance tests for the comparisons to give a deeper insight on the significance of the results. It is worth noting that empirical studies carried out so far have been rarely used such tests.

At the same time other combinations of evolutionary algorithms with existing estimation techniques could be explored. For example, a genetic algorithm could be exploited to optimise a crucial step in the application of the CBR technique, namely the feature subset selection. Moreover, other evolutionary algorithms should be investigated (Harman, 2007), such as Tabu Search (Glover and Laguna, 1997), never used for estimating software development effort, and Simulated Annealing (Metropolis, Rosenbluth, Rosenbluth, Teller and Teller, 1953), employed only in a very preliminary case study (Uysal, 2008). The estimation process should also combine two heuristic methods. In particular, a global search can be performed to find a set of good estimation models. To this end a Genetic Algorithm (Goldberg, 1989) or a Particle Swarm Optimization algorithm (Kennedy and Eberhart, 1995) can be used. Then, this set is refined in a second step in order to achieve the best estimation model. Such a step can be performed by using a local search,

e.g., a Simulated Annealing algorithm (Metropolis et al., 1953).

Finally, the observation that so far there is no study that took into account new emerging development environments, such as model-driven development, agile techniques, web applications, suggests the need to apply evolutionary approaches in these contexts.

REFERENCES

Abran, A., & Robillard, P. N. (1996). Function Points Analysis: An Empirical Study of its Measurement Processes. *IEEE Transactions on Software Engineering*, *22*(12), 895–910. doi:10.1109/32.553638

Albrecht, S. J., & Gaffney, J. R. (1983). Software Function, Source Lines of Code, and Development Effort Prediction: A Software Science Validation. *IEEE Transactions on Software Engineering*, *9*(6), 639–648. doi:10.1109/TSE.1983.235271

Bernroider, E., & Koch, S. (2001). ERP Selection Process in Midsize and Large Organizations. *Business Process Management Journal*, *7*(3), 251–257. doi:10.1108/14637150110392746

Boehm, B. W. (1981). *Software Engineering Economics*. Englewood Cliffs, NJ: Prentice-Hall.

Braga, P. L. Oliveira, A. L. I. & Meira, S. R. L. (2008). A GA-based Feature Selection and Parameters Optimization for Support Vector Regression Applied to Software Effort Estimation. In *Proceedings of the 23rd ACM symposium on Applied computing*, Galé in Fortaleza, Ceará, Brazil, (pp. 1788-1792).

Braga, P. L., Oliveira, A. L. I., & Meira, S. R. L. (2007-a). Software Effort Estimation Using Machine Learning Techniques with Robust Confidence Intervals. In *Proceedings of the 19th IEEE International Conference on Tools with Artificial Intelligence*, Patras, Greece, (vol. 1, pp. 181-185).

Braga, P. L., Oliveira, A. L. I., Ribeiro, G. H. T., & Meira, S. R. L. (2007-b). Bagging Predictors for Estimation of Software Project Effort. In *Proceedings of the 20th IEEE International Joint Conference on Neural Networks*, Orlando, FL, (pp. 1595-1600).

Briand, L., El Emam, K., Surmann, D., Wiekzorek, I., & Maxwell, K. (1999). An Assessment and Comparison of Common Software Cost Estimation Modeling Techniques. In *Proceedings of the 21st International Conference on Software Engineering*, Los Angeles, CA, (pp. 313–322).

Briand, L., Langley, T., & Wiekzorek, I. (2000). A Replicated Assessment and Comparison of Common Software Cost Modeling Techniques. In *Proceedings of the 22nd International Conference on Software Engineering*, Limerick, Ireland, (pp. 377–386).

Briand, L. C., & Wieczorek, I. (2002). *Software Resource Estimation* (pp. 1160–1196). Encyclopaedia of Software Engineering.

Burgess, C. J., & Lefley, M. (2001). Can Genetic Programming Improve Software Effort Estimation: A Comparative Evaluation. *Information and Software Technology*, *43*(14), 863–873. doi:10.1016/S0950-5849(01)00192-6

Chiu, N. H., & Huang, S. (2007). The Adjusted Analogy-based Software Effort Estimation based on Similarity Distances. *Journal of Systems and Software*, *80*(4), 628–640. doi:10.1016/j.jss.2006.06.006

Conte, D., Dunsmore, H., & Shen, V. (1986). *Software Engineering Metrics and Models*. San Francisco, CA: The Benjamin/Cummings Publishing Company, Inc.

Cortes, C., & Vapnik, V. (1995). Support-vector networks. *Machine Learning*, *20*(3), 273–297. doi:10.1007/BF00994018

Deng, J. (1989). Introduction to Grey System Theory. *Journal of Grey System*, *1*, 1–24.

Desharnais, J. M. (1989). *Analyse Statistique de la Productivitie des Projets Informatique a Partie de la Technique des Point des Function*. Unpublished Masters Thesis, University of Montreal, Montreal, Canada.

Dolado, J. J. (2000). A Validation of the Component-based Method for Software Size Estimation. *IEEE Transactions on Software Engineering*, *26*(10), 1006–1021. doi:10.1109/32.879821

Finnie, G. R., Wittig, G. E., & Desharnais, J. M. (1997). A Comparison of Software Effort Estimation Techniques: Using Function Points with Neural Networks, Case-based Reasoning and Regression Models. *Journal of Systems and Software*, *39*(3), 281–289. doi:10.1016/S0164-1212(97)00055-1

Glover, F., & Laguna, M. (1997). *Tabu Search*. Boston: Kluwer Academic Publishers.

Goldberg, D. E. (1989). *Genetic Algorithms in Search, Optimization, and Machine Learning*. Reading, MA: Addison-Wesley.

Harman, M. (2007). The Current State and Future of Search Based Software Engineering. In Proceedings of Future of Software Engineering, Minneapolis, MN, (pp. 342-357).

Harman, M., & Jones, B. F. (2001). Search based software engineering. *Information and Software Technology*, *43*(14), 833–839. doi:10.1016/S0950-5849(01)00189-6

Holland, J. (1975). *Adaptation in Natural and Artificial Systems*. Ann Arbor, MI: University of Michigan Press.

Huang, C. L., & Wang, C. J. (2006). A GA-based Feature Selection and Parameters Optimization for Support Vector Machines. *Expert Systems with Applications*, *31*(2), 231–240. doi:10.1016/j.eswa.2005.09.024

Huang, S. J., Chiu, N. H., & Chen, L. W. (2008). Integration of the Grey Relational Analysis with Genetic Algorithm for Software Effort Estimation. *European Journal of Operational Research, 188*(3), 898–909. doi:10.1016/j.ejor.2007.07.002

ISBSG. (2009). *International Software Benchmarking Standards Group.* Retrieved from www.isbsg.org

Kemerer, C. F. (1987). An Empirical Validation of Software Cost Estimation Models. *Communications of the ACM, 30*(5), 416–429. doi:10.1145/22899.22906

Kennedy, J., & Eberhart, R. C. (1995). Particle Swarm Optimization. In *Proceedings of IEEE International Conference on Neural Networks,* Beijing, China, (pp. 1942–1948).

Kitchenham, B., Pickard, L. M., MacDonell, S. G., & Shepperd, M. J. (2001). What Accuracy Statistics Really Measure. *IEEE Software, 148*(3), 81–85. doi:10.1049/ip-sen:20010506

Koch, S., & Mitlöhner, J. (2009). Software Project Effort Estimation with Voting Rules. *Decision Support Systems, 46*(4), 895–901. doi:10.1016/j.dss.2008.12.002

Lefley, M., & Shepperd, M. J. (2003). Using Genetic Programming to Improve Software Effort Estimation based on General Data Sets. In *Proceedings of Genetic and Evolutionary Computation Conference,* Chicago, (pp. 2477–2487).

Li, Y. F., Xie, M., & Goh, T. N. (2009). A Study of Project Selection and Feature Weighting for Analogy based Software Cost Estimation. *Journal of Systems and Software, 82*(2), 241–252. doi:10.1016/j.jss.2008.06.001

Matson, J. E., Barrett, B. E., & Mellichamp, J. M. (1994). Software Development Cost Estimation using Function Points. *IEEE Transactions on Software Engineering, 20*(4), 275–287. doi:10.1109/32.277575

Metropolis, N., Rosenbluth, A., Rosenbluth, M., Teller, A., & Teller, E. (1953). Equation of State Calculations by Fast Computing Machines. *The Journal of Chemical Physics, 21*(6), 1087–1092. doi:10.1063/1.1699114

Oliveira, A. L. I. (2006). Estimation of Software Project Effort with Support Vector Regression. *Neurocomputing, 69*(13-15), 1749–1753. doi:10.1016/j.neucom.2005.12.119

Parlos, A. G., Fernandez, B., Atyla, A., Muthusami, J., & Tsai, W. (1994). An Accelerated Algorithm for Multilayer Preceptor Networks. *IEEE Transactions on Neural Networks, 5*(3), 493–497. doi:10.1109/72.286921

Rumelhart, D. E., Hinton, G. E., & Williams, R. J. (1988). Learning representations by backpropagating errors. In Neurocomputing: foundations of research, (pp. 696-699).

Shan, Y., Mckay, R. I., Lokan, C. J., & Essam, D. L. (2002). Software Project Effort Estimation using Genetic Programming. In *Proceedings of International Conference on Communications Circuits and Systems,* Chengdu, China, (Vol. 2, pp. 1108–1112).

Shepperd, M., & Schofield, C. (2000). Estimating Software Project Effort using Analogies. *IEEE Transactions on Software Engineering, 23*(11), 736–743. doi:10.1109/32.637387

Shin, M., & Goel, A. L. (2000). Empirical Data Modeling in Software Engineering using Radical Basis Functions. *IEEE Transactions on Software Engineering, 26*(6), 567–576. doi:10.1109/32.852743

Shukla, K. K. (2000). Neuro-Genetic Prediction of Software Development Effort. *Information and Software Technology, 42*(10), 701–713. doi:10.1016/S0950-5849(00)00114-2

Srinivasan, K., & Fisher, D. (1995). Machine Learning Approaches to Estimating Software Development Effort. *IEEE Transactions on Software Engineering, 21*(2), 126–137. doi:10.1109/32.345828

Uysal, M. (2008). Estimation of the Effort Component of the Software Projects Using Simulated Annealing Algorithm. In *Proceedings of World Academy of Science* (pp. 258–261). Buenos Aires, Argentina: Engineering and Technology.

Chapter 3
The Application of Genetic Algorithms to the Evaluation of Software Reliability

Angel Fernando Kuri-Morales
Instituto Tecnológico Autónomo de México, México

ABSTRACT

The evaluation of software reliability depends on a) The definition of an adequate measure of correctness and b) A practical tool that allows such measurement. Once the proper metric has been defined it is needed to estimate whether a given software system reaches its optimum value or how far away this software is from it. Typically, the choice of a given metric is limited by the ability to optimize it: mathematical considerations traditionally curtail such choice. However, modern optimization techniques (such as Genetic Algorithms [GAs]) do not exhibit the limitations of classical methods and, therefore, do not limit such choice. In this work the authors describe GAs, the typical limitations for measurement of software reliability (MSR) and the way GAs may help to overcome them.

1. INTRODUCTION

The IEEE defines reliability as "The ability of a system or component to perform its required functions under stated conditions for a specified period of time." Rosenberg, L., Hammer, T., Shaw, J. (1998) wrote that to most project and software development managers, reliability is equated to correctness. That is, they look to testing and, thereafter, finding and fixing the "bugs" thus yielding the "correct" software. Typically we are not satisfied with merely

"correct" software. Rather we also seek software which also displays a certain amount of quality. Intuitively, one of the basic elements of software's quality is its correctness, i.e. a program's characteristic of outputting adequately (correctly) for all possible inputs. On first look it would seem that correctness is the least one could ask of reliable software. Unfortunately, one of the basic theoretical consequences of the analysis by Turing (1936) is that there is no algorithm (or program) which will, in all cases, be able to determine whether another algorithm (or program) will behave correctly. In other words, correctness is incomputable. Therefore,

DOI: 10.4018/978-1-61520-809-8.ch003

the assessment of software's correctness turns out to be formally undecidable. In practice, therefore, one has to acquiesce with the fact that practical "correctness" results from conscientious testing, and practically finding and (hopefully) fixing bugs.

Since finding and fixing bugs discovered in testing is necessary to assure reliability, a methodology leading to the development of a robust, high quality product through all of the stages of the software lifecycle is most desirable. That is, the reliability of the delivered code is related to the quality of all of the processes and products of software development; the requirements documentation, the code, test plans, and testing.

Software reliability is not a well defined concept, but there are important efforts striving to identify and apply metrics to software products that promote and assess reliability. Reliability is a by-product of quality, and software quality can be measured. Quality metrics assist in the evaluation of software reliability.

ISO 9126 (1991) defines six quality characteristics, one of which is reliability. Gillies (1992) indicates that "A software reliability management program requires the establishment of a balanced set of user quality objectives, and identification of intermediate quality objectives that will assist in achieving the user quality objectives." Since reliability is an attribute of quality, it can be concluded that software reliability depends on high quality software.

1.1 Optimizing from Quality Criteria

If we are able to objectively define the elements on which software's quality depends then we will be able to define an objective measure of it. Furthermore, we will also be able to compare different software systems purportedly solving the same set of problems and establish a solid figure of relative merit. Once having defined the most adequate metrics the assessment of software quality becomes one of optimization: namely, the maximization of the figure of merit. The problem of how to achieve

efficient optimization has led to the development of computer intensive methods which differ from the classical ones in various respects. The classical optimization techniques are useful in finding the optimum solution or unconstrained maxima or minima of continuous and differentiable functions. These are analytical methods and make use of differential calculus in locating the optimum solution. The classical methods have limited scope in practical applications as some of them involve objective functions which are not continuous and/or differentiable. These methods typically assume that the function is twice differentiable with respect to the design variables and that the derivatives are continuous. The quality criteria related to software quality which are to be optimized do not satisfy the above requirements. In fact, they do not usually even correspond to a closed form function. Therefore a new approach to the optimization is needed, one which is not dependent on the mathematical properties just mentioned. Several such optimization techniques have been advanced and analyzed during the past years. They were inspired by natural evolution and are collectively called "Evolutionary Computation" (EC).

1.2 Evolutionary Computation

Throughout the years since their inception there have been several attempts to mimic (albeit partially) the process of biological evolution. The primary motivation arises from the fact that living beings are seen as advanced solutions to the problem of adaptation to a dynamic but (relatively) stable environment; they are the by-product of optimal adaptation to dynamic habitats. Some of the evolutionary methods are more mathematically demanding while others are more intuitive. In a work of this kind it is impossible to even skim over all of them. It is enough, in this context, to say that examples of EC are Evolution Strategies, Evolutionary Programming, Genetic Programming, Learning Classifier Systems and Genetic Algorithms (GAs). Among these the most popular technique is the one corresponding to GAs. GAs are simple to understand and program. More importantly, they are reasonably well understood. We, therefore, restrict our attention to them.

The basic aim of this work is to analyze the possible usefulness of GAs to the problem of evaluating software reliability. Therefore, we must establish a link between the use of adequate quality metrics and evolutionary optimization techniques. We start by discussing GAs. The treatment of the basic characteristics of GAs is aimed at the non-mathematically inclined reader and we have tried to retain an intuitive feeling when introducing the concepts although some mathematical background is still required.

2. BASIC TENETS OF GENETIC ALGORITHMS

Genetic Algorithms and Evolutionary Computation at large are often referred to as "optimum solution search methods which partially simulate the process of natural evolution". Although this definition is evocative and useful as an analogy, it has the disadvantage of suggesting (given the obvious complexity involved in the accurate simulation of biological evolutionary mechanisms) that it may consist of a set of informal and heuristic techniques which may or may not achieve their goal. Nothing is further from the truth. In fact, GAs have several interesting mathematically proven characteristics.

1. The function to be optimized does not have to comply with any preset mathematical requirements. In fact, in many of the more interesting applications such function is not even known and is replaced by an adequate simulation of the system under study.

2. The GA will always converge to the global optimum as Rudolph (1994) proved. This is true in general and given this proven fact the attention of the practitioner shifts from effectiveness to efficiency.

3. The said convergence does not depend (as many other numerical methods do) on the way the starting points are chosen. In fact, it is better to randomly generate the initial set of starting points (the "population").

There are many ways to implement the characteristics mentioned above in an evolutionary algorithm. That is, there is not "a Genetic Algorithm". Rather, there are many possible alternatives. For historical reasons, the so-called Simple Genetic Algorithm is the best known.

2.1 The Canonical Genetic Algorithm

The Canonical (or Simple) GA is as follows.

Outline of the Basic (Simple) Genetic Algorithm

1. Generate random population of n individuals (suitable solutions for the problem)
2. Evaluate the fitness $f(x)$ of each individual x in the population.
3. If the end condition is satisfied, stop, and return the best solution in current population.
4. Create a new population by repeating steps A, B, and C until the new population is complete.
   a. Select two individuals (the *parents*) from a population according to their fitness (the better fitness, the larger chance to be selected).
   b. With probability Pc (crossover probability) cross over the parents to form two new individuals (the *offspring*). If no crossover is performed, offspring are an exact copy of the parents.
   c. With probability Pm (mutation probability) mutate new offspring at each locus (position in individual).
5. Place the new offspring in a new population; discard the previous population.
6. Go to step 2

This algorithm, as stated, is called the "Simple" or "Canonical" GA (CGA). The CGA was initially proposed in Holland (1975). It is easy to analyze (to a certain extent) but it does have several shortcomings. It is possible to envision a number of variations which improve the CGA's performance as will be discussed in the sequel. Therefore, the CGA is NOT the best choice but it is the one that we are likely to find in most references, hence the name "canonical". Since it is well understood it may be used as a standard against which other GA variations may be compared. The CGA (as all other GAs) is sensitive to the proliferation of copies of the best individuals at an early stage, which hampers its convergence speed. On the other hand, in order to obtain the probabilistic behavior outlined above, one must cope with the fact that some fitness values may be negative. Therefore, negative fitness values must be mapped into positive ones[1]. Besides, the CGA does not include provisions for elitism. All of these shortcomings may be satisfactorily solved as will be shown in the sequel.

2.2 General Considerations on Genetic Algorithms

In what follows we discuss the underlying principles of a GA trying not to veer into the peculiarities of any one particular breed unless otherwise noted. To emphasize the mathematical underpinnings of the optimization process involved, we choose to describe a GA as follows:

A Genetic Algorithm is an optimization method which:

1. Explicitly works on a discrete search space.
2. Considers a small number of plausible solutions.
3. Randomly determines the initial set of points.
4. Searches the solution space by probing several points (plausible solutions) simultaneously.

5. Iteratively refines the quality of the set of points.
6. Replaces the set of original points by processing the information obtained during each iteration using the so-called *genetic operators*. Typically [there are many more possible choices as discussed in Bäck (1996)] the operators are *selection*, *crossover* and *mutation*.
7. Retains a copy of the *n* best evaluated individuals (where $n \geq 1$) in a process called *elitism*.
8. Repeats steps (d), (e), (f) and (g) for a predefined number of times.

2.2.1 Comments Regarding the Operation of a Genetic Algorithm

We make some explanatory comments regarding points (a) to (g).

2.2.1.1 It Explicitly Works on a Discrete Search Space

Comment. Although any computerized method ultimately works in a finite space a GA does so explicitly. The "real" variables in a computer are, actually, binary numbers somehow encoding an alleged real variable. But this fact normally remains hidden from the user. In a GA the representation is explicit. A number is encoded according to the problem in a convenient way. A frequent way of encoding is by using the weighted binary code. One possible binary format for real number representation demands for one sign bit ("1" is minus; "0" is plus), "I" bits for the integer part of a variable and "F" bits for the fractional part[2]. Thus, for I = 4 and F = 20 a "real" variable consists of 25 bits. With this format (to which we will refer as the *sif* format) the number $x=-8.75$ is encoded as $x=1100011000000000000000000$. Let us say, for example, that we wish to maximize the function $f(x,y)=-(x-5)^2-(y-3)^2$. Using the said conventions we need 50 bits to represent the possible values of x and y. There are 2^{50} binary combinations of

50 bits (approximately 1.126×10^{15}). This number expresses the different choices for the values of x and y. Were we to evaluate all possible combinations of $f(x,y)$ at the rate of 1 million per second we would find the solution in about 10^9 seconds (close to 36 years worth of uninterrupted processing time). A GA will find the optimum values $(x=5, y=3)$ in a fraction of a second.

2.2.1.2 It Searches the Solution Space by Evaluating a Small Set of Plausible Solutions

Comment. The basic idea is that a set of individuals (called the *population*) is evaluated to check how good an individual is in terms of the problem to solve (the *fitness* of the individual). Consider the maximization of $z=f(x,y)=-(x-5)^2-(y-3)^2$. One possible individual is the vector *(4,-2)* *(4,-2)*; another is the vector *(10,-15)*. Notice that any plausible solution (i.e. any pair of real numbers) is a candidate individual. In this regard, the complex vector *(3+2i,-5+3i)* is NOT a plausible solution because we have defined our domain as the set of real numbers. Clearly, *f(4,-2)=-26* while *f(10.-15)=-349*. In this sense, individual *(4,-2)* is better than individual *(10,-15)* because *f(4,-2)* is larger than *f(10,-15)*. The fitness of *(4,-2)* and *(10,-15)* are *-26* and *-349* respectively; and $f(x,y)=-(x-5)^2-(y-3)^2$ is, here, the fitness function. The number of individuals is selected beforehand. It is not immediately intuitive that the analysis of a restricted set of initial individuals will allow the algorithm to target on the best solution. As it may be formally proven that is, however, the case. The size of the population influences the dynamics of the process but not its final result.

2.2.1.3 It Randomly Determines the Initial Set of Points

Comment. As opposed to typical non-evolutionary optimization methods, GAs are not subject to specific starting points to ensure the proper behavior of the algorithm. A GA will reach the optimum value regardless of its starting configuration. In other words, for a large variety of population sizes and regardless of the values of the starting individuals the GA will find the global optimum. On the other hand, only in very particular cases does the knowledge of the problem (and the ensuing possibility of specifically selecting the initial values of the individuals) will guarantee faster convergence. Perhaps anti-intuitively, GAs will typically be more efficient if the starting elements of the population are randomly chosen. In very broad terms this is due to the fact that starting points inserted "by hand" will focus the initial search on a sub-space which may easily become an attractor. Such attractors are not necessarily close to the global optimum. The GA will eventually exit the zone of attraction but it will do so at the expense of extra computation.

2.2.1.4 Searches the Solution Space by Probing Several Points (Plausible Solutions) Simultaneously

Comment. Virtually all non-evolutionary optimization methods start on *one* preselected "seed" point and try to iteratively refine the solution[3]. Hopefully, every step will get us closer to the global optimum. For instance, in the popular (and classical) *Steepest Ascent method* we take advantage of the fact that the gradient of a function $f(x)$ [denoted by $\nabla f(x)$] is a vector which points in the direction of largest increment of f. Given a point $x_0 \in R^n$ of the domain of $f: R^n \rightarrow R$ if $\lambda 0_\in R+$ is a positive scalar then in the vector $x0_+ \lambda 0 \nabla_f(x0)$ the value of f is larger than in x0. Taking advantage of this fact we define an iterative process where $xi =_x i-1_{+\lambda} i-1_{\nabla f} xi-1_)$. In this expression $\lambda i-1$ _max_imizes $\varphi(\lambda)=xi-1+\lambda i_{-1\nabla} f(x_{i-1})$. T_o_i llustrate let us maximize $z=f(x,y)=-(x-5)2-(y-3)^2$. We a^{t}bitrarily select as a starting point v0=(1,1) *For z* we obtain $\nabla(x,y)=(-2(x-5),-2(y-3))$ *from* which $\nabla(1,1)=(8,4)$. *We mu*st find a t0 such $_i$hat f(t0) is $_m_a$ximized thus:

$$
\begin{aligned}
f(t_0) &= f(1,1) + t_0(8,4) \\
&= f(1 + 8t_0, 1 + 4t_0) \\
&= -(8t_0 - 4)^2 - (4t_0 - 2)^2 \\
&= -80t_0^2 + 80t_0 - 20
\end{aligned}
\tag{1}
$$

Differentiating this and equating to 0 we get f'(t0)=-$_8$0(2t0-1)_0; t0=1/$_2$. The new point is, therefore, v1=(*1 1*)+(*1/2*)(*8,4*)=(*5,3*). Now $\nabla f(5,3)=0$ *and* the process ends. In this simple problem the seed is the point (1,1). It is fairly obvious that, in general, it is difficult to establish a point which is adequate a pr*iori sin*ce, in some cases, the steps of the method will not lead us to a point closer to the solution; that is, the method will diverge. GAs, on the other hand, rely not on one but on seve*ral po*ints ("individuals") from which the GA tries to extract information that leads its search to the global optimum. Furthermore, regardless of how the initial values of the individuals are set, the GA will converge to an adequate solution. This unobvious fact may be proven by noticing that a GA may be modeled as a Markov chain (MC). Markov (1971) showed that the probability that a given state of the MC is reached is independent of the initial state.4

2.2.1.5 Iteratively Refines the Quality of the Set of Points

Comment. Every individual is graded according to a set of criteria which, taken together, comprise the *fitness function.* The fitness is that which is being optimized. It may or may not have a well defined mathematical expression. To a GA it makes no difference as long as one is able to assign a figure of merit to each particular individual. In contrast, typical optimization methods rely on the fact that the functions to optimize are differentiable and/or convex and/or have some other mathematical properties which yield an adequate behavior. To the GA the only requirement is that it is computable. Most problems in a finite space are computable.

A GA, therefore, starts by evaluating a set of plausible alternatives (the individuals in the population) and iteratively replaces the initial population by the following ones which are found on an individual-by-individual basis. However, the behavior of the population as a whole is improved as a consequence of the individual's improvement.

2.2.1.6 It Replaces the Set of Original Points by Combining the Information Obtained During Each Iteration Using the So-Called Genetic Operators

Comment. The typical operators are *selection, crossover* and *mutation.*

2.2.1.6.1 *Selection* refers to the way an individual in a population is chosen to "survive". It is here that the phrase "survival of the fittest" is invoked. The most frequently cited selection mechanism (called *proportional* selection) yields a random subset of the original individuals giving preference to those whose fitness is proportionally better in terms of the average fitness of the population. Assume, for example, function *z* (see above) and a population that consists of 50 individuals $(x_p y_p)$. The fitness of individual *i* will be denoted by f_i while the population's cumulative fitness f_c is given by

$$f_c = \sum_{i=1}^{50} -(x_i - 5)^2 - (y_i - 3)^2 .$$

Accordingly, individual *i* will be selected with probability $P(i)=f_i/f_c$. For the purpose of this example, assume that f_c is *-200*. Then the individual *(+4,-2)* be selected with probability

$$P_{(+4,-2)} = \frac{f_{(+4,-2)}}{f_c} = \frac{-26}{-200} = 0.13 .$$

Likewise, individual (+10,-10) will be selected with probability

$$P_{(+10,-10)} = \frac{-194}{-200} = 0.97 .$$

The idea is that the *genes* of the individuals (i.e. the bits by which an individual is encoded) will be selected more frequently when they convey the characteristics which make them better suited to solve the fitness problem.

2.2.1.6.2 *Crossover* refers to the process of randomly interchanging segments of couples of individuals. Assume we use the *sif* format outlined above. The individuals I_1=(*+4,-2*) and I_2=(*_10,-15*) would be encoded as follows. +4 is encoded as "00100 00000 00000 00000 00000", -2 as "10010 00000 00000 00000 00000" and the vector (+4, -2) is simply obtained by concatenating both codes, thus:

I_1 = *(+4,-2)* → "**00100 00000 00000 00000 00000 10010 00000 00000 00000 00000**"

Likewise,

I_2 = *(+10,-15)* → "01010 00000 00000 00000 00000 11111 00000 00000 00000 00000".

We can easily calculate the fitness of I_1 to be -26 whereas the one of I_2 is -349. A hypothetical random choice of position 27 of the *chromosome* (the encoded version of an individual) as the crossover point would take the full code of *(+4,-2)*(consisting of 25 bits) plus the leftmost 2 bits of *(+10,-15)*and concatenate to it the rightmost 23 bits of *(+10,-15)* to get:

I_{12}= "**00100 00000 00000 00000 00000 10**111 00000 00000 00000 00000"

which corresponds to the vector (+4,-7) with a fitness of -101. The complementary code [25 bits of *(+10,-15)* plus the two leftmost bits of *(+4,-2)* concatenated with the rightmost 23 bits of *(+4,-2)*] yields

I_{21} = "01010 00000 00000 00000 00000 11**010 00000 00000 00000 00000**"

This corresponds to the vector (+10,-10) with a fitness of -194.

We have, thus, produced two new (*offspring*) numbers by mixing the elements of the two original (*parent*) ones. It is from this process that the name *genetic* comes from. In a suggestive analogy, the code of the individual corresponds to the *genotype* of a living being and its numerical value to the *phenotype*. The elements of the code correspond to the *genes* of a species. Crossing over two individuals is an analogy of the DNA exchange during the sexual reproduction phase of living beings. I_{12} and I_{21} are the descendants of I_1 and I_2. In this particular example the two offspring have a better fitness (-101 and -194) than one of their parents (-26). Individuals *(+10,-10)* and *(+10,-15)* would tend to be retained in the populations of following generations. Every iteration is called a *generation* in obvious reference to the biological counterpart. The crossover scheme illustrated here is called "1-point crossover" for obvious reasons. But other alternatives (annular or uniform crossover, for instance {for which see Kuri (1998)}) are possible.

2.2.1.6.3 *Mutation.* It should be clear that every evaluation of our function is an exploration of the solution space. Evidently the number of possible combinations of a limited population (even for relatively small ones) does not guarantee that the GA will explore all points of the space and, therefore, it does not guarantee that it will find the solution. To enrich the scope of the search, random alterations are forced in the bits of the individuals. This is done with low probability lest the convergence process be importantly disturbed. Consider again I_1=*(+4,-2)*. As before, it is encoded by "00100 00000 00000 00000 0000 10010 00000 00000 00000 00000". Recall it has a fitness of -26. Now assume that bit 6 of its chromosome changes from its original value of "0" to "1" (i.e. bit 6 *mutates*). The numerical value of the mutated vector is now (+4.5,-2) and its fitness is -25.25. It has slightly improved but, more importantly, the *genetic pool* has been positively enriched.

In fact, it is mutation which guarantees that a GA will reach a global optimum. For assume that at any given time a bit encoding the optimum solution is not present in any of the individuals of the population. There is a non-zero probability of this bit to mutate into the correct value. Therefore, by this process, eventually all possible combinations will be tested and no element of the search space will remain unexplored. This, of course, is not satisfactory in itself since the time needed for convergence is not bounded. It is for this reason that combination and selection form an integral part of any GA.

2.2.1.7 It Retains a Copy of the *n* Best Evaluated Individuals (Where *n≥1*) in a Process called *Elitism*

Comment. Intuitively a GA as described above (*without* elitism) will *not* find the solution to the optimization problem. Since the individuals of the population are continuously crossed over and mutated eventually the code corresponding to the solution (if it has been found) will be altered with probability 1 because of the mutation operator's action. The GA's process typically stops after a predetermined number of generations. Therefore, there is a nonzero probability of stopping after the best value has been lost. This situation is reversed if the GA is run *with* elitism. Elitism simply means that the best fitness value (and the corresponding individual) up to iteration *t* is preserved. Clearly, once a good value is found it will be retained until (and if) a better one is found. This ensures that the GA will halt having stored the best possible value. Notice that the GA will sometimes come up, in generation *t*, with a best individual that is worse than the best of generation *t-1*. However, if the best individual is stored, the best value up to generation *t* may never suffer a setback. This is particularly advantageous once the global solution has been reached. It may be that best value of the last generation is NOT the best. But if the solution was found in the previous generation it may never be lost.

2.2.1.8 Conclusion

GAs are optimization tools which may yield the best solution to an optimization problem every time. On the other hand, even if a GA is stopped before having reached the optimum value, Goldberg (1989) argues that it will reach a point *close* to the best value in logarithmic time. However, the convergence process is not bounded in time. Two recognized causes for a CGA (or any GA, for that matter) to get temporarily trapped in local

Table 1. Relative performance of different breeds of genetic algorithms

Algorithm	Relative Performance	Number of Optimized Functions
VGA	1.000	2,736
EGA	1.039	2,484
TGA	1.233	2,628
SGA	1.236	2,772
CGA	1.267	3,132
RHC	3.830	3,600

minima (and thus slowing down the process of convergence) are the so-called *deceptive functions* and the *spurious correlation* [both discussed in Mitchell (1992)]. Suffice it to say here that both are related to the fact that the genetic pool lacks the needed variety. Hence, the next issue in our agenda is to find a way such that the process of convergence is not only effective but efficient as well. In other words, since a GA will eventually zero-in on the best value, how does one make this process to be *fast*?

2.3 An Improved Genetic Algorithm

In Kuri (2002) a statistical analysis was performed by minimizing a large *(17,352)* number of functions and comparing the relative performance of six optimization methods[5] of which five are GAs. The ratio of every GA's absolute minimum (with probability *P=0.95*) relative to the best GA's absolute minimum may be found in Table 1 under the column "Relative Performance". The number of functions which were minimized to guarantee the mentioned confidence level is shown under "Number of Optimized Functions".

It may be seen that the so-called Vasconcelos' GA (VGA) in this study was the best of all the analyzed variations. Interestingly the CGA comes at the bottom of the list with the exception of the random mutation hill climber (RHC) which is not an evolutionary algorithm. According to these results, the minima found with the VGA are, on the average, more than 25% better than those found with the CGA. The interested reader may find the detailed description of the different GAs in Kuri and Gutiérrez (2002). Due to its tested efficiency, we now describe in more detail the VGA.

2.3.1 Vasconcelos' Genetic Algorithm

Outline of Vasconcelos' Genetic Algorithm (VGA)

1. Generate random population of *n* individuals (suitable solutions for the problem)
2. Evaluate the fitness *f(x)* of each individual *x* in the population
3. Order the *n* individuals from best (top) to worst (bottom) for *i=1, 2,..., n* according to their fitness.
4. Repeat steps A-D for *i=1,2,..., ⌊n/2⌋*.
   a. *Deterministically* select the *i-th* and the *(n-i+1)-th* individuals (the *parents*) from the population.
   b. With probability *Pc* cross over the selected parents to form two new individuals (the *offspring*). If no crossover is performed, offspring are an exact copy of the parents.
   c. With probability *Pm* mutate new offspring at each locus (position in individual).
   d. Add the offspring to a new population
5. Evaluate the fitness *f(x)* of each individual *x* in the new population
6. Merge the newly generated and the previous populations
7. If the end condition is satisfied, stop, and return the best solution.
8. Order the *n* individuals from best to worst (*i=1, 2,..., n*) according to their fitness
9. Retain the top *n* individuals; discard the bottom *n* individuals
10. Go to step 4

2.3.1.2 Comment

As opposed to the CGA, the VGA selects the candidate individuals deterministically picking the two extreme performers of the generation for crossover. This would seem to fragrantly violate the survival-of-the-fittest strategy behind evolutionary processes since the genes of the more apt individuals are mixed with those of the least apt ones. However, the VGA also retains the best *n* individuals out of the *2n* previous ones. The net effect of this dual strategy is to give variety to the genetic pool (the lack of which, remember, is a cause for slow convergence) while still retaining a high degree of elitism. This sort of elitism, of course, guarantees that the best solutions are not lost. On the other hand, the admixture of apparently counterpointed plausible solutions is aimed at avoiding the proliferation of similar genes in the pool. In nature as well as in GAs variety is needed in order to ensure the efficient exploration of the space of solutions[6]. As stated before, all GAs will eventually converge to a global optimum. The VGA does so in less generations. Alternatively we may say that the VGA will outperform other GAs given the same number of generations. Besides, it is easier to program because we need not to simulate a probabilistic process. Finally, the VGA is impervious to negative fitness values.

We, thus, have a tool which allows us to identify the best values for a set of predefined metrics possibly reflecting complementary goals. This metric(s) may be arbitrary and this suits us well because one way to establish which of a set of software systems is better than the other is to: a) Define a metric or set of metrics. b) Determine the one system whose combination is best for the systems.

3. MEASUREMENT OF SOFTWARE RELIABILITY

Software reliability engineering (SRE) is a disciplined approach to software quality assurance that efficiently directs testing resources to critical and/or frequently used functions of the software system. SRE ensures that the test effort realistically emulates the actual uses the software will see in the field. This approach leads to an improvement in quality as viewed from the point of view of the user. SRE should not be confused with software testing. The latter is a more generic term which includes attempting to verify all aspects of software quality. Software reliability engineering, on the other hand, is a focused, quantitative approach to testing. It concentrates resources on reducing software faults which will become observable failures to users. By focusing on user-oriented concerns, SRE excludes such software testing measurements such as unit-test code coverage which is a developer-oriented measure.

In the field of software reliability engineering, a number of models have been proposed for predicting the failure intensity of systems over time. The ability to predict failure intensity rates in the future is important as it allows for practitioners to better set release schedules. These models make use of simplifying assumptions in order to achieve their goals. In Far, B.H. (2005) we can find that they assume that the chance of discovering a failure in the system at any given time follows a random distribution. As such, it can be modeled using statistical random distributions. Another assumption is that the observed failure intensity for any time interval is independent of all other intervals [Musa, (1998)]. The use of evolutionary optimization techniques, however, opens a new avenue to SRE: the possibility of evaluating the quality of the software as it is being developed. In essence, this means that software's reliability may be quantified and modified accordingly as the software matures.

The IEEE defines reliability as *The ability of a system or component to perform its required functions under stated conditions for a specified period of time*. We already remarked that reliability is one of the criteria, attribute or characteristic that is incorporated. IEEE Std 982.2-1988 states "A software reliability management program requires the establishment of a balanced set of user quality objectives, and identification of intermediate quality objectives that will assist in achieving the user quality objectives."

Building high reliability software depends on the application of quality attributes at each phase of the development life cycle with the emphasis on error prevention, especially in the early life cycle phases. Metrics are needed at each development phase to measure applicable quality attributes.

3.1 Software Reliability Engineering and Genetic Algorithms

In focusing on error prevention for reliability, we need to identify and measure the quality attributes applicable at different life cycle phases. We need to specifically focus on requirements, design, implementation, and test phases. GAs require the definition of precise elements to determine the fitness function. The fitness function may be arbitrarily complicated. Its optimization (even partial), therefore, becomes impossible to tackle using traditional techniques. But to a GA, as already discussed, the optimization of such functions is perfectly feasible. Ultimately, the optimization of the desired fitness will lead to better more reliable software. The question is, therefore, what criteria should be included in the fitness function in order to achieve reliable software? In what follows we shall analyze some of the objective criteria which will lead to the definition of the proper function to optimize. We rely on the discussion of Rosenberg, L., Hammer, T., Shaw, J. (1998) which focused on the efforts of the Software Assurance Technology Center (SATC) at NASA. Specific software metrics are being used to help improve system reliability by identifying areas of the software requirements specification and code that can potentially cause errors.

Three life cycle phases where software metrics can be applied to impact the reliability are:

1. Requirements
2. Coding
3. Testing.

We now address each of them.

3.1.1 Metrics for Requirements Reliability

Requirements specify the functionality that must be included in the final software. It is critical that the requirements be written such that there is no misunderstanding between the developer and the user. The requirements must be structured, complete, and easy to apply. Formats for requirement specification structure have been defined [see, for instance, IEEE Standard 982.2 (1987), NASA Software Assurance guidebook (1989), Department of Defense (1994)] which specify the content of the requirement specification outside the requirements themselves. Consistent use of a format such as this ensures that critical information, such as operational environment, is not omitted. Complete requirements ought to be stable and thorough, specified in adequate detail to allow design and implementation to proceed. In order to develop reliable software from the requirements phase forward, the requirements must not contain ambiguous terms or any terminology that could be interpreted as an optional requirement. The importance of correctly documenting requirements has led the software industry to produce a significant number of aids to the creation and management of the requirements specification documents and individual specification statements. Tools have been developed to parse requirement documents. The Automated Requirements Measurement (ARM) software was developed for scanning a file that contains the text of the requirement specification. During this scan process, it searches each line of text for specific words and phrases. These search arguments (specific words and phrases) are an indicator of the document's quality as a specification of requirements.

3.1.1.1 Automated Requirements Measurement

Seven measures were developed:

1. **Lines of Text:** Physical lines of text as a measure of size.
2. **Imperatives:** Words and phrases that command that something must be done or provided. The number of imperatives is used as a base requirements count.
3. **Continuances:** Phrases that follow an imperative and introduce the specification of requirements at a lower level, for a supplemental requirement count.
4. **Directives:** References provided to figures, tables, or notes.
5. **Weak Phrases:** Clauses that are apt to cause uncertainty and leave room for multiple interpretation measure of ambiguity.
6. **Incomplete:** Statements within the document that have TBD (To be Determined) or TBS (To Be Supplied).
7. **Options:** Words that seem to give the developer latitude in satisfying the specifications but can be ambiguous.

3.1.2 Metrics for Design and Code Reliability

Although there are design languages and formats, these do not lend themselves to an automated evaluation and metrics collection. It is needed to analyze the code for the structure and architecture to identify possible error prone modules based on

1. Complexity
2. Size
3. Modularity

3.1.2.1 Complexity

It is generally accepted that more complex modules are more difficult to understand and have a higher probability of defects than less complex modules [as discussed in Kitchenham, B., Pfleeger, S. (1996)]. Thus, complexity has a direct impact on overall quality and specifically on maintainability. There are many different types of complexity measurements. An adequate one is logical (Cyclomatic) complexity, which is computed as the number of linearly independent test paths.

3.1.2.2 Size

This is one of the oldest and most common forms of software measurement. Size of modules is itself a quality indicator. Size can be measured by: total lines of code, counting all lines; non-comment non-blank which decreases total lines by the number of blanks and comments and executable statements as defined by a language dependent delimiter.

3.1.2.3 Modularity

The most effective evaluation is a combination of size and complexity. The modules with both a high complexity and a large size tend to have the lowest reliability. Modules with low size and high complexity are also a reliability risk because they tend to be very terse code, which is difficult to change or modify. [Rosenberg, L., and Hammer, T. (1998)].

3.1.2.4 Object Oriented Code

These metrics are also applicable to object oriented code for which additional metrics are needed to evaluate the quality of the object oriented structure. For object oriented quality analysis we may consider: Weighted methods per class (WMC), Response for a Class (RFC), Coupling Between Objects (CBO), Depth in Tree (DIT), and Number of Children (NOC). Since there are very few industry guidelines for these metrics, a possible guideline based is called Weighted Methods per Class (WMC).

WMC is a predictor of how much time and effort is required to develop and maintain the class. The higher the WMC, the more testing necessary and maintenance is increased. In general, classes should have less than 20 methods, but up to 40 is acceptable. The complexity of a method should not exceed 5. Therefore, WMC is preferred to be

less than 100 and should not exceed 200. Classes with higher WMC will require extensive testing for comprehensive coverage. They also will be difficult to maintain. These classes have a low reliability.

3.1.3 Metrics for Testing Reliability

Testing metrics must take two approaches to comprehensively evaluate the reliability.

1. The evaluation of the test plan, ensuring that the system contains the functionality specified in the requirements. This activity should reduce the number of errors due to lack of expected functionality.
2. The evaluation of the number of errors in the code and rate of finding/fixing them. A model to simulate the finding of errors and projects the number of remaining errors and when they will all be identified has been developed in Triantafyllos, Vassiliadis and Kobrosly (1995).

To ensure that the system contains the functionality specified, test plans are written that contain multiple test cases; each test case is based on one system state and tests some functions that are based on a related set of requirements. The objective of an effective verification program is to ensure that every requirement is tested, the implication being that if the system passes the test, the requirement's functionality in included in the delivered system. An assessment of the traceability of the requirements to test cases is needed.

In the total set of test cases, each requirement must be tested at least once, and some requirements will be tested several times because they are involved in multiple system states in varying scenarios and in different ways. While each requirement should, in principle, be comprehensively tested, limited time and budget are always constraints upon writing and running test cases. To this effect it is convenient to apply statistical tests which will ensure the validity of the results to a given pre-specified level [Hammer, T., Rosenberg, L., Huffman, L., Hyatt, L. (1997)]. From an error trending perspective, the model developed by the SATC employs a straightforward implementation of the Musa Model to compute a nonlinear approximation to the cumulative errors found to date.

3.1.3.1 Musa Basic Model

The Musa model is named "basic" as it provides a simple approach to modeling failure intensity. It assumes that the execution time between failures is exponentially distributed. As well, the per-fault hazard rate is assumed to be constant. The failure intensity (λ) is a function of failure intensity at the start of execution (λ_o), the expected number of failures at a given time (μ), and the total number of failures occurring in an infinite time (ν_o).

$$\lambda(\mu) = \lambda_o \left(1 - \frac{\mu}{\nu_o} \right) \qquad (2)$$

Given this formulation, it is clear the Musa Basic model requires existing failure data be gathered from a running system such as a beta-test in order to be applied. This model is particularly recommended for use in a majority of industry situations by its author. He stresses its applicability to a wide variety of software projects as evidenced by its usefulness in a number of efficacy trials in industry performed by many researchers listed in the Musa text. The Basic model meets the goals defined by Musa for an effective model in that is widely applicable, simple, computes useful quantities, and is based on sound assumptions.

Rather than using the probabilistic approach to determine model parameters, however, an "iterative" process that employs a non-linear optimization technique to fit the model-generated cumulative error distribution curve to the actual cumulative error distribution curve is applied by SATC. A sum-of-difference-squared is used to de-termine the "best fit." Using the computed values and other functions defined by Musa allow us to estimate: (a) the number of errors remaining in the product, and (b) the time needed to detect the remaining errors. To relate manpower utilization to detecting the errors remaining in the product a modified version of the Musa Model where the linear term in the exponential is replaced by the integral of a Rayleigh function is used. Manpower utilization and cumulative manpower utilization curves can be computed, and then extrapolated to include the manpower needed to detect the remaining errors.

3.2 Applications

Metrics to measure software reliability do exist and can be used starting in the requirements phase. At each phase of the development life cycle, metrics can identify potential areas that may lead to problems or errors. Finding these areas in the phase they are developed decreases the cost and prevents potential ripple effects from the changes, later in the development life cycle. Metrics used early can aid in detection and correction of requirement faults that will lead to prevention of errors later in the life cycle. The cost benefits of finding and correcting problems in the requirements phase has been demonstrated to be at least a factor of 14, making a strong argument for pursuing this approach and building in reliability starting at the requirements phase.

3.3 Considering Constraints in Genetic Algorithms

The alert reader will have noticed, however, that there are no provisions in a GA (as we have defined it) to handle constraints in the values of the variables. And most of the problems of interest must consider restrictions to a certain degree. Without loss of generality a minimization with restrictions problem may be formulated as follows:

Minimize $\quad f(\vec{x}) \qquad \vec{x} \in \Re^n$

Subject to $\quad h_i(\vec{x}) = 0 \qquad i = 1,...m \qquad (3)$

$\qquad\qquad g_i(\vec{x}) \leq 0 \qquad i = m+1,...p$

Constraints define the feasible region, meaning that if the vector $\vec{x}$ complies with all constraints $h_i(\vec{x}) = 0$ and $g_i(\vec{x}) \leq 0$ then it belongs to the feasible region. Traditional methods relying on calculus demand that the functions and constraints have very particular characteristics (continuity, differentiability, second order derivability, etc.) while those based on GAs have not such limitations, as already pointed out. It is of practical interest to be able to ascertain which of the many proposed constraint handling strategies is best. The most popular approach to constrained optimization is the application of penalty functions as discussed in Coello (2001). In this approach, a constrained problem is transformed into a non-constrained one. The function under consideration is transformed as follows:

$$F(\vec{x}) = \begin{cases} f(\vec{x}) & \vec{x} \in \textit{feasible region} \\ P(\vec{x}) & \vec{x} \notin \textit{feasible region} \end{cases} \qquad (4)$$

and the problem described in (3) turns into the one of minimizing (4) if a proper selection of the penalty function is achieved. A successful and simple strategy discussed in Kuri and Gutiérrez (2002) consists of defining the penalty function $P(\vec{x})$ as follows:

$$P(\vec{x}) = \left[K - s\frac{K}{p} \right] \qquad (5)$$

where K is a large[7] constant $[O(10^9)]$, p is the number of constraints and s is the number of these which have been satisfied. K's only restriction is that it should be large enough to ensure that any non-feasible individual is graded much more poorly than any feasible one. Here the algorithm

receives information as to how many constraints have been satisfied but is not otherwise affected. The basic idea is that all individuals which do not satisfy *all* the constraints should be graded much more poorly than those who do. Hence, they are assigned a large value (remember that we are minimizing the function). Those individuals which do not satisfy all constraints may satisfy *some* of them. In this case they are assigned a value proportional to the number of constraints. The less constraints the individual satisfies, the closer to K their fitness will be. This allows for the GA to prefer those individuals which satisfy c constraints to those satisfying $c-1$ of them. However, we want any individual satisfying all constraints to be considered much better than one which does not comply with even one, which is why K is made *very* large. A simple example is the following. Assume that we wish to solve the following problem:

$W(x,y,z) = 2x^3 + 3x^2 + sin(2x) - y^2 + sin(xy) + cos(yz) + y - z^2 - z + 4 \qquad (6)$

Subject to:

$$F_1 = 3x^2 + sin(xy) - z^2 + 2 \geq 0$$
$$F_2 = 2x^3 - y^2 - z + 3 \geq 0 \qquad (7)$$
$$F_3 = sin(2x) + cos(yz) + y - 1 \geq 0$$

Let N be the number of individuals in the population, G the number of generations of the GA and K the penalty value. Then by setting *N=70, G=100,* and *K=10^9* we run a VGA to get *W(-0.029444882, 1.2638376802, 1.4009605795) = 0.010926.* We verify the conditions to get

$$F_1 = 0.002705488$$
$$F_2 = 0.001702681 \qquad (8)$$
$$F_3 = 0.006517990$$

Table 2. Quality variables and their acronyms

Requirements	Design and Code	Reliability	Object oriented code
Lines of Text (LOT) [L]	Complexity (COM) [X]	Test plan (TPL) [T]	Weighted methods per class (WMC) [H]
Imperatives (IMP) [I]	Size (SZE) [Z]	Number of errors in the code (NEC) [N]	Response for a Class (RFC) [F]
Continuances (CON) [C]	Modularity (MOD) [Y]	Rate of finding/fixing them (RFF) [R]	Coupling Between Objects (CBO) [B]
Directives (DIR) [D]			Depth in Tree (DIT) [J]
Weak Phrases (WPH) [W]			Number of Children (NOC) [K]
Incompletion (INC) [M]			
Options (OPT) [O]			

Indeed, all conditions F_1, F_2, F_3 are greater than zero, as required. This problem is non-linear on the function as well as on the conditions. Typical optimization methods would result ineffective when faced by this problem [see, for instance, Ruszczynski, A., (2006)] but, as shown, a GA may solve it easily. With this strategy in hand we may now tackle problems as the one above. And this allows us to establish the desirable values which make a high quality software system.

3.4 Software Reliability Engineering and Genetic Algorithms

Once the adequate metrics are identified and the measurement tools have been deviced one is able to apply GAs to optimize the fitness function which will reflect the priorities of the design team. In accordance with the previous discussion we may identify 13 variables to assess; 18 in the case we include those of object oriented code. We list them along with an identifying acronym in Table 2.

There are various ways in which one may take advantage of the optimization characteristics of a GA. We address with some detail the problem of establishing, given a set of specifications of a system and the possibility to determine the qualifications of the modules comprising such system, how to best combine the modules to target on the best software under the defined metrics.

The fitness function for software quality of an optimizing algorithm may be set in the following terms.

$$F(quality) = min(F_{req} + F_{dec} + F_{rel} + F_{oo}) \quad (9)$$

This function is to be minimized for high quality of software to be attained. It has been defined as the association of 4 metrics. Each one of these **metrics** contributes linearly to the overall grade of the system. The particular functions composing *F(quality)* are:

$$F_{req} = \rho(k_1 L + k_2 I + k_3 C + k_4 D + k_5 W + k_6 M + k_7 O) \quad (10)$$

$$F_{dec} = \delta(k_8 X + k_9 Z - k_{10} Y) \quad (11)$$

$$F_{rel} = \lambda(-k_{11} T + k_{12} N - k_{13} R) \quad (12)$$

$$F_{oo} = \omega(k_{14} H - k_{15} F + k_{16} B + k_{17} J + k_{18} K) \quad (13)$$

In order to allow the setting of particular preferences for the case in hand we have introduced 22 weighing constants. Variables $\rho \delta \lambda$ and ω weigh the relative importance assigned to each of the four metrics as described above while variables k1 to k18 s_{et} the relative values of the variables of each metric. In what follows we shall restrict our attention to those not having to do with object oriented code since there is not a general agreement on their relative importance. For the purposes of this argument we may simply consider that $\omega = 0$. *We* may, therefore, assign relative importance to each one of the metrics. Constants k1 - $_k7$ we_igh each of the seven elements of the requirements metric; constants k8, k_9 an_d k10 w_{ei}gh those of the design/code metric. Notice that the term for k10 h_{as} a negative sign attached to it, reflecting the fact that modularity (variable Y) i*s* desirable and we wish to maximize it. Since we have defined a minimization function, this sign is required. Constants k11, $_{kl}2$ a_{nd} k13, $_{ll}$kewise, affect the reliability metric. Again, negative signs have been assigned to the terms corresponding to k11 $(_{va}$riable T) and k13 $(_{va}$riable R).

The way we assign the values to the constants is a matter of choice. But an experienced system's analyst may assign reasonable values for the ran*ges of* such variables with ease. And here is where a GA may become a valuable tool. The method is as follows.

1. Determine the acceptable ranges to all variables.
2. Set the conditions for each of the variables as inequalities of the form8

$$c_{min(i)} \leq k_i \leq c_{max(i)} \qquad \forall i \qquad (14)$$

3.5 Run A GA

The GA will deliver the values of all the variables which:

1. Satisfy the constraints of (2)
2. Minimize the value of (1)

We assume that one has the tools outlined in section 3 allowing us to automatically determine the values of the variables. Then any system or subsystem will be adequately evaluated and assigned an objective grade. Our aim is to find the values within the specified ranges which will yield the best fitness function. Determining the values of the constants which will optimize the performance of a system is no easy task. But the GA will output such values efficiently. Furthermore, the designer is able to experiment with several different ranges and, upon multiple optimization runs, decide which set is the one that better suits his/her objectives.

3.5.1 Case Studies

In order to exemplify the application of the concepts outlined above we include two case studies. In the first one we illustrate by assigning numerical values to the parameters of Equation (9). Then we select appropriate values for the algorithm's parameters. In the second one we impose non-linear conditions on the constraints. In that case it is much more difficult to find the values of the parameters of Equation (9) fulfilling the constraints.

3.5.1.1 Case Study 1

In what follows we present a case study which illustrates the linear process outlined above. From Equations (9) we have:

$$F(quality) = min(F_{req} + F_{dec} + F_{rel} + F_{oo}) \qquad (15)$$

$$F_{req} = \rho(k_1L + k_2I + k_3C + k_4D + k_5W + k_6M + k_7O) \qquad (16)$$

$$F_{dec} = \delta(k_8X + k_9Z - k_{10}Y) \qquad (17)$$

$$F_{rel} = \lambda(-k_{11}T + k_{12}N - k_{13}R) \qquad (18)$$

In principle there are 16 variables whose values we would like to optimize in any specific case. To make the illustration simple we shall assume that the *requirements* have already been evaluated as a whole, yielding a grade of 3. We assume that the elements in our system are graded on a scale from 1 to 5, where "5" is best. In other words, we assume that

$$k_1L + k_2I + k_3C + k_4D + k_5W + k_6M + k_7O = 3 \tag{19}$$

We shall also assume that the design and code attributes of the system have already been evaluated yielding a grade of 4. That is, we also know that

$$k_8X + k_9Z - k_{10}Y = 4 \tag{20}$$

We have also measured the reliability items having to do with the costs associated to the test plan (T), the number of errors found in the code (N) and the cost involved in finding and fixing such errors (R). The grades for T, N and R have been given as follows: T = 5, N = 4 and R = 3. What we would like to determine are the following issues.

1. What relative importance should we assign to the quality of the requirements?
2. What relative importance should we assign to the design and code?
3. What relative importance should we assign to the reliability phase?

We establish, a priori, that the reliability phase is more important than the requirements and design/code phases. To this effect we set the following bounds:

$$0.2 \leq \rho \leq 0.4$$
$$0.1 \leq \delta \leq 0.5 \tag{21}$$
$$0.6 \leq \lambda \leq 1.0$$

Furthermore, the particular issues pertaining to the reliability phase are assigned the following bounds:

$$2 \leq k_{11} \leq 3$$
$$3 \leq k_{12} \leq 5 \tag{22}$$
$$4 \leq k_{13} \leq 6$$

What relative weights should we assign to the test plan, the cost of errors and the cost of debugging such errors in our systems? We also want to answer: What are the best values for the six parameters which will minimize the cost function given by Equation (15)?

The function to minimize becomes

$$F = 3\rho + 4\delta + \lambda(-5k_{11} + 4k_{12} - 3k_{13}) \tag{23}$$

As remarked, this function (which has been kept relatively simple for the purposes of this example; it could be arbitrarily complex) may be minimized by a GA. First, we decide to represent the six parameters with an S3.25 format. It is easy to see, from the upper bounds we imposed on the values of the parameters, that we will never need more than 3 bits for the integer part of the value (with 3 bits we may represent an upper value of "7", which is enough in this case). 25 binary decimals, on the other hand, yield a precision of close to 3 hundredths of a million ($2^{-25} \approx 3 \times 10^{-8}$). The individual in this simple example has, therefore, a length of 174 bits. Recall that we use a bit for the sign and, hence, every parameter requires 1 + 3 + 25 = 29 bits. Given that we have 6 such parameters we end up with 29×6=174 bits in the representation of a possible solution to our problem.

Once having decided on the representation, we also establish the following conditions for the GA:

- **Population size:** 200 individuals.
- **Number of generations:** 200.
- **Crossover ratio:** Pc = 0.9
- **Mutation ratio:** Pm = 0.005

With these values we proceed to run the algorithm. The values we obtained from one run are the following:

$$\rho = 0.2000178695$$
$$\delta = 0.1000171006$$
$$\lambda = 0.9999959469$$
$$k_{11} = 2.9999994040$$
$$k_{12} = 3.0000078976$$
$$k_{13} = 5.9999670684$$

(24)

Clearly, the algorithm has chosen the largest possible value of λ (within the constraints). It has performed similarly for k_{11}, k_{12} and k_{13}. The values of ρ and δ are not as direct. The overall minimum value found was -19.999659.

3.5.1.2 Case Study 2

The preceding example presented us with a problem whose conditions were simple enough and could have been tackled with several alternative methods. We now introduce a set of non-linear conditions to further illustrate the power of the genetic process. As above, the function to minimize is F=3ρ+4δ+λ(-5k$_{11}$+4k$_{12}$-3k$_{13}$). To make things more interesting we impose the following conditions:

$$\rho \approx \delta^3 + 2\delta - \delta$$
$$+10 \geq \delta \geq \text{-10}$$

(25)

$$\lambda \approx 2k_{11}^2 - 3k_{11} - 1$$
$$+10 \geq k_{11} \geq -10$$

(26)

$$k_{12} \approx 2\sin(k_{13}) - 2\tan(k_{13}) + (k_{13})^2$$
$$0.88 \geq k_{13} \geq 0.01$$

(27)

The constraints are not intended to necessarily be a reflection of common everyday cases.

Nonetheless they are perfectly feasible. In order to make clear the computational meaning of the "≈" symbol we replace each approximate equality with two inequalities, as follows:

$$\delta^3 + 2\delta - \delta + 0.01 \geq \rho \geq \delta^3 + 2\delta - \delta - 0.01$$

(28)

$$2k_{11}^2 - 3k_{11} - 0.99 \geq \lambda \geq 2k_{11}^2 - 3k_{11} - 1.01$$

(29)

$$2\sin(k_{13}) - 2\tan(k_{13}) + (k_{13})^2 + 0.01 \geq k_{12} \geq$$
$$2\sin(k_{13}) - 2\tan(k_{13}) + (k_{13})^2 - 0.01$$

(30)

Therefore, there are 12 constraints to be satisfied.

Now we represent the six parameters with an S4.25 format. The slight difference in representation is important. Here the upper bounds imposed on the values of the parameters require maximum values of size ±10. Thus, we need 4 bits for the integer part. As before, 25 binary decimals yield a precision of $2^{-25} \approx 3 \times 10^{-8}$. The individual in this example has a length of 180 bits since every parameter requires 1 + 4 + 25 = 30 bits. Given that we have 6 such parameters there are 30×6=180 bits in the representation of a possible solution to our problem. For this example we set

- **Population size:** 400 individuals.
- **Number of generations:** 1000.
- **Crossover ratio:** Pc = 0.9
- **Mutation ratio:** Pm = 0.005

The values we obtained from this run are the following:

$$\rho = \text{-3.911916435}$$
$$\delta = \text{-1.366312534}$$
$$\lambda = \text{-1.475757897}$$

(31)

$$k_{11} = 1.315355778$$
$$k_{12} = 0.008594364 \qquad (32)$$
$$k_{13} = 0.010186106$$

From which the minimized value of the fitness function is -7.50090218. The reader may verify that all constraints are satisfied.

The values of the parameters, clearly, are not as intuitive as in the former case. This is to be expected from the non-linearity of the constraints. And this is, precisely, the point to be made. We remarked in the introduction that genetic algorithms are powerful optimization techniques and, if properly handled, they are apt to find reasonable solutions where classical methods are not effective. This is the case in hand. Even though the constraints are non-linear the algorithm is able to find the best (minimum) value.

3.6 Modeling the Most Reliable Software System

With the method outlined it is possible to model the development path of the software so that it is best as the development proceeds. For assume that the initial design goals are reflected in the choice of the ranges and the values of the values for the metrics as defined above. Then the designer will be able to test the sensitivity of the software to the different values and ranges. Of course these values and ranges will depend, to a certain extent, on external variables not necessarily associated to the technical issues. Given such case it is simple to incorporate the new values of the development parameters into de model and perform a new evaluation of the best choices. The point is, of course, that even if these decisions have to be taken in order to ensure the successful completion of complex software systems, this is usually done informally. It is not our claim that a process of decision in these instances is to be assigned to a strictly formal method. However, as less and less importance is assigned to subjective decisions the

probability of success will increase. Furthermore, a knowledge base may be established and enriched by storing the elements involved on the case decisions. This possibility is interesting and would be difficult to achieve via non evolutionary methods.

In conclusion, evolutionary computation (here illustrated with genetic algorithms) is a tool enabling the designer to tackle the software reliability problem by solving the complex optimization involved in evaluating the status of the systems and taking the appropriate decisions in line with the development of the system.

REFERENCES

Bäck, T. (1996). *Evolutionary Algorithms in Theory and Practice*. Oxford, UK: Oxford University Press.

Coello, C. (2001). *Theoretical and Numerical Constraint-Handling Techniques used with Evolutionary Algorithms: A Survey of the State of the Art*. Computer Methods in Applied Mechanics and Engineering.

Department of Defense (1994). Military Standard Software Development and Documentation. MIL-STD-498.

Dorigo, M., Maniezzo, V., & Colorni, A. (1996). *The Ant System: Optimization by a colony of cooperating agents*. IEEE Transactions on Systems, Man and Cybernetics - Part B.

Far, B. H. (2005). Course Notes. *SENG 635: Software Reliability and Testing*. Date Accessed February 2005 from http://www.enel.ucalgary.ca/People/far/Lectures/SENG635/p1/02_files/v3_document.html

Gillies, A. C. (1992). *Software Quality, Theory and management*. London: Chapman Hall Computing Series.

Goldberg, D. (1989). *Genetic Algorithms in Search, Optimization and Machine Learning*. Boston: Addison-Wesley.

Hammer, T., Rosenberg, L., Huffman, L., & Hyatt, L. (1997). Measuring Requirements Testing. In *Proc. International Conference on Software Engineering*. Boston: IEEE Computer Society Press.

Holland, J. (1975). *Adaptation in Natural and Artificial Systems*. Ann Arbor, MI: University of Michigan Press.

Kitchenham, B., & Pfleeger, S. (1996). Software Quality: The Elusive Target. *IEEE Software, 13*(1), 12–21. doi:10.1109/52.476281

Kuri, A. (1998). An Alternative Model of Genetic Algorithms as Learning Machines. In *Expert Systems with Applications* (pp. 173–184). New York: Elsevier Science.

Kuri, A. (2002). In Coello, C., Albornoz, A., Sucar, E., & Cairó, O. (Eds.), *A Methodology for the Statistical Characterization of Genetic Algorithms, (LNAI 2313* (pp. 79–88). Berlin: Springer-Verlag.

Kuri, A., & Gutiérrez, J. (2002). In Coello, C., Albornoz, A., Sucar, E., & Cairó, O. (Eds.), *Penalty Function Methods for Constrained Optimization with Genetic Algorithms: a Statistical Analysis, (LNAI 2313* (pp. 79–88). Berlin: Springer-Verlag.

Markov, A. A. (1971). *Extension of the limit theorems of probability theory to a sum of variables connected in a chain*. Chichester, UK: John Wiley and Sons.

Mitchell, M. (1996). *Introduction to Genetic Algorithms*. Cambridge, MA: MIT Press.

Mitchell, M., Forrest, S., & Holland, J. (1992). The Royal Road for genetic algorithms: Fitness Landscapes and GA Performance. In F.J. Varela & P. Bourgine, (eds.), *Toward a practice of autonomous Systems: Proceedings of the First European Conference on Artificial Life*. Cambridge, MA: MIT Press.

Musa, J. (1998). *Software Reliability Engineering*. New York: McGraw-Hill.

NASA Software Assurance guidebook (1989). *NASA GSFC MD, Office of Safety and Mission Assurance*.

Rennard, J.-P. (2002). *Vie Artificielle où la biologie rencontre l'informatique*. Vuibert.

Rosenberg, L., & Hammer, T. (1998). Metrics for Quality Assurance and Risk Assessment. In *Proc. Eleventh International Software Quality Week*, San Francisco, CA.

Rosenberg, L., Hammer, T., & Shaw, J. (1998). Software Metrics and Reliability (ISSRE 1998 Best Paper). *IEEE International Symposium on Software Reliability Engineering*.

Rudolph, G., Convergence Analysis of Canonical Genetic Algorithms, (1994). *IEEE Transactions on Neural Networks, 5*(1), 96-101. doi:10.1109/72.265964

Ruszczynski, A. (2006). *Nonlinear Optimization*. Princeton, NJ: Princeton University Press.

IEEE Standard 982.2 (1987). Guide for the Use of Standard Dictionary of Measures to Produce Reliable Software.

Triantafyllos, G., Vassiliadis, S., & Kobrosly, W. (1995, February). On the Prediction of Computer Implementation Faults Via Static Error Prediction Models. *Journal of Systems and Software, 28*(2), 129–142. doi:10.1016/0164-1212(94)00050-W

Turing, A. (1936). On Computable Numbers, with an Application to the Entscheidungsproblem. *Proceedings of the London Mathematical Society, 42*, 230–265. doi:10.1112/plms/s2-42.1.230

ENDNOTES

[1] A discussion of the way to do this may be found in Mitchell (1996).

[2] Alternative coding methods may be found in Rennard (2002).

[3] One notable exception are the so-called "ant systems", for which see Dorigo (1996).

[4] This is true if the MC is irreducible and its states are positive recurrent. The MCs for a GA satisfy both criteria.

[5] VGA: Vasconcelos' GA; EGA: Eclectic GA; TGA: Elitist GA; SGA: Statistical GA; CGA: Canonical (or Simple) GA; RMH: Random Mutation Hill Climber.

[6] The Latin American philosopher José Vasconcelos proposed that the admixture of all races would eventually give rise to a better one he called the *cosmic* race; hence the algorithm's name.

[7] The term "large" is relative. The value suggested implies that feasible individuals will convey values of the fitness function smaller than, say, 100.

[8] In equation (14) we include constants $\rho, \delta, \lambda, \omega$.

Chapter 4
Synthesis of Object–Oriented Software Structural Models Using Quality Metrics and Co–Evolutionary Genetic Algorithms

André Vargas Abs da Cruz
Pontifícia Universidade Católica do Rio de Janeiro, Brazil

Dilza Szwarcman
Pontifícia Universidade Católica do Rio de Janeiro, Brazil

Thiago S. M. Guimarães
Pontifícia Universidade Católica do Rio de Janeiro, Brazil

Marco Aurélio C. Pacheco
Pontifícia Universidade Católica do Rio de Janeiro, Brazil

ABSTRACT

One of the biggest challenges for the developer of object-oriented software is the modeling and developing of the objects themselves, so that they are easily reusable in complex systems. The final quality of the software depends mostly on the quality of the modeling developed for it. Modeling and specification of software are fundamental steps for making the software development an activity of engineering. Design is the activity in which software behavior and structure are elaborated. During this phase many models are developed anticipating several views of the final product and making software evaluation possible even before the software is implemented. Consequently, the synthesis of a software model can be seen as a problem of optimization, where the attempt to find a better configuration among the elements chosen through the object-oriented paradigm, such as classes, methods and attributes that meet quality design criteria. This work studies a possibility to synthesize higher quality modelings through the evolution of Genetic Algorithms, a technique that has proved to be efficient in dealing with problems involving large

DOI: 10.4018/978-1-61520-809-8.ch004

search spaces. The work was divided in three main stages: a study of object-oriented software engineering; the definition of a model using genetic algorithms; and co-evolution of species for the synthesis of object-oriented software modeling, aiming at quality improvement; and at the implementation of a model for case study. The study of object-oriented software engineering involved the establishment of software development phases and the characterization of the representation used in modeling phase and, in particular, the characterization of class diagrams based on UML. The study also investigated software quality metrics such as Reutilization, Flexibility, Understandability, Functionality, Extensibility and Effectiveness. The specification of genetic algorithm consisted in the definition of the structure of the chromosome that could provide a good representation of modeling diagram and a function of evaluation of the design that could take the software quality metrics in to consideration. As a result, the chromosomes represent metadata of a simplified UML diagram of classes, which may later be used as an entry of a CASE (Computer Aided Software Engineering) Tool that can create the implementation code in the chosen pattern. The evaluation function was defined focusing at the synthesis of a higher quality object-oriented software modeling. In order to observe the use of more than one objective at the same time the Pareto technique for multi objective problems was used. The evolution is directed towards the improvement of quality metrics by searching for a qualitatively better modeling, based on Bansiya's (Bansiya and Davis, 2002) study. The construction of a co-evolutionary model consisted in defining distinct species so that each one would represent part of the problem to be evolved, thus enabling a more efficient representation of the model. The co-evolutionary model allowed the evolution of more complex structures, which would not be possible in a simple Genetic Algorithm. The chromosomes related to each species codify metadata and that is why the solution assembly (design) makes use of a decoder. A case study was done to synthesize the modeling of an elevator controller. The results achieved in this section were compared to the modelings produced by specialists, and the characteristics of these results were analyzed. The GA performance in the optimization process was compared to that of a random search and, in every case, the results achieved by the model were always better.

1. INTRODUCTION

1.1. Motivation

The concern and the efforts to improve the practices of software development, looking for productivity, quality growth and lower costs, bring to evidence new perspectives for software development.

The difficulty and delay in implementing a complex system can be reduced if the previously developed and tested components can be used. However, a big initial effort to accomplish this goal is necessary for a software development company to create a repository of reusable software components.

Nowadays, the object-oriented programming paradigm is widely used and, as a consequence, huge effort has been made to reuse software. A new technique has been developed by Dandashi (Dandashi, 1998) to infer the re-usability of a software component by means of measurements taken directly from the implementation.

The object-orientation paradigm has changed the elements that are used to infer the quality of the software. Traditional metrics of software products such as size, complexity, performance and quality had to be changed to include new concepts such as encapsulation, inheritance, and polymorphism, which are innate to object orientation. This way, new metrics have been defined (Chidamber & Kemerer, 1994; Hitz & Montazeri, 1996; Li &

Henry, 1993) to measure the object-orientation products.

Bansiya (Bansiya & Davis, 2002) has developed a hierarchical model called Quality Model for Object-Oriented Design (QMOOD), which aims at mapping metric modeling into quality attributes. These quality attributes are: Re-usability, Flexibility, Understandability, Functionality, Extendibility and Effectiveness.

The idea of improving the modeling of object-oriented software based on metrics of quality must lead to an automated process, creating higher-quality models based on characteristics of the problem. This automated process can be achieved by the use of advanced computing techniques such as the ones from the field of Computational Intelligence.

The Computational Intelligence focuses, through the techniques inspired in Nature, on the development of intelligent systems that are able to imitate aspects of human behaviors, as learning, perception, reasoning, evolution and adaptation. The Genetic Algorithms are intelligent models inspired in biological evolution that, through adaptable methods, are able to find potential solutions by not completely exhausting all possible solutions for the problem (Bäck, Fogel, & Michalewicz, 1997; Davis, 1996; Goldberg, 1989; Michalewicz, 1996).

The Computational Intelligence Techniques, especially Evolutionary Algorithms, have been applied in problems of object-oriented code generation. In his doctoral dissertation, Bruce (Bruce, 1995) used genetic programming to automate the process considering more specific problems of code generation and its functionality.

Due to the demand growth for software products, there is a clear need for faster development and higher quality in each phase of the process to make the reuse possible. That is why models that help to automate and control the quality of each phase of the development are becoming more popular, thus this research investigates one of the possible paths for this development.

1.2. Related Works

This research area is still largely unexplored, therefore, the research that are related to this work are few, and most of them use the Genetic Programming technique, as shown on the chart below.

The Genetic Programming (GP), created by John Koza (Koza, 1992) in the early nineties, shows a mechanism similar to genetic algorithms. However, there are differences between GP and GA and instead of using binary words to represent possible solutions, data structures in the shape of *trees* of arbitrary size are used.

In Genetic Programming there is a population of computer programs and the purpose of the algorithm is, through the evolution of these programs, to reach the program that best solves a specific problem.

One of the distinguished works was the one done by Blickle (Blickle, 1996). His work examines the application of Evolutionary Algorithms in the synthesis of complex digital systems composed by *hardware* and *software* elements. Blickle also shows the synthesis of implementations for H.261 *Codec* video chip demonstrating the methodology and capacity of Evolutionary Algorithm to reach good solutions for the problem.

Throughout the years, the techniques for Genetic Programming had to be adapted in order to be able to follow the Object-Oriented paradigm. One of the major works based on Object-Oriented Genetic Programming (OOGP) was done by Bruce (Bruce, 1995), but this area still needs further research and analysis. Bruce deals with more specific problems of code generation and its functionality, and even though he mentions the evolution of reusable codes, he does not thoroughly discuss it.

Recent researches have been carried out, such as the one in Lucas' (Lucas, 2004) article, where more advanced techniques of Object-Oriented Genetic Programming have been considered. In his article Lucas still suggests the possible use of Software Metrics to evaluate synthesized programs.

2. SOFTWARE ENGINEERING

2.1. Object-Oriented System Design

The Object-Oriented Systems are no longer a novelty, since they have been on the market for many years. The object-orientation allows for better modeling of the problems, providing for better abstractions and making the treatment of more complex problems possible.

Some of the main concepts of object orientation are essential for the development of any software model. These concepts are: objects, classes, methods and attributes. Their specifications are as follows:

- **Objects:** The fundamental unit of any object-oriented system. An object is anything that is either real or abstract, for which one wants to store data about.
- **Classes:** Patterns from which objects are created and that specify the common behavior of such objects. Classes contain the declaration of Methods and Attributes.
- **Methods:** Represent the dynamic behavior of Classes, by defining the behavior of services offered by the Class.
- **Attributes:** Define the static behavior of the instances and are usually accessed through the Methods of the class.

These concepts are part of any object-oriented structure. It is worth highlighting some definitions of relations between classes, such as the relation of inheritance and dependency.

Inheritance represents a hierarchy of classes, allowing for the specialization, evolution and, mainly the reutilization of classes. The concept of inheritance enables methods and attributes of more generic classes to be inherited by more specialized classes. For example, if class B inherits from class A, it is said that class A is superclass

Figure 1. Example of an Inheritance relationship

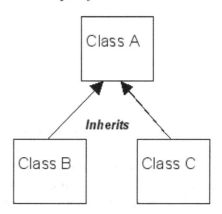

of B. Usually a class can usually have only one superclass. It may, however, have many heirs.

An example of inheritance relationship is shown in Figure 1.

In the example above, Class A has more generic functionalities and Classes B and C are specializations of Class A. The following might be found in an application:

- **Class A**: Means of transportation
- **Class B**: Car
- **Class C**: Train

The relationships of dependency simply specify that one class is dependent on the other. Here, this dependency is understood as follows: If class A is dependent on class B, class A has an attribute of class B, therefore, class A contains a reference to class B.

An extension of the example of the above dependency relationship is shown in Figure 2:

In Figure 2, Class A has an attribute of the Class C type. An example of application could be:

- **Class A**: Car
- **Class C**: Engine

Thus, if Class C ought to be modified, classes dependent on C are likely to suffer some impacts

Figure 2. Example of dependency relationship

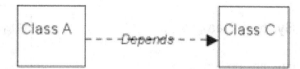

and; in this case the dependence class would be Class A.

These concepts have been used by software engineering to modularize complex problems and have been included in most of Computer-Aided Software Engineering (CASE) tools. CASE tools are becoming more complex as a result of software engineering improvements, and often provide support for the development of documents in UML (Unified Modeling Language) (OMG –UML, 2003).

UML is a language that was standardized by the Object Management Group (OMG) for the representation of object-oriented systems. The utilization of UML in an object-oriented model allows for a more efficient integration of the stages of the development process.

UML has 12 main diagrams. In this paper, only one of them, the class diagram, will be used. This diagram shows the static structure of a model, especially the elements existing in the system, their internal structure, and their relationship with other elements. Classes, methods, attributes, inheritance and dependency between classes are represented in the class diagram, concepts were described above.

The use of UML in the development of object-oriented software facilitates the modeling of more complex problems and improves the quality of the final product. This quality might be monitored throughout the various phases of the development process, but quality control in early phases is more important and efficient, for it can help the developer make better decisions. There are also metrics used to help evaluate the quality of UML diagrams, making the developer's work easier (Genero, Piattini, Manso, & Cantone, 2003).

2.2. Software Quality Metrics

It is possible to identify a set of quality attributes in each software modeling. Modelings that satisfy quality attributes can be classified as good modelings. When software is projected focusing on specific quality attributes, the extension, maintenance and reuse of modeling is done in a much simpler and easier way. For example, modelings that are flexible, trustworthy and effective in terms of system architecture, as well as in terms of the resources (time and space) are good candidates for reuse, since they have valuable time and expenditures time when extensions and modifications are needed.

Considering that there are many different points of view concerning quality concept, the task of determining and evaluating the presence of quality attributes is neither easy nor direct. Most of the times, the concept involving a set that represents quality attributes may be subjective. Besides, there is no way to directly evaluate the products of the process of software development in order to detect the existence or lack of these attributes, which are considered by the majority of the experts as quality representative.

The quality attributes on which this research is based are the attributes used by Bansiya (Bansiya & Davis, 2002), in QMOOD. Those attributes are: Reutilization, Flexibility, Understandability, Functionality, Extendibility and Effectiveness.

These quality attributes, as well as quality as a whole, are abstract concepts, so they are not directly observable. As for qualities, there is no universal agreement to define each of those high quality attributes. A brief description of definitions and problems related to quality attributes is given

Table 1. Definition of quality attributes

Quality Attributes	Definition
Reutilization	It reflects the presence of the characteristics of object-oriented modeling, characteristics that allow its reutilization for the solution of a new problem without significant efforts.
Flexibility	It is the characteristic that allows for the incorporation of changes in modeling and modeling ability to be adapted to provide different, however similar capacities.
Understandability	It comprises the modeling properties, which enable it to be easily learned and understood. This is directly related to the complexity of the modeling structure.
Functionality	It is concerned about responsibilities attributed to the modeling classes, which are made by classes through public interfaces.
Extendability	It refers to the presence and usage of properties in an existing modeling that allows for the incorporation of new requirements in the modeling.
Efectiveness	It is about the ability of the modeling to reach the desired functionality and behavior by using object orientation concepts and techniques.

Figure 3. Description of the synthesis process of the modeling

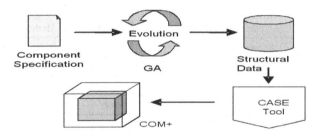

in the next sub-sections. There is a summary of these definitions in Table 1.

3. DESIGN EVOLUTION SYSTEM BASED ON OBJECT-ORIENTED QUALITY

3.1. Architecture of the Proposed System

The purpose of System Design Evolution based on Object-Oriented Quality Software is to synthesize software modeling following quality metrics specified in Bansiya's work (Bansiya & Davis, 2002), described above.

The architecture of the proposed synthesis process is shown in Figure 3.

It is possible to have a better understanding of the figure above through the description of its phases:

Component Specification

In this phase it is necessary to have a full knowledge of the problem that will be approached by the modeling to be synthesized. For instance, if the goal is to synthesize a modeling of a system that would represent a model of Neural Network, the work of a specialist will be necessary (Haykin, 1999).

The specialist shall estimate all relevant characteristics of the model, as well as the relationship among them, thereby representing Initial Specifications of the component to be synthesized. These specifications comprise a set of initial methods and attributes, which characterize the behavior of

Table 2. Attributes specifications

Code Attribute	Attribute Name
Integer	Label for the Attribute, so it can be easily identified in the final solution.

Table 3. Methods specification

Code Method	Method Name
Integer	Label for Methodology, so it can be easily identified in the final solution.

Table 4. Specifications of the relationships

Relationship Code	Method Code	Attribute Code	Type
Integer	Integer	Integer	1/0

Table 5. Example of specifications of attributes

Code Attribute	Attribute Name
1	Attribute_1
2	Attribute_2

Table 6. Example of specification of methods

Code Method	Method Name
1	Method_1
2	Method_2
3	Method_3

Table 7. Example of specification of relationships

Code Relationship	Code Method	Code Attribute	Type
1	1	2	0
2	2	1	0
3	2	2	0
4	3	2	1

the component, besides including possible restrictions and relationships that indicate connections among methods and attributes.

The Component Specifications can be divided into three charts, as shown in Tables 2, 3 and 4.

Tables 2 and 3 represent only the lists of Attributes and Methods. Each Attribute and Method has a code that is used on Table 4 to define the relationships among them.

Table 4, as previously mentioned, represents a list of relationships between Attributes and Methods – Methods and Methods. Attributes and Methods are indicated by their own codes and their types determine if the field "Code Attribute" represents an Attribute or a Method. If the type is "0", the relationship is between Attribute and Method, however, if the type is "1", the relationship is between Methods and Methods.

Tables 5, 6 and 7 below show a simple example of Specification.

A look at Table 7 leads us to the following conclusion:

- Method_1 uses Attribute_2
- Method_2 uses Attribute_1 and Attribute_2
- Method_3 uses Method_2

Evolution

This is the phase where the synthesis occurs. The evolution of the modeling occurs through the use of one Genetic Algorithm (GA).

In order to carry out the evolutionary process, the GA uses information from the Component Specifications and generates a configuration of *metadata* from synthesized modeling. The strategic action is then to create random configurations of metadata that contain Classes created with Methods and Attributes distributed by the classes. Next, the corresponding modeling is evaluated through Quality Metrics.

The GA, which forms the main part of the model, is described in the following section.

Metadata

The use of *metadata* is usual between software that automate the modeling and the code generation. Therefore, it has been decided to focus the evolution on the *modeling* of the component and not directly on its code, expressing the modeling by *metadata*. As a result, a modeling will be represented by *metadata* structures that describe the classes and their relationships.

Metadata are defined as *data about data*, that is, in this case they represent structured information (data) on a modeling (data).

CASE tool

As mentioned before, CASE (Computer-Aided Software Engineering) tools try to automate the phases of the process of the object-oriented process. Thence, a CASE tool is able to receive *metadata* generated by the GA and provide several treatments on synthesized modeling using UML language, being also able to generate the code referring to the UML modeling.

In this stage a specialist may possibly make changes to the modeling, so as to fit it in accordance with the specialist's purposes.

Component

The last phase of the process simply represents the mapped component generated by CASE tool. In Figure 3, the component was generated and standardized according to Microsoft COM+ (Component Object Model) (Iseminger, 2000).

3.2. Synthesis of Design by Co-Evolutionary Genetic Algorithms

The most important part of the system is the modeling of the Genetic Algorithm (GA). The GA is responsible for the optimization and synthesis of the desired solution.

The evolutionary process performed by the GA has some components that should be carefully developed for its proper functioning. The components are the following: Representation, Genetic Operators, Decoding and Evaluation.

3.2.1. Species Representation

One of the crucial aspects for the solution of problems by Genetic Algorithm is the choice of the chromosome representation that will be evolved.

As the model used requires the treatment of various aspects from object-oriented programming, such as inheritance, dependencies and the definition of where to allocate each method and attribute, it has been decided to use Genetic Algorithms advanced techniques, such as the Co-evolutionary model, allowing the analysis of the problem. This Co-Evolutionary model presents an important aspect that should be taken into consideration and is related to the evolution of interdependent subcomponents. If it is possible to break down the problem into independent subcomponents, each of which can evolve without concerning about the evolution of the other.

Therefore, the proposed solution was modeled through a Co-evolutionary Genetic Algorithm with four species:

- Classes
- Dependencies
- Methods
- Attributes

Each species represents one part of the problem to be evolved and deserves an independent representation. A general view of the Co-evolutionary Genetic Algorithm modeling is shown in Figure 4. The representations of each species are described below.

Species Classes

The species *Classes* deal with problems of definition of "*who may inherit from whom*" and with the

Figure 4. General view of the genetic model with four species

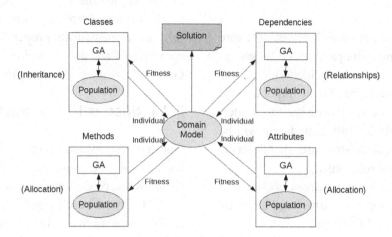

Figure 5. Simplified diagram of classes

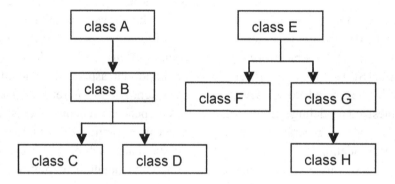

number of classes of the components. A diagram of classes, where inheritances are shown, can be seen as several disconnected graphs and with no cycles, in other words, several trees, as shown in the simplified example shown in Figure 5. In the example, the arrows represent the inheritance relationship.

This species is represented by order based model, which is widely used and studied on problems similar to the Traveling Salesman Problem (TSP). Therefore, the chromosome comprises an ordered list where each gene represents a class, and the position of the gene indicates the priority of the class: the ones positioned closer to the left have a higher priority. An example of chromosome from the species *Classes* is shown in Table 8. This ordered list indicates the order in which

Table 8. Example of chromosome with up to 8 classes

Class	B	C	F	A	G	H	D	E
Priority	1	2	3	4	5	6	7	8

the class will be chosen for building the trees of the class diagram.

As already mentioned, the number of classes of the modeling must be able to vary, reason why the quantity of classes must also be a parameter to be optimized. In order to solve this problem, a chromosome of variable size approached by Zebulum (Zebulum, Pacheco and Vellasco, 2001) in his research applied to the evolution of electronic circuits was used. In this approach, each

Table 9. Example of activation mask activating 4 classes

Class	A	B	C	D	E	F	G	H
Mask	1	0	0	1	1	1	0	0

Table 10. Mask representing an incidence matrix corresponding to the diagram of classes of Figure 5

	A	B	C	D	E	F	G	H
A	0	0	0	0	0	0	0	0
B	1	0	0	0	0	0	0	0
C	0	1	0	0	0	0	0	0
D	0	1	0	0	0	0	0	0
E	0	0	0	0	0	0	0	0
F	0	0	0	0	1	0	0	0
G	0	0	0	0	1	0	0	0
H	0	0	0	0	0	0	1	0

element of the list can be found active or inactive, and this is why an *activation mask* is used. When an element is deactivated, it is not considered in the problem solution. This mask, as well as the chromosome, has a maximum size defined by a parameter called *Max-classes*. An example of activation mask is shown in Table 9.

It is important to note that the order held by the classes in the list that represents the activation mask is alphabetical, and does not change during the evolution, allowing for the activation and deactivation of classes, but not their positions. For example, in the activation mask in Table 9, classes A, D, E and F are active, although in the chromosome in Table 8 these classes occupy positions 4, 7, 8 and 3.

These two lists enable the evolution of the order in which the classes will be introduced in the diagram, the numbers of classes, and which classes are active. Furthermore, it is necessary to represent the inheritance relationships between classes. The inheritance relationship is a relationship between two classes and, according to the *software* engineering, they are represented in the UML *Classes Diagram*. In Figure 5, for example, class B *inherits* from class A. Another binary mask was used to represent the inheritance of the entire diagram.

The simplified example shown in Figure 5 can be considered as a set of directed graphs and can be represented by an incidence matrix. This incidence matrix would be a new mask, an example of which can be seen in Table 10.

The individual of this species has, therefore, three parts which are: a list of classes, an activation mask and an inheritance mask. Each of these parts is submitted to specific genetic operators.

The genetic operators that act in the list of classes are order-based operators; however, the operators that act in masks are binary operators. Details on these types of operators will be given later on in this section.

The reading of this chromosome and the construction of the graph are made by a decoder which uses an incidence matrix and respects the order defined by the ordered list of the chromosome. This decoder uses the four species to build a solution. Its algorithm will be shown further on.

The masks shown in Tables 9 and 10 can be seen as an extension of the chromosome of the species *Classes*, in other words, each chromosome of this species has an activation mask for the incidence matrix. These two masks could be considered as two new species, however, this would increase even more the computational cost of the evolution, and for this reason they were kept linked to the chromosome of the species *Classes*.

Dependency Species

The dependency relationship in the diagram of classes points out that, if class A *depends* on class B, in some ways class A uses class B, and, probably, if any change occurs in class B, class A will go through adjustments. The representation of the species *Dependencies* indicates the dependency between classes, therefore the relation between classes is of N:N. So, a binary matrix of

Table 11. Example of the species chromosome dependencies

	C_1	C_2	C_3	C_4	C_5	C_6
C_1	0	1	0	0	0	0
C_2	1	0	0	0	0	0
C_3	0	0	0	1	1	0
C_4	0	1	0	0	0	0
C_5	0	0	0	0	0	0
C_6	1	0	0	0	1	0

Figure 6. Graphic representation of the dependencies of the chromosomes from Table 11

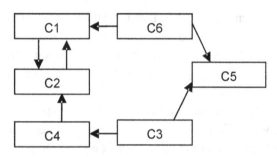

Max classes X Max classes dimension was used, where each gene corresponds to a class and is represented by another list of classes. Each allele has value 1 for a class that depends on the other class, or 0 for the opposite case. The number of active classes is indicated by the activation mask of the species *Classes*.

An example of the representation that was described is available in the Table 11 and the graphic representation of the dependencies can be seen in Figure 6. In Figure 6, the direction of the arrow indicates the direction where the dependency occurs, for example, Class 6 *depends* on Class 5 and so on.

Species Methods

The species *Methods* must indicate *where* each method will be placed, in other words, it must indicate its distribution by the classes of the system.

The chromosome has a representation similar to the species *Classes*, being formed by a list of methods that will be permuted forming several configurations. In addition to methods, this list has markers, and their function is to represent the division of classes. The function of the markers will become clearer later, after the description of the decoder is presented. The number of markers that are present in the list is *Maxclasses – 1*. Naturally, each marker has only one code which cannot be repeated, as well as each method.

This list has the methods of the *initial specification* and the order that it appears in the gene indicates the *priority* on which the method should be tested. An example of a chromosome of species *Methods* is represented in the Table 12. The positions with an M represent the markers.

Species Attributes

The species *Attributes* should indicate *where* each attribute will be placed and it is very similar to the species *Methods*.

The representation of the chromosome is identical to the representation of methods; again it has a list of priority attributes with markers that indicate the classes. The attributes that form the list belong to the *initial specification*, and the order that this list appears in the gene indicates the *priority on* which the attribute should be placed in the class. Table 13 shows an example of this chromosome.

3.2.2 Genetic Operators

Each species has specific genetic operators for its representation. The genetic operators used in each species are presented below.

The first species to be examined is the one responsible for the class of the system. As it has been already said, the species *Classes* has an ordered-based chromosome, similar to the representation used for the Traveling Salesman Problem – TSP (Fagerholt & Christiansen, 2000; Moon, Kim, Choi, & Seo, 2002) where the genetic algorithm is responsible for creating new permutations of

Table 12. Example of a chromosome of the species methods with the MaxClasses = 6

M1	M4	M	M5	M	M3	M6	M2	M	M	M7	M

Table 13. Example of chromosome of the species Attribute with MaxClasses = 6

A3	M	A7	A1	A5	M	A6	M	A2	M	A4	M

an ordered list, which in the case of the Traveling Salesman Problem represents the round-trip way to visit the cities in the order described.

The species *Classes* uses the same representation, with the difference that each round-trip is replaced with a Class to be created.

According to Michalewicz (Michalewicz, 1996), until recently, three types of different crossover were defined to represent the round-trip: *Partially Mapped Crossover (PMX), Order Crossover (OX),* and *Cycle Crossover (CX).*

For the genetic mutation operators there are basically four types of operators: Swap, Position Inversion – (PI) Rotation Left Mutation – (RLM) and Rotation Right Mutation – (RRM) (Michalewicz, 1996).

The chromosome of species *Classes* has two types of masks that also undergo through the action of specific genetic operators of mutation (the *crossover* operator was not used for the masks). The masks are binary representations in one and two dimensions, respectively, as shown in Tables 10 and 11 above. Therefore, genetic operators are simpler and intuitive. They are: ADD, SUB, FLIPBITS.

The ADD operator is responsible for adding a value 1 to the mask. Thus, if a mask is the activation mask of classes, it is adding a new class in the system. It is possible to see in the example (1), a mask before and after the application of the operator.

(1 0 $\underline{0}$ 1 0 0 1 1 0) – Before (1 0 $\underline{1}$ 1 0 0 1 1 0) - After (1)

The SUB operator is the opposite of the ADD. Its function is to add a value 0 to the mask. Thus, if a mask is an activation mask of classes, it is removing a class from the system. In example (2) it is possible to see a mask before and after the application of the operator.

(1 0 $\underline{1}$ 1 0 0 1 1 0) - Before (1 0 $\underline{0}$ 1 0 0 1 1 0) - After (2)

Note that in both operators a position of the chromosome is chosen and the value in this position is transformed in 1 or 0 depending on the operator, but there is a chance that the position has a new value already, and so, the resulting chromosome will be identical to the parent.

The FLIPBITS operator acts inverting the value of a chosen gene. This operator can end up inserting or removing a class from system, if the mask is an activation mask of classes. The problem that happens to the ADD and SUB mentioned above does not happen with FLIPBITS operator, for it is guaranteed that the resulting chromosome will always have a gene with an inverted value in relation to the parent.

Species *Dependencies* also has a representation of a binary matrix, therefore the mutation operator FLIBITS is also used in it, as already explained above. Now, a *crossover* operator is used, the ONEPOINT *crossover* for the two dimensions. Figure 7 shows the ONEPOINT crossover performance. Since the chromosome has two dimensions, two division points should

Figure 7. Example of the ONEPOINT crossover in two dimensions

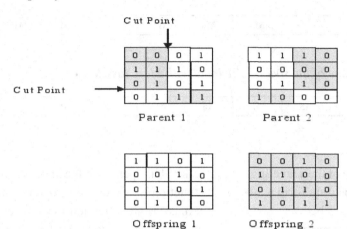

be chosen and then the exchange of the genetic material should be carried out.

The genetic operators used for the species *Methods* and *Attributes* are the same, since the chromosome representations are the same. The operators used are the same ones used in species *Classes*, which also applies an ordered-based representation.

3.2.3. Decoding

Decoding consists basically in forming the real solution of the problem from the chromosomes. The decoding process forms the solution so that it can be evaluated by the algorithm.

In the developed model, the four species have indirect representations of the solution and each one represents part of the solution. Therefore, the decoder needs to use the four species for the formulation of the solution that will be evaluated.

The decoding algorithm has the following steps:

```
Add active classes in the solutions
•   Go through Classes type chro-
    mosome from left to right.
•   Check the position of the
    class in the classes activa-
    tion mask;
```

```
•   If the class is active:
    ○   Add class in the solution
        ▪   create inheritance
            relationships:
•   For each class i in the
    solution;
•   Go through the line that re-
    fers to the class in the in-
    heritance mask
    ○   For each column j with
        value '1'
        ▪   If the formation of
            cycles does not occur
            Class j is i
            superclass
Create dependency relationships
•   For each i class in the
    solution
•   Go through the line that
    refers to the class in the
    chromosome of the species
    Dependencies.
    ○   For each j column with
        '1' value
        ▪   Class j depends on
            class i
Allocate methods
•   ClassIndex = 0
•   Go through the chromosome of
```

```
Species Methods from left to
right
```
- `If the gene is a marker`
  - `ClassIndex = ClassIndex + 1`
  - `ClassIndex = ClassIndex MOD (number of classes in a solution)`
- `Add method to the class that refers to the ClassIndex`

`Allocate attributes`
- `ClassIndex = 0`
- `Go through the chromosome of species Attributes from left to right`
- `If the gene is a marker`
  - `ClassIndex = ClassIndex + 1`
  - `ClassIndex = ClassIndex MOD (number of classes in the solution)`
- `. Add attribute to the class that refers to ClassIndex`

This algorithm builds up a solution that will be evaluated by the metrics in the evaluation function. The evaluation method is described in the next section.

3.2.4. Multi-Objective Evaluation

The evaluation of the solution is one of the main phases of a GA. It is the evaluation that indicates if a solution is rather good or not, therefore, it is the evaluation of the solution that directs the evolutionary process in order to reach an optimum solution.

The evaluation function focus on the quality attributes described in the previous section. The calculation of the attributes is based on Bansiya's (Bansiya & Davis, 2002) research in QMOOD. The quality attributes to be calculated are the following: Reutilization, Flexibility, Understandability,

Functionality, Extendibility and Effectiveness. According to Bansiya`s research, these attributes can be inferred through modeling properties. These properties are available in Table 14.

In his research, Bansiya inferred a relationship between the properties of the modeling described in Table 14 and the quality attributes already mentioned. This relationship is detailed in equation in Table 15 below.

For the calculation of the properties of the modeling in the equations, metrics that can estimate these values in a certain modeling are used. There are several metrics that in some way measure the software quality. In his research, Bansiya studied a set of more than 30 metrics and he selected the ones that can best estimate the main properties of a structural software modeling. These metrics are described in Table 16.

The relationship between these metrics and properties of the modeling is what is lacking, so that values can be calculated for the quality attributes. This relationship is intuitive and is described in Table 17.

It is possible to see that the property *Modularity* does not appear in the equations in the Table 16, therefore, this eliminates the metric *MFM*. Another point to be considered is related to the *CIS* and *NOM* metrics, for in this research instance, where only the public methods of classes have been considered, these two metrics reflect the same measurement, but only the metric *CIS* will be used.

By applying the relation above, the equations to estimate quality attributes are formed in the following way:

- **Reutilization** = -0.25 *DCC + 0.25 *CAM + 0.5 *CIS + 0.5 *DSC
- **Flexibility** = 0.25 *DAM - 0.25 *DCC + 0.5 * MOA + 0.5 *NOP
- **Understandability** = -0.33 * ANA + 0.33 * DAM - 0.33 * DCC + 0.33 * CAM - 0.33 * NOP - 0.33 * CIS - 0.33 * DSC

Table 14. Definition of modeling properties

Propriety	Definition
Modeling size	It is The measure of the number of classes that are used in modeling.
Hierarchies	Hierarchies are used to represent different concepts of generalization – specialization in a modeling. It is the counting of the number of classes that have descendents, but do not have super class in the modeling.
Abstraction	It is the measure of the aspect of the generalization – specialization of the modeling. The classes which have one or more descendants in a modeling have this quality of abstraction.
Encapsulation	In object-oriented modeling this encapsulation property focus on the modeling of classes, which prevent access to the declaration of the attributes, by its declaration as private, thus protecting the internal representation of the objects.
Modularity	It is the measure of deviation of the average number of services provided by classes in a project. The intention is to identify modelings that have classes with a large deviation of the average number of services.
Coupling	It defines the interdependency of an object with other objects in a modeling. It is the measurement of the number of other objects that need to be accessed by an object, so that it can function correctly.
Cohesion	It infers in the relationship of methods and attributes in a class. Strong superposition in method parameters and attribute types indicates strong cohesion.
Composition	It measures the "part-of", "consists of" and "part-whole", which are aggregation relationships in an object-oriented modeling.
Inheritance	It is the measurement of the "is-a" relationship between classes. This relationship is related to the level of nesting of classes in an inheritance hierarchy.
Polymorphism	It is the ability to substitute an object for another one that has the same interface at the runtime. It is the measurement of services that are dynamically determined in an object during runtime.
Messaging	It is the counting of the number of public methods that are available as services for other classes. This is a measure of services that is offered by a class.
Complexity	It is the measurement of the level of difficulty in understanding the internal and external structure of classes and their relationships.

Table 15. Equation for the inference of quality attributes

Quality Attribute	Equation
Reusability	-0.25 * Coupling + 0.25 * Cohesion + 0.5 * Messaging + 0.5 * modeling size
Flexibility	0.25 * Encapsulation - 0.25 * Coupling + 0.5 * Composition + 0.5 * Polymorphism
Understandability	-0.33 * Abstraction + 0.33 * Encapsuling - 0.33 * Coupling + 0.33 * Cohesion - 0.33* Polymorphism - 0.33 * Complexity - 0.33 *modeling Size
Functionality	0.12 * Cohesion + 0.22 * Polymorphism + 0.22 * Messaging + 0.22 * Modeling Size + 0.22 * Hierarchies
Extendability	0.5 * Abstraction - 0.5 * Coupling + 0.5 * Inheritance + 0.5 * Polymorphism
Effectiveness	0.2 * Abstraction + 0.2 * Encapsulation + 0.2 * Composition + 0.2 * Inheritance + 0.2 * Polymorphism

- **Functionality** = 0.12 * CAM + 0.22 * NOP + 0.22 * CIS + 0.22 * DSC + 0.22 * NOH
- **Extendability** = 0.5 * ANA - 0.5 * DCC + 0.5 * MFA + 0.5 * NOP
- **Efectiviness** = 0.2 * ANA + 0.2 * DAM + 0.2 * MOA + 0.2 * MFA + 0.2 * NOP

The metrics are obtained from the basic components of the modeling.

These basic components are: attributes, methods and classes. This relationship causes some contradictions among the metrics, in other words, two metrics that are based in the same component of the modeling can be opposites and one cannot be improved without harming the other. Table

Table 16. Metrics description

Sigla	Name	Description
DSC	Modeling Size in Classes	Number of public methods in a class.
NOH	Number of Hierarchies	The number of class hierarchies in the modeling.
ANA	Average Number of Ancestors	The average number of classes wherefrom a class inherits information.
DAM	Data Access Metric	The ratio of the number of private (protected) attributes by the total number of attributes declared in the class. A high value is desired.
MFM	Measure of Functional Modularity	This metric computes the modularity based on the deviation of the number of methods in a class from the average number of methods by a class in the modeling. A value close to zero is preferred. A small value indicates smaller deviation between classes in the number of services provided.
DCC	Direct Class Coupling	The counting of different number of classes that a class is directly related to. The metric includes classes that are directly related by attribute declarations and message passing (parameters) in methods.
CAM	Cohesion Among Methods in Class	This metric computes the relationship between methods of a class based on the parameter lists of the methods. The metric is calculated by using the summation of the intersection of parameters of method with the maximum independent set of all types of parameter in the class. A value close to 1 is preferred.
MOA	Measure of Aggregation	This metric measures the extent of the part-whole relationship, done by the use of attributes. It is a counting of the number of data declarations of which types are classes that are defined by the developer.
MFA	Measure of Functional Abstraction	It is the ratio in the number of methods inherited by a class and the total number of methods accessible by members in the class.
NOP	Number of Polymorphic Methods	It is the counting of every methos that can exhibit polymorphic behavior. Such methods in C++ are defined as virtual.
CIS	Class Interface Size	It is the counting of the number of public methods in the class.
NOM	Number of Methods	It is the counting of all the methods defined in a class.

Table 17. Relationship of metrics with the properties of modeling

Modeling Property	Metric
Modeling Size	DSC
Hierarchies	NOH
Abstraction	ANA
Encapsulation	DAM
Modularity	MFM
Coupling	DCC
Cohesion	CAM
Composition	MOA
Inheritance	MFA
Polymorphism	NOP
Messaging	CIS
Complexity	NOM

18 shows the relationship among metrics and components of the modeling.

The metrics are calculated and normalized to be applied in the equations of the quality attributes. So, the values for each metric vary from 0 to 1.

Each quality attribute represents an objective to be optimized by the GA. Therefore, the evaluation function might use of a strategy to deal with multiple objectives.

Some penalizations are used in the evaluation function in order to eliminate undesirable solutions, such as: solutions with no classes, solutions with empty classes, that is, those with no methods and no attributes, and solutions with invalid dependencies. The invalid dependencies are: dependency of a class with itself, or the dependencies of a class with another class that belongs to the same hierarchy. These penaliza-

Table 18. Relationship of metrics with the basic components of the modeling

Metric	Attribute	Method	Class
DSC			X
NOH			X
ANA			X
DAM	X	X	X
MFM			X
CAM		X	X
DCC	X	X	X
CIS		X	X
MFA			X
MOA	X		
NOP		X	X
NOM	X	X	X

tions work in the equations of the calculation of quality attributes by subtracting the normalized value of the penalized from the attribute value. This prevents the GA from searching for solutions in the search space parts that, according to the specialist's knowledge, do not make sense.

By applying the Pareto technique, the evaluation process of the individuals is divided in three steps:

1. Calculation of the value for each objective for all the individuals of the population;
2. Determination of the individuals that belong to the optimal Pareto set (not dominated);
3. Differentiation of the individuals that belong to the optimal Pareto set.

The first phase consists simply in the calculation of the metrics and the application of the equations for the determination of quality attributes.

The second phase follows an algorithm described by Fonseca (Fonseca and Flaming, 1993) for the determination of optimal Pareto set. In this algorithm a *raking* is done among the individuals and, at the end, a desired set is obtained.

The third phase is necessary in order to avoid large oscillations in the choice of the best individual in each generation. Without this differentiation among individuals of the optimal Pareto set, all of them have the same chance to be chosen as the best individual; therefore this causes large variation through the generation. In order to accomplish this differentiation a new *ranking* inside the optimal Pareto set is created according to the following algorithm:

For each individual i that belong to optimal Pareto set:

- Calculate the number of individuals of the entire population that is dominated by i.
- Elaborate a new *rank*, favoring the individual that has higher dominance in the population.
- Reorder the population considering the *rank* among the non dominated individuals.
- The *fitness* of each individual receives the value of interpolation from the best (*rank = 1*) to the worse (*rank = n* pop_size) in the usual manner, according to a linear function.
- Calculate the average of the *fitness* of the individuals with the same *rank*, in a way that they have the same chance in the selection process.

At the end of the three phases, the population will be put in order and the best individual will be in the first position and with better chances to be chosen by the selection operator. In order to favor even more the chances of the non-dominated set so that they can remain in the population, an interpolation of the *fitness* is done in a way that the optimal Pareto set receives higher values and moves away from the rest of the population. An example of interpolation is shown below:

- Be $P = \{I_1, I_2, I_3, I_4\}$ the optimal Pareto set already in order according to the algorithm described in the third phase.

- Go through *P* in the order by filing in the *fitness* using interpolation: *2*pop_size, 2*pop_size-2, 2*pop_size-4, 2*pop_size-6.*
- Be I_5 the next individual of the population, which does not belong to *P*.
- Fill in the *fitness* of I_5 with *pop_size-3* and the next ones with *pop_size-4, pop_size-5,...*

By using this Pareto strategy, a mixture of objectives does not occur, and even the priority may be given to one or other objective. During the evolution it is possible to observe each objective in development, although when considering all the objectives together one influences the development of the other, for they are calculated by the same metrics and the GA tries to find a balance between them.

4. CASE STUDY

For the case study, it was necessary to implement a tool that is able to simulate the model proposed on the previous section. For the tests and analysis of the tool and the model, three case studies with different levels of complexity were chosen. The system was tested, initially, for the synthesis of minor modelings. Next, more complex modelings were tested to facilitate the analysis of the results.

All the necessary information for the functioning of the system is given by an XML file and by database with the *initial specification.*.

In this configuration file is possible to modify the general parameters of the evolution, such as the size of the population, number of generations and number of experiments. In it the user also chooses the maximum number of classes of the modeling to be synthesized (*Max Classes*) and the quality attributes that will be optimized. After this configuration, the parameters for each species of the model must be configured.

In case the *crossover* and *mutation* rates are equal to zero, the system will execute a random search. This configuration is allowed in order to compare the genetic algorithm with the random search.

After several tests with different rates for the genetic operators of the four species, the values displayed in the configuration file shown above were considered satisfactory and were used for the case studies. An analysis of the tests will be shown in the next sections by considering the GA performance and the synthesized modeling.

4.1. Elevator Control

This case study aimed at using a modeling that has practical use, so that it can be compared to a modeling created by a specialist. The chosen modeling is presented as an example from the book *"Object-Oriented and Classical Software Engineering"* by Stephen R. Schach, pgs. 407-415 (Schach, 2002). The modeling is based on a system to control an elevator.

4.1.1. Design

In his book, Schach presents several phases and diagrams of the modeling of the problem to control the elevator. In order to apply the model proposed, the characteristics of the suggested problem were analyzed, based on the book and information that was taken from it, in order to form the *initial specification*.

The simplified diagram of classes that was formulated by Schach can be seen in Figure 8.

The initial specification deduced by a specialist for the model was the following:

Methods
turn_button_on, turn_button_off, check_requests, update_requests, start_timer, close_doors, open_doors, move_down_one_floor, move_up_one_floor, elevator_event_loop
Attributes
illuminated, requests, doors_open

Figure 8. A modeling elaborated by a specialist in the elevator problem

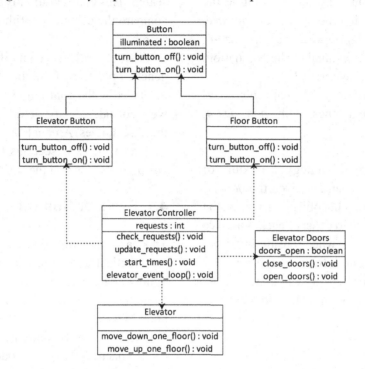

Relationships
turn_button_off uses illuminated
turn_button_on uses illuminated
check_requests uses requests
update_requests uses requests
close_doors uses doors_open
open_doors uses doors_open
elevator_event_loop uses check_requests
elevator_event_loop uses turn_button_on
elevator_event_loop uses move_up_one_floor
elevator_event_loop uses uses open_doors
elevator_event_loop uses turn_button_off
elevator_event_loop uses start_timer
elevator_event_loopusesmove_down_one_floor
elevator_event_loop uses close_doors
elevator_event_loop uses update_requests

The modeling in Figure 8 was placed in the model and evaluated. The values achieved for quality attributes were:

- Reutilization: 0,2571
- Flexibility: 0,7470
- Understandability: -0,0891
- Functionality: 0,3796
- Extendibility: 0,6274
- Efectiviness: 0,4819

4.1.2. Results

The analysis of the results was done based on various aspects. First of all, the performance of the GA can be analyzed through the evolution graphs of each objective. Figures 9 through 14 show these graphs; they are compared with the random search algorithm. The bold line represents the GA and the dashed line represents the random search algorithm. The graph shows the average of the best ones in 150 generation.

These graphs were generated based on the average of the best individuals from 15 experiments with 150 generations each. It is possible to see that

Figure 9. The GA performance graph for the objective Reusability

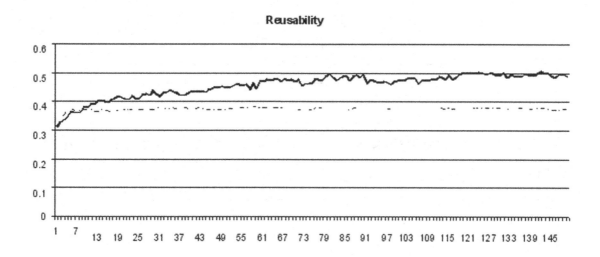

Figure 10. The GA performance graph for the objective Flexibility

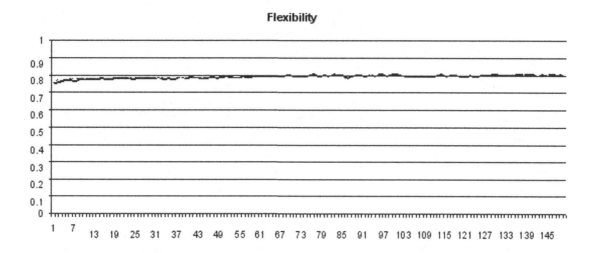

in the *Reutilization* and *Functionality* attributes the GA has a better performance if compared to the random search and a better evolution can also be observed. In other objectives the evolution remains basically constant and the GA performance is not very different from the random search algorithm. Some elements have influence in this fact. The consideration of all the objectives together ends up harming their evolution, since some of them are considered contradictory. Further on, the graphs separately developed for each objective will be shown and it will facilitate the understanding.

Next, the analysis will focus on the synthesized modelings that were done in the various tests. First of all, all objectives were considered and the modeling that was generated can be seen in Figure 15. The values reached for the attributes are in the Table 19, where they are compared

Figure 11. The GA performance graph for the objective Understandability

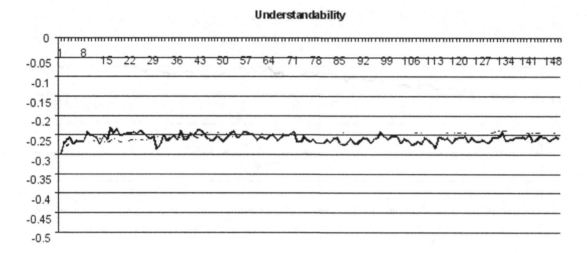

Figure 12. The GA performance Graph for the objective Functionality

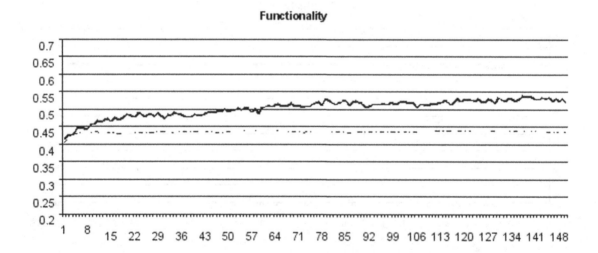

with those that were measured for the modeling elaborated by the specialist.

By analyzing Table 19, it is concluded that the synthesized modeling has better values for all quality attributes, except for the *Understandability*, where the modeling created by a specialist has a value of 65% better. This can also be seen in the comparison of the Figures 26 and 47. This characteristic occurred in most of the tests, showing that in order to improve the other five attributes the *Understandability* is harmed. Therefore, by analyzing Figure 15, it is possible to identify a lot of meaningless information, which a project technician would not do. This shows that when a specialist creates a modeling he ends up prioritizing *Understandability*, as we could see in the first case study in this paper.

Figure 13. The GA performance graph for the objective Extendibility

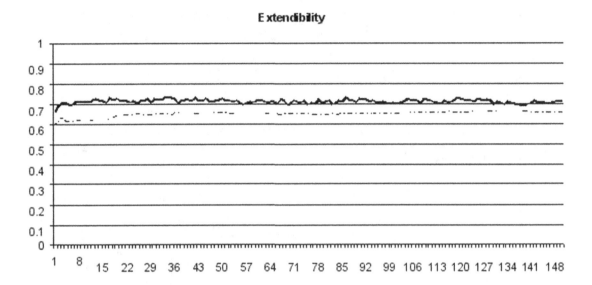

Figure 14. The GA performance graph for the objective Effectiveness

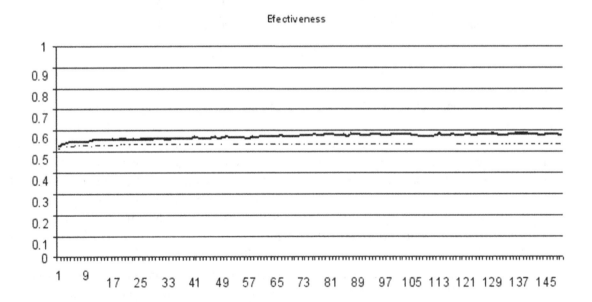

An interesting case of analysis is the synthesis of modeling which only prioritizes the objective *Understandability*. The result is in Figure 16.

Only one class was created in the optimization and the value reached for the attribute *Understandability* was -0,055, only 3, 8% better than the modeling of the attribute described in the book. This suggests that the best modeling might be obtained through combinations among the objectives, *Understandability* being one of

Figure 15. Modeling synthesized in the optimization of all the quality attributes

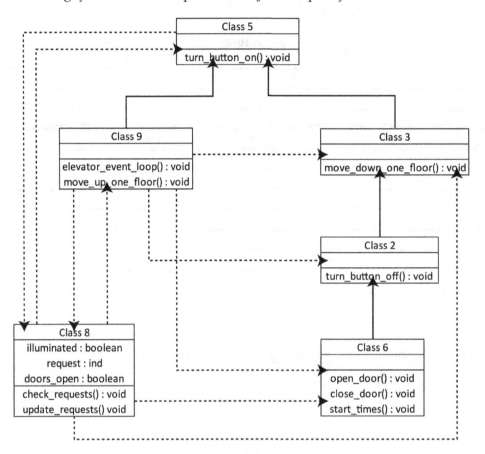

them, for it is the one that is close to a clear and objective modeling.

Considering the studied evaluation technique, the solution created by a specialist would be a solution that belongs to the Optimum Pareto set,

Table 19. Comparison of the quality attributes of the modelings

Attribute	Model	Expert
Reutilization	0,4669	0,2571
Flexibility	0,8055	0,7470
Understand-ability	-0,2559	-0,0891
Functionality	0,4994	0,3796
Extensibility	0,7555	0,6274
Efectiviness	0,5911	0,4819

and it could continue in the evolution. Thus, the new test performed was the one of inserting the specialist's solution as a seed in the first population. In this test, the GA made use of the solution that was created in the beginning and several combinations of objectives were tested, the best one was the one in which the *Understandability* and *Flexibility* attributes were used. The generated modeling can be seen in Figure 17.

In this case, several characteristics of the initial seed in the solution can be seen. The values reached for the quality attributes were the following:

- Flexibility: 0,7857
- Understandability: -0,0827

Figure 16. Synthesized modeling in the optimization of Understandability

Classe 4
requests : int
doors_open : int
illuminated : int
turn_button_off() : void
turn_button_on() : void
move_down_one_floor() : void
move_up_one_floor() : void
close_doors() : void
open_doors() : void
start_timer() : void
update_requests() : void
check_requests() : void
elevator_event_loop() : void

The value of the attribute *Understandability* is very close to the one found for the specialist's modeling. Another characteristic that can be seen is the grouping of methods and attributes, which was maintained, basically, resembling the initial seed. All these indicate that the solution given by the specialist is really a good one, since its characteristics were used in the evolution.

5. CONCLUSION AND FUTURE WORK

The goal of this work was to elaborate and evaluate a model able to combine the technique of the Co-evolutionary Genetic Algorithm to the object oriented software engineering and to the metrics proposed by Bansiya (Bansiya & Davis 2002), in his QMOOD model (Quality Models for Object-Oriented Modeling), in order to synthesize software modelings with better quality. Therefore, studies in Software Engineering have been done focusing on the aspects that belong to the object-oriented paradigm which are: classes, dependencies, methods, and attributes, metrics for Software Quality and its practical use. For the development of the model, the study of the representations of chromosomes in Genetic Algorithms, Co-evolutionary models and evaluation technique for multi-objective problems was necessary.

Furthermore, this research evaluated the performance of the model before the random search by its application, in order to optimize the different quality attributes in simple and more complex modeling problems. It is important to point out that the use of genetic algorithms with the use of co-evolution has always shown consistent results in relation to the optimization of the desirable objectives. The decoupling in the representation

Figure 17. Understandability and flexibility optimization using initial seed

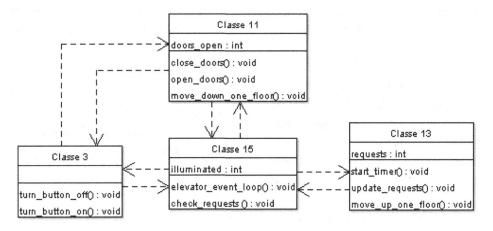

of the solution in co-evolutionary model was essential to make the consideration of a greater number of the characteristics of the object orientation paradigm in the evolution possible, allowing their independent evolution.

The results of this work turned out to be very promising in some of the cases, for the problem in evaluating software modeling is very subjective. This characteristic is what differentiates this problem from the problem of circuit synthesis, for example, in situations where the goal is to optimize parameters, such as velocity and consumption, where the best value is just what really counts, even if the synthesized circuit is not definable, or if it has useless components. It is very important to understand the diagrams in software modeling, as it is the starting point for the software implementation.

However, it is important to point out that even though the synthesized modelings cannot be promptly used without any modifications, the evolutionary synthesis that was developed can be applied as a help for the project technician, generating several types of modelings, in which different quality attributes are optimized and new good characteristics can be detected. Nevertheless, the proposed model does not replace the work of a project technician; it just helps him to find new solutions that may not have been thought of.

It was identified that the use of modelings as seeds from the first generation can help in the evolution and benefit the final solution with good characteristics. For this reason, the work of a project technician, is and will always be very important.

The model makes the standardization of modeling possible by benefiting the developer in many ways. The detection of problems in the modeling, in one of the first phases of the development process can significantly reduce time consuming and cost to solve problems when identified too late.

Another contribution of the methodology developed in this research is its use as a laboratory for the evaluation of metric sets for the measurement of the quality of the software. This can be done together with other publications, such as Bansiya`s work (Bansiya & Davis 2002).

We also observed that, in some situations, the consideration of several objectives did not allow the evolution for good solutions due to the contradiction between metrics and quality attributes. In some cases the GA was not able to reach better results than the random search. However, in problems of a larger scale this difficulty might not occur.

It is important to point out that the metrics suggested by Bansiya (Bansiya 2002), which were applied in this research, were empirically conceived and they do not necessarily correctly reproduce the objectives sought after quality software. A more meticulous study on this theme might clarify the problem of designs evaluation further on.

6. REFERENCES

Bäck, T., Fogel, D. B., & Michalewicz, Z. (1997). *Handbook of Evolutionary Computation.* Philadelphia: IOP Publishing. doi:10.1887/0750308958

Bansiya, J., & Davis, C. G. (2002). A Hierarchical Model for Object-Oriented Design Quality Assessment. *IEEE Transactions on Software Engineering, 28*(1), 4–17. doi:10.1109/32.979986

Blickle, T. (1996). *Theory of Evolutionary Algorithms and Application to System Synthesis.* PhD Thesis, Swiss Federal Institute of Technology, Zurique, Switzerland.

Bruce, W. S. (1995). *The Application of Genetic Programming to the Automatic Generation of Object-Oriented Programs.* Ph.D. Dissertation, School of Computer and Information Sciences, Nova Southeastern University, Fort Lauderdale.

Chidanber, S. R., & Kemerer, C. F. (1994). A Metrics Suite For Objected-Oriented Design. *IEEE Transactions on Software Engineering, 20*(6), 476–493. doi:10.1109/32.295895

Dandashi, F. (1998). *A Method for Assessing the Reusability of Object-oriented Code Using a Validated Set of Automated Measurements*. Ph.D. Dissertation, SITE, George Mason University, Fairfax, VA.

Davis, L. (1996). *Handbook of Genetic Algorithms*. New York: Van Nostrand Reinhold.

Fagerholt, K., & Christiansen, M. (2000). A Travelling Salesman Problem with Allocation, Time Window, and Precedence Constraints – an Application to Ship Scheduling. Intl. Trans. In Op. Res., 7, 231-244.

Fonseca, C. M., & Fleming, P. J. (1993). Genetic Algorithms for Multiobjective Optimization: Formulation, Discussion and Generalization. Genetic Algorithms. In S. Forrest, (ed.), *Proceedings of the Fifth International Conference*. San Mateo, CA: Morgan Kaufmann.

Genero, M., Piattini, M., Manso, E., & Cantone, G. (2003). Building UML Class Diagram Maintainability Prediction Models Based on Early Metrics. In *IEEE Proceedings of the Ninth International Software Metrics Symposium*.

Goldberg, D. E. (1989). *Genetic Algorithms in Search, Optimization, and Machine Learning*. Reading, MA: Addison-Wesley Publishing Company, Inc.

Haykin, S. (1999). *Neural Networks: A Comprehensive Foundation* (2nd ed.). Upper Saddle River, NJ: Prentice-Hall.

Hitz, M., & Montazeri, B. (1996). Chidamber and Kemerer's Metrics Suite: A Measurement Theory Perspective. *IEEE Transactions on Software Engineering, 22*(4), 267–271. doi:10.1109/32.491650

Iseminger, D. (2000). *Com+ Developer's Reference Library*. Redmond, WA: Microsoft Press.

Koza, J. R. (1992). *Genetic Programming: On the Programming of Computers by Means of Natural Selection*. Cambridge, MA: MIT Press.

Li, W., & Henry, S. (1993). Object-Oriented Metrics That Predict Maintainability. *Journal of Systems and Software, 23*, 111–122. doi:10.1016/0164-1212(93)90077-B

Lorenz, M., & Kidd, J. (1994). *Object-Oriented Software Metrics*. Upper Saddle River, NJ: Prentice Hall.

Lucas, S. M. (2004). Exploiting Reflection in Object Oriented Genetic Programming. In *European Conference on Genetic Programming*.

Michalewicz, Z. (1996). *Genetic Algorithms + data structures = evolution programs*. Berlin: Springer-Verlag.

Moon, C., Kim, J., Choi, G., & Seo, Y. (2002). An Efficient Genetic Algorithm for the Traveling Salesman Problem with Precedence Constraints. *European Journal of Operational Research, 140*, 606–617. doi:10.1016/S0377-2217(01)00227-2

OMG Unified Modeling Language Specification. (2003). Version 1.5, formal/03-03-01.

Schach, S. R. (2002). *Object-Oriented and Classical Software Engineering* (5th ed.). New York: McGraw-Hill.

Zebulum, R. S., Pacheco, M. A. C., & Vellasco, M. M. B. R. (2001). *Evolutionary Electronics: Automatic Design of Electronic Circuits and Systems by Genetic Algorithms*. Boca Raton, FL: CRC Press.

Chapter 5
Application of Artificial Immune Systems Paradigm for Developing Software Fault Prediction Models

Cagatay Catal
Information Technologies Institute, Turkey

Soumya Banerjee
Birla Institute of Technology, International Center, Mauritius

ABSTRACT

Artificial Immune Systems, a biologically inspired computing paradigm such as Artificial Neural Networks, Genetic Algorithms, and Swarm Intelligence, embody the principles and advantages of vertebrate immune systems. It has been applied to solve several complex problems in different areas such as data mining, computer security, robotics, aircraft control, scheduling, optimization, and pattern recognition. There is an increasing interest in the use of this paradigm and they are widely used in conjunction with other methods such as Artificial Neural Networks, Swarm Intelligence and Fuzzy Logic. In this chapter, we demonstrate the procedure for applying this paradigm and bio-inspired algorithm for developing software fault prediction models. The fault prediction unit is to identify the modules, which are likely to contain the faults at the next release in a large software system. Software metrics and fault data belonging to a previous software version are used to build the model. Fault-prone modules of the next release are predicted by using this model and current software metrics. From machine learning perspective, this type of modeling approach is called supervised learning. A sample fault dataset is used to show the elaborated approach of working of Artificial Immune Recognition Systems (AIRS).

1. INTRODUCTION

Today's software systems are becoming more and more complex and their lines of codes will reach to billions from millions of lines of code in near future. Therefore, innovative Validation & Verification (V&V) techniques are required more than ever to manage the complexity of current and future systems. Software Engineering Institute

DOI: 10.4018/978-1-61520-809-8.ch005

Figure 1. The scope of this chapter

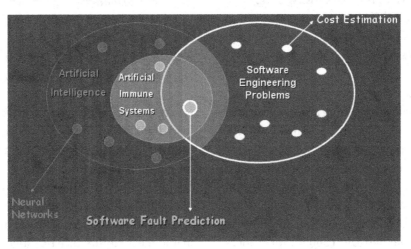

(SEI) published a report in 2006 and proposed a research agenda for U.S. Department of Defense about ultra-large-scale systems which will likely to have billions of lines of code. These kind of systems and large scale systems pose extraordinary challenges in Validation and Verification area and this chapter's subject, software fault prediction, is a proven quality assurance activity in achieving highly reliable systems.

Artificial Immune Systems (AIS) embody the principles and advantages of vertebrate immune systems. They are used for intrusion detection, classification, optimization, clustering and search problems. Recently, there is an increasing interest in the use of AIS paradigm to solve complex problems. In this chapter, a popular AIS based classification algorithm, AIRS, is explored on a software fault prediction dataset. The scope of this chapter is shown in Figure 1 and the yellow point which has "software fault prediction" label shows that this model is the intersection of AIS paradigm and a software engineering problem.

Immune system has two mechanisms that interact with each other. The first one is the innate immune system and there is no need being interacted with the relevant pathogen in the past for this type of mechanism. The second one is the adaptive immune system that enhances its ability

in order to detect more pathogens after the interaction. Lymphocytes are classified as B-cells and T-cells. Each lymphocyte can bind to a particular invader which is known as antigens. The similarity degree between B-cell and antigen is called affinity. If the antigen is detected by B-cell, B-cell is cloned with a process called "clonal expansion". These clones are mutated using "somatic hypermutation process" according to the affinity level. Some of these clones are differentiated into B memory cells in order to respond rapidly for the next attack from same invader and therefore immune system is said to have memory feature. Best matching clones with antigens survive and this process is known as "clonal selection".

The rest of this chapter is organized as follows: Section 2 describes the role of Artificial Immune System in software engineering domain along with its background and contemporary works. Section 3 elaborates the basic AIRS algorithm for software fault prediction followed by sequential diagrammatic representation of the algorithm in 3.1. Case study example is presented to validate the algorithm in section 4 and section 4.1. Section 5 gives conclusion.

2. ROLE OF ARTIFICIAL IMMUNE SYSTEM IN SOFTWARE ENGINEERING DOMAIN: MOTIVATION AND EXAMPLES

Distributed control, learning by experience, adaptation and parallel processing are main features of immune systems. These features make the AIS paradigm very powerful for solving complex problems and we developed several software fault prediction models based on AIS paradigm (Catal & Diri, 2009b, 2008, 2007a, 2007b). A systematic review of software fault prediction studies was published by Catal and Diri (2009a) for readers who want to see the current trends in this area.

Artificial Immune Recognition System (AIRS) is a supervised learning algorithm, inspired by the vertebrate immune system. Until 2001, most of the studies in AIS were focused on unsupervised learning algorithms. Watkins (2001) decided to show that artificial immune systems could be used for classification problems. The only exception was Carter's study (Carter, 2000), introduced a complex classification system based on AIS. Watkins (2001) demonstrated that AIS paradigm can be used for classification problems. Watkins' algorithm uses the resource-limited approach of Timmis and Neal's study (2000) and the clonal selection principles of De Castro and Von Zubben's (2000) study. After the first AIRS algorithm, some researchers proposed modified AIRS, which had a better algorithmic complexity with a little reduction of accuracy. Watkins (2005) also developed a parallel AIRS during his PhD studies. AIRS algorithm has powerful features that can be listed as follows:

- *Generalization:* The algorithm does not need all the dataset for generalization and it has data reduction capability
- *Parameter Stability:* Even though user-defined parameters are not optimized for the problem, the performance degradation is very small

- *Performance:* There has been demonstrated that its performance is excellent for some datasets
- *Self-Regulatory:* There is no need to choose a topology before training.

When we apply Artificial Neural Network paradigm for any problem, we need to identify the topological features such as the number of hidden or output nodes before training, but this is not a valid case for AIRS. Furthermore, the performance variation of AIRS is not significant after using the optimized parameters. This feature is known as parameter stability of AIRS algorithm.

Software quality engineering comprises of several quality assurance activities such as testing, formal verification, inspection, fault tolerance, and software fault prediction. Testing is the most important one but other approaches such as fault prediction are extremely helpful to improve the quality and reach dependable systems. The approaches to reach dependable systems can be categorized to four groups:

- *Fault Avoidance:* Software engineering practices such as code inspection and code walk-through help to avoid the faults
- *Fault Removal:* Unit and integration testing are some of the software engineering practices used to remove faults
- *Fault Tolerance:* Recovery block scheme and n-version programming scheme techniques can be used to tolerate faults
- *Fault Prediction:* Faults may be predicted before they occur. Therefore, fault-prone modules are tested much more than not fault-prone modules

The quality of software components should be tracked continuously during the development of high-assurance systems such as telecommunication infrastructures, medical devices, and avionics systems. Quality assurance group can improve the product quality by allocating necessary budget and human resources to low quality modules identified with different quality estimation models. Recent advances in software quality estimation yield building defect predictors with a mean probability of detection of 71 percent and mean false alarms rates of 25 percent (Menzies, Greenwald, & Frank, 2007). Software metrics are used as independent variables and fault data are regarded as dependent variable in software fault prediction models. The aim of building this kind of models is to predict the fault labels (fault-prone or not fault-prone) of the modules for the next release of the software.

Machine learning algorithms are trained with previous software metrics and fault data. Then, created models are used to predict the labels of new version's modules according to the new software metrics. Until now, many researchers developed and validated several fault prediction models by using machine learning and statistical techniques. There have been used different kinds of software metrics and diverse feature reduction techniques in order to improve the models' performance. Fault-prone modules can be automatically identified before testing phase by using the software fault prediction models. Generally, these models mostly use software metrics of earlier software releases and previous fault data collected during the testing phase. The benefits of these prediction models for software development practices are shown as follows:

- Refactoring candidates can be identified from the fault prediction models, which require refactoring
- Software testing process and software quality can be improved by allocating more resources on fault-prone modules
- The best design approach can be selected from design alternatives after identifying the fault-prone classes by using class-level metrics
- As fault prediction is an approach to reach dependable systems, we can have a highly

assured system by using fault prediction models during development.

Since 1990s, researchers have applied different kinds of algorithms based on machine learning and statistical methods to build high-performance fault predictors. However, most of them used non-public datasets to validate their models. Even though some of the researchers claimed that their models provided the highest performance in fault prediction, some of these models revealed to be unsuccessful when evaluated on public datasets. Therefore, it is extremely crucial to benchmark available fault prediction models under different conditions on public datasets.

Software fault prediction process uses the method-level metrics (Halstead and McCabe metrics), but additionally it can use class-level metrics, too. Method-level metrics are suitable for both procedural and object-oriented programming paradigms, whereas, class-level metrics can be only calculated for programs developed with object-oriented programming languages. Researchers used different methods such as Genetic Programming, Decision Trees, Neural Networks, Naive Bayes, Dempster-Shafer Networks, Case-based Reasoning, Fuzzy Logic and Logistic Regression for software fault prediction.

The following activities belong to traditional fault prediction:

- *Metrics gathering:* Previous software metrics from a version control system such as Clearcase or Subversion are gathered using an automatic tool developed in-house or manually (Metrics Gathering Tool)
- *Fault data gathering:* Previous fault data from change management such as ClearQuest are gathered using an automatic tool (Fault Data Gathering Tool)
- *Dataset construction:* Metrics and fault label of each module is combined in a dataset for further exploration and model building

Figure 2. This shows software fault prediction process

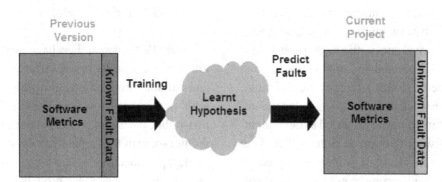

- ***Machine learner training:*** Recently machine learning algorithms are chosen to construct fault prediction model
- ***Machine learner testing:*** K-fold cross validation is used for testing or a part of dataset is used as test dataset
- ***Module fault prediction:*** Fault label of modules are predicted using current software metrics
- ***Action plan preparation:*** Some organizations may decide to do refactoring for fault-prone modules and others can use this information to prioritize modules to be tested

A typical software fault prediction process includes two major steps, as shown in Figure 2. First, a fault prediction model is built using previous software metrics and fault data belonging to each software module (class or method level). After this training phase, fault labels of program modules can be estimated using this model.

Menzies et al. (2007) showed that Naive Bayes with a logNum filter is the best software prediction model, even though it is a very simple algorithm. They also stated that there is no need to find the best software metrics group for software fault prediction because the performance variation of models with different metrics group is not significant. Almost all the software fault

prediction studies use metrics and fault data of previous software release to build fault prediction models, which are called "supervised learning" approaches in machine learning community. However, in some cases, there are very few or no previous fault data. Consequently, we need new models and techniques for these two challenging prediction problems.

Unsupervised learning approaches such as clustering methods can be used when there are not any previous fault data, whereas semi-supervised learning approaches can be used when there are very few fault data. Zhong, Khoshgoftaar and Seliya (2004) used Neural-Gas and K-means clustering algorithms to create the clusters and then an expert examined representative modules of clusters to assign the fault-proneness label. The performance of their model was comparable with classification algorithms (Zhong et al., 2004). In the cases when a company does not have previously collected fault data, or when a new project type is initiated, unsupervised learning approaches could be incorporated. Seliya, Khoshgoftaar, and Zhong (2004) used Expectation-Maximization (E-M) algorithm for semi-supervised software fault prediction problem showing that their model had comparable results with classification algorithms. Therefore, the semi-supervised fault prediction models are required especially in the

Figure 3. This shows no fault data problem

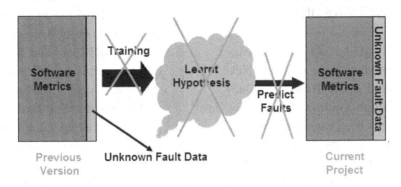

Figure 4. This shows limited fault data problem

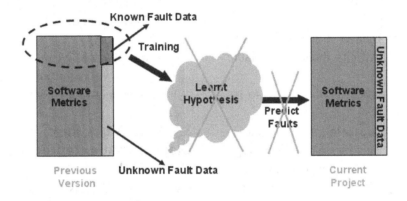

Figure 5. This shows a sample fault prediction dataset

```
15,2,1,2,42,168,0.11,9,18.67,1512,0.06,84,12,0,1,0,9,7,false
25,2,1,2,34,132.83,0.12,8.57,15.5,1138.58,0.04,63.25,13,6,4,0,8,7,true
15,2,1,2,43,191.76,0.15,6.67,28.76,1278.37,0.06,71.02,8,2,2,0,10,12,false
9,2,1,2,20,74.01,0.13,7.88,9.4,582.82,0.02,32.38,4,2,1,0,9,4,true
16,2,1,2,44,196.21,0.15,6.67,29.43,1308.1,0.07,72.67,9,2,2,0,10,12,false
```

de-centralized software projects, where most of the companies find difficulties to collect fault data.

Figure 3 depicts no fault data problem and unsupervised learning approaches can be applied in this case whereas Figure 4 shows limited fault data problem and semi-supervised learning approaches can be applied for this case.

A sample training dataset, including software metrics and known fault data, is shown in Figure 5. All the metrics are separated with commas in this figure and the last column presents whether this module caused fault or not during the testing phase. This last feature (column) consists of false and true values.

3. AIRS ALGORITHM FOR SOFTWARE FAULT PREDICTION

Artificial Immune Systems is a biologically inspired computing paradigm such as Neural Networks, and Swarm Intelligence. Brownlee (2005) implemented this algorithm in Java. Performance of AIRS algorithm has been examined for various machine learning datasets. Each data point in datasets is called antigen. Activity diagram of this algorithm is given in Figure 6. Details of the algorithm are explained below. Step 2, 3, 4 are used for each data point in dataset and Step 1 and 5 are applied only one time.

1. *Initialization:* Dataset is normalized into [0, 1] interval. Affinity threshold variable is computed.
    a. Training dataset is normalized to [0, 1] range.
    b. Affinity Threshold (AT) variable is prepared. This variable is the average value of affinities between antigens.
    c. Memory cell pool and ARB pool are initialized.
2. *Antigen Training:* Each data point in training set is provided to the memory pool to stimulate the recognition cells in memory pool. Stimulation values are assigned to the recognition cells and the cell, which has maximum stimulation value, is marked as the best memory cell. This cell is used for affinity maturation and cloned, then mutated. These clone cells are put into the Artificial Recognition Ball (ARB) pool. Equation 1 depicts the stimulation formula. Equation 2 shows how to compute the number of clones (**These are two core formulas**).

$$stim = 1 - affinity. \tag{1}$$

$$numClones = stim * clonalRate * hypermutationRate. \tag{2}$$

3. *Competition for limited resource:* After mutated clones are added to the ARB pool, competition starts. Antigen is used to stimulate the ARB pool and limited resource is computed with respect to stimulation values. ARBs with very limited resource or no limited resource are deleted from ARB pool. This step continues until stopping criteria is met. Otherwise, mutated clones of ARBs are produced.
4. *Memory cell selection:* Candidate memory cell that has a maximum stimulation score from ARB pool is chosen. ARB is copied to the memory cell pool if ARB's stimulation value is better than the original best matching memory.
5. *Classification:* Memory cell pool is used for cross-validation and K-nearest neighbor approach is applied for classification.

3.1 AIRS Algorithm: Diagrammatic Representation

Figure 7, 8, 9 depicts the second step of the algorithm. Figure 10 and Figure 11 show the third step of the algorithm; Figure 12 and Figure 13 show the fourth step of AIRS algorithm. Fifth step of the algorithm is the classification. The figures given below depict the training phase of AIRS algorithm.

4. CASE STUDY: APPLICATION OF AIRS FOR FAULT PREDICTION

In this section, the application of AIRS algorithm for software fault prediction problem will be explained with one numerical example. To prepare this example, a sourceforge project, wekaclassalgos (http://wekaclassalgos.sourceforge.net) was used. We debugged step by step the source code of this project and examined the data locating in memory cell pool and Artificial Recognition Ball (ARB) pool. ARB represents the B cells in

Figure 6. This diagram shows the activity diagram of AIRS algorithm

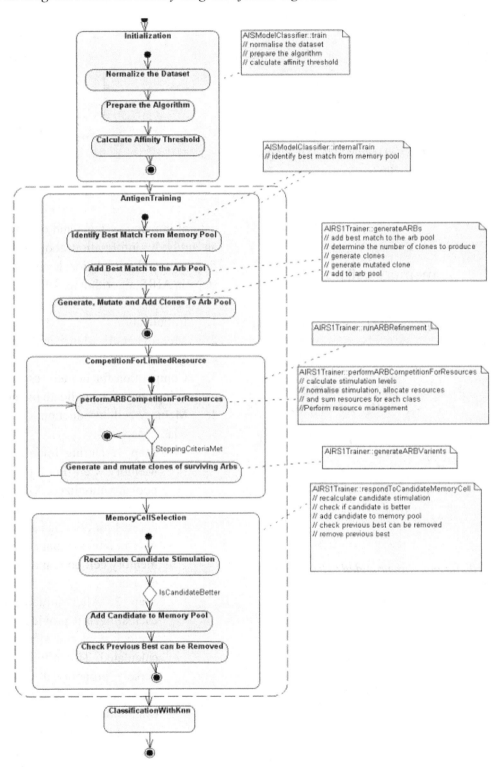

Figure 7. Antigen is provided to the memory cell pool (Timmis, 2008)

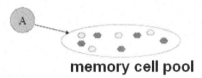

Figure 8. Best matching memory cell (MCmatch) is identified (Timmis, 2008)

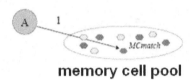

Figure 9. Mutants are added to the ARB pool (Timmis, 2008)

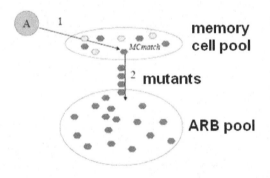

Figure 10. Antigens are provided to the ARB pool (Timmis, 2008)

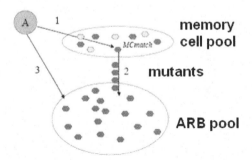

Figure 11. Candidate memory cell (Timmis, 2008)

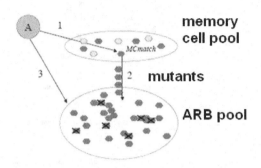

natural immune systems and one ARB includes an antibody, information about the number of resources and stimulation level. There are five steps in AIRS algorithm as follows:

1. Initialization
2. Memory cell identification and ARB generation
3. Competition for limited resources and development of a candidate memory cell
4. Memory cell introduction
5. Classification
   ○ **Step 1:** During initialization phase, Memory Cell Pool (M) and ARB pool are initialized. A data point from dataset can be used to initialize these pools. From biological point of view, we can imagine that antibodies are in memory cell pool and antigens are in dataset.
   ○ **Step 2:** After initialization phase, each antigen is provided to the memory cell pool and affinity values are calculated. This affinity value is inversely propotional with Euclidean distance between two vectors. Stimulation values are calculated by using Equation 1 given in previous sections. If the Euclidean distance is small, stimulation level is high and this means that memory cell is

Figure 12. Comparison of best matching cell and candidate memory cell (Timmis, 2008)

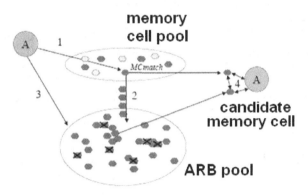

Figure 13. Candidate memory cell is added to the memory cell pool (Timmis, 2008)

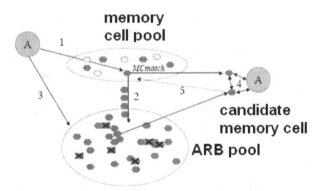

stimulated enormously by this antigen. At the second step of the algorithm, the cell which has the highest stimulation value in the M is identified and this cell is cloned and clones are mutated. After mutation, mutations are added to the ARB pool.

- **Step 3:** At this step, a competition starts in ARB pool for limited resources and the total number of resources which can be used by ARBs in the system is limited. The antigen used in previous step is also provided to this pool and resources are assigned according to the affinity values. ARBs which do not have sufficient resources are removed from ARB pool. If the stopping criteria is

not met, each surviving ARB produces mutated clones and this process goes on until stopping criteria is met. Stopping criteria checks if ARBs are stimulated enough. The most stimulated ARB is selected as "candidate memory cell".

- **Step 4:** If the affinity value between "candidate memory cell" and antigen is higher than the affinity value between "best matching cell" and the same antigen, this "candidate memory cell" is added to the memory cell pool (M). There is another control to decide whether best matching cell should be removed from M or not. We will show this control in our numerical example. Cells which reside

Figure 14. A sample fault prediction dataset

```
@RELATION  FaultPredictionDataset
@ATTRIBUTE CyclomaticComplexity    REAL
@ATTRIBUTE LinesOfCode             REAL
@ATTRIBUTE NumberOfUniqueOperand   REAL
@ATTRIBUTE NumberOfUniqueOperator  REAL
@ATTRIBUTE class {yes, no}
@DATA
40.0, 220.0, 140.0, 240.0, yes
2.0, 12.0, 8.0, 8.0, no
65.0, 42.0, 430.0, 260.0, yes
3.0, 10.0, 13.0, 8.0, no
5.0, 14.0, 7.0, 6.0, no
100.0, 240.0, 160.0, 234.0, yes
65.0, 45.0, 430.0, 260.0, yes
8.0, 9.0, 13.0, 8.0, no
9.0, 24.0, 7.0, 6.0, no
150.0, 640.0, 160.0, 234.0, yes
```

in M pool will be used to find out the class label of test data points.

○ **Step 5:** Step 1 and Step 2 work one time when AIRS is called. Step 2, 3, 4 work for each data point locating in dataset. At the last step of the algorithm, test data point is provided to the cells in M and *k* number of most stimulated memory cells are identified. The majority of the labels of these most stimulated memory cells decide what the class label should be.

Example given here is based on AIRS version 1 algorithm. At the second version of this algorithm, general principles were preserved but minor modifications were implemented. AIRS version 1 is more complex than AIRS version 2 but provides better performance compared to AIRS version 2. We debugged the first version of the algorithm because it is the starting point of AIRS algorithms. A sample fault prediction dataset with ARFF format is given in Figure 14. Each row represents one software module and each column except the last column shows a software metric such as lines of code. Last column of each row indicates whether that module caused fault or not during system testing or operational phase. *Yes* label at that column means that this module cause at least one fault and *No* label means that

Figure 15. Training set chosen from the sample dataset

```
5.0, 14.0, 7.0, 6.0, no
8.0, 9.0, 13.0, 8.0, no
40.0, 220.0, 140.0, 240.0, yes
150.0, 640.0, 160.0, 234.0, yes
3.0, 10.0, 13.0, 8.0, no
```

this module did not cause any fault during system testing.

N-fold cross validation technique is used to evaluate the performance of machine learning algorithms if the test is done in the training dataset. Some researchers suggest to repeat N-fold cross validation technique M times and this is represented with N*M validation. This approach provides statistically reliable results. In this example, we used 2-fold cross validation (N=2) one time (M=1) because there exist just a few data points and this is just an example for readers. During the debugging, we noticed that modules shown in Figure 15 were chosen for training set and the rest were chosen for test set. This is a 2-fold cross validation, modules shown in Figure 15 will be in test set for the second calculation and the rest will be in the training set. However, we will explain only the first part of 2-fold cross validation due to page limitations.

During initialization phase, dataset is normalized and WEKA library functions were used for this normalization. WEKA is an open source machine learning tool and *wekaclassalgos* sourceforge project is based on this open source tool. Normalization in WEKA is done by using Equation 3 and Equation 4 according to the column values.

Interval = MaximumColumnValue – MinimumColumnValue   (3)

NormalizedValue = (ValueToBeNormalized – MinimumColumnValue) / Interval   (4)

Figure 16. Normalized training set

```
0.013605, 0.007924, 0, 0, no
0.034014, 0, 0.039216, 0.008547, no
0.251701, 0.33439, 0.869281, 1, yes
1, 1, 1, 0.974359, yes
0, 0.001585, 0.039216, 0.008547, no
```

Figure 17. Content of ARB pool after initialization

```
0.013605,0.007924,0,0,1
```

Figure 18. Content of memory cell pool after initialization

```
1,1,1,0.974359,0
```

For example; let's examine how the first element in first row of Figure 15, value 5, is normalized. Interval = 150 − 3 = 147 and Normalized Value = (5-3) / 147 = 0.013605 are calculated. Therefore, the normalization value of 5 is 0.013505 and the similar operations for all the other elements locating in dataset. The normalized training set is shown in Figure 16.

Following sections will show how each steps of AIRS algorithm work by using this normalized training dataset and at some points, some of the cells will be presented as sample because the other ones can be calculated with similar logic.

4.1. Initialization

There are three major steps during initalization as follows:

a.   *Normalization:* We already showed how to calculate the normalized training set in previous section.

b.   *AT value calculation:* Affinity threshold value (AT) should be calculated during initialization phase. This value is the mean of Euclidean distances between all the normalized values shown in Figure 15. For this dataset, AT is 0.497 according to the debugging screens. User specifies *numInstancesAffinityThreshold* parameter before executing AIRS algorithm and if this variable is -1, all the data points in dataset are used to calculate the AT value. In this example, this value was -1 before the execution.

c.   *Initialization of memory cell pool and ARB pool:* Memory cell pool and ARB pool are

initalized at the first step of AIRS algorithm. User can specify *arbInitialPoolSize* and *memInitialPoolSize* parameters prior to the execution of AIRS. Default value for these parameters are 1 and during our debugging process, these values were 1, too. Therefore, one data point for ABR pool and one data point for memory cell pool are randomly chosen from training set to initialize them. We noticed that row 4 of the training set [1, 1, 1, 0.0974359, 0] was initialized for memory cell pool and first row of the training set [0.013605, 0.0007924, 0, 0, 1] was initialized for ARB pool. Because user parameters were 1 before execution, only one data point was copied for each pool. After the initialization phase, the contents of ARB and memory cell pool are shown in Figure 17 and Figure 18 respectively. Class label {yes} was represented with 0 value and {no} label was represented with 1 value.

After this initialization of these pools, the first step of the algorithm finishes.

4.2. Memory Cell Identification and ARB Generation

In this step, an antigen is provided to the memory cell pool and the first row in the training dataset [0.013605, 0.007924, 0, 0, 1] is chosen as first antigen. At later loops, the other rows are chosen

Figure 19. New content of memory cell pool

```
1, 1, 1, 0.974359, 0
0.013605, 0.007924, 0, 0, 1
```

as antigens. Because this antigen's class label is different than the antibody's class label locating in memory cell pool, the function which identifies the best matching memory cell returns *null* and this null value is assigned to *bestMatch* variable. *Current* antigen [0.013605, 0.007924, 0, 0, 1] will be added to the memory cell pool and hence, no such an event will occur any more. New content of the memory cell pool is shown in Figure 19.

New current antigen vector will be the second row of the training set which is represented with [0.034014, 0, 0.039216, 0.008547, no] vector. The affinity between this current antigen vector and memory cells in memory cell pool are calculated. Euclidean distance is used to calculate the affinity between two vectors and this value is substracted from value 1 to find the stimulation value. As mentioned in previous sections, {no} label is represented with 1 value and hence, only the stimulation value between this current vector and the second row of memory cell pool is meaningful and the function does not return *null*. However, the first row of the memory cell pool has different class label than the current antigen vector and the stimulation value calculated for this cell is not important to identify the best matching cell. Therefore, [0.013605, 0.007924, 0, 0, 1] vector is chosen as best matching memory cell and the stimulation value is 0.9795.

$$mc_{match} = [0.013605, 0.007924, 0, 0, 1]$$

If the stimulation value would be value 1, that would be the maximum stimulation value and this cell would not be copied to the ARB pool. In that case, this cell would be added to the memory cell pool and it would be the best recognising cell for

that antigen. Because the stimulation value is not value 1, clones are produced from this cell and they are mutated and transferred to the ARB pool.

The number of clones that will be produced from the best matching cell is proportional with the stimulation value and it is calculated with the Equation 5.

# of clones = Math.round(stimulation_value * clonal_rate * hypermutation ratio)   (5)

Default values for clonal rate and hypermutation ratio are 10 and 2 respectively. Therefore, the maximum number of clones can be (1 * 10 * 2 = 20) 20. According to this example, 20 clones (Math. round(0.975 * 10 * 2) = 20) will be produced from this best matching cell. To mutate these clones, a random number is generated in the interval [0, 1] and this value is compared with *mutationRate* parameter. Default value for *mutationRate* is 0.1 and it can be customized by the user prior to the execution of the algorithm. If the random number generated with *rand* function is smaller than the *mutationRate*, feature's value is changed with a value generated with *rand* function. If it is not smaller than the *mutationRate*, second feature is chosen and mutation process is tried be realized at this feature. In this AIRS implementation, class label can be mutated too and integer value depending on the number of classes is assigned. Let's assume that mutation occurs at the class feature but the new value of this feature is assigned again 1. Even though this is a mutated clone, it's all features are totally same with the mc_{match} cell. During debugging process, we encountered with this case and hence, this mutated clone called mutant 1 was added to the ARB pool. New content of the ARB pool is shown in Figure 20. Last row shown in Figure 20 shows the mutant1 and the first row is the cell chosen at the initialization step. Second row of the memory cell pool is the best matching cell.

20 clones are mutated and added to the memory cell pool. Therefore, ARB will include 22 ARB

Figure 20. New content of ARB pool after mutant1

```
0.013605, 0.007924, 0, 0, 1
0.013605, 0.007924, 0, 0, 1
0.013605, 0.007924, 0, 0, 1
```

Figure 21. Content of ARB pool after mutant2

```
0.013605, 0.007924, 0, 0, 1
0.013605, 0.007924, 0, 0, 1
0.013605, 0.007924, 0, 0, 1
0.7617, 0.007924, 0, 0, 1
...
```

after the second step of AIRS finishes. During the mutation process of the second clone, we observed that the mutation occurred at the first feature of the clone and the random value was 0.7617 generated with *rand* function. That's why, mutant2 is represented with [0.7617, 0.007924, 0, 0, 1] vector and this vector is added to the memory cell pool. The content of the ARB pool after mutant2 is shown in Figure 21.

4.3. Competition for Limited Resources

At the end of the second step, there were 22 ARB in ARB pool and we will calculate 22 stimulation values when antigen is provided to the ARB pool. The last antigen we worked was [0.034014, 0, 0.039216, 0.008547, 1]. This antigen is provided to ARBs. Stimulation value between this antigen and first row of the ARB pool is 0.9953. As first, second and third rows of ARB pool are same, stimulation values will be same, 0.9953. Stimulation value between antigen and the last row of the pool is 0.234 according to the debugging screens. According to these stimulation values, resources are assigned to the ARBs. Stimulation values are multiplied with *clonalRate* (10) and result is the number of assigned resources. If the class label of the ARB is different than the class label of antigen,

stimulation value is subtracted from value 1 and this is the new stimulation value of ARB. If they have the same label, no subtraction is done. This implementation was done in AIRS version 1 but in second version of AIRS algorithm, resources are only assigned to the ARBs that have same class label with the antigen.

After resources are assigned, total number of assigned resources are calculated for each class separately. During debugging process, we observed that *resources[0]* and *resources[1]* were 0.0093 and 112.92 respectively. Default value of *totalResources* parameter is 150 and hence, total number of resources for each class should be smaller than 75. Because *resources[0] = 0.0093* is smaller than 75, there is no reason to remove some resources of ARBs which have "yes" class label. However, *resources[1] = 112.92* and it is bigger than 75. Therefore, we will start to delete from the ARBs which have the smallest number of resources. ARBs are sorted according to the number of resources they have and we have to delete (112.92 – 75 = 37.12) approximately 37 resources. First ARB which has 0.5570 resource value is deleted and this goes on until threshold value 75 is reached. After 75 value is reached, ARB which has the maximum number of resources and has the same class label with the antigen, is chosen as *mostStimulatedSameClass* ARB. During debugging phase, we observed that this *mostStimulatedSameClass* was [0.04104, 0.007924, 0, 0, 1]. Number of resources of this ARB was 10 and stimulation value was 1. This ARB is also *candidate memory cell* but we cannot confirm it yet because we did not check the stopping condition.

At this point, we should check if the stopping criteria is met or not. Mean stimulation values belonging to two classes will be compared with stimulation threshold (0.9). During debugging phase, we observed that *meanStimulation[0]* is *0.0046* and it is smaller than 0.9. Therefore, we see that stopping condition is not met yet. That's why, ARBs will be cloned and mutated. For the first control, even if the condition is met, clones are produced according to this implementation. The number of clones which can be produced from an ARB are calculated with (stimulation_value * clonalRate). That's why, the maximum number of clones are 10 (1 * 10 =10). However, maximum number of clones for memory cell pool was 20 because of hypermutation parameter. The reason why we produce more cells in memory cell pool is to provide more diversity in that pool.

Let's assume that one of the surviving cells in ARB pool is [0.013605, 0.007924, 0, 0, 1]. Antigen was [0.034014, 0, 0.039216, 0.008547, 1]. Euclidean distance between these vectors is near to 0 and stimulation value is near to 1. Therefore, number of clones will be 10. Each clone will be mutated and are added to the ARB pool. This process is done for all the ARBs which are still alive. Because stopping condition is not met yet, competition for limited resources is done again. Antigen is again provided to the ARB pool and ARBs which do not have sufficient resources will be removed.

After stopping condition is met, we observed that ARB which has the maximum resources is [0.04104, 0.07924, 0.03916, 0, 1]. This cell is called *candidate memory cell* and this is the end of this step (Step 3 of AIRS algorithm). At the next step, we will examine which cell (mc$_{match}$ or candidate memory cell) matches better with the antigen.

4.4. Memory Cell Introduction

In previous steps, we identified the following cells:

mc$_{match}$ = [0.013605, 0.007924, 0, 0, 1]

CandidateMemoryCell = [0.04104, 0.07924, 0.03916, 0, 1]

Antigen = [0.034014, 0, 0.039216, 0.008547,1]

Figure 22. New content of memory cell pool

$$1, 1, 1, 0.974359, 0$$
$$0.04104, 0.007924, 0.03916, 0, 1$$

First, stimulation value between antigen and mc$_{match}$ is calculated. Then, stimulation value between antigen and candidate memory cell is calculated. The first stimulation value is 0.9795 and second one is 0.99391. Because the second value is bigger than the first one, candidate memory cell is copied into the memory cell pool. After this process, a control is done to decide whether mc$_{match}$ should be removed from the pool or not. For this control, affinity between mc$_{match}$ and candidate memory cell is calculated. If this value is smaller than the cut-off value, mc$_{match}$ is removed. This cut-off value is equal to the multiplication of Affinity Threshold (AT) and Affinity Threshold Scalar (ATS). Default value for ATS is 0.2 and AT value was calculated during the initialization phase of AIRS algorithm. During debugging phase, we observed that cut-off value is 0.99391 and affinity between mc$_{match}$ and candidate memory cell is 0.021138. Because this affinity value is smaller than the cut-off value, mc$_{match}$ is removed from the memory cell pool. New content of the memory cell pool is shown in Figure 22.

During debugging process, we noticed that there are 521 ARBs in ARB pool after memory cell pool is updated. Now 2nd, 3rd, 4th steps of AIRS algorithm were completed for that antigen. After this antigen, next antigen from the training set will be the current antigen and the same process will be executed. New current vector will be the vector represented with [0.251701, 0.33439, 0.869281, 1, 0]. After this antigen passes the steps 2, 3, 4 sequentially, the new content of the memory cell pool will change. New content of the memory cell pool is shown in Figure 23.

The other antigens locating in training dataset will pass from the steps 2, 3, 4 and the memory cell

Figure 23. New content of memory cell pool after new antigen

```
1, 1, 1, 0.974359, 0
0.04104, 0.007924, 0.03916, 0, 1
0.27105, 0.2215, 0.84256, 0.8412, 0
```

Figure 24. Final form of the memory cell pool

```
0.04104, 0.007924, 0.03916, 0, 1
0.27105, 0.2215, 0.84256, 0.8412, 0
1, 1, 1, 0.974359, 0
```

Figure 25. Test dataset

```
2, 12, 8, 8, ?
65, 42, 430, 260, ?
100, 240, 160, 234, ?
65, 45, 430, 260, ?
9, 24, 7, 6, ?
```

pool will be produced. Final form of the memory cell pool is shown in Figure 24.

4.5. Classification

We had identified five training data points and five test points. Test data points will be provided to the memory cell pool and the majority label of K number of most stimulated memory cells will be assigned for that data point. Test dataset is shown in Figure 25. These data points locating in this dataset will also be normalized as done in training dataset.

The first row of test dataset will be [0, 0, 0.000236, 0.00787, ?]. Stimulation values between this data point and memory cells are calculated. During stimulation calculation, class labels are not used and hence, stimulation values are easily calculated at this step. Prior to the execution of AIRS algorithm, k parameter of k-nn was 3.

Therefore, there is no need to sort the stimulation values from biggest to the smallest. Class labels of memory cells will be used to decide the class label of test point. There are two cells which have {yes} label and only one cell which has {no} label, all the test points will have {yes} label. This was a very simple dataset and our aim was to demonstrate how AIRS algorithm can be used for software fault prediction problem. In case of real datasets intelligent predictions are collected from AIRS based software fault prediction model.

5. CONCLUSION

Software fault prediction is a very active software engineering research topic and different machine learning and adaptive and evolutionary algorithms have been used to reach the best classification result. Artificial Immune Systems is an emerging computational intelligence technique that provides promising results for many problems and we are working on developing better algorithms with this paradigm. In this chapter, we investigated the use of Artificial Immune Systems paradigm for software fault prediction problem during the research implementation. The study showed the elaborated working steps of AIRS algorithm with a software engineering dataset. Public datasets for this problem can be accessed from http://promisedate.org. A sample fault prediction dataset was used to show how AIRS algorithm works in this challenging software engineering problem. We expect core research in this area to achieve a mature software engineering discipline and better fault prediction models. Researchers may apply this classification algorithm, AIRS, for other software engineering problems too. In addition, there exist different clustering and optimization algorithms that are based on AIS paradigm. Some of these algorithms could be appropriate for the other diversified software engineering problems.

ACKNOWLEDGMENT

This project is supported by The Scientific and Technological Research Council of Turkey (Tubitak) under Grant 107E213 and Birla Institute of Technology, International Center, Mauritius. The findings and opinions in this study belong solely to the authors, and are not necessarily those of the sponsors.

REFERENCES

Brownlee, J. (2005). *Artificial immune recognition system: A review and analysis* (Report No. 1-02). Melbourne, Australia: Swinburne University of Technology.

Carter, J. H. (2000). The immune system as a model for pattern recognition and classification. *Journal of the American Medical Informatics Association, 7*(1), 28–41.

Catal, C., & Diri, B. (2007a). Software defect prediction using artificial immune recognition system. In *Proceedings of 25th IASTED International Multi-Conference on Software Engineering, Innsbruck, Austria,* (pp. 285-290).

Catal, C., & Diri, B. (2007b). Software fault prediction with object-oriented metrics based artificial immune recognition system. In *Proceedings of Product-Focused Software Process Improvement Conference (PROFES 2007), Riga, Latvia,* (pp. 300-314).

Catal, C., & Diri, B. (2008). A fault prediction model with limited fault data to improve test process. *Proceedings of Product Focused Software Process Improvement Conference (PROFES 2008),* Frascati, Italy, (pp. 244-257).

Catal, C., & Diri, B. (2009a). A systematic review of software fault prediction studies. *Expert Systems with Applications, 36*(4), 7346–7354. doi:10.1016/j.eswa.2008.10.027

Catal, C., & Diri, B. (2009b). Investigating the effect of dataset size, metrics sets, and feature selection techniques on software fault prediction problem. *Information Sciences, 179*(8), 1040–1058. doi:10.1016/j.ins.2008.12.001

De Castro, L. N., & Von Zubben, F. J. (2000). The clonal selection algorithm with engineering applications. In *Proceedings of Genetic and Evolutionary Computation Conference, Las Vegas, Nevada,* (pp. 36–37).

Menzies, T., Greenwald, J., & Frank, A. (2007). Data mining static code attributes to learn defect predictors. *IEEE Transactions on Software Engineering, 33*(1), 2–13. doi:10.1109/TSE.2007.256941

Seliya, N., Khoshgoftaar, T. M., & Zhong, S. (2004). Semi-supervised learning for software quality estimation. In *Proceedings of the 16th International Conference on Tools with Artificial Intelligence,* Boca Raton, FL, (pp. 183-190).

Timmis, J. (2008). *Collaborative bio-inspired algorithms.* Retrieved August 13, 2009, from www.artificial-immune-systems.org/courses/Lectures/lecture6.pdf

Timmis, J., & Neal, M. (2000). Investigating the evolution and stability of a resource limited artificial immune systems. In *Proceedings of Genetic and Evolutionary Computation Conference, Las Vegas, Nevada,* (pp. 40-41).

Watkins, A. (2001). *AIRS: A resource limited artificial immune classifier.* Master Thesis, Mississippi State University. Retrieved from http://www.cse.msstate.edu/~andrew/research/publications/watkins_thesis.pdf

Watkins, A. (2005). *Exploiting immunological metaphors in the development of serial, parallel, and distributed learning algorithms.* Doctoral Dissertation, Mississippi State University. Retrieved from http://www.cse.msstate.edu/~andrew/research/publications/watkins_phd_dissertation.pdf

Zhong, S., Khoshgoftaar, T. M., & Seliya, N. (2004). Unsupervised learning for expert-based software quality estimation. In *Proceedings of the 8th International Symposium on High Assurance Systems Engineering*, Tampa, FL, (pp. 149-155).

Chapter 6
Genetic Programming for Cross–Release Fault Count Predictions in Large and Complex Software Projects

Wasif Afzal
Blekinge Institute of Technology, Sweden

Richard Torkar
Blekinge Institute of Technology, Sweden

Robert Feldt
Blekinge Institute of Technology, Sweden

Tony Gorschek
Blekinge Institute of Technology, Sweden

ABSTRACT

Software fault prediction can play an important role in ensuring software quality through efficient resource allocation. This could, in turn, reduce the potentially high consequential costs due to faults. Predicting faults might be even more important with the emergence of short-timed and multiple software releases aimed at quick delivery of functionality. Previous research in software fault prediction has indicated that there is a need i) to improve the validity of results by having comparisons among number of data sets from a variety of software, ii) to use appropriate model evaluation measures and iii) to use statistical testing procedures. Moreover, cross-release prediction of faults has not yet achieved sufficient attention in the literature. In an attempt to address these concerns, this paper compares the quantitative and qualitative attributes of 7 traditional and machine-learning techniques for modeling the cross-release prediction of fault count data. The comparison is done using extensive data sets gathered from a total of 7 multi-release open-source and industrial software projects. These software projects together have several years of development and are from diverse application areas, ranging from a web browser to a robotic controller software. Our quantitative analysis suggests that genetic programming (GP) tends to have better consistency in terms of goodness of fit and accuracy across majority of data sets. It also has

DOI: 10.4018/978-1-61520-809-8.ch006

comparatively less model bias. Qualitatively, ease of configuration and complexity are less strong points for GP even though it shows generality and gives transparent models. Artificial neural networks did not perform as well as expected while linear regression gave average predictions in terms of goodness of fit and accuracy. Support vector machine regression and traditional software reliability growth models performed below average on most of the quantitative evaluation criteria while remained on average for most of the qualitative measures.

1. INTRODUCTION

The development of quality software on time and within stipulated cost is a challenging task. One influential factor in software quality is the presence of software faults, which have a potentially considerable impact on timely and cost-effective software development. Thus fault prediction models have attracted considerable interest in research (as shown in Section 2). A fault prediction model uses historic software quality data in the form of metrics (including software fault data) to predict the number of software faults in a module or a release (Taghi and Naeem, 2002). Fault predictions for a software release are fundamental to the efforts of quantifying software quality. A fault prediction model helps a software development team in prioritizing the effort spent on a software project and also for selective architectural improvements. This paper presents both quantitative and qualitative evaluations of using genetic programming (GP) for cross-release predictions of fault count data gathered from open source and industrial software projects. Fault counts denotes the cumulative faults aggregated on a weekly or monthly basis. We quantitatively compare the results from traditional and machine learning approaches to fault count predictions and also assess various qualitative criteria for a better trade-off analysis. The main purpose is to increase empirical knowledge concerning innovative ways of predicting fault count data and to apply the resulting models in a manner that is suited to multi-release software development projects.

Regardless of large number of studies on software fault prediction, there is little convergence of results across them. This non-convergence of results is also highlighted by other authors such as (Stefan, Bart, Christophe & Swantje, 2008; Magnus and Per, 2002). This necessitates further research to increase confidence in the results of fault prediction studies. Stefan et al. (2008) identifies three sources of bias in fault prediction studies: use of small and proprietary data sets, inappropriate accuracy indicators and limited used of statistical testing procedures. Magnus and Per (2002) further highlight the need for the authors to provide information about context, data characteristics, statistical methods and chosen parameters; so as to encourage replications of these studies. These factors, more or less, contribute to a lack of benchmarking in software fault prediction studies. Therefore, *benchmarking*, although recommended by (Susan, Steve & Richard, 2003) as a way to advance research, is still open for further research in software fault prediction studies.

One challenge in having trustworthy software fault prediction models is the nature of typical software engineering data sets. Software engineering data come with certain characteristics that complicate the task of having accurate software fault prediction models. These characteristics include missing data, large number of variables, strong co-linearity between the variables, heteroscedasticity[1], complex non-linear relationships, outliers and small size (Gray and MacDonell, 1997). Therefore, "it is very difficult to make valid assumptions about the form of the functional relationship between the variables" (Lionel, Victor & William, 1992, pp. 931). Moreover, the acceptability of models has seen little success due to lack of meaningful explanation of the relationship among different variables and lack of generalizability of model results (Gray and MacDonell, 1997). Applications of computational and artificial intelligence have attempted to deal with some of these challenges, see e.g. (Zhang and Tsai, 2003), mainly because of their inherent intelligent modeling mechanisms to deal with data. There are several reasons for using these techniques for fault prediction modeling:

1. They do not depend on assumptions about data distribution and relationship between independent and dependent variables.
2. They are independent of any assumptions about the stochastic behavior of software failure process and the nature of software faults (Yu-Shen and Chin-Yu, 2007).
3. They do not conceive a particular structure for the resulting model.
4. The model and the associated coefficients can be evolved based on the fault data collected during the initial test phase.

While the use of artificial intelligence and machine learning is applied with some success in software reliability growth modeling and software fault predictions, only a small number of these studies make use of data from large industrial software projects; see e.g. (Tian and Noore, 2005). Performing large empirical studies is hard due to difficulties in getting necessary data from large software projects, but if we want to generalize the use of some technique or method, larger type software need to be investigated to gain better understanding. Moreover, due to the novelty of applying artificial intelligence and machine learning approaches, researchers many times focus more on introducing new approaches on a smaller scale than validating existing approaches on a larger scale. In this paper we try to focus on the latter part.

Another dimension that lacks researchers' attention is cross-release prediction of faults. With the growing adoption of agile software development methodologies, prediction of faults in subsequent releases of software will be an important decision tool. With short-timed releases, the software development team might not be inclined towards gathering many different program metrics in a current release of a project. Therefore, machine-learning techniques can make use of less and commonly used historical data to become a useful alternative in predicting the number of faults across different releases of a software project.

The goals of this study differ in some important ways from related prior studies (Section 2). Our main focus is on evaluating genetic programming (GP) for cross-release prediction of fault counts on data set from large real world projects; to our knowledge this is novel. We evaluate the created models on fault data from several large and real world software projects, some from open-source and some from industrial software systems (See Section 3).

Our study is also unique in comparing multiple different fault count modeling techniques, both traditional and several machine learning approaches. The traditional approaches we have selected are three software reliability growth models (SRGMs) that represent the fault count family of models (Goel, 1985). These three models are Goel-Okumoto non-homogeneous Poisson process model (GO) (Goel and Okumoto, 1979), Brooks and Motley's Poisson model (BMP) (Brooks and Motley, 1980) and Yamada's S-Shaped growth model (YAM) (Yamada and Osaki, 1983). We selected them because these models provide a fair representation of the fault count family of models (representing different forms of growth curves). In particular, GO and BMP are concave (or exponential) while YAM is S-shaped. We also include a simple and standard least-squares linear regression as a baseline.

The machine learning approaches we compare with are artificial neural networks (ANN) and support vector machine regression (SVM). We selected these because they are very different/disparate and have seen much interest in the machine learning (ML) communities of late, see e.g. (Tian and Noore, 2007; Raj and Ravi, 2008, Khoshgoftaar and Yi, 2007) for some examples. Our main goal is to answer the question:

Is GP a better approach for cross release prediction of fault counts compared to traditional and machine learning approaches on fault data from large and real-world software projects?

To answer it we have identified a number of more detailed research questions listed in Section 4. By applying the model creation approaches described above and by answering the research questions the paper makes the following contributions:

1. Quantitative and qualitative assessment of the generalizability and real-world applicability of different modeling techniques by the use of extensive data sets covering both open source and industrial software projects.
2. Use of GP for *cross-release* fault predictions.
3. Comparative evaluations with both traditional and machine learning models for *cross-release* prediction of fault count data.

The remainder of this paper is organized as follows. In Section 2, we present the background for this study. Section 3 elaborates on the data collection procedure. Section 4 describes the research questions, while Section 6 provides a brief introduction to the techniques used in the study. Section 5 describes the different evaluation measures used in the study while Section 7 covers the application of different techniques and the corresponding evaluation. Validity evaluation is presented in Section 8 while discussion and conclusions are presented in Section 9.

2. RELATED WORK

The research into software quality modeling based on software metrics is "used to predict the response variable which can either be the class of a module (e.g. fault-prone and not fault-prone) or a quality factor (e.g. number of faults) for a module" (Khoshgoftaar and Seliya, 2003, pp. 256). The applicable methods include statistical methods (random-time approach, stochastic approach), machine learning methods and mixed algorithms (Venkata, Farokh, Yen and Raymond, 2005). Despite the presence of large number of models, there is little agreement within the research community about the best model (Stefan et al. 2008). The result is that the prediction problem is seen as being largely unsolvable and NP-hard (Venkata et al., 2005; Martin and Gada, 2001). Due to a large number of studies covering software quality modeling (for both classifying fault-proneness and predicting software faults), the below references are more representative than exhaustive.

Kehan and Khoshgoftaar (2007) empirically evaluated eight statistical count models for software quality prediction. They showed that with a very large number of zero response variables, the zero inflated and hurdle count models are more appropriate. The study by Yu, Shen & Dunsmore (1988) used number of faults detected in earlier phases of the development process to predict the number of faults later in the process. They compared linear regression with a revised form of, an earlier proposed, Remus-Zilles model. They found a strong relationship between the number of faults during earlier phases of development and those found later, especially with their revised model. Taghi, John, Bibhuti, & Gary (1992) showed that the typically used least squares linear regression and least absolute value linear regression do not predict software quality well when the data does not satisfy the normality assumption and thus two alternative parameter estimation procedures (relative least square and minimum relative error) were found more suitable in this case. In (Munson and Khoshgoftaar, 1992), discriminant analysis technique is used to classify the programs into either fault prone and not fault prone based upon the uncorrelated measures of program complexity. Their technique was able to yield less Type II errors (mistakenly classifying a fault prone module as fault prone) on data sets from two commercial systems.

In (Lionel, Victor & Christopher, 1993), optimized set reduction classifications (that generates logical expressions representing patterns in the data) were found to be more accurate than multivariate logistic regression and classification trees in modeling high-risk software components. The less optimistic results of using logistic regression are not in agreement with Khoshgoftaar's study (Khoshgoftaar and Allen, 1999), which supports using logistic regression for software quality classification. Also the study by (Giovanni and Mauro, 2002) used logistic regression to successfully classify faults across homogeneous applications. Victor, Lionel, Walc & Lio (1996) verified that most of Chidamber and Kemerer's object-oriented metrics are useful quality indicators for fault-prone classes. Niclas, Christin & Mary, (1997) investigated the use of metrics for release n to identify the most fault prone modules in release $n+1$. In (Niclas, Ming & Mary, 1998), principal component analysis and discriminant analysis was used to rank the software modules in several groups according to fault proneness.

Using the classification and regression trees (CART) algorithm, and by balancing the cost of misclassification, Taghi, Edward, Wendell and John (1999) showed that the classification-tree models based on several product, process and execution measurements were useful in quality classification for successive software releases. Lionel, Walcelio and Wust (2002) proposed Multivariate Adaptive Regression Splines (MARS) to classify object-oriented (OO) classes as either fault prone or not fault prone. MARS outclassed logistic regression with an added advantage that the functional form of MARS is not known *a priori*. In (Jeremy and Art, 2007), the authors show that static code attributes like McCabe's and Halstead's are valid attributes for fault prediction. It was

further shown that naive Bayes outperformed the decision tree learning methods.

We also find numerous studies making use of machine intelligence techniques for software fault prediction. Applications of artificial neural networks to fault predictions and reliability growth modeling mark the beginning of several studies using machine learning for approximations and predictions.

Neural networks have been found to be a powerful alternative when noise in the input-generating process complicates the analysis, a large number of attributes describe the inputs, conditions in the input-generating process change, available models account for some but not all of the data, the input-generating distribution is unknown and probably non-Gaussian, it is expensive to estimate statistical parameters, and nonlinear relationship are suspected (Laura, 1991, pp. 212).

These characteristics are also common to data collected from a typical software development process. Karunanithi et al. published several studies (Karunanithi, Malaiya & Whitley, 1991; Nachimuthu, Darrell & Yashwant, 1992; Nachimuthu, Darrell & Yashwant, 1992; Karunanithi and Malaiya, 1996; Karunanithi, 1993) using neural network architectures for software reliability growth modeling. Other examples of studies reporting encouraging results include (Tian and Noore, 2005; Raj and Ravi, 2008; Khoshgoftaar, Pandya, & More, 1992; Khoshgoftaar, Allen, Hudepohl & Aud, 1997; Khoshgoftaar and Szabo, 1996; Tadashi, Yasuhiko & Shunji, 1999; Sitte, 1999; Aljahdali, Sheta & Rine, 2001; Adnan, Yaakob, Anas & Tamjis, 2000; Guo and Lyu, 2004; Nidhi and Pratap, 2005; Ho, Xie & Goh, 2003; Tian and Noore, 2004; Tian and Noore, 2005; Tian and Noore, 2005). Kai-Yuan, Lin, Wei-Dong, Zhou-Yi, & David (2001) observed that the prediction results of ANNs show a positive overall pattern in terms of probability distribution but were found to be poor at quantitatively estimating the number of software faults.

A study by (Gray and MacDonell, 1997) showed that neural network models show more predictive accuracy as compared with regression-based methods. The study also used a criteria-based evaluation on conceptual requirements and concluded that not all modeling techniques suit all types of problems. CART-LAD (least absolute deviation) performed the best in a study by Khoshgoftaar et al. (Khoshgoftaar and Seliya, 2003) for fault prediction in a large telecommunications system in comparison with CART-LS (least squares), S-plus, regression tree algorithm, multiple linear regression, artificial neural networks and case-based reasoning.

Tibor, Rudolf & Istvan (2005) used OO metrics for predicting number of faults in classes using logical and linear regression, decision tree and neural network methods. They found that the results from these methods were nearly similar. A recent study by Stefan et al. (2008) also concluded that with respect to classification, there were no significant differences among top 17 of the classifiers used for comparison in the study.

Apart from artificial neural networks, some authors have proposed using fuzzy models, as in (Cai, Wen & Zhang, 1991; Cai, Wen & Zhang, 1993; So, Cha & Kwon, 2002; Utkin, Gurov & Shubinsky, 2002), and support vector machines, as in (Tian and Noore, 2007), to characterize software reliability.

In the later years, interest has shifted to evolutionary computation approaches for software reliability growth modeling. Genetic programming has been used for software reliability growth modeling in several studies (Eduardo, Silvia, Aurora & Gustavo, 2005; Eduardo, Aurora & Silvia, 2006; Costa, de Souza, Pozo, & Vergilio, 2007; Yongqiang and Huashan, 2006; Afzal, Torkar & Feldt, 2008; Wasif & Richard, 2008; Wasif and Richard, 2008). The comparisons with traditional software reliability growth models indicate that genetic programming has an edge with respect to predictive accuracy and does not need assumptions common in these traditional models. There are

also several studies where genetic programming has been successfully used for software quality classification (Khoshgoftaar and Yi, 2007; Taghi, Yi & Naeem, 2004).

There are also studies that use a combination of techniques, e.g. (Tian and Noore, 2007), where genetic algorithms are used to determine an optimal neural network architecture and in (Donald, 2002), where principal component analysis is used to enhance the performance of neural networks.

As mentioned in Section 1, very few studies have looked at cross-release predictions of fault data on a large scale. Thomas and Elaine (2002) presented a case study using 13 releases of a large industrial inventory tracking system. Among several goals of that study, one was to investigate the fault persistence in the files between releases. The study concluded with moderate evidence supporting that files containing high number of faults in one release remain `high fault files' in later releases. The authors later extend their study in (Elaine, Thomas & Robert, 2005) by including four further releases. They investigated which files in the next release of the system were most likely to contain the largest number of faults. A negative binomial regression model was used to make accurate predictions about expected number of faults in each file of the next release of a system.

3. SELECTION OF FAULT COUNT DATA SETS

We use fault count data from two different types of software projects: Open source software and industrial software. For all of these projects we have data for multiple releases of the same software system. Between releases there can be both changes and improvements to existing functionality as well as additions of new features. The software projects involved together represent several man years of development and span a multitude of different software applications targeting e.g.

home users, small business users and industrial, embedded systems.

The included open source systems are: Apache Tomcat[2], OpenBSD[3] and Mozilla Firefox[4]. Apache Tomcat is a servlet container implementing the Java servlet and the JavaServer Pages. Members of the Apache Software Foundation (ASF), and others, contribute in developing Apache Tomcat. OpenBSD is a UNIX-like operating system developed at the University of California, Berkley. OpenBSD supports a variety of hardware platforms and includes several extra security options like built-in cryptography. Mozilla Firefox is an open-source web-browser from the Mozilla Corporation, supporting a variety of operating systems.

In the following, the fault count data from these open source software projects are referred to as OSStom, OSSbsd and OSSmoz, respectively.

The industrial fault count data sets come from three large companies specializing in different domains. The first industrial data set (IND01) is from a European company in the space industry. The multi-release software is for an on-board computer used in a satellite system. It consists of about 70,000 lines of manually written C code for drivers and other low-level functions and about 230,000 lines of C code generated automatically from Simulink models. The total number of man-hours used to develop the software is on the order of 30,000. About 20% of this was spent in system testing and 40% in unit tests. The faults in the data set is only from system testing, the unit testing faults are not logged but are corrected before the final builds.

The second and third fault count data sets (IND02, IND03) are taken from a power and automation company specializing in power products, power systems, automation products, process automation and robotics. IND02 comes from one of their robotic controller software that makes use of advanced motion technology to program robot systems. This software makes use of a state-of-the-art self-optimizing motion

technology, security and error handling mechanism and advanced user-authorization system. IND03 consists of fault count data from a robotic packaging software. This software comes with an advanced vision technique and integrated conveyor tracking capability; while being open to communicate with any external sensor. The total number of man-hours used to develop the two projects is on the order of 2,000.

The last data set, IND04, comes from a large mobile hydraulics company specializing in engineered hydraulic, electric and electronic systems. The fault count data set comes from one of their products, a graphical user interface integrated development environment, which is a part of family of products providing complete vehicle control solutions. The software allows graphical development of machine management applications and user-specific service and diagnostic tools. The software consists of about 350000 lines of hand written Delphi/Pascal code (90%) and C code (10%). Total development time is about 12000 man-days, 30% of this has been on system tests.

3.1. Data Collection Process

The fault count data from the three open source projects: Apache Tomcat (OSStom), OpenBSD (OSSbsd) and Mozilla Firefox (OSSmoz), come from web-based bug reporting systems.

As an example, Figure 1 shows a bug report for Mozilla Firefox. For OSStom and OSSmoz, we recorded the data from the `Reported' and `Version' fields as shown in the Figure 1. For OSSbsd, the data was recorded from the 'Environment' and 'Arrival-Date' fields of the bug reports. We include all user-submitted bug reports in our data collection because the core development team examines each bug report and decides upon a course to follow (Paul, Mary, Jim, Bonnie, & Santhanam, 2004). The severity of the user submitted faults was not considered as all submitted bug reports were treated equally. A reason for treating all user submitted bug reports as equal was to eliminate

Figure 1. A sample bug report

*Figure 2. Data collection from open source and industrial software projects, time span mentioned in ()
in the second column is same for the releases preceding*

Software	Data collected from releases and time span	Training and test sets	Length of training set	Length of testing set
OSStom	6.0.10, 6.0.11, 6.0.13 (Mar.–Aug. 2007), 6.0.14 (Aug.–Dec. 2007)	Train on 6.0.10, 6.0.11, 6.0.13 Test on 6.0.14	24	20
OSSbsd	4.0, 4.1 (Jan.–Jul. 2007), 4.2 (Oct.–Dec. 2007)	Train on 4.0, 4.1 Test on 4.2	28	12
OSSmoz	1.0, 1.5 (Jul.–Dec. 2005), 2.0 (Jan.–Jun. 2006)	Train on 1.0, 1.5 Test on 2.0	72	24
IND01	4.3.0, 4.3.1, 4.4.0, 4.4.1, 4.5.0 (Oct. 2006–Feb. 2007), 4.5.1 (Mar.–Apr. 2007)	Train on 4.3.0, 4.3.1, 4.4.0, 4.4.1, 4.5.0 Test on 4.5.1	20	8
IND02	5.07, 5.09 (Feb. 2006–Apr. 2007), 5.10 (Feb.–Dec. 2007)	Train on 5.07, 5.09 Test on 5.10	38	11
IND03	5.09, 5.10 (Sept. 2005–Dec. 2007)	Train on 5.09 Test on 5.10	19	11
IND04	3.0, 3.1 (Jan. 2007–Mar. 2008), 3.2 (Sept.–Dec. 2008)	Train on 3.0, 3.1 Test on 3.2	60	16

inaccuracy and subjective bias in assigning severity ratings. We were assisted by our industrial partners in provision of the fault count data sets IND01, IND02, IND03 and IND04.

Figure 2 show more details regarding the data collected from the open source and industry software projects, respectively. The data sets were impartially split into training and test sets. In line with the goals of the study (i.e. cross-release prediction), we used a finite number of fault count data from multiple releases as a training set. The resulting models were evaluated on a test set, comprising of fault count data from subsequent releases of respective software projects. The length

of the test sets also determined the prediction strength x time units into future where x equals the length of the test set and is different for different data sets. We used the cumulative weekly count of faults for all the data sets, except for IND02 and IND03 for which the monthly cumulative counts were used due to the availability of the fault data in monthly format.

4. RESEARCH QUESTIONS

Before presenting the empirical study in detail, where we compare different fault count modeling methods, we need to detail the specific research questions to be answered. Informally, we want to evaluate if GP can be a better approach for cross-release prediction of fault count data in general when compared with traditional and machine learning approaches. We quantify this evaluation in terms of goodness of fit, predictive accuracy, model bias and qualitative criteria:

- **RQ 1:** What is the *goodness of fit (gof)* of the GP-evolved model as compared with traditional and machine learning models for cross-release predictions?
- **RQ 2:** What are the levels of *predictive accuracy* of GP-evolved model for cross-release predictions as compared with traditional and machine learning models?
- **RQ 3:** What is the *prediction bias* of the GP-evolved model for cross-release prediction of fault count data as compared with traditional and machine learning models?
- **RQ 4:** How do the prediction techniques compare *qualitatively* in terms of generality, transparency, configurability and complexity?

5. EVALUATION MEASURES

Selecting appropriate evaluation measures for comparing the predictability of competing models is not trivial. A number of different accuracy indicators have been used for comparative analysis of models; see e.g. (Shepperd, Cartwright & Kadoda, 2000). Since a comparison of different measures is out of scope for this paper, we used multiple evaluation measures to increase confidence in model predictions; a recommended approach since we would have a hard time relying on a single evaluation measure (Nikora and Lyu, 1995).

However, quantitative evaluation of predictive accuracy and bias are not the only important aspects for real-world use of the modeling tech-

niques. Thus we also compare them on a set of qualitative aspects. Below we describe both of these types of evaluation.

5.1. Quantitative Evaluation

On the quantitative front, we test the models' results for goodness of fit, predictive accuracy and model bias. A goodness of fit test measures the difference between the observed and the fitted values after a model is fitted to the training data. We are interested here to test whether the two samples (actual fault count data from the testing set and the predicted fault count data from each technique) belong to identical distributions. Therefore, the Kolmogorov-Smirnov (K-S) test is applied which is a commonly used statistical test for measuring goodness of fit (Stringfellow and Andrews, 2002; Matsumoto, Inoue, Kikuno & Torii, 1988). The K-S test is distribution free, which suited the samples as they failed the normality tests. Since goodness of fit tests do not measure predictive accuracy *per se*, we use prequential likelihood ratio (PLR), absolute average error (AAE) and absolute relative error (ARE) and prediction at level *l* (*pred (l)*) as the measures for evaluating predictive accuracy. Specifically, PLR provides a measure for short-term predictability (or next-step predictability) while AAE and ARE provides measures for variable-term predictability (Taghi, Naeem & Nandini, 2006; Malaiya, Karunanithi & Verma, 1990). We further test a particular model's bias, which gives an indication of whether the model is prone to overestimation or underestimation (Malaiya et al., 1990). To measure a particular model's bias, we examine the distribution of residuals to compare models as suggested in (Kitchenham, Pickard, MacDonell & Shepperd, 2001; Lesley, Barbara & Susan, 1999). We also formally test for significant differences between competing prediction systems as recommended in e.g. (Shepperd et al, 2000). In the following we describe the evaluation measures in more detail.

Kolmogorov-Smirnov (K-S) test. The K-S test is a distribution-free test for measuring general differences in two populations. The statistic J for the two-sample two-sided K-S test is given by,

$$J = \frac{mn}{d} \max_{-\infty < t < +\infty} \{| F_m(t) - G_n(t) |\} \qquad (1)$$

where $F_m(t)$ and $G_n(t)$ are the empirical distribution functions for the two samples respectively, m and n are the two sample sizes and d is the greatest common divisor of m and n. In our case, the two samples were, i) the training part of the actual fault count data and ii) the actual predictions from the technique under test. For detailed description of the test, see (Hollander and Wolfe, 1999).

Prequential likelihood ratio (PLR). PLR is used to investigate the relative plausibility of the predictions from two models (Abdel-Ghaly, Chan & Littlewood, 1986). The prequential likelihood (PL) is the measure of closeness of a model's probability density function to the true probability density function. It is defined as the running product of one-step ahead predictions $f_i(t_i)$ of next fault count intervals $T_{j+1}, T_{j+2},... T_{j+n}$:

$$PL_n = \prod_{i=j+1}^{j+n} \hat{f}_i(t_i) \qquad (2)$$

The PLR of two prediction systems, A and B, is then the running product of ratio of their successive on-step ahead predictions $\hat{f}_j^A(t_j)$ and $\hat{f}_j^B(t_j)$ respectively (Sarah and Bev, 1996):

$$PLR_i^{AB} = \prod_{j=s}^{j=i} \frac{\hat{f}_j^A(t_j)}{\hat{f}_j^B(t_j)} \qquad (3)$$

In our case, we select the actual time distribution of fault count data as a reference and conduct pair-wise comparisons of all other models' predictions against it. Then the model with the relatively smallest prequential likelihood ratio can be expected to provide the most trust worthy predictions. For further details on PLR, see (Sarah and Bev, 1996).

Absolute average error (AAE). The AAE is given by,

$$AAE = \frac{1}{n} \sum_{i=1}^{n} | y_i - \hat{y}_i | \qquad (4)$$

where y_i is the predicted value against the original y_i, n is the total number of points in the test data set.

Absolute relative error (ARE). The ARE is given by,

$$ARE = \frac{1}{n} \sum_{i=1}^{n} \frac{| y_i - \hat{y}_i |}{| y_i |} \qquad (5)$$

where y_i is the predicted value against the original y_i, n is the total number of points in the test data set.

Prediction at level l. The Prediction at level l, *pred(l)*, represents a measure of the number of predictions within $l\%$ of the actuals. We have used the standard criterion for considering a model as acceptable which is pred(0.25) $\geq$ 0.75 which means that at least 75% of the estimates are within the range of 25% of the actual values (Jos and Javier, 2000).

Distribution of residuals. To measure a particular model bias, we examine the distribution of residuals to compare models (Kitchenham et al., 2001; Shepperd et al., 2000). It has the convenience of applying significance tests and visualizing differences in absolute residuals of competing models using box plots.

5.2. Qualitative Evaluation

In addition to the quantitative evaluation factors, there are other qualitative criteria, which need to be accounted for when assessing the usefulness of a particular modeling technique. Qualitative criterion-based evaluation evaluates each method based on conceptual requirements (Gray and MacDonell, 1997). One or more of these requirements might influence model selection. We use the following qualitative criteria (Gray and MacDonell, 1997; Carolyn et al. 2000; Michael & Allen, 1992; Burgess and Lefley, 2001), which we believe are important factors influencing model selection:

1. Configurability (ease of configuration), i.e. how easy is it to configure the technique used for modeling?
2. Transparency of the solution (explanatory value regarding output), i.e. do the models explain the output?
3. Generality (applicability in varying operational environments), i.e. what is the extent of generality of model results for diverse data sets?
4. Complexity, i.e. how complex are the resulting models?

6. SOFTWARE FAULT PREDICTION TECHNIQUES

This section describes the techniques used in this study for software fault prediction. The techniques include genetic programming (GP), artificial neural networks (ANN), support vector machine regression (SVM), Goel-Okumoto non-homogeneous Poisson process model (GO), Yamada's S-shaped growth model (YAM) and Brooks and Motley's Poisson model (BMP). We have used GPLAB version 3 (Silva, 2007) (for running GP), Weka software version 3.4.13 (Witten & Frank, 2005) (for running ANN, SVM and LR) and SMERFS3 version 2 (Farr, 2009) (for running GO, YAM and BMP).

6.1. Genetic Programming (GP)

GP is an evolutionary computation technique and is an extension of genetic algorithms (Koza, 1992). The population structures (individuals) in GP are not fixed length character strings, but programs that, when executed, are the candidate solutions to the problem. For the symbolic regression application of GP, programs are expressed as syntax trees, with the nodes indicating the instructions to execute and are called functions (e.g. *min*, *, +, /), while the tree leaves are called terminals which may consist of independent variables of the problem and random constants (e.g. *x*, *y*, *3*). The worth of an individual GP program in solving the problem is assessed using a fitness evaluation. The fitness evaluation of a particular individual in this case is determined by the correctness of the output produced for all of the fitness cases (Bäck, Fogel & Michalewicz, 2000). The control parameters limit and control how the search is performed like setting the population size and probabilities of performing the genetic operations. The termination criterion specifies the ending condition for the GP run and typically includes a maximum number of generations (Burke and Kendall, 2005). GP iteratively transforms a population of computer programs into a new generation of programs using various genetic operators. Typical operators include crossover, mutation and reproduction. Crossover takes place between two parent trees with swapping branches at randomly chosen nodes, while in tree mutation a random node within the parent tree is substituted with a new random tree created with the available terminals and functions. Reproduction causes a proportion of trees to be copied to the next generation without any genetic operation (Silva, 2007).

Initially we experimented with a minimal set of functions and the terminal set containing the independent variable only. We incrementally in-

Figure 3. GP control parameters

Control parameter	Value
Population size	200
Number of generations	450
Termination condition	450 generations
Function set (for OSStom, OSSbsd, IND01 & IND02)	$\{+,-,*,sin,cos,log,sqrt\}$
Function set (for OSSmoz, IND03, IND04)	$\{+,-,*,/,sin,cos,log\}$
Terminal set	$\{x\}$
Tree initialization (for OSStom, OSSbsd, OSSmoz, IND03, IND04)	Ramped half-and-half method
Tree initialization (for IND01, IND02)	Full method
Genetic operators	Crossover, mutation, reproduction
Selection method	Lexictour
Elitism	Replace

creased the function set with additional functions and later on also complemented the terminal set with a random constant. For each data set, the best model having the best fitness was chosen from all the runs of the GP system with different variations of function and terminal sets. The GP programs were evaluated according to the sum of absolute differences between the obtained and expected results in all fitness cases, $\sum_{i=1}^{n} | e_i - e_i^* |$, where e_i is the actual fault count data, e_i^* is the estimated value of the fault count data and n is the size of the data set used to train the GP models.

The control parameters that were chosen for the GP system are shown in Figure 3. The selection method used is *lexictour* in which the best individuals are selected from a random number of individuals. If two individuals are equally fit, the tree with fewer nodes is chosen as the best (Silva, 2007). For a new population, the parents and off springs are prioritized for survival according to elitism. The elitism level specifies the members of the new population, to be selected from the current population and the newly generated individuals. The elitism level used in this study is *replace* in which children replace the parent population having received higher priority of survival, even if they are worse than their parents (Silva, 2007).

6.2. Artificial Neural Networks (ANN)

The development of artificial neural networks is inspired by the interconnections of biological neurons (Russell and Norvig, 2003). These neurons, also called nodes or units, are connected by direct links. These links are associated with numeric weights, which show both the strength and sign of the connection (Russell and Norvig, 2003). Each neuron computes the weighted sum of its input, applies an activation (step or transfer) function to this sum and generates output, which is passed on to other neurons.

A neural network structure can be feed-forward (acyclic) network and recurrent (cyclic) network. Feed-forward neural networks do not contain any cycles and a network's output is only dependent on the current input instance (Witten & Frank, 2005). Recurrent neural networks feeds its output back into its own inputs, supporting short-term memory. Feed-forward neural network are more common and may consist of three layers: Input, hidden and output. The feed-forward neural network having one or more hidden layers is called multilayer feed-forward neural networks. Back-propagation is the common method used for learning the multilayer feed-forward neural network whereby the error from the output layer back-propagates to the hidden layer. The ANN models for this study were obtained using multilayer feed-forward neural networks containing one input layer, one hidden layer and one output layer. The multilayer perceptron implemented in Weka software version 3.4.13 was used for training. The output layer had one node with linear transfer function and the two nodes in the hidden layer had sigmoid transfer function.

6.3. Support Vector Machine (SVM)

Support vector regression uses support vector machine algorithm for numeric prediction. Support vector machine algorithms classify data points by finding an optimal linear separator which possess the largest margin between it and the one set of data points on one side and the other set of examples on the other. The largest separator is found by solving a quadratic programming optimization problem. The data points closest to the separator are called support vectors (Russell and Norvig, 2003). For regression, the basic idea is to discard the deviations up to a user specified parameter ε (Witten & Frank, 2005). Apart from specifying ε, the upper limit C on the absolute value of the weights associated with each data point has to be enforced (known as capacity control). The support vector regression implemented in Weka software version 3.4.13 was used for training which uses Smola and Scholkopf sequential minimization algorithm (Smola and Schölkopf, 2004) for training. More details on support vector regression can be found in (Smola and Schölkopf, 2004; Gunn 1998).

6.4. Linear Regression (LR)

The linear regression used in the study performs a standard least-squares linear regression (Kachigan, 1982). Simple linear regression helps to find a relationship between the independent (x) and dependent (y) variables. It also allows for prediction of dependent variable values given values of the independent variable. The general form of a simple linear regression is,

$$y = \alpha + \beta x \qquad (6)$$

where α (y-intercept) and β (slope) are unknown and are estimated from data.

6.5. Traditional Software Reliability Growth Models

As discussed in Section 1, we use three traditional software reliability growth models for comparisons. Below is a brief summary of these models while further details, regarding e.g. the models' assumptions, can be found in (Goel and Okumoto, 1979; Brooks and Motley, 1980; Yamada and Osaki, 1983).

The Goel-Okumoto non-homogeneous Poisson process model (GO) (Goel and Okumoto, 1979) is given by,

$$m(t) = a \left[1 - e^{-bt} \right] \qquad (7)$$

while Yamada's S-shaped growth model (YAM) (Yamada and Osaki, 1983) is also a non-homogeneous Poisson process model given by,

$$m(t) = a \left(1 - (1+bt)\, e^{-bt} \right) \qquad (8)$$

where in both above equations a is the expected total number of faults before testing, b is the failure detection rate and $m(t)$ is the expected number of faults detected by time t, also called as the mean value function. In the above two models, the failure arrival process is viewed as a stochastic non-homogeneous Poisson process (NHPP), with the number of failures $X(t)$ for a given time interval $(0,t)$ given by the probability $P[X(t) = n]$ as (Jeff, 1996):

$$P[X(t) = n] = \frac{[m(t)]^n e^{-m(t)}}{n!} \qquad (9)$$

Brooks and Motley's model come in two variations, depending upon the assumption of either a Poisson or a binomial distribution of failure observations. We make use of the Poisson model. Specifically, Brooks and Motley's Poisson model (BMP) (Brooks and Motley, 1980) with Poisson distribution of failure observations n_i over all possible X for i-th period of length t_i gives the probability $P[X=n_i]$ of number of failures for a given time interval,

$$P[X = n_i] = \begin{cases} \dfrac{(N_i\phi_i)^{n_i} e^{-N_i\phi_i}} \\ \phi_i = 1 - (1 - \phi)^{t_i} \end{cases} \qquad (10)$$

where N_i is the estimated number of defects at the beginning of i-th period and ϕ is Poisson constant.

7. EXPERIMENT AND RESULTS

We have collected data from a total of seven multi-release open source and industrial software projects for the purpose of cross-release prediction of fault count data. The data sets have been impartially split in to training and test sets. The training set is used to build the models while the *independent* (hold-out) test set is used to evaluate the models' performance. The training and test data sets are given in Figure 2. For all our data sets, we had the complete data set available upfront because they were based on projects having a historical pool of data. Therefore we were required to select a split mechanism that was impartial and also preserve the time-series nature of data. A generally accepted practice for data mining algorithms is to hold out one-third of the data for testing and use the remaining two-thirds for training (Witten & Frank, 2005), however, owing to the *cross-release* nature of this study, we resorted to a training set comprising of fault data from previous releases of the software under consideration while the testing set was comprised of fault data from the forthcoming release.

The performance is assessed both quantitatively (goodness of fit, predictive accuracy, model bias) and qualitatively (ease of configuration, solution transparency, generality and complexity). The independent variable in our case is the week number while the corresponding dependent variable is the count of faults. Week number is taken as the independent variable because it is controllable and potentially has an effect on the dependent variable, i.e. the count of faults, in which the effect of the treatment is measured. All our data sets were uni-variate, which suited the cross-release nature of this study since collecting multivariate data across releases is quite difficult and also would have severely complicated the cross-release modeling. The design type of our experiment is one factor with more than two treatments (Box, Hunter & Hunter, 1978). The factor is the prediction of fault count data while the treatments are the application of GP, traditional approaches and the machine learning approaches. In this section, we further present the results of goodness of fit, predictive accuracy, model bias and qualitative evaluation for different techniques applied to the different data sets in the study.

7.1. Evaluation of Goodness of Fit

We make use of K-S test statistic to test whether the two samples (in this case, the predicted and actual fault count data from the test set part of the data set for each technique) have the same probability distribution and hence represent the same population. The null hypothesis here is that the predicted and the actual fault count data have the same probability distribution (Hollander and Wolfe, 1999) i.e.,

$$H_0\text{: } [F(t) = G(t), \text{ for every } t] \qquad (11)$$

At significance level $\propto = 0.05$, if the K-S statistic J is greater than or equal to the critical value J_α, the null hypothesis (Eq. 11) is rejected in favor of the alternate hypothesis, i.e. that the two samples do *not* have the same probability distribution.

Figure 4 shows the results of applying K-S test statistic for each technique for every data set. The (--) in the Figure 4 indicates that the algorithm was not able to converge for the particular data set. The instances where the K-S statistic J is less than

Figure 4. Results of applying Kolmogorov-Smirnov test. The bold values indicate $J < J_\alpha$, (--) indicates lack of model convergence, J_α is the critical J value at $\alpha = 0.05$

	Sample size	J_{GP}	J_{ANN}	J_{SVM}	J_{LR}	J_{GO}	J_{YAM}	J_{BMP}	$J_{\alpha=0.05}$
OSStom	20	**0.20**	0.95	**0.30**	**0.25**	–	**0.25**	**0.25**	0.43
OSSbsd	12	**0.17**	**0.50**	0.75	**0.50**	**0.42**	**0.58**	**0.50**	0.68
OSSmoz	24	0.46	**0.37**	1.00	1.00	–	**0.17**	0.46	0.39
IND01	8	**0.37**	0.87	1.00	1.00	–	–	**0.62**	0.75
IND02	11	**0.27**	**0.45**	**0.27**	**0.27**	**0.27**	**0.54**	**0.27**	0.64
IND03	11	**0.54**	**0.54**	–	**0.54**	–	–	0.82	0.64
IND04	16	0.50	1.00	1.00	1.00	–	1.00	1.00	0.48

Figure 5. Summary statistics for K-S test showing the mean, median, min and max corresponding to the respective number of data sets

Technique	No. of data sets	K-S test statistic			
		Mean	Median	Min	Max
GP	7	0.36	0.37	0.17	0.54
BMP	7	0.56	0.50	0.25	1.00
LR	7	0.65	0.54	0.25	1.00
ANN	7	0.67	0.54	0.37	1.00
YAM	6	0.55	0.56	0.17	1.00
SVM	6	0.72	0.87	0.27	1.00
GO	2	0.34	0.34	0.27	0.42

the critical value J_α are shown in bold in Figure 4. It is evident from Figure 4 that GP was able to show statistically significant goodness of fit for the maximum number of data sets (i.e. five). The other close competitors were ANN (4), LR (4), YAM (4) and BMP (4). This indicates that, at significance level $\alpha = 0.05$, GP is better in terms of having statistically significant goodness of fit on more data sets than other, competing, techniques.

Figure 5 shows the summary of K-S test statistic for all the techniques. Since some techniques did not converge for some data sets, the number of data sets applicable for techniques is different. GP, ANN, LR and BMP were able to converge for all seven data sets. However, the same did not happen with other techniques, as can be seen from the second column of Figure 5. We can observe that in comparison with ANN, LR and BMP with seven data sets each, GP appears to be a better technique (shows a comparatively closer fit to

the set of observations) when ranked based on mean and median.

We conclude that the goodness of fit of GP models for cross-release predictions is promising in comparison with traditional and machine learning models as they were able to show better goodness of fit, both in terms of K-S test statistic and ranking based on mean and median, on more data sets.

7.2. Evaluation of Predictive Accuracy

Figure 6 shows the final *log* result of the running product of the ratio of the successive one-step ahead predictions of actual fault count data and other techniques' prediction. Since the actual time distribution of weekly/monthly fault count data is chosen as the reference, the PLR values closer to 0 are better. We observe from Figure 6 that the

Figure 6. log(PLR}) values for one-step-ahead predictions. The values shown are the final log result of the running product of ratio of the successive on-step ahead predictions of actual fault count and other models' predictions. Values closer to 0 are better

	Sample size	GP	ANN	SVM	LR	GO	YAM	BMP
OSStom	20	2.66	8.77	0.81	**0.38**	–	−2.00	−1.20
OSSbsd	12	**−0.10**	−0.30	−2.80	−1.60	−1.31	−1.69	1.03
OSSmoz	24	11.28	−3.14	12.45	7.78	–	**−0.19**	−2.20
IND01	8	**−0.29**	−2.17	44.28	4.67	–	2.11	0.97
IND02	11	0.15	0.74	0.39	**0.07**	−0.55	−0.88	0.56
IND03	11	**7.21**	7.21	–	7.21	–	–	−8.62
IND04	16	**0.56**	1.14	−6.63	−6.75	–	−7.58	−7.17

log(PLR) values are closest to 0 on four occasions for GP while thrice for LR. The winner from each data set is shown in bold in Figure 6. This shows that for most data sets (four out of seven), the probability density function of the GP model is closer to the true probability density function.

Figure 7 depicts the PLR analysis for all the data sets which shows the pair wise comparisons of each technique with the actual weekly/monthly fault count data which has been chosen as the reference model (indicated as a dotted straight line in the plots of Figure 7). We see that for OSStom (Figure 7a), the prediction curves for LR and SVM are closer to the reference in comparison with other curves. For OSSbsd (Figure 7b), the prediction curve for GP follows the reference more closely than other curves. Same behavior is also evident for IND01, IND03 and IND04 (Figures 2d, 2e and 2g). However, for OSSmoz (Figure 7c), YAM is better at following the reference compared to any other curve, while for IND03 (Figure 7f), the curves for GP, ANN and LR are much closer to the *log*(PLR) of actual fault count data. Overall, GP was able to show more consistent predictive accuracy, across four of the seven data sets.

Figure 8 shows the computed values of AAE for all the data sets. The lowest AAE values from each data set are shown in bold. GP gave the lowest AAE values for the maximum number of data sets (data sets OSStom, OSSbsd, IND01, IND03 and IND04), followed by LR, which remained successful in case of data sets IND02, and IND03.

Since the AAE samples from different methods did not satisfy the normality assumption, we used the non-parametric Wilcoxon rank sum test to test the null hypothesis that data from two samples have equal means. We tested for following pairs of AAE samples: GP vs. ANN, GP vs. SVM, GP vs. LR, GP vs. YAM and GP vs. BMP. The corresponding *p*-values for these tests came out to be 0.27, 0.02, 0.13, 0.03 and 0.22 respectively. At significance level of 0.05, the result indicated that the null hypothesis is rejected for GP vs. SVM and GP vs. YAM, while showing that there is no statistically significant difference between the AAE means of GP, ANN, LR and BMP at the 0.05 significance level.

Apart from statistical testing, Figure 9 presents the summary statistics of AAE for all the techniques. We can observe that having a ranking based on median, GP has the lowest value in comparison with ANN, LR and BMP having 7 data sets each. For a ranking based on mean, GP appears to be very close to the best mean AAE value for BMP, which is 12.05.

Figure 10 shows the computed values of ARE for all the data sets. It is evident from the Table that GP resulted in the lowest ARE values for most of the data sets (five out of seven). The other closest technique was LR that was able to produce lowest ARE values for two data sets. This shows that GP is generally a better approach for variable-term predictability.

Figure 7. log(PLR) plots for the data sets OSStom, OSSbsd, OSSmoz, IND01, IND02, IND03 and IND04

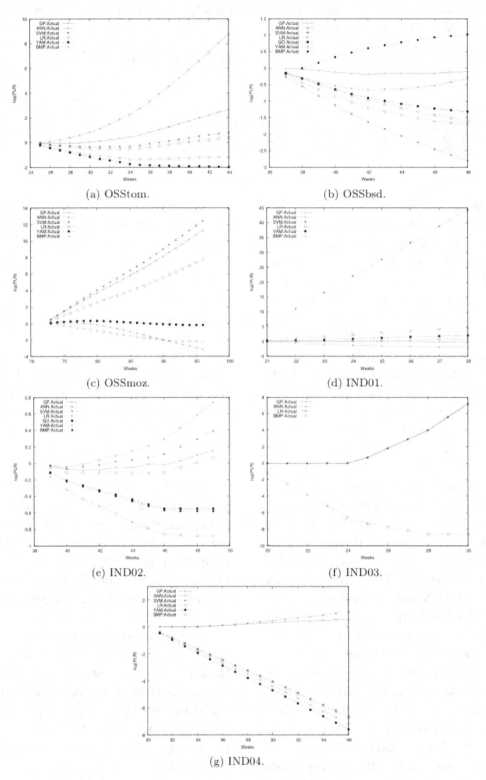

(a) OSStom.

(b) OSSbsd.

(c) OSSmoz.

(d) IND01.

(e) IND02.

(f) IND03.

(g) IND04.

Figure 8. AAE values for different techniques for all data sets. The bold values indicate the lowest AAE values from each data set. (--) indicates lack of model convergence

	Sample size	GP	ANN	SVM	LR	GO	YAM	BMP
OSStom	20	**6.35**	35.38	7.55	6.91	--	8.36	**6.35**
OSSbsd	12	**3.78**	14.08	44.01	23.72	18.93	24.79	19.44
OSSmoz	24	64.71	45.18	114.69	78.61	--	**9.77**	26.12
IND01	8	**2.90**	8.49	27.64	12.29	--	6.51	3.47
IND02	11	5.07	12.05	7.57	**4.58**	7.80	12.60	8.25
IND03	11	**1.36**	**1.36**	--	**1.36**	--	--	1.90
IND04	16	**1.18**	2.31	17.08	17.46	--	20.12	18.80

Figure 9. Summary statistics for AAE showing the mean, median, min and max corresponding to the respective number of data sets

Technique	No. of data sets	AAE statistic			
		Mean	Median	Min	Max
BMP	7	12.05	8.25	1.90	26.12
GP	7	12.19	3.78	1.18	64.71
ANN	7	16.98	12.05	1.36	45.18
LR	7	20.70	12.29	1.36	78.61
YAM	6	13.69	11.18	6.51	24.79
SVM	6	36.42	22.36	7.55	114.69
GO	2	13.36	13.36	7.80	18.93

Figure 10. ARE values for different techniques for all data sets. Bold values indicate the lowest ARE values from each data set. (--) indicates lack of model convergence

	Sample size	GP	ANN	SVM	LR	GO	YAM	BMP
OSStom	20	**0.06**	0.33	0.07	0.07	--	0.11	0.08
OSSbsd	12	**0.02**	0.08	0.26	0.14	0.12	0.15	0.12
OSSmoz	24	0.22	0.15	0.40	0.28	--	**0.03**	0.10
IND01	8	**0.10**	0.31	1.00	0.44	--	0.23	0.11
IND02	11	0.03	0.07	0.04	**0.02**	0.05	0.08	0.05
IND03	11	**0.37**	**0.37**	--	**0.37**	--	--	1.49
IND04	16	**0.03**	0.07	0.51	0.52	--	0.61	0.57

As with AAE, ARE samples from different methods also did not satisfy the normality assumption. We used the non-parametric Wilcoxon rank sum test for testing the following pairs of ARE samples: GP vs. ANN, GP vs. SVM, GP vs. LR, GP vs. YAM and GP vs. BMP. The corresponding *p*-values for these tests came out to be 0.18, 0.07, 0.15, 0.29 and 0.17 respectively. This shows that, for significance level of 0.05, there is no statistical difference between the ARE means of GP, ANN, SVM, LR, YAM and BMP.

Apart from statistical testing, we can observe from Figure 11 that having a ranking based on both mean and median; GP has the lowest value in comparison with ANN, LR and BMP having 7 data sets each.

We further applied the measure of *pred(l)* to judge on the predictive ability of the prediction

Figure 11. Summary statistics for ARE showing the mean, median, min and max corresponding to the respective number of data sets

Technique	No. of data sets	ARE statistic			
		Mean	Median	Min	Max
GP	7	0.12	0.06	0.02	0.37
ANN	7	0.20	0.15	0.07	0.37
LR	7	0.26	0.28	0.02	0.52
BMP	7	0.26	0.11	0.05	0.80
YAM	6	0.20	0.13	0.03	0.61
SVM	6	0.37	0.33	0.04	0.96
GO	2	0.08	0.08	0.05	0.12

Figure 12. Pred(0.25) calculation for different techniques for all data sets. (--) shows lack of model convergence

	Sample size	GP (%)	ANN (%)	SVM (%)	LR (%)	GO (%)	YAM (%)	BMP (%)
OSStom	20	100	30	100	100	–	99	100
OSSbsd	12	100	100	50	100	100	100	100
OSSmoz	24	41.67	100	0	16.67	–	100	100
IND01	8	100	37.5	100	0	–	37.5	100
IND02	11	100	45.45	100	100	100	100	100
IND03	11	45.45	45.45	–	44.45	–	–	18.18
IND04	16	100	100	0	0	–	0	0

systems. The result of applying *pred (l)* is shown in Figure 12. The standard criterion of *pred (0.25)* ≥ 75 for stable model predictions was met by different techniques for different data sets but GP and BMP were able to meet this criterion on most data sets i.e. five. The application of these two techniques on the five data sets resulted in having 100% of the estimates within the range of 25% of the actual values.

We conclude that while the statistical tests for AAE and ARE do not give us a clear indication of a particular technique being (statistically) significantly better compared to other techniques, the summary statistics (Tables 7 and 9) together with the evaluation of pred(0.25) and PLR show that the predictive accuracy of GP for cross-release prediction of fault count data is promising in comparison with other techniques.

7.3. Evaluation of Model Bias

We examined the bias in predictions by making use of box plots of model residuals. The box plots of residuals for all the data sets are shown in Figure 13. For OSSbsd (Figure 13b) and IND04 (Figure 13g), the box plot of GP show two important characteristics:

1. Smaller or equivalent length of the box plot as compared with other box plots.
2. Presence of majority of the residuals close to 0 as compared with other box plots.

For IND03 (Figure 13f), the length of the box plot and its proximity close to 0 appear to be similar for GP, ANN and LR. For OSStom (Figure 13a), SVM and LR are better placed than rest of the techniques while for OSSmoz (Figure 13c), YAM appears to be having a smaller box plot positioned in the proximity of 0. For IND01, although the

Figure 13. Charts showing Box plots of residuals for the seven data sets

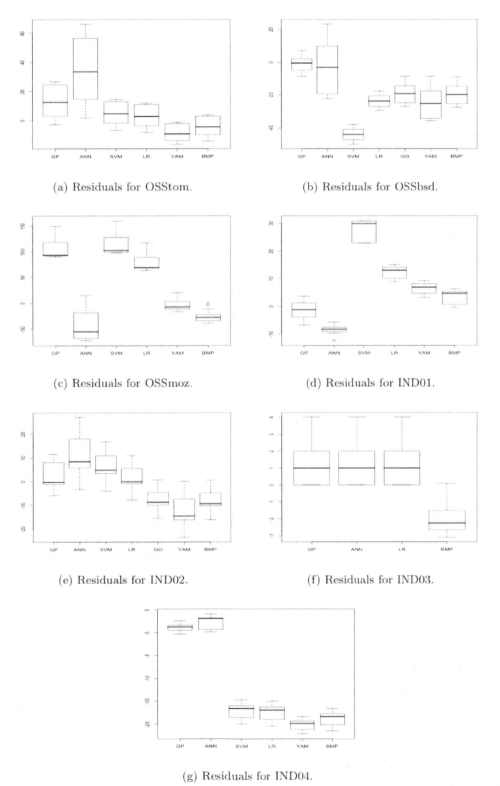

(a) Residuals for OSStom.

(b) Residuals for OSSbsd.

(c) Residuals for OSSmoz.

(d) Residuals for IND01.

(e) Residuals for IND02.

(f) Residuals for IND03.

(g) Residuals for IND04.

Figure 14. Kruskal-Wallis statistic h for different data sets for testing difference in residuals. v is the degrees of freedom

Data sets	Kruskal-Wallis statistic, h
OSStom, $\chi^2_{0.05}=11.07,\ v=5$	83.49
OSSbsd, $\chi^2_{0.05}=12.60,\ v=6$	58.51
OSSmoz, $\chi^2_{0.05}=11.07,\ v=5$	122.95
IND01, $\chi^2_{0.05}=11.07,\ v=5$	43.76
IND02, $\chi^2_{0.05}=12.60,\ v=6$	42.9
IND03, $\chi^2_{0.05}=7.81,\ v=3$	21.45
IND04, $\chi^2_{0.05}=11.07,\ v=5$	75.57

Figure 15. p-values after applying the Wilcoxon rank sum test on residuals (values rounded to two decimal places). Values in bold indicate p > 0.05

	$P_{GP:ANN}$	$P_{GP:SVM}$	$P_{GP:LR}$	$P_{GP:GO}$	$P_{GP:YAM}$	$P_{GP:BMP}$
OSStom, $\alpha = 0.05$	0.00	0.00	0.01	–	0.00	0.00
OSSbsd, $\alpha = 0.05$	**0.79**	0.00	0.00	0.00	0.00	0.00
OSSmoz, $\alpha = 0.05$	0.00	0.02	0.00	–	0.00	0.00
IND01, $\alpha = 0.05$	0.00	0.00	0.00	–	0.00	0.02
IND02, $\alpha = 0.05$	**0.09**	**0.32**	**0.95**	0.00	0.00	0.00
IND03, $\alpha = 0.05$	–	–	–	–	–	0.00
IND04, $\alpha = 0.05$	0.02	0.00	0.00	–	0.00	0.00

length of the box plot seems to be small for ANN, it still appears below the 0-mark indicating that the predictions from ANN are overestimating the actual fault count data. The GP box plot, however, appears to be better positioned in this respect. The same is the case with IND02 (Figure 13e) where GP and LR show a good trade-off between length and actual position of the box plot.

Since the box plots of the residuals were skewed, we resorted to using the non-parametric Kruskal-Wallis test to examine if there is a statistical difference between the residuals for all the data sets and to confirm the trend observed from the box plots. The results of the application of the Kruskal-Wallis test appear in Figure 14. For each of the data sets, the Kruskal-Wallis statistic h is greater than the critical value $\chi^2_{0.05}$. Therefore, we had sufficient evidence to reject the null hypothesis that the residuals for different techniques within a project were similar.

In order to further investigate if the residuals obtained from GP are different from those of other techniques, we used the Wilcoxon rank sum test. The p-values obtained are shown in Figure 15. The table shows that except for four cases, the p-values were found to be less than 0.05, which rejects the null hypothesis that the samples are drawn from identical continuous distributions. The four cases where the null hypothesis was not rejected coincide with data sets OSSbsd and IND02, where the comparisons of the residuals of GP were not found to be different from those of ANN, SVM and LR. (These cases are shown in bold in Figure 15.)

We conclude that in terms of model bias, the examination of residuals show the greater consistency of GP as compared with other traditional and machine learning models in having predictions that result in smaller box plots that are positioned near the 0-mark. Further, application of the Wilcoxon rank sum test shows that except for four combinations (GP:ANN-OSSbsd, GP:SVM-IND02, GP:LR-IND02, GP:ANN-IND02), there is sufficient evidence to show that the residuals from GP are different from those of other competing techniques.

7.4. Qualitative Evaluation of Models

The selection of a particular model for fault count predictions is influenced not only by the quantitative factors (e.g. goodness of fit, predictive accuracy and bias) but also by certain conceptual requirements, which we term as qualitative measures. We believe that it is important to take into account these qualitative measures (in addition to quantitative ones) to reach an informed decision about a suitable technique or combination of techniques to use for fault count predictions.

Ease of configuration. The parametric models including BMP, GO, YAM and linear regression require an estimation of certain parameters. The number of these parameters and the ease with which these parameters can be measured affects measurement cost (Michael & Allen, 1992). With automated reliability measurement using tools such as CASRE (Computer-Aided Software Reliability Estimation) and SMERFS (Statistical Modeling and Estimation of Reliability Functions for Systems) (Farr, 2009; Nikora, 2009), the estimation of parameters may have eased but such tools are limited by the number of supported models and numerical approximation methods. Linear regression, in comparison, is much simpler to use having several tools available for automation.

For the machine learning methods used in this study, the ease of configuration concerns setting algorithmic control parameters. For ANN, some initial experimentation is required to reach a suitable configuration of number of layers and associated number of neurons. For GP, there are several parameters that control the adaptive evaluation of fitter solutions, such as selection of function and terminal sets and probabilities of genetic operators. For SVM, one needs to take care of capacity control and the loss function. But once these algorithmic control parameters are set, an approximation is found by these methods during training. However, there seems to be no clear differentiation among different techniques with respect to ease of configuration. This is in our opinion a general problem and indicates a need for further research.

Transparency of the solution. The resulting equations for traditional models are partially transparent however; GP is capable of producing transparent solutions because the resulting model is an algebraic expression (which is not the case with ANN and SVM). Thus, transparency of solutions is one distinct advantage of using GP. Transparency of the solutions "can be important for the purpose of verification as well as theory building and gaining an understanding of the process being modeled" (Gray and MacDonell, 1997, pp. 435). In our case, with one independent variable (week number) and one dependent variable (count of faults), typical GP solutions are of the form below:

$$times(minus(sin(minus(cos(x),x)),minus(log(cos(log(sin(log(x)))))),sin(x))),log(x)) \qquad (12)$$

where x is the independent variable and *minus, times, sin, cos, log* represents the function set (as outlined in Figure 3). While eq. 12 is transparent, it is still difficult to explain the relationship between the independent and dependent variables. Therefore, simplification of resulting GP solutions is important which has to do with finding solutions with less nodes to make the results understandable analytically.

Generality. The extent of generality of model results for diverse data sets is better for machine learning and evolutionary methods than the traditional methods. This is because of the fact that machine learning and evolutionary models do not depend on prior assumptions about data distribution and form of relationship between independent and dependent variables. The model and the associated coefficients are evolved based on the fault data collected during the initial test phase. In this sense, the applicability of the models derived from machine learning and evolutionary methods for different development and operational environments and life-cycle phases, appear to be better suited than traditional modeling techniques.

Complexity. The complexity criterion is especially important to discuss with respect to GP since GP has the potential of evolving transparent solutions. However the solutions can become complex as the number of nodes in the GP solution increases (as in Eq. 12), a phenomenon known as bloating. Although there are different ways to control this (see e.g. Sean and Liviu, 2006), in the context of canonical GP, this is still an important consideration. For ANN, the complexity can be connected to the potential complex and inefficient structures that can evolve in an attempt to discover difficult data patterns. For SVM and traditional software reliability growth models, being essentially black box, the complexity is difficult to discuss. However, for linear regression, where the reasoning process is partially visible, the complexity is apparently minimal.

There can be another way to evaluate complexity in terms of suitability of a technique to incorporate complex models. This can be connected back to the theory of whether the modeling technique determines its own structure or requires the engineer to provide the structure of the relationship between independent and dependent variables (Gray and MacDonell, 1997). The machine learning and evolutionary models certainly scores high in this respect in comparison with traditional methods.

8. VALIDITY EVALUATION

There can be different threats to the validity of the empirical results (Claes et al., 2000).

Conclusion validity, refers to the statistically significant relationship between the treatment and outcome. We have used non-parametric statistics in this study, particularly Kolmogorov-Smirnov goodness of fit test, Kruskal-Wallis statistic and Wilcoxon rank sum test. Although the power of parametric tests is known to be higher than for non-parametric tests, we were uncertain about the corresponding parametric alternatives meeting the tests' assumptions. Secondly, we used a significance level of 0.05, which is a commonly used significance level for hypothesis testing (Juristo and Moreno, 2001); however, facing some criticism lately (Ioannidis, 2005). Therefore, it can be considered as a limitation of our study and a potential threat to conclusion validity. One potential threat to conclusion validity could have been that the fitness evaluation used for GP (Subsection 6.1) is similar to the quantitative evaluation measures for comparing different techniques (Subsection 5.1). This is, however, not the case with this study since the GP fitness function differs from the quantitative evaluation measures and also we have used a variety of different quantitative evaluation measures not necessarily based on minimization of standard error. A potential threat to conclusion validity is that the fault count data sets did not consider the severity level of faults, rather treated all faults equally. This is a limitation of our study and we acknowledge that by considering severity levels, the conclusion validity of the study would have improved; but at the same time we are also apprehensive that subjective bias might result in wrong assignment of severity levels. Another potential threat to conclusion validity is the different lengths of training and test data sets, depending upon the fault counts from respective releases. We were not sure if this is an influential factor in our study. We plan to investigate this in the future. A similar threat is the data set size available for training and subsequently testing the models. This is our limitation that the actual fault counts of different releases determined the data set size that varied across different software.

Internal validity, refers to a causal relationship between treatment (independent variable) and outcome (dependent variable). It concerns all the factors that are required for a well-designed study. As for the selection of different data sets, we opted for having data sets from varying domains. Moreover, for each data set, we used a consistent scheme of impartially splitting the data set into testing and training sets for all the techniques. A possible threat to internal validity is that we cannot publicize our industrial data sets due to proprietary concerns; therefore other researchers cannot make use of these data sets. However, we encourage other researchers to emulate our results using other publicly available data sets. The best we could do is to clearly state our research design and apply recommended approaches like statistical hypothesis testing to minimize the chances of unknown bias. Also, the different techniques were applied over different data sets in approximate standard parameter settings. For the GP algorithm there are no standard setting for the function and terminal sets so we had to test a few different ones, while keeping other parameters constant, until some search success was seen. Even though this is standard practice when using GP systems, a potential threat is that it could bias the results.

The used data sets were grouped on a weekly or monthly basis. One reason for this is that one of the industrial data sets was only available at this level of detail. While some studies (e.g. Wood, 1996) have indicated that the grouping of data is not a threat, it is possible that more detailed and frequent date and time resolution, and thus prediction intervals, could affect the applicability of different modeling techniques. For example, linear regression models might have a relative advantage for data that is more regular, with less frequent changes. However, it is hard to predict such effects and without further study we cannot determine if it is really a threat.

Construct validity, is concerned with the relationship between the theory and application. We attempted to present both quantitative and qualitative evaluation factors in the study for defining the different constructs. There is a threat

that we might have missed one or more evaluation criteria; however the evaluation measures used in the study reflect the ones commonly used for evaluating prediction models.

External validity, is concerned with generalization of results outside the scope of the study. We used data sets from both open source and commercial software projects that we believe adds to the generalizability of the study. Also the data sets cannot be regarded as toy problems as each one of them represented real-life fault data from multiple software releases. One threat to external validity is the selection of machine learning algorithms for comparison. Being a large field of research, new data mining algorithms are continuously being proposed. We used a small subset of the machine learning algorithms but we are confident that our subset is a representative one, being based on techniques which have different modeling mechanism and are currently active fields of research.

9. DISCUSSION AND CONCLUSION

In this paper, we compared the cross-release predictions of fault count data from models evolved using GP with common machine learning and traditional models. The comparisons were based on measures of goodness of fit, predictive accuracy and model bias. We also presented an analysis of some of the conceptual requirements for a successful model (including ease of configuration, transparency of solution, generality and complexity). These conceptual requirements are important when considering the applicability of a prediction system (Carolyn et al. 2000) and should be taken into account along with the quantitative performance.

The results of K-S test statistic showed statistically significant goodness of fit for the GP-evolved models for the majority of the data sets. The predictive accuracy of the competing models was assessed using PLR, AAE, ARE and pred *(l)*. Using PLR, GP-evolved models showed consistently better predictive accuracy across four of the seven data sets. For the measure of AAE and ARE, GP models were able to give the respective lowest values for largest number of data sets. Finally, GP models were able to meet the standard criterion of pred (0.25) ≥ 75 for stable model predictions for the most number of data sets (compared to other techniques). This observation regarding the accuracy of GP predictions is in agreement with Arthur (2006) where the GP models performed with acceptable quality within 20% outside the training data range. We also assessed the model bias of competing techniques using distribution of residuals, and in that analysis GP models showed a tendency of having less biased predictions as compared with other traditional and machine learning approaches. In terms of conceptual requirements, though ease of configuration might not be the favorable aspect of GP models, the transparency of solution and generality are factors that add further value to the quantitative potential of GP-evolved models.

The fact that no prior assumptions have to be made in terms of actual model form is a distinct advantage of machine learning approaches over linear regression and traditional models. The traditional techniques need to satisfy the underlying assumptions, which means that there is no assurance that these techniques would converge to a solution. This does not happen with GP and ANN machine learning techniques. This shows that the machine learning techniques tend to be more *flexible* than its traditional counterparts. This flexibility also contributes to the greater *generalizability* of machine learning models in a greater variety of software projects. GP offers flexibility by adjusting a variety of functions to the data points; thereby both structure and complexity of the model evolve during subsequent generations.

Considering the different trade-offs among competing models, it appears crucial to define the *success criterion* for an empirical modeling effort. Such a definition of success would help exploit

the unique capabilities of different modeling techniques. For instance, if success is defined in terms of having only accurate predictions without the need of examining the relationship among variables in the form of a function, then artificial neural networks (ANN) might be a worthy candidate for selection (being known as universal approximators), provided that the requisite levels of model accuracy are satisfied. But selecting ANN as a modeling technique would mean that we have to be aware of its potential drawbacks:

1. Less flexible as the neural nets cannot be manipulated once the learning phase finishes (Dolado, Fernandez, Otero & Urkola, 1999). This means that neural networks require frequent retraining once specific process conditions change and hence adds to the maintenance overhead.
2. Black-box approach, thus disadvantageous for experts who want to have an understanding and potential manipulation of variable interactions.
3. Possibility of having inefficient and non-parsimonious[5] structures.
4. Potentially poor generalizability outside the range of the training data (Kordon, Smits, Jordaan & Rightor, 2002).

In contrast, GP possesses certain unique characteristics considering the above issues. Symbolic regression using GP is flexible because of its ability to adjust variety of functions to the data points and the models returned by symbolic regression are open for interpretation. This also helps to identify significant variables, which in the longer run could be used in subsequent modeling to increase the efficiency of the modeling effort (Kotanchek, Smits & Kordon, 2003). This might also be useful for an easy integration in existing industrial work processes whereby only those variables could be used.

A brief summary of the relative performance of different techniques is presented in Figure 16. The

Figure 16. Summary of the relative strengths of the methods on different criteria; techniques are ranked according to the relative performance for maximum number of times on all the data sets

	GP	ANN	SVM	LR	GO	YAM	BMP
Goodness of fit	+ +	-	-	0	-	-	-
Accuracy	+ +	-	- -	0	- -	-	-
Bias	+ +	+	-	0	- -	-	- -
Ease of configuration	0	0	0	+	0	0	0
Transparency of solution	+	-	-	0	0	0	0
Generality	+	+	+	-	-	-	-
Complexity	0	0	0	+	0	0	0
Key:							
+ + very good, + good, 0 average, - bad, - - very bad							

performance indicators are given as to summarize the detailed evaluation done in the study based on several measures (Section 5). The indicators (++, +, 0, -, - -) for the quantitative measures of goodness of fit, accuracy and model bias represent the relative performance of different techniques for largest number of times on different data sets, e.g. GP is ranked (++) on accuracy because of performing comparatively better on accuracy measures for greater number of data sets. The indicators for the qualitative measures represent the relative merits of the techniques as discussed in Subsection 7.4. Figure 16 shows that GP has the advantage of having better goodness of fit and accuracy as compared to other techniques, even though no special adaptions were made to the canonical GP algorithm taking into account the time series nature of the data (GP and ANN are expected to perform better for time series prediction if there is a possibility to save state information between different steps of prediction which can be used to identify trends in the input data; however, we wanted to compare the performance for standard algorithms and any enhancements to these techniques is not addressed in this study). Figure 16 shows that the GP models also exhibit less model bias. On the other hand, the ease of configuration and complexity are not necessarily stronger points for GP models. It is interesting to observe that ANN does not perform as well as expected in terms of goodness of fit and accuracy. Linear regression was able to show normal predictions in terms of goodness of fit and accu-

racy but scores higher on ease of configuration; they however lack generality due to the need of satisfying underlying assumptions. SVM and the traditional models (GO, YAM, BMP) appear to have similar advantages and disadvantages, with YAM showing a slightly improved quantitative performance, while SVM possesses better generality across different data sets.

The most encouraging result of this study shows the feasibility of using GP as a prediction tool across different releases of software. This indicates that the development team can use GP to make important decisions related to the quality of their deliverables. GP models also showed a decent ability to adapt to different time spans of releases (on the basis of the different lengths of the testing sets for different data sets); which is also a positive indicator. It shows that GP is least affected by moderate differences in the release durations and can predict decently with variable time units into future. Additionally, having evaluated the performance on diverse data sets from different application domains shows the flexibility of GP, i.e. suits a variety of data sets.

In short, the use of GP can lead to improved predictions with the additional capabilities of solution transparency and generality across varying operational environments. Secondly the GP technique used in this paper followed a standard\slash canonical approach. Several adaptations to the GP algorithm (e.g. Pareto GP and grammar-guided GP) can potentially lead to further improved GP search process. We intend to investigate this in the future. Another future work involves evaluating the use of GP in an *on-going* project in an industrial context and to compare the relative short-term and long-term predictive strength of the GP-evolved models for different lengths of training data. Lastly, evaluation of ensemble methods presents another opportunity for future research.

REFERENCES

Abdel-Ghaly, A. A., Chan, P. Y., & Littlewood, B. (1986). Evaluation of competing software reliability predictions. *IEEE Transactions on Software Engineering, 12*(9), 950–967.

Adnan, W. A., Yaakob, M., Anas, R., & Tamjis, M. R. (2000). *Artificial neural network for software reliability assessment.* Paper presented at the Proceedings of TENCON 2000.

Afzal, W., Torkar, R., & Feldt, R. (2008). *Prediction of fault count data using genetic programming.* Paper presented at the proceedings of INMIC 2008 IEEE International Multitopic Conference.

Aljahdali, S. H., Sheta, A., & Rine, D. (2001). *Prediction of software reliability: A comparison between regression and neural network nonparametric models.* Paper presented at the proceedings of ACS/IEEE International Conference on Computer Systems and Applications.

Arthur, K. (2006). Evolutionary computation at Dow Chemical. *SIGEVOlution, 1*(3), 4–9. doi:10.1145/1181964.1181965

Arthur Karl, K., Guido, F. S., & Mark, E. K. (2007). *Industrial evolutionary computing.* Paper presented at the Proceedings of the 2007 GECCO conference companion on Genetic and evolutionary computation.

Bäck, T., Fogel, D. B., & Michalewicz, Z. (2000). [–*Basic algorithms and operators*: San Francisco: Taylor & Francis Group.]. *Evolutionary Computation, 1*.

Barry, B., & Victor, R. B. (2001). Software Defect Reduction Top 10 List. *Computer, 34*(1), 135–137.

Box, G. E. P., Hunter, W. G., & Hunter, J. S. (1978). *Statistics for experimenters: An introduction to design, data analysis, and model building.* Mahwah, NJ: Wiley-Interscience.

Brooks, W., & Motley, R. (1980). *Analysis of discrete software reliability models.* IBM Federal Systems.

Bugzilla homepage. (Last checked: October 2008). from http://www.bugzilla.org

Burgess, C. J., & Lefley, M. (2001). Can genetic programming improve software effort estimation? A comparative evaluation. *Information and Software Technology, 43*(14), 863–873. doi:10.1016/S0950-5849(01)00192-6

Burke, E. K., & Kendall, G. (2005). *Search methodologies–Introductory tutorials in optimization and decision support techniques.* Berlin: Springer Science and Business Media.

Cai, K.-Y. (1996). Fuzzy methods in software reliability modeling. In *Introduction to fuzzy reliability.* Amsterdam: Kluwer International Series in Engineering and Computer Science, Kluwer Academic Publishers.

Cai, K.-Y., Wen, C., & Zhang, M. (1991). A critical review on software reliability modeling. *Reliability Engineering & System Safety, 32*(3), 357–371. doi:10.1016/0951-8320(91)90009-V

Cai, K.-Y., Wen, C., & Zhang, M. (1993). A novel approach to software reliability modeling. *Microelectronics and Reliability, 33*(15), 2265–2267. doi:10.1016/0026-2714(93)90066-8

Carolyn, M., Gada, K., Martin, L., Keith, P., Chris, S., & Martin, S. (2000). An investigation of machine learning based prediction systems. *Journal of Systems and Software, 53*(1), 23–29. doi:10.1016/S0164-1212(00)00005-4

Claes, W., Per, R., Martin, H., Magnus, C. O., Björn, R., & Wesslén, A. (2000). *Experimentation in software engineering: An introduction.* Amsterdam: Kluwer Academic Publishers.

Costa, E. O., de Souza, G. A., Pozo, A. T. R., & Vergilio, S. R. (2007). Exploring Genetic Programming and Boosting Techniques to Model Software Reliability. *Reliability. IEEE Transactions on, 56*(3), 422–434.

Dolado, J. J., Fernandez, L., Otero, M. C., & Urkola, L. (1999). *Software effort estimation: The elusive goal in project management.* Paper presented at the Proceedings of the International Conference on Enterprise Information Systems.

Donald, E. N. (2002). An Enhanced Neural Network Technique for Software Risk Analysis. *IEEE Transactions on Software Engineering, 28*(9), 904–912. doi:10.1109/TSE.2002.1033229

Eduardo, O., Aurora, P., & Silvia Regina, V. (2006). *Using Boosting Techniques to Improve Software Reliability Models Based on Genetic Programming.* Paper presented at the Proceedings of the 18th IEEE International Conference on Tools with Artificial Intelligence.

Eduardo Oliveira, C., Silvia, R. V., Aurora, P., & Gustavo, S. (2005). *Modeling Software Reliability Growth with Genetic Programming.* Paper presented at the Proceedings of the 16th IEEE International Symposium on Software Reliability Engineering.

Elaine, J. W., & Thomas, J. Ostrand & Robert, M. B. (2005). Predicting the Location and Number of Faults in Large Software Systems. *IEEE Transactions on Software Engineering, 31*(4), 340–355. doi:10.1109/TSE.2005.49

Farr, W. (Last checked March 2009). SMERFS3 homepage. Retrieved from http://www.slingcode.com/smerfs/downloads/

Giovanni, D., & Mauro, P. (2002). *An empirical evaluation of fault-proneness models.* Paper presented at the Proceedings of the 24th International Conference on Software Engineering.

Goel, A. L. (1985). Software Reliability Models: Assumptions, Limitations, and Applicability. *Software Engineering. IEEE Transactions on, SE-11*(12), 1411–1423.

Goel, A. L., & Okumoto, K. (1979). Time dependent error detection rate model for software reliability and other performance measures. *IEEE Transactions on Reliability, R-28*(3), 206–211. doi:10.1109/TR.1979.5220566

Gray, A. R., & MacDonell, S. G. (1997). A comparison of techniques for developing predictive models of software metrics. *Information and Software Technology, 39*(6), 425–437. doi:10.1016/S0950-5849(96)00006-7

Gunn, S. R. (1998). *Support vector machines for classification and regression. School of electronics and computer science.* UK: University of Southampton.

Guo, P., & Lyu, M. R. (2004). A pseudoinverse learning algorithm for feedforward neural networks with stacked generalization applications to software reliability growth data. *Neurocomputing, 56*, 101–121. doi:10.1016/S0925-2312(03)00385-0

Ho, S. L., Xie, M., & Goh, T. N. (2003). A study of the connectionist models for software reliability prediction. *Computers & Mathematics with Applications (Oxford, England), 46*(7), 1037–1045. doi:10.1016/S0898-1221(03)90117-9

Hollander, M., & Wolfe, D. A. (1999). *Nonparametric statistical methods.* New York: John Wiley and Sons, Inc.

Ioannidis, J. P. A. (2005). Why most published research findings are false. *PLoS Medicine, 2*(8), 696–701. doi:10.1371/journal.pmed.0020124

Jeff, T. (1996). An integrated approach to test tracking and analysis. *Journal of Systems and Software, 35*(2), 127–140. doi:10.1016/0164-1212(95)00092-5

Jeremy, G., & Art, F. (2007). Data mining static code attributes to learn defect predictors. *IEEE Transactions on Software Engineering, 33*(1), 2–13. doi:10.1109/TSE.2007.256941

Jos, & Javier, D. (2000). A validation of the component-based method for software size estimation. *IEEE Trans. Softw. Eng., 26*(10), 1006-1021.

Juristo, N., & Moreno, A. M. (2001). *Basics of software engineering experimentation*. Amsterdam: Kluwer Academic Publishers.

Kachigan, S. K. (1982). *Statistical analysis - An interdisciplinary introduction to univariate and multivariate methods*. New York: Radius Press.

Kai-Yuan, C., Lin, C., Wei-Dong, W., Zhou-Yi, Y., & David, Z. (2001). On the neural network approach in software reliability modeling. *Journal of Systems and Software, 58*(1), 47–62. doi:10.1016/S0164-1212(01)00027-9

Karunanithi, N. (1993). *A neural network approach for software reliability growth modeling in the presence of code churn*. Paper presented at the Proceedings of Fourth International Symposium on Software Reliability Engineering.

Karunanithi, N., & Malaiya, Y. K. (1996). Neural networks for software reliability engineering. In *Handbook of software reliability and system reliability*. Hightstown, NJ: McGraw-Hill Inc.

Karunanithi, N., Malaiya, Y. K., & Whitley, D. (1991). *Prediction of software reliability using neural networks*. Paper presented at the proceedings of the 1991 International Symposium on Software Reliability Engineering.

Kehan, G., & Khoshgoftaar, T. M. (2007). A Comprehensive Empirical Study of Count Models for Software Fault Prediction. *IEEE Transactions on Reliability, 56*(2), 223–236. doi:10.1109/TR.2007.896761

Khoshgoftaar, T., Allen, E., Hudepohl, J., & Aud, S. (1997). Application of neural networks to software quality modeling of a very large telecommunications system. *IEEE Transactions on Neural Networks, 8*(4). doi:10.1109/72.595888

Khoshgoftaar, T. M., & Allen, E. B. (1999). Logistic regression modeling of software quality. *International Journal of Reliability Quality and Safety Engineering, 6*(4), 303–317. doi:10.1142/S0218539399000292

Khoshgoftaar, T. M., Pandya, A. S., & More, H. B. (1992). *A neural network approach for predicting software development faults*. Paper presented at the Proceedings of the Third International Symposium on Software Reliability Engineering.

Khoshgoftaar, T. M., & Seliya, N. (2003). Fault Prediction Modeling for Software Quality Estimation: Comparing Commonly Used Techniques. *Empirical Software Engineering, 8*(3), 255–283. doi:10.1023/A:1024424811345

Khoshgoftaar, T. M., & Szabo, R. M. (1996). Using neural networks to predict software faults during testing. *IEEE Transactions on Reliability, 45*(3), 456–462. doi:10.1109/24.537016

Khoshgoftaar, T. M., & Yi, L. (2007). A Multi-Objective Software Quality Classification Model Using Genetic Programming. *IEEE Transactions on Reliability, 56*(2), 237–245. doi:10.1109/TR.2007.896763

Kitchenham, B. A., Pickard, L. M., MacDonell, S. G., & Shepperd, M. J. (2001). What accuracy statistics really measure? *Software. IEE Proceedings, 148*(3), 81–85. doi:10.1049/ip-sen:20010506

Kordon, A., Smits, G., Jordaan, E., & Rightor, E. (2002). *Robust soft sensors based on integration of genetic programming, analytical neural networks, and support vector machines.* Paper presented at the Proceedings of the CEC '02 Proceedings of the 2002 Congress on Evolutionary Computation, 2002.

Kotanchek, M., Smits, G., & Kordon, A. (2003). Industrial strength genetic programming. In *Genetic programming theory and practice* (pp. 239–256). Amsterdam: Kluwer.

Koza, J. (1992). *Genetic programming: on the programming of computers by means of natural selection.* Cambridge, MA: MIT Press.

Langdon, W. B. (2008). *A Field Guide to Genetic Programing.* Published via http://lulu.com and freely available at http://www.gp-field-guide.org.uk

Laura Ignizio, B. (1991). Introduction to artificial neural systems for pattern recognition. *Computers & Operations Research, 18*(2), 211–220. doi:10.1016/0305-0548(91)90091-5

Lesley, P., Barbara, K., & Susan, L. (1999). *An Investigation of Analysis Techniques for Software Datasets.* Paper presented at the Proceedings of the 6th International Symposium on Software Metrics.

Leung, H., & Varadan, V. (2002). *System modeling and design using genetic programming.* Paper presented at the Proceedings of First IEEE International Conference on Cognitive Informatics.

Li, P. L., Shaw, M., & Herbsleb, J. (2003). *Selecting a defect prediction model for maintenance resource planning and software insurance.* Paper presented at the proceedings of the Fifth Workshop on Economics-Driven Software Research.

Lionel, C. B., Victor, R. B., & Christopher, J. H. (1993). Developing Interpretable Models with Optimized set Reduction for Identifying High-Risk Software Components. *IEEE Transactions on Software Engineering, 19*(11), 1028–1044. doi:10.1109/32.256851

Lionel, C. B., Victor, R. B., & William, M. T. (1992). A Pattern Recognition Approach for Software Engineering Data Analysis. *IEEE Transactions on Software Engineering, 18*(11), 931–942. doi:10.1109/32.177363

Lionel, C. B., Walcelio, L. M., & Wust, J. (2002). Assessing the applicability of fault-proneness models across object-oriented software projects. *IEEE Transactions on Software Engineering, 28*(7), 706–720. doi:10.1109/TSE.2002.1019484

Magnus, C. O., & Per, R. (2002). *Experience from Replicating Empirical Studies on Prediction Models.* Paper presented at the Proceedings of the 8th International Symposium on Software Metrics.

Malaiya, Y. K., Karunanithi, N., & Verma, P. (1990). *Predictability measures for software reliability models.* Paper presented at the Proceedings of COMPSAC 90 Fourteenth Annual International Computer Software and Applications Conference.

Martin, S., & Gada, K. (2001). Comparing Software Prediction Techniques Using Simulation. *IEEE Transactions on Software Engineering, 27*(11), 1014–1022. doi:10.1109/32.965341

Matsumoto, K., Inoue, K., Kikuno, T., & Torii, K. (1988). *Experimental evaluation of software reliability growth models.* Paper presented at FTCS-18, Digest of Papers, the proceedings of Eighteenth International Symposium on Fault-Tolerant Computing.

Michael, R. L., & Allen, N. (1992). Applying Reliability Models More Effectively. *IEEE Software, 9*(4), 43–52. doi:10.1109/52.143104

Munson, J. C., & Khoshgoftaar, T. M. (1992). The detection of fault-prone programs. *IEEE Transactions on Software Engineering, 18*(5), 423–433. doi:10.1109/32.135775

Nachimuthu, K., Darrell, W., & Yashwant, K. M. (1992). Using Neural Networks in Reliability Prediction. *IEEE Software, 9*(4), 53–59. doi:10.1109/52.143107

Nachimuthu, K., Darrell, W., & Yashwant, K. M. (1992). Prediction of Software Reliability Using Connectionist Models. *IEEE Transactions on Software Engineering, 18*(7), 563–574. doi:10.1109/32.148475

Niclas, O., Ann Christin, E., & Mary, H. (1997). Early Risk-Management by Identification of Fault-prone Modules. *Empirical Software Engineering, 2*(2), 166–173. doi:10.1023/A:1009757419320

Niclas, O., & Hans, A. (1996). Predicting Fault-Prone Software Modules in Telephone Switches. *IEEE Transactions on Software Engineering, 22*(12), 886–894. doi:10.1109/32.553637

Niclas, O., Ming, Z., & Mary, H. (1998). Application of multivariate analysis for software fault prediction. *Software Quality Control, 7*(1), 51–66. doi:10.1023/A:1008844909795

Nidhi, G., & Manu Pratap, S. (2005). Estimation of software reliability with execution time model using the pattern mapping technique of artificial neural network. *Computers & Operations Research, 32*(1), 187–199. doi:10.1016/S0305-0548(03)00212-0

Nikora, A. P. (2009). *CASRE homepage*. Retrieved from http://www.openchannelfoundation.org/projects/CASRE_3.0

Nikora, A. P., & Lyu, M. R. (1995). *An experiment in determining software reliability model applicability*. Paper presented at the Proceedings of the Sixth International Symposium on Software Reliability Engineering.

Palu, S. (Last checked November 2008). *Instance-based learning: A Java implementation*. Retrieved from http://www.developer.com/java/other/article.php/10936_1491651_1

Paul Luo, L., Mary, S., Jim, H., Bonnie, R., & Santhanam, P. (2004). *Empirical evaluation of defect projection models for widely-deployed production software systems*. Paper presented at the Proceedings of the 12th ACM SIGSOFT twelfth international symposium on Foundations of software engineering.

Raj Kiran, N., & Ravi, V. (2008). Software reliability prediction by soft computing techniques. *Journal of Systems and Software, 81*(4), 576–583. doi:10.1016/j.jss.2007.05.005

Raymond, E. S. (1999). Cathedral and the bazaar. Sebastopol, CA: O'Reily & Associates.

Reformat, M., Pedrycz, W., & Pizzi, N. J. (2003). Software quality analysis with the use of computational intelligence. *Information and Software Technology, 45*(7), 405–417. doi:10.1016/S0950-5849(03)00012-0

Russell, S., & Norvig, P. (2003). *Artificial intelligence-A modern approach*. New York: Prentice Hall Series in Artificial Intelligence.

Sarah, B., & Bev, L. (1996). Techniques for prediction analysis and recalibration. In *Handbook of software reliability engineering* (pp. 119–166). New York: McGraw-Hill, Inc.

Sean, L., & Liviu, P. (2006). A comparison of bloat control methods for genetic programming. *Evolutionary Computation, 14*(3), 309–344. doi:10.1162/evco.2006.14.3.309

Shepperd, M., Cartwright, M., & Kadoda, G. (2000). On Building Prediction Systems for Software Engineers. *Empirical Software Engineering, 5*(3), 175–182. doi:10.1023/A:1026582314146

Silva, S. (2007). *GPLAB - A Genetic Programming Toolbox for MATLAB*. Retrieved from http://gplab. sourceforge.net (Last checked 27 February 2009)

Sitte, R. (1999). Comparison of software-reliability-growth predictions: neural networks vs parametric-recalibration. *IEEE Transactions on Reliability, 48*(3), 285–291. doi:10.1109/24.799900

Smola, A. J., & Schölkopf, B. (2004). A tutorial on support vector regression. *Statistics and Computing, 14*(3), 199–222. doi:10.1023/B:STCO.0000035301.49549.88

So, S. S., Cha, S. D., & Kwon, Y. R. (2002). Empirical evaluation of a fuzzy logic-based software quality prediction model. *Fuzzy Sets and Systems, 127*(2), 199–208. doi:10.1016/S0165-0114(01)00128-2

Stefan, L., Bart, B., Christophe, M., & Swantje, P. (2008). Benchmarking Classification Models for Software Defect Prediction: A Proposed Framework and Novel Findings. *IEEE Transactions on Software Engineering, 34*(4), 485–496. doi:10.1109/TSE.2008.35

Stringfellow, C., & Andrews, A. A. (2002). An Empirical Method for Selecting Software Reliability Growth Models. *Empirical Software Engineering, 7*(4), 319–343. doi:10.1023/A:1020515105175

Susan Elliott, S., Steve, E., & Richard, C. H. (2003). *Using benchmarking to advance research: a challenge to software engineering*. Paper presented at the Proceedings of the 25th International Conference on Software Engineering.

Tadashi, D., Yasuhiko, N., & Shunji, O. (1999). Optimal software release scheduling based on artificial neural networks. *Annals of Software Engineering, 8*(1-4), 167–185.

Taghi, M. K., Edward, B. A., Wendell, D. J., & John, P. H. (1999). *Classification Tree Models of Software Quality Over Multiple Releases*. Paper presented at the Proceedings of the 10th International Symposium on Software Reliability Engineering.

Taghi, M. K., John, C. M., Bibhuti, B. B., & Gary, D. R. (1992). Predictive Modeling Techniques of Software Quality from Software Measures. *IEEE Transactions on Software Engineering, 18*(11), 979–987. doi:10.1109/32.177367

Taghi, M. K., & Naeem, S. (2002). *Tree-Based Software Quality Estimation Models For Fault Prediction*. Paper presented at the Proceedings of the 8th International Symposium on Software Metrics.

Taghi, M. K., Naeem, S., & Nandini, S. (2006). An empirical study of predicting software faults with case-based reasoning. *Software Quality Control, 14*(2), 85–111.

Taghi, M. K., Yi, L., & Naeem, S. (2004). *Module-Order Modeling using an Evolutionary Multi-Objective Optimization Approach*. Paper presented at the Proceedings of the 10th International Symposium on Software Metrics.

Thomas, J. O., & Elaine, J. W. (2002). *The distribution of faults in a large industrial software system*. Paper presented at the Proceedings of the 2002 ACM SIGSOFT international symposium on software testing and analysis.

Tian, L., & Noore, A. (2004). Software reliability prediction using recurrent neural network with Bayesian regularization. *International Journal of Neural Systems, 14*(3), 165–174. doi:10.1142/S0129065704001966

Tian, L., & Noore, A. (2005). Dynamic software reliability prediction: An approach based on Support Vector Machines. *International Journal of Reliability Quality and Safety Engineering, 12*(4), 309–321. doi:10.1142/S0218539305001847

Tian, L., & Noore, A. (2005). Evolutionary neural network modeling for software cumulative failure time prediction. *International Journal of Reliability Quality and Safety Engineering, 87*(1), 45–51.

Tian, L., & Noore, A. (2005). On-line prediction of software reliability using an evolutionary connectionist model. *Journal of Systems and Software, 77*(22), 173–180.

Tian, L., & Noore, A. (2007). Computational intelligence methods in software reliability prediction. *Computational Intelligence in Reliability Engineering, 39*, 375–398. doi:10.1007/978-3-540-37368-1_12

Tibor, G., Rudolf, F., & Istvan, S. (2005). Empirical Validation of Object-Oriented Metrics on Open Source Software for Fault Prediction. *IEEE Transactions on Software Engineering, 31*(10), 897–910. doi:10.1109/TSE.2005.112

Utkin, L., Gurov, S., & Shubinsky, M. (2002). A fuzzy software reliability model with multiple-error introduction and removal. *International Journal of Reliability Quality and Safety Engineering, 9*(3). doi:10.1142/S0218539302000780

Venkata, U. B. C., Farokh, B. B., Yen, I. L., & Raymond, A. P. (2005). *Empirical Assessment of Machine Learning based Software Defect Prediction Techniques*. Paper presented at the Proceedings of the 10th IEEE International Workshop on Object-Oriented Real-Time Dependable Systems.

Victor, R. B., & Lionel, C. B., Walc, & lio, L. M. (1996). A Validation of Object-Oriented Design Metrics as Quality Indicators. *IEEE Transactions on Software Engineering, 22*(10), 751–761. doi:10.1109/32.544352

Wasif, A., & Richard, T. (2008). *A Comparative Evaluation of Using Genetic Programming for Predicting Fault Count Data*. Paper presented at the Proceedings of The Third International Conference on Software Engineering Advances.

Wasif, A., & Richard, T. (2008). *Suitability of Genetic Programming for Software Reliability Growth Modeling*. Paper presented at the Proceedings of the International Symposium on Computer Science and its Applications.

Witten, I. H., & Frank, E. (2005). *Data mining-Practical machine learning tools and techniques*. San Francisco: Morgan Kaufmann Publishers.

Wood, A. (1996). Predicting software reliability. *Computers, 29*(11), 69–77. doi:10.1109/2.544240

Yamada, S., Ohba, M., & Osaki, S. (1983). S-shaped reliability growth modeling for software error detection. *IEEE Transactions on Reliability, R-32*(5), 475–478. doi:10.1109/TR.1983.5221735

Yongqiang, Z., & Huashan, C. (2006). *Predicting for MTBF Failure Data Series of Software Reliability by Genetic Programming Algorithm*. Paper presented at the Proceedings of the Sixth International Conference on Intelligent Systems Design and Applications - Volume 01.

Yu, T. J., Shen, V. Y., & Dunsmore, H. E. (1988). An Analysis of Several Software Defect Models. *IEEE Transactions on Software Engineering, 14*(9), 1261–1270. doi:10.1109/32.6170

Yu-Shen, S., & Chin-Yu, H. (2007). Neural-network-based approaches for software reliability estimation using dynamic weighted combinational models. *Journal of Systems and Software, 80*(4), 606–615. doi:10.1016/j.jss.2006.06.017

Zhang, D., & Tsai, J. (2003). Machine Learning and Software Engineering. *Software Quality Journal, 11*(2), 87–119. doi:10.1023/A:1023760326768

ENDNOTES

[1] A sequence of random variables with different variances.

[2] http://tomcat.apache.org/

[3] http://www.openbsd.org

[4] http://www.mozilla.com/

[5] The parsimonious factor takes into account that the model with the smallest number of parameters is usually the best.

Chapter 7
Exploring a Self Organizing Multi Agent Approach for Service Discovery

Hakima Mellah
Research Centre in Scientific and Technical Information - CERIST, Algeria

Soumya Banerjee
Birla Institute of Technology, International Center, Mauritius

Salima Hassas
University of Lyon, France

Habiba Drias
USTHB, Algeria

ABSTRACT

The chapter presents a Multi Agent System (MAS) approach, for service discovery process to consider the user in the service discovery process involoving his interactions under constraints. The service discovery has become an emerging phenomena in software engineering and process engineering as well. The proposed MAS has demonstrated significant self oranizining potential. This feature is very crucial for assuring a correct service delivery, to avoid failures or mal-function for the service discovery environment. The requirement for self organizing choreographed services have been well realized, in case of operational, functional and behavioral faults. Self organization within the MAS is adopted by the recourse to a self organizing protocol conceived from bacteria colony and evolutionary computation paradigm.

1. INTRODUCTION

Service orientation promotes a new way to design and implement large scale distributed applications across organizational and technical boundaries. However, it does not provide sufficient means to cope with the increasing complexity in service-oriented software applications. A promising way to get rid of the dilemma is to enable self-organization in service oriented computing (Gonzalez, 2005) (Martin, 2006). The emphasis could be given to the service orientation in the architectural design facilitates reusability, flexibility, interoperability, and agility

DOI: 10.4018/978-1-61520-809-8.ch007

for the software engineering part of those kind of system. Broadly, the service autonomy raises the question of how to establish proper operation status on the system level especially in presence of possible failures in some service elements. The research exhibit that the intelligent agent could be self organized to anticipate and follow up the failure part of software engineering. Practically, the proposed model has the pragmatic feature to trace he distributed problem and it is also capable to adopt the instant maintainability of the system. In this context, it is important to reciprocate the service of agents within the system and to get back the re-engineered system with minimum alterations. The agents are participating in these processes and re-discover the ambiguous part of the system itself by tracing the protocol exchanged through agents and the system.

The rest of the chapter is organized as follows: Section 2 describes background and related works of the Web Services which is one of the prominent examples of Multi Agent System. Section 3 elaborates the self organization principle within the Multi Agent System. Section 4 presents a brief outline on protocol and its primitives followed by the detailed service discovery approach in section 5. Section 6 is devoted about the different failure of system and section 7 discusses a case study presenting the applicability of the proposal. Section 8 presents the necessary tools being used to implement the system. Finally section 8 and 9 present the conclusion and further research in this direction.

2. BACKGROUND

Web Services (WS) reliability is strongly dependent on the fault handling mechanisms of the communication protocols and on the messaging infrastructure mediating their interactions (Erradi, Maheshwari, & Tosic, 2006). Correct service delivery continuity defines web services reliability. This implies zero, or at worst, relatively

few failures and rapid recovery time (Erradi, Maheshwari, & Tosic, 2006). WS are managed by different geographically distributed providers The unreliability of any of the constituent WS could lead to the failure or QoS degradation, even if other constituent seem to be reliable. A service management middleware is proposed in (Erradi, Maheshwari, & Tosic, 2006), it is based on some recovery policies (eg retry, skip, use). In (Ardissono L., Furnari, Goy, Petrone, & Segnan, 2006) a framework is proposed for WS orchestration, as environment of this latter could present some exceptions that are not able to identify precisely their causality. WS are used to diagnose exceptions in a more precise manner. In (Ardissono L., Furnari, Goy, Petrone, & Segnan, 2007) an interaction protocol for every cooperating web service WS_i is represented by an abstract process. The local view of WS_i on choreography is determined by associating its abstract process to the final WS. In this context, a WS monitor is responsible of checking the choreographed services by receiving their status messages during choreography. The problem is also posed when the WS monitor itself does not respond in time.

(Pat, Lyu, & Malek, 2006) proposed a general approach in system fault tolerance that can be applicable to WS. It is based on a replication driven WS system and on a replication manager. The replication manager keeps check the WS availability by the polling method. All the checking process is centralized on the replication manager and its abstract process. The whole system seems to be non-functioning in absence of replication manager. The several other contemporary proposals are published in supporting the development of reliable composite web services and in centralized WS orchestration (Ardissono L., Furnari, Goy, Petrone, & Segnan, 2006). In decentralized orchestration, the state of the composite WS depends on its distribution across nodes. To discover and utilize services, human based approaches, is not only time consuming, but also requires continuous user interaction. Software agents have been subject to research in many inter-related fields. They are long-lived, having persistent computations that can perceive reason, act, and communicate. They have the ability to make decisions independently, without human intervention and without influence from other agents, notably when they are some failures during the service discovery process. Chafle (Ardissono L., Furnari, Goy, Petrone, & Segnan, 2006) proposes a framework, based on local monitoring agents, for checking the state of the orchestrated WS; all the monitoring agents interact with a Status Monitor. Palathingal and his colleagues (Palathingal & Chandra, 2004) developed a multi agents approach for service discovery and utilization. The MAS proposed in his work is restricted within the UDDI (Universal Description Discovery and Integration). An agent is created, when a service provider expresses the need to publish services. Each software agent is specialized in a category of services. In this approach there is no indication on the adopted interaction protocol while agents are interacting, or on failure production, within the system, even the services are being choreographed.

In the chapter, the MAS for services discovery are based principally on data duplication within the services provider, whereas interaction between agents is based on a self organizing protocol conceived from evolutionary agents.

3. SELF ORGANIZATION AND MULTI AGENT SYSTEM: BIO-INSPIRED EVOLUTIONARY APPROACH

The most concrete example of a self organization is the way in which the ants produce pheromone like traces between the foods sources. The bacteria colonies also reorganize by forming patterns in order to fight against the adverse life conditions within the environment. They develop a sophisticated co-operative behavior and complex possibilities of communication, in order to be able to change their pattern. They prefer to reorganize,

like the direct cell-cell physical interactions by the intermediary of additional membrane polymers, which is useful for the model formation in "without-life" systems. Based on these models, we have elaborated a communication model (Mellah, Hassas, & Drias, 2006) and a self organizing (Mellah, Hassas, & Drias, 2007) principally based on communication primitives that demonstrates how, through interactions (communication), interacting information sources could be self -organized. Moreover, the latter is regarded as an interaction cellular program and complexity is ensured by the composition of blocks (primitives).

As mentioned, the prominent distributed service is Web Services, therefore model of interaction on web paradigm should also be discussed. The W3C (W3C Glossary) define orchestrations as "the model of interaction that must comply a Web service agent to achieve its goal". However, even if orchestrations are a support for incremental programming in response to the introduction of a new event or the coordination with a new service, they do not support their own composition (Peltz, 2003).

While orchestration describes, in terms of service, interactions it may have with other services, and internal stages of data processing or invocations of internal modules (Peltz, 2003), choreography describes the collaboration between a collections of services, whose aim is achieving a given objective. The achievement of this objective is done by exchanging messages (Austin, Barbir, Peters, & Ross-Talbot, 2004). Therefore, in choreography it is possible to have multiple orchestrations and in each one, one service will act as an orchestra chef.

The model proposed by (Mellah, Hassas, & Drias, 2006) emphasized organization functioning influences, it's structuring; the key factors commonly from the tasks and activities, competences and responsibilities including their interactions network. Instead of considering information sources connection, we consider the whole of WS that are choreographed to respond to a user request. These WS translate existence of a discovery structure. As in an organization, choreographed WS, constituting a discovery structure, are connected by varied and complex flows which are all significant. They explain how the discovery process has been achieved, or which services are implied and composed relatively to the user query. The complex flows represent the organizational structure and choreographed services are mapped to this organizational structure's elements. The interactions networks connect the organizational positions (geographical positions on which services are located). The information network must be self organized in this context.

In services discovery process, information retrieval includes two orthogonal components which must be complementary and that are:

1. **The construction of the network:** is a self-organizing process which requires an adaptive behavior while respecting the network consumption.

2. **Research:** is ensured by a distributed algorithm which will exploit the structure of the emergent network.

In (Heylighen, 2003) (Mellah, Hassas, & Drias, 2006) a trigger factor for self organizing distributed information sources (IS) is **IS** delay response time, which can avoid a failure production in the whole system. Services may encapsulate IS interaction for responding to a user query. The encapsulation will be based on a service discovery structure that needs to maintain its connectivity (between services). In order to avoid resources bottleneck or single points of failures during interaction, services components or resources should maintain connectivity with each others. This connectivity can be assured by the recourse to self organizing resources or services components. Services fault causalities are varied and three main categories have been distinguished (Erradi, Maheshwari, & Tosic, 2006):

1. Functional faults that are caused by a non completion of task execution or some incorrect results delivered by service (for example: price limits or delivery deadline), and behavioral exceptions that are caused by an incorrect service invocation, message loss during service.

2. Environmental faults that refer to communication infrastructure exceptions and middleware failures of the hosting servers and database servers (for example: service response time, service availability).

3. Contractual fault that are linked to the violation of Service Level Agreement (SLAs) and collaboration policies; in this case the service execution might be completed without the conformity of results to the negotiated SLAs.

In this chapter, we emphasize more on the two first categories, and consider delayed service response time or non service availability when:

• Machines or network connections of a particular service provider are currently overloaded. The information may influence an agent to choose a different provider offering the same or a similar service.

• A transaction was involved by a user, such as the provider identity and network locations of specific services within a composed service, we should avoid situation like resource bottlenecks or single point of failure within the network.

Therefore, instead to affect a provider of services to a single machine, services are duplicated on several machines and at each one, agent software is associated. Each provider will be corresponded with several machines. When a service does not respond any more or there is a resource bottleneck, another machine will be ready to provide the same or similar service.

Based on these postulates, services will be considered as the tasks transferred between agents

Figure 1. The self organizing protocol primitives' interactions

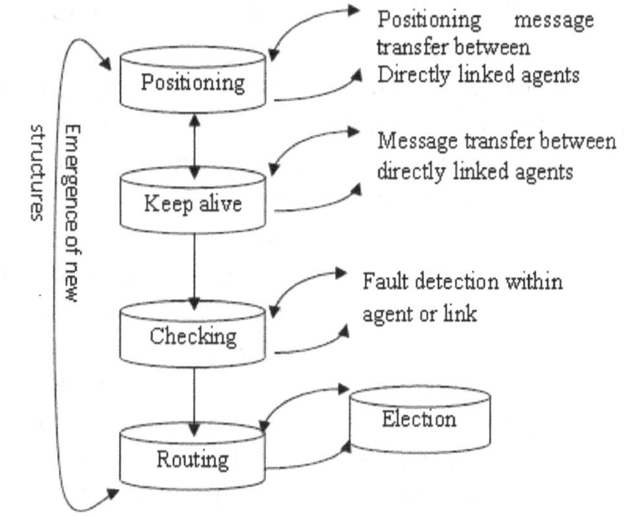

machines. The latter's interaction will be based on the self organizing protocol (Mellah, Hassas, & Drias, 2007), and failures are detected by the checking primitive that keeps alive interactions between agents machines. The positioning primitive computes the distance between agent machines that do not responds to a service request (without the duplication of data). Similarly, the routing primitive elaborates the way to follow for reaching the required service from other machines. After finding the addresses, the new service will be updated within the (Web Service Description Language)WSDL document.

4. THE PROTOCOL

We describe in this section the commonly used protocol primitives that interact to maintain connectivity between agents (Figure1):

4.1 Positioning Primitive

It provides information on agent position relatively to set of agents, which means that an agent-machine considered as a source broadcasts a message containing its identity, the services that are duplicated in its machine and a position value(namely *Pos*). Each agents that receives the message, broadcasts it in its neighborhood with *Pos* value incremented by "1". An agent may receive this message several times, so it stores the minimum value of *Pos* and identity of the issuing agent source.

4.2 Election Primitive

Once a fault is detected, one agent triggers the election process by sending a message containing a fitness value, to elect the leader of the agent group. The leader agent will have the privilege to delete an agent which is not able to perform its role and create another one to replace it, it is also useful for all decision making.

4.3 Routing Primitive

This primitive is important for maintaining connectivity between agents, and is triggered when an agent is breakdown, or when a communication link is lost. Two algorithms have been proposed in this process, the first is for allocating tasks of the breakdown agent to the neighborhood, the second is triggered by the agent that detect the communication link problem, and it is for seeking another path to communicate. The failure recovery process is also an integral part of service discovery scenario discussed in this chapter. The failure could be repaired by a troubleshooting service algorithm.

4.4 Checking Primitive

Each agent periodically broadcasts a message to its neighbors to mark its keep-alive. After a period, if no message arrives to one agent, the checking primitive tries to localize the problem within the agent or the communication link. Once the problem is localized, the routing primitive in launched to correct the situation.

5. SERVICE DISCOVERY PROCESS: STEP WISE IMPLEMENTATION

In order to propose the necessary MAS for service discovery, the process's steps are summarized briefly as follows:

- The service provider deploys a WS in a server and generates a WS description (in WSDL file).
- The service provider publishes the service in UDDI registry
- after introducing a request, the system searches the needed information in the UDDI registry
- UDDI registry sends the description of all the corresponding services (in WSDL file)
- Once the service is selected, the service is invoked by its provider via a SOAP request.
- The request in the executed by the provider and results are transferred to the user.

5.1 The Multi Agent System for Service Discovery

The scope of this paper is not to assure the semantic discovery of services since a lot of works have been done in this area (Kunal & Amit, 2007) using ontologies and semantic annotations. During service discovery process, several problems of non availability of services and request overloading within the corresponding supplier may arise. This may lead to delay or even blocking the entire system. In the proposed MAS, we point at services duplication, in different machines, since its mechanism reduces recovery time and increases system availability. As in the literature of the MAS, agents interact according to an interaction protocol such as the contract net and acquaintances models, the proposed MAS is mainly based on a self-organization protocol that is inspired by bacterial colony life (Mellah, Hassas, & Drias, Towards a self organizing protocol for a Multi Agents System, 2007).

The MAS is composed by three agents that are: Request Analyzer Agent (RAA), Composer Agent (CA), several Machine Agents (MA), those are described below:

Request Analyzer Agent (RAA): Commonly known as RAA, represents the interface between the user and the system which look for the service. Its principal role is analyzing user query. The latter is decomposed into simple sub queries when it is complex. For each simple query, a matching is done between the query's keyword and the most appropriate service. Then a service discovery process is launched within the **UDDI**(Universal Description Discovery and Integration).

Composer Agent (CA): It is responsible of receiving web services WSDL documents that results from the discovery process. By considering the user constraints on the desired WS, the CA makes its selection. The WS references that are not selected are saved in a table. The chosen WS is invoked by the CA by sending a **SOAP**(Simple

Figure 2. Task table

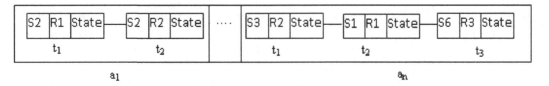

| S2 | R1 | State | S2 | R2 | State | .... | S3 | R2 | State | S1 | R1 | State | S6 | R3 | State |

t_1 t_2 t_1 t_2 t_3

a_1 a_n

Figure 3. The proposed service discovery MAS architecture

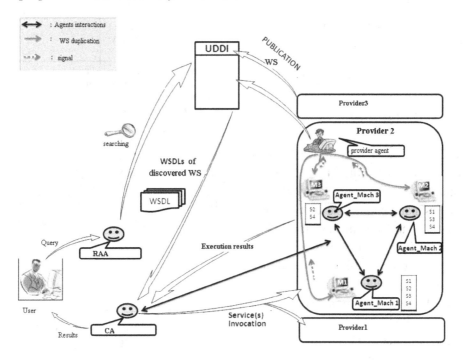

Object Access Protocol) query. Once all needed services for a request are invoked, the CA composes the results of WS execution and presents them to the user. In case of a problem appearance within the WS, and based on the saved table, another provider is selected.

Machine Agent (MA): To avoid resources bottleneck or service non availability problems, we suggest the data duplication on one or several machines within the providers. Each machine is marked by a MA. Its role is to ensure reliable delivery of a WS by monitoring regularly the status of the: machine, state of the service, and status of communication link that connects agents machines each others. The MA will keep track of all the services duplicated in the machine, as well as MA neighbor's identities (through messages). MA In case of service failures, the same service located in another machine replaces it immediately (Figure 3).

A tasks table corresponds to the MAS, and each record correspond at one MA a_i (Figure 2). The list structure of a_i is described as:

- The **SOAP** query for executing a WS
- Service name requested by the query
- State of the query (in execution or in failure).

Table 1. Query through RAA

QueryID	Keywords	Attributes
R1	Hotel	Hotel-type="5*"∧ country="Algeria"∧city="Algiers"∧ room-rate<=" 10000DA";
R2	Car	Country="Algeria" ∧city= "Algiers"∧car-type= »Nissan » ∧ price<= « 5000DA »;

While a machine is invoked for executing a WS, the machine agent corresponding inserts the query in the list. Once the execution is achieved the task t_i is removed from AM table.

5.2 System Functioning

Once the user query is introduced, the RAA analyses the request and if it is complex, it decomposes it into sub queries. A simple query consists of two parts: the first part contains the keyword and the second contains the assigned attributes. For example, by considering a user with an aim to book a room in a five star hotel for a period of 3 days from 15 June 2009, with room rates below or equal to 10000DA/day, and renting a car (Peugeot), during the period, with a rate less than or equal to 5000DA/day. Within the user interface, the user introduces his keywords that are hotel booking and car rental, and then adds related attributes such as: hotel-type: 5*, Country: Algeria, City: Algiers. The query is then summarized in a table. The RAA constitutes the summarize query in a table summary query (Refer Table 1)

RAA translates each simple query into a SOAP query before sending it to UDDI registry via the HTTP protocol. The UDDI discovers the most pertinent services that correspond to the user query based on keywords and attributes. Once the search is accomplished, UDDI sends all corresponding WSDLs documents to the CA, who analyses them to browse to the user functions assured by each service.

Table 2. Services search results

Service execution results	Service URL
«City=Algiers, room-cost=10000 DA/ night»(more informations...)	http://www.hotel1.com/informations
«City=Algiers, room-cost=10000 DA/night" (more informations...)	http://www.hotel2.com/informations
«City=Algiers, Car-typ=disponible, Car-Name= disponible, Car-cost= 5000 DA/day » (more informations...)	http://www.AgenceLocationVoiture1.com/informations
«City=Tipaza,Car-name = disponible, Car-type= disponible, Car-cost= 2 500 DA/ day » informations...)	http://www.AgenceLocationVoiture2.com/informations

Table 3. An example of rescue table

User query	Rescue WSDL
R1	WSDL1, WSDL3
R2	WSDL2

Suppose that the search with R1, finds three services $WSDL_1$, $WSDL_2$, $WSDL_3$, and the CA analyzes the WDL(s) to detect the constraints introduced by the user. If S_1 and S_2 are the corresponding services, then they will be invoked by CA via a SOAP query.

The CA saves temporarily WS, that are not selected by the user, in a rescue table (Table 3), it will be used in case of problem apparition within the chosen service. And then it sends SOAP query to invoke services.

Once the invocation is done, the CA will be linked with the MA from the machine that has been chosen to execute the query. The corresponding MA monitors the query execution. In case of WS execution failure, the MA asks for another MA in its neighborhood. If it is the MA itself that fails, all its neighbors will try to replace it, to shorten the user query response time. At the end of execution, the MA sends the result to the CA, which composes all results of executions it has invoked, and returns the final result to the user. If the system fails in the execution of a service, the CA uses the secure table for invoking a similar service provided by another provider. Assuring successful' agents communication will facilitate designing reliable MAS, since many problems can occur in the system. Failures could appear at different system level such as: agent level, agents communication link level, and at service level. When failures happen, agents had to reason, decide and adapt to new decision themselves. In this context, we solicit a self organizing protocol can establish the reliable communication between agents.

The scope of chapter is not only to describe the bio-inspired protocol, also we mention its most important primitives, its interaction (presented in Figure 1), and their interpretation in the paradigm of service discovery. The referenced protocol among the agents is visualized in the form of the distributed tasks in an abstract manner. As MAS in this chapter is proposed for discovering services, the tasks that will be exchanged among agents machines (AM) primarily are represented by services.

6. FAILURES OCCURRING WITHIN THE SYSTEM

In each failure level different decisions had to be adopted by agents especially when failure is within:

- Agent.
- Communication link.
- Service.

6.1 Agent Failures

As there are various types of agents in the system, behavior or decision they take is different within each type.

6.1.1 Agent Machines(AM)

One can consider that an agent machine $(AM)a_i$ does not respond anymore; all its services, awaiting to be executed, will be distributed among the rest of AM in the system, in this context two cases distinguished:

1. The breakdown AM a_i is the alone neighbor of an agent a_j

```
Begin
a_j consults the field a_i of the
tasks vector (to know what are the
services non yet executed by a_i)
If a_j is able to excute all a_i
services
    Then
    -Task[a_j]= Task[a_j]+ Task[a_i]
    * a_j adds all a_i services in
    its table *
    -a_j launches election process
    (the leader removes a_i, in-
    forms the provider to repair
    the failure).
    -a_j launches the positioning
    process.
    Else
    -a_j inserts only the servic-
    es that is able to execute.
    -a_j launches the routing process
    (to find agents that accept to
    take the rest of services)
        - If a_j finds a_x (agent that
        is able to execute the rest
        of services)
            Then
            -a_x launches election
            process(the leader re-
            moves a_i, informs the pro-
            vider to repair the fail-
            ure and reconstructs a_i).
            -a_x launches the position-
            ing process.
```

```
    Else
    -a  launches election
      x
    process(the leader removes
    a , informs the provider
     i
    to repair the failure and
    reconstructs a ).
                   i
  EndIf;
Endif
END
```

2. The breakdown agent a_i has several neighbors

Repairing the failure of a_i consists in attributing all its services to the neighborhood; several cases can be considered:

```
Begin
If each agent a  pertaining to a
                v                 i
neighborhood is able to take a sub
set of a  services
         i
  Then
    -each  a  adds  to  task[a ],
            v                   v
    a  sub  set  of  task[a ].
                           i
    -each agent a  launches elec-
                 v
    tion process (the leader removes
    a ,informs the provider to repair
     i
    the failure and reconstructs a ).
                                  i
    -each a  launches positioning
           v
    process.
  Else (no agent is able to
  take a sub set of a  services)
                     i
      -Each a  launches routing
             v
      process (to find agents
      that can take the rest of
      services)
    -If no agent a  are found
                  x
    to fix a  problem
            i
      Then
      -Each neighbour a  launch-
                       i
      es election process.
      Else
      - each agent a  accepts
                    x
      services that can execute
      and  launches  election
      process.
```

```
    EndIf
    - the leader removes a , in-
                          i
    forms the provider to repair
    the failure and reconstructs a
                                  i
    -the leader launches posi-
    tioning process.
  EndIf;
End
```

It should be noted that when a provider is informed that a MA a_x is in a failure state it must fix the problem on the machine M_x (hardware problem), and redefines a_x agent. Once the agent is integrated into the system as a MA, it launches the *election process* to be recognized in the agent network architecture (Only the leader can add or remove an agent), and then a_x launches positioning process.

6.1.2 Request Analyzer Agent or Composer Agent Failure

The most considered failures in this work are within the service provider; the following solutions for RAA or CA are: When a failure is considered within a RAA, it means that the discovery process is not launched yet, and the repair is done by restarting the process another time. Whereas when the failure is within CA the user will not receive the result and he has to introduce its query again by the mean of user interface.

6.2 A Communication Link Failure

Three different cases are considered:

6.2.1 The MAS is Decomposed Into Two Systems

The group of agents is decomposed into two subnets where one agent in a subnet is connected to another agent in another subnet. In this case, if the link connecting these two agents is destroyed,

Figure 4. The MAS is decomposed into two sub systems S1 and S2

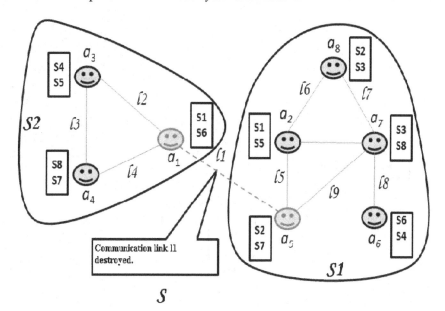

we will have two separate subsystems as shown in Figure 4.

While the destroyed link divided the MAS into two subsystems, it will be no path leading S_1 to S_2. And there is no path leading a_1 to a5 (Figure 4). For this, one possibility might be that a_1 (and/or a_5) changes its port address and sends a keep-alive to its lost neighbor, the agent a_2 responds with a keep-alive signal too, to say that it accepted this new address.

6.2.2 The Isolated Agent Is a Neighbor of an Agent Pertaining To a Subsystem

This situation could happen within the Agent Machine MAS interactions or within the interaction between CA and one of AM as shown in Figure 5.

By the destruction of the link l_1, AC will be isolated. In this case it will change its port address and send a keep-alive signal to the lost agent(a_1), which responds by the same that it agrees for the new address.

6.2.3 The Two Agents Pertain To the Same System

In this case the two separated agents launched the *routing process* to find another way to communicate and the *positioning process* in launched (Figure 6).

6.3 Service Failure

An algorithm is given below to fix a services execution problem:

a_{src}: agent source
a_{emet}: agent sender of message
Rec: boolean variable
Task: Each record represents an AM, and contains key words to execute.
Neighbors$\{a_i\}$: the set of a_i neighbors
$Id_{service}$: the service identifier
Id-Req: it is the keyword

$$task[a_i]head \rightarrow state = \begin{cases} 1: \text{service failure} \\ 0: \text{if not} \end{cases}$$

Figure 5. A destroyed communication link between AC and AM

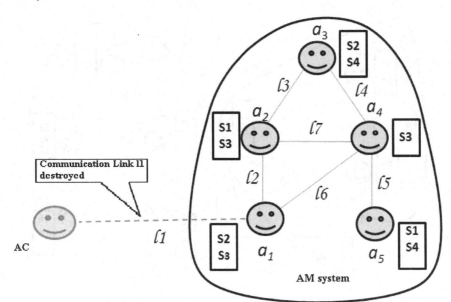

Figure 6. A communication link destruction between two agents of the same MAS

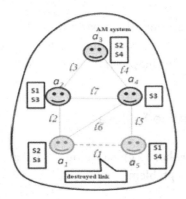

Algorithm

Agent$_{src}$
Begin
-Task [a$_{src}$].state:= 0 ;
-send **Repair_service (a**$_{src,}$
a$_{emet'}$ **Id**$_{service'}$ **Id-Req)** to all
direct neighbors;
-send **Redeploy (S**$_i$**, M**$_i$**)** to the
provider ;
End

Agent$_j$
Begin
when the message **Repair_service**
(a$_{src'}$ **a**$_{emet'}$ **Id**$_{service'}$ **Id-Req)** from **a**$_{emet}$
do
　　If rec = False
　　　Then
　　　　-rec = Vrai;
　　　　-**If** Task [a$_{src}$].state
　　　　= 0 //service not yet
　　　　repaired
　　　　　Then
　　　　　　-**If** Id$_{service}$ ∈
　　　　　　service{a$_j$}
　　　　　Then
　　　　　-Task [a$_{src}$].
　　　　　state=1 ;
　　　　　-insert the
　　　　　task in Task
　　　　　[a$_j$];
　　　　　-remove the
　　　　　task from Task
　　　　　[a$_{src}$];
　　　　Else
　　　　-send message

Figure 7. A failure is detected within S_2 on a_1

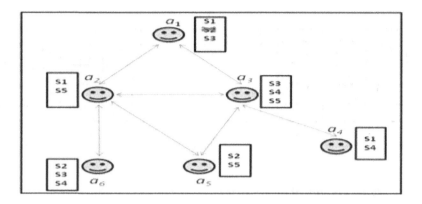

```
    Repair_Service
    (a_src, a_j, Id-
         Id-Req)
    service,
    to
    neighbors{a_j}-
    {a_j};
         endif
      Endif
    EndIf
  Done
End
```

7. CASE STUDY AND ANALYSIS

When a MA agent detects that a service has failed in its machine it tries to shoot the trouble. It affects "0", to the state of failed service, in the Tasks table. Broadcasts the message *Repair_Service (A_{src}, A_{emet}, $Id_{service}$, Id-Req)* to its neighbors, and then informs the provider that the service is down by sending the message *Redeploy(S_{fail}, $Id_{machine}$)* to repair it, with S_{fail}: service being in failure, and $Id_{machine}$ is the corresponding machine.

A neighbor by receiving the troubleshooting message for the first time attributes "true" to *Rec* variable. It checks the status of the failed service in the tasks table; if it is "1", this means that the service has already been supported by another agent, otherwise it will verify if the failed service is within its services list. If so, it updates the service status to "1", inserts the query in the tasks table and removes it from the source agent tasks table. Otherwise it broadcasts the *repair service ()* message to it's directs neighbors.

7.1 Example

Suppose The MAS of AM composed of agents (a_1, a_2,..., a_6) where a_1 detected a failure within S_2 service (Figure 7),

As illustrated above the tasks table associated is presented in Figure 8:

- a_1 sends message Repair-service(a_1, a_1, S_2, Id_{req}) to its directs neighbors a_2, a_3.
- a_2, a_3 don't have S_2 within their services list, so:
  - a_2 broadcasts the message Repair_Service (a_1, a_2, S_2, Id_{req}) to its directs neighbors a_3, a_5, a_6.
  - a_3 broadcasts the message Repair_Service (a_1, a_3, S_2, Id_{req}) to its directs neighbors a_2, a_4, a_5.

By receiving the repair message, a_5 finds that S_2 of M_1 machine is not repaired, and it is within its services list. Its updates the state of S_2 (by affecting the value "1"), removes t_1 from Task[a_1], inserts it in Task[a_5]. After receiving

Figure 8. Tasks table before service repair. R_i: User request

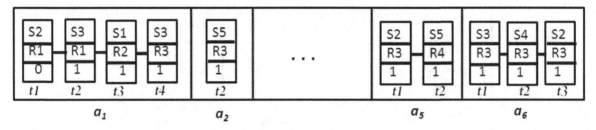

Figure 9. Service repair by creating a link with a_6

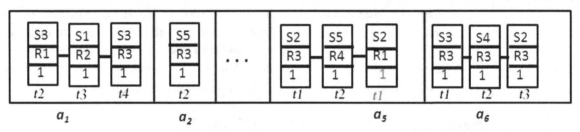

Figure 10. Tasks table after service repair. R_i: User request

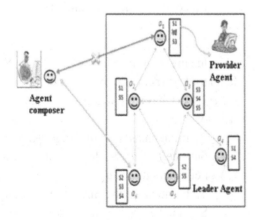

the repair message, a_6 finds that the state of S_2 is 1(it has already been repaired), it ignores the message(Figure 9). a_5 launches election process to select a leader, the latter destructs the link between a_6 and AC (Figure 10).

8. IMPLEMENTATION ASPECTS

The implementation of the Multi Agent System is a work in progress. However, we are using Jade(Java Agent Development Framework) for developing the user interface that collects the user constraints on the query he introduces (in terms of keywords). The request is queried in OWL_S concepts via Jena2.2 API(Application Programming Interface). Jena is a Java Kit for the semantic web. Messages transferred among agents are FIPA-ACL type, whereas the primitives used by agents are programmed in Java.

9. CONCLUSION AND FUTURE RESEARCH

In this chapter the service discovery has been presented referring bio-inspired and evolutionary agents. The emphasis has been initiated a model for service failure detection and recovery in distributed environment with the help of the proposed self organized Multi Agent. The positioning of the self organized agents and its protocol has been elaborated in the chapter with a brief service case model. The relevance and potential applications of self organized agents in service discovery paradigm is an emerging field of research in different flavors of software engineering and recommender system. The critical software services and models like health care, banking and disaster management could be harnessed including more sophisticated human like agents. Collective intelligence from nature has already been envisaged effectively in the service response and failure coverage; hence service discovery through self organized agents could be treated as major mile stone of software engineering research.

REFERENCES

Ardissono, L., Furnari, R., Goy, A., Petrone, G., & Segnan, M. (2006). *Fault tolerant WS orchestraion by means of diagnosis* (pp. 2–16). Berlin: Springer verlag.

Ardissono, L., Furnari, R., Goy, R., Petrone, G., & Segnan, M. (2007). Monitoring choreographed services. In Sobth, S. V. T. (Ed.), *Innovations and advanced techniques in computer and information sciences and engineering* (pp. 283–288). doi:10.1007/978-1-4020-6268-1_51

Austin, D., Barbir, A., Peters, E., & Ross-Talbot, S. (2004). *Web Services Choreography Requirements W3C Working Draft.* World Wide Web Consortium (W3C).

Erradi, A., Maheshwari, P., & Tosic, V. (2006). Recovery policies for enhancing web services reliability. In *IEEE International Conference on Web Services, ICWS*, (pp. 189-196).

Gonzalez, F. (2005). Comprendre l'approche orientée service. Saint Maurice, France: BG informatique.

Heylighen, F. (2003). The science of self organization and Adaptativity. In *Knowledge Management, organizational intelligence and learning and complexity*. Boca Raton, FL: E. P. Ltd.

Kunal, V., & Amit, S. (2007). Semantically Annotating a Web Service. *IEEE Internet Computing, 11*(2), 83–85. doi:10.1109/MIC.2007.48

Martin, D. (2006). Putting web services in context. In *Electronic notes in theoretical Computer Science* (pp. 3–16). New York: Elsevier.

Mellah, H., Hassas, S., & Drias, H. (2006). A communication model of distributed information sources bacteria colonies inspired. In *10th IEEE International Conference on Intelligent Engineering Systems, INES'06*, London.

Mellah, H., Hassas, S., & Drias, H. (2006). Information systems self organization: Problematic, principles and methodologies. In *2nd International conference on Advanced Database Conference-IADC*, (pp. 170-175), USA.

Mellah, H., Hassas, S., & Drias, H. (2007). Towards a self organizing protocol for a Multi Agents System. In Proceeding IEEE of the sixth international conference on Networking ICN 07, (pp. 60-66), France.

Palathingal, P., & Chandra, S. (2004). Agent Approach for Service Discovery and Utilization. In *Proceedings of the 37th Hawaii International Conference on System Sciences*, Hawaii.

Pat, P., Lyu, M., & Malek, M. (2006). Making services fault tolerant. In Penkler, D., Reitenspiess, M., & Tam, F. (Eds.), *ISAS 2006* (pp. 43–61). Berlin: Springer Verlag.

Peltz, C. (2003). Web Services Orchestration and Choreography. *Computer, 26*(10), 46–52. doi:10.1109/MC.2003.1236471

Chapter 8
Innovative Hybrid Genetic Algorithms and Line Search Method for Industrial Production Management

Pandian Vasant
University Technology Petronas, Malaysia

ABSTRACT

Many engineering, science, information technology and management optimization problems can be considered as non linear programming real world problems where the all or some of the parameters and variables involved are uncertain in nature. These can only be quantified using intelligent computational techniques such as evolutionary computation and fuzzy logic. The main objective of this research chapter is to solve non linear fuzzy optimization problem where the technological coefficient in the constraints involved are fuzzy numbers which was represented by logistic membership functions by using hybrid evolutionary optimization approach. To explore the applicability of the present study a numerical example is considered to determine the production planning for the decision variables and profit of the company.

INTRODUCTION

It is well known that optimization problems arise in a variety of situations. Particularly interesting are those concerning management problems as decision makers usually state their data in a vague way: "high benefits", "as low as possible", "important savings", etc. Because of this vagueness, managers prefer to have not just one solution but a set of them, so that the most suitable solution can be applied according to the state of existing deci-

sion of the production process at a given time and without increasing delay. In these situations fuzzy optimization is an ideal methodology, since it allows us to represent the underlying uncertainty of the optimization problem, while finding optimal solutions that reflect such uncertainty and then applying them to possible instances, once the uncertainty has been solved. This allows us to obtain a model of the behavior of the solutions based on the uncertainty of the optimization problem.

Fuzzy constrained optimization problems have been extensively studied since the seventies. In the linear case, the first approaches to solve the so-called

DOI: 10.4018/978-1-61520-809-8.ch008

fuzzy linear programming problem appeared in Bellman & Zadeh (1970), Tanaka, Okuda & Asai (1974), Zimmermann (1976), Sengupta, Vasant & Andreeski (2008). Since then, important contributions solving different linear models have been made and these models have been the subject of a substantial amount of work. In the nonlinear case (Ali, 1998; Ekel, Pedrycz & Schinzinger, 1998; Ramik & Vlach, 2002; Vasant & Barsoum, 2008; Vasant, Barsoum, Khatun & Abbas, 2008; Jimenez, Sanchez & Vasant, 2008) the situation is quite different, as there is a wide variety of specific and both practically and theoretically relevant nonlinear problems, with each having a different solution method.

In this chapter, the new methodology of modified s-curve membership function using fuzzy linear programming in production planning and their applications to decision making are carried out. Especially, fuzzy linear programming based on vagueness in the fuzzy parameters such as objective coefficients, technical coefficients and resource variables given by a decision maker is analyzed.

Various types of membership functions were used in fuzzy linear programming problem and its application such as a linear membership function (Zimmermann, 1976; 1978; Elamvazuthi, Sinnadurai, Khan & Vasant, 2009), a tangent type of a membership function (Leberling, 1981), an interval linear membership function (Hannan, 1981), an exponential membership function (Carlsson and Korhonen, 1986), inverse tangent membership function (Sakawa, 1983), logistic type of membership function (Watada, 1997), concave piecewise linear membership function (Inuiguchi, Ichihachi and Kume, 1990) and piecewise linear membership function (Hu and Fang, 1999). As a tangent type, of a membership function, an exponential membership function, and hyperbolic membership function are non-linear function; a fuzzy mathematical programming defined with a non-linear membership function

results in a non-linear programming. Usually a linear membership function is employed in order to avoid non-linearity. Nevertheless, there are some difficulties in selecting the solution of a problem written in a linear membership function. Therefore, in this chapter a modified s-curve membership function is employed to overcome such deficits, which a linear membership function has. Furthermore, S-curve membership function is more flexible enough to describe the vagueness in the fuzzy parameters for the production planning problems (Vasant, 2003; 2006; 2008). Moreover, the application of modified s-curve membership functions in production management and industrial manufacturing problems are widely available in Vasant, Bhattacharya & Abraham (2008), Peidro & Vasant (2009), Tsoulos & Vasant (2009) and Vasant & Nader (2009).

Due to limitations in resources for manufacturing a product and the need to satisfy certain conditions in manufacturing and demand, a problem of fuzziness occurs in industrial production planning systems. This problem occurs also in chocolate manufacturing when deciding a mixed selection of raw materials to produce varieties of products. This is referred here to as the Product-mix Selection Problem (Tabucanon, 1996). The objective of the company is to maximize its profit, which is, alternatively, equivalent to maximizing the gross contribution to the company in terms of US$. That is to find the optimal product mix under uncertain constraints in the technical, raw material and market consideration. Furthermore, it is possible to show the relationship between the optimal profits and the corresponding membership values (Zimmermann, 1978; Bhattacharya, Abraham & Vasant, 2008). According to this relationship, the decision maker can then obtain his optimal solution with a trade-off under a predetermined allowable imprecision.

The chapter is outlined as follows. The construction of modified s-curve membership functions are presented in Section 2. Formulation of

Figure 1. Modified S-Curve membership function

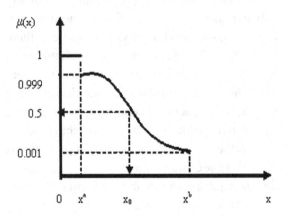

the fuzzy product-mix selection problem (FPSP) for three cases is considered in Section 3. The case study of FPSP is given in Section 4. In Section 5, we examine the outcome of real life application problem of FPSP and its solution. The chapter ends with conclusion and future research work.

DEVELOPMENT OF MEMBERSHIP FUNCTION

The modified S-curve membership function is a particular case of the logistic function with specific values of B, C and α. These values are to be found out. This logistic function as given by Equation (1) and depicted in Figure 1 is indicated as S-shaped membership function by Gonguen (1969), Zadeh (1971) and Vasant (2008).

We define, here, a modified S-curve membership function as follows:

$$\mu(x) = \begin{cases} 1 & x < x^a \\ 0.999 & x = x^a \\ \dfrac{B}{1 + Ce^{\alpha x}} & x^a < x < x^b \\ 0.001 & x = x^b \\ 0 & x > x^b \end{cases}$$

$$(1)$$

where μ is the degree of membership function. Notation α determine the shapes of membership function $\mu(x)$, where α > 0. The larger parameter α get, the less their vagueness becomes. It is necessary that parameter α, which determines the figures of membership functions, should be heuristically and experientially decided by experts.

Figure 1 shows the modified S-curve. The membership function is redefined as $0.001 \leq \mu(x) \leq 0.999$. This range is selected because in manufacturing system the availability of materials need not be always 100% of the requirement. At the same time the availability of materials will not be 0%. Therefore there is a range between xa and xb with $0.001 \leq \mu(x) \leq 0.999$. This concept of range of $\mu(x)$ is used in this research paper.

We rescale the x axis as xa = 0 and xb = 1 in order to find the values of B, C and α. Novakowska (1977) has performed such a rescaling in his work of social sciences.

The values of B, C and α are obtained from Equation (1) as

$$B = 0.999\,(1 + C) \qquad (2)$$

$$\frac{B}{1 + Ce^{\alpha}} = 0.001 \qquad (3)$$

By substituting Equation (2) into Equation (3):

$$\frac{0.999(1 + C)}{1 + Ce^{\alpha}} = 0.001 \qquad (4)$$

Rearranging Equation (4)

$$\alpha = \ln \frac{1}{0.001} \left(\frac{0.998}{C} + 0.999 \right) \qquad (5)$$

Since, B and α depend on C, we require one more condition to get the values for B, C and α

Let, when $x_0 = \dfrac{x^a + x^b}{2}$, $\mu(x_0) = 0.5$; Therefore

$$\frac{B}{1 + Ce^{\frac{\alpha}{2}}} = 0.5 \qquad (6)$$

and hence

$$\alpha = 2 \ln\left(\frac{2B - 1}{C}\right) \qquad (7)$$

Substituting Equation (5) and Equation (6) in to Equation (7), we obtain

$$2 \ln\left(\frac{2(0.999)(1 + C) - 1}{C}\right) = \ln\frac{1}{0.001}\left(\frac{0.998}{C} + 0.999\right) \qquad (8)$$

Rearranging Equation (8) yields

$$(0.998 + 1.998C)^2 = C(998 + 999C) \qquad (9)$$

Solving Equation (9):

$$C = \frac{-994.011992 \pm \sqrt{988059.8402 + 3964.127776}}{1990.015992} \qquad (10)$$

Since C has to be positive, Equation (10) gives $C = 0.001001001$ and from Equation (2) and (5), $B = 1$ and $\alpha = 13.81350956$.

In this paper a real-life industrial problem for product mix selection involving 21 constraints and 8 decision variables has been considered. This problem occurs in production planning in which a decision-maker plays a pivotal role in making decision under a highly fuzzy environment. Decision maker should be aware of his/her level of satisfaction as well as degree of vagueness while making the product mix decision. Thus, the authors have

analyzed using the sigmoid membership function, the fuzziness patterns and fuzzy sensitivity of the solution. In Vasant (2006; 2004) and Abraham, Vasant & Bhattacharya (2008) a linear case of the fuzzy objective function problem is solved by using a linear programming iterative method which is repeatedly applied for different degrees of satisfaction values. In this chapter, a non linear case of the problem is considered and we propose a multi-objective optimization approach in order to capture solutions for different degrees of satisfaction and vagueness factors with a simple run of the algorithm. This multi-objective optimization approach has been proposed by authors in Jimenez, Gomez-Skarmeta & Sanchez (2004a; 2004b) and Jimenez, Cadenas, Sanchez, Gmez-Skarmeta & Verdegay (2006) within a fuzzy optimization general context.

Given this background, the chapter is organized as follows: In the following section a non linear case study in chocolate manufacturing firm is described and its mathematical formulation stated. It followed by proposed a non-linear objective optimization approach for this problem and an ad hoc hybrid evolutionary algorithm. The next section shows results obtained with the proposed non-linear objective evolutionary algorithms and the line search algorithm. Finally, the last section offers the main conclusions and future research direction.

CASE STUDY CHOCOLATE MANUFACTURING

Due to limitations in resources for manufacturing a product and the need to satisfy certain conditions in manufacturing and demand, a problem of fuzziness occurs in industrial systems. This problem occurs also in chocolate manufacturing when deciding a mixed selection of raw materials to produce varieties of products. This is referred

Table 1. Profit coefficients c_i, d_i and e_i (profit function in US $ per 10^3 units)

Product (x_i)	Synonym	c_i	d_i	e_i
x_1 = Milk chocolate, 250g	MC 250	$c_1 = 180$	$d_1 = 0.18$	$e_1 = 0.01$
x_2 = Milk chocolate, 100g	MC 100	$c_2 = 83$	$d_2 = 0.16$	$e_2 = 0.13$
x_3 = Crunchy chocolate, 250g	CC 250	$c_3 = 153$	$d_3 = 0.15$	$e_3 = 0.14$
x_4 = Crunchy chocolate, 100g	CC 100	$c_4 = 72$	$d_4 = 0.14$	$e_4 = 0.12$
x_5 = Chocolate with nuts, 250g	CN 250	$c_5 = 130$	$d_5 = 0.13$	$e_5 = 0.15$
x_6 = Chocolate with nuts, 100g	CN 100	$c_6 = 70$	$d_6 = 0.14$	$e_6 = 0.17$
x_7 = Chocolate candy	CANDY	$c_7 = 208$	$d_7 = 0.21$	$e_7 = 0.18$
x_8 = Chocolate wafer	WAFER	$c_8 = 83$	$d_8 = 0.17$	$e_8 = 0.16$

here to as the product-mix selection problem (Tabucanon, 1996).

There are a number of products to be manufactured by mixing different raw materials and using several varieties of processing. There are limitations in resources of raw materials and facility usage for the varieties of processing. The raw materials and facilities usage required for manufacturing each product are expressed by means of fuzzy coefficients. There are also some constraints imposed by marketing department such as product-mix requirement, main product line requirement and lower and upper limit of demand for each product. It is necessary to obtain maximum profit with certain degree of satisfaction of the decision-maker.

Problem Statement

Optimization techniques are primarily used in production planning problems in order to achieve optimal profit, which maximizes certain objective function by satisfying a number of constraints. The first step in an optimal production planning problems is to formulate the underlying nonlinear programming (NLP) problem by writing the mathematical functions relating to the objective and constraints.

Given a degree of satisfaction value μ, the fuzzy constrained optimization problem can be formulated (Vasant, 2008) as the non linear constrained optimization problem shown below. Table 1, 2, 3 and 4 provide the input data for the Equation (1) in the problem statement.

Maximize $\sum_{i=1}^{8} \left(c_i x_i - d_i x_i^2 - e_i x_i^3 \right)$

Subject to:

$$\sum_{i=1}^{8} \left[a_{ij}^l + \left(\frac{a_{ij}^h - a_{ij}^l}{\alpha} \right) \ln \frac{1}{C} \left(\frac{B}{\mu} - 1 \right) \right] x_i - b_j \le 0, \quad j = 1, 2, \dots, 17$$

$$\sum_{i=7}^{8} r_i x_i - 0.15 \sum_{i=1}^{6} r_i x_i \le 0$$

$x_1 - 0.6 x_2 \le 0$

$x_3 - 0.6 x_4 \le 0$

$x_5 - 0.6 x_6 \le 0$

$0 \le x_i \le \mu i,\ i = 1, 2, \dots, 8$ \hfill (11)

In the above non-linear programming problem, the variable vector x represents a set of variables

Table 2. Raw material and facility usage required (per 10^3 units) ($\tilde{a}_{ij} = [a^l_{ij}, a^h_{ij}]$) and availability ($b_j$)

Material or Facility	MC 250	MC 100	CC 250	CC100	CN250	CN100	Candy	Wafer
Cocoa (kg)	[66, 109]	[26, 44]	[56,9]	[22,37]	[37,62]	[15,25]	[45, 75]	[9, 21]
Milk (kg)	[47, 78]	[19, 31]	[37,6]	[15,25]	[37,62]	[15,25]	[22, 37]	[9, 21]
Nuts (kg)	[0, 0]	[0, 0]	[28,4]	[11,19]	[56,94]	[22,37]	[0, 0]	[0, 0]
Cons. sugar (kg)	[75, 125]	[30, 50]	[66,109]	[26,44]	[56,94]	[22,37]	[157,262]	[18,30]
Flour (kg)	[0, 0]	[0, 0]	[0, 0]	[0, 0]	[0, 0]	[0, 0]	[0, 0]	[54,90]
Alum. foil (ft²)	[375,625]	[0, 0]	[375,625]	[0, 0]	[0, 0]	[0, 0]	[0, 0]	[187,312]
Paper (ft²)	[337,562]	[0, 0]	[337,563]	[0, 0]	[337,562]	[0, 0]	[0, 0]	[0, 0]
Plastic (ft²)	[45, 75]	[95, 150]	[45, 75]	[90,150]	[45,75]	[90, 150]	[1200,200]	[187,312]
Cooking (ton-hours)	[0.4, 0.6]	[0.1, 0.2]	[0.3, 0.5]	[0.1, 0.2]	[0.3,0.4]	[0.1, 0.2]	[0.4, 0.7]	[0.1,0.12]
Mixing (ton-hours)	[0, 0]	[0, 0]	[0.1, 0.2]	[0.04,0.07]	[0.2, 0.3]	[0.07,0.12]	[0, 0]	[0, 0]
Forming (ton-hours)	[0.6, 0.9]	[0.2, 0.4]	[0.6, 0.9]	[0.2, 0.4]	[0.6, 0.9]	[0.2, 0.4]	[0.7, 1.1]	[0.3, 0.4]
Grinding (ton-hours)	[0, 0]	[0, 0]	[0.2, 0.3]	[0.07,0.12]	[0, 0]	[0, 0]	[0, 0]	[0, 0]
Wafer making (ton-hours)	[0, 0]	[0, 0]	[0, 0]	[0, 0]	[0, 0]	[0, 0]	[0, 0]	[0.2, 0.4]
Cutting (hours)	[0.07,0.2]	[0.07,0.1]	[0.07,0.12]	[0.07,0.12]	[0.07,0.12]	[0.07,0.12]	[0.15,0.25]	[0, 0]
Packaging1 (hours)	[0.2, 0.3]	[0, 0]	[0.2, 0.3]	[0, 0]	[0.2, 0.3]	[0, 0]	[0, 0]	[0, 0]
Packaging2 (hours)	[0.04,0.6]	[0.2, 0.4]	[0.04,0.06]	[0.2, 0.4]	[0.04,0.06]	[0.2, 0.4]	[1.9, 3.1]	[0.1, 0.2]
Labour (hours)	[0.2, 0.4]	[0.2, 0.4]	[0.2, 0.4]	[0.2, 0.4]	[0.2, 0.4]	[0.2, 0.4]	[1.9, 3.1]	[1.9, 3.1]

Table 3. Demand (u_k) and revenues/sales (r_k) in US $ per 10^3 units

Product (x_k)	Synonym	Demand (u_k)	Revenues/Sales (r_k)
x_1 = Milk chocolate, 250g	MC 250	u_1 = 500	r_1 = 375
x_2 = Milk chocolate, 100g	MC 100	u_2 = 800	r_2 = 150
x_3 = Crunchy chocolate, 250g	CC 250	u_3 = 400	r_3 = 400
x_4 = Crunchy chocolate, 100g	CC 100	u_4 = 600	r_4 = 160
x_5 = Chocolate with nuts, 250g	CN 250	u_5 = 300	r_5 = 420
x_6 = Chocolate with nuts, 100g	CN 100	u_6 = 500	r_6 = 175
x_7 = Chocolate candy	CANDY	u_7 = 200	r_7 = 400
x_8 = Chocolate wafer	WAFER	u_8 = 400	r_8 = 150

x_i, i = 1, 2,…, 8. The above optimization problem contains eight continuous variables and 21 inequality constraints. A test point x_i satisfying constrains is called feasible, if not infeasible. The set satisfying constrains is called the feasible domain. The aim of the optimization is to maximize the total production profit for the industrial production planning problems.

HYBRID GENETIC ALGORITHM FOR SOLVING OPTIMIZATION PROBLEMS

Genetic algorithms (GAs) have been used successfully to find optimal or near-optimal solutions for a wide variety of optimization problems (Gen and Cheng, 1996; Goldberg, 1989) since its introduction by Holland (1992). GAs is intelligent

Table 4. Raw material availability (b)

Material or Facility	Availability
Cocoa (kg)	100000
Milk (kg)	120000
Nuts (kg)	60000
Cons. sugar (kg)	200000
Flour (kg)	20000
Alum. foil (ft^2)	500000
Paper (ft^2)	500000
Plastic (ft^2)	500000
Cooking (ton-hours)	1000
Mixing (ton-hours)	200
Forming (ton-hours)	1500
Grinding (ton-hours)	200
Wafer making (ton-hours)	100
Cutting (hours)	400
Packaging 1 (hours)	400
Packaging 2 (hours)	1200
Labour (hours)	1000

stochastic optimization techniques based on the mechanism of natural selection and genetics. GAs start with an initial set of solutions, called population. Each solution in the population is called a chromosome (or individual), which represents a point in the search space. The chromosomes are evolved through successive iterations, called generations, by genetic operators (selection, crossover and mutation) that mimic the principles of natural evolution. In a GA, a fitness value is assigned to each individual according to a problem- specific objective function. Generation by generation, the new individuals, called offspring, are created and survive with chromosomes in the current population, called parents, to form a new population.

GAs often performs well in global search, but they are relatively slow and trapped in converging to a local optimal (Wang & Wu, 2004). On the other hand, the local improvement methods such as gradient based (Line Search, LS) procedures, can find the local optimum in a small region of the search space, but they are typically poor in

a global search. Therefore, various strategies of hybridization have been suggested to improve performance of simple GAs (Cheng & Gen, 1996; Wang & Wu, 2004). These hybridizations usually involve incorporating a neighborhood search (NS) heuristic as a local improver into a basic GA loop of recombination and selection. That is, local improver is applied to each newly generated offspring to move it to a local optimum one before inserting it into the enlarged population (Turabieh, Sheta & Vasant, 2007). In this manner, GA is used to perform global exploration among a population (i.e. as a diversification tool), while the local improver is used to perform local exploitation around chromosomes (i.e. as an intensification tool). The general structure of the proposed hybrid genetic algorithm (HGA) for the problem is described as follows:

- **Step 1:** Initialization: Create an initial population of population size solutions using constructive heuristics and randomly generated solutions.
- **Step 2:** Recombination: Recombine the solutions in the current population using genetic operators to create new individuals.
- **Step 3:** Improvement: Apply the local improvement method (Line Search, LS) to replace each offspring with a local optimum one, and insert the improved offspring into the enlarged population.
- **Step 4:** Selection: Select population size solutions from the chromosomes in the enlarged population to form the next generation, and determine the best solution in the new population.
- **Step 5:** Iteration: Repeat Steps 2–4 until the termination condition reaches.

Therefore, the best solution in the last population will be final solution for the problem that ideally may be an optimal or near-optimal solution.

However, due to high computational burden of the optimal solution method, an efficient and effective hybrid genetic algorithm is proposed in this research work. In HGA, four following ways of hybridization are used:

- Incorporating simple and effective uniform heuristics into initialization step to generate good initial population.
- Incorporating two effective mutation operator of adaptive feasible and crossover operator of arithmetic to complete continuous solution of the problem with constraints.
- Incorporating an efficient neighborhood search method of gradient based (Line Search, LS) as an add-on extra to the main GA algorithms to obtain optimal solutions.
- Incorporating an enumeration method into fitness evaluation function in the stopping criteria for complete continuous solution of the problem.

Computational results indicate that the performance of HGA is very promising, and it outperforms the optimal enumeration method in particular at medium and large-scaled problems in terms of computation times and also solution quality at majority of the test problems.

L. "Dave" Davis states in the Handbook of Genetic Algorithms, "Traditional genetic algorithms, although robust, are generally not the most successful optimization algorithm on any particular domain" (1991). Davis argues that hybridizing genetic algorithms with the most successful optimization methods for particular problems gives one the best of both worlds: correctly implemented, these algorithms should do no worst than the (usually more traditional) method with which the hybridizing is done. Of course, it also introduces the additional computational overhead of a population based search.

Davis often uses real valued encodings instead of binary encodings, and employs, "recombination operators" that may be domain specific. Other researchers, such as Michalewicz (1993) also use non-binary encodings and specialized operations

in combination with a genetic based model of search. Muhlenbein (1991) takes a similar opportunistic view of hybridization. In a description of a parallel genetic algorithm Muhlenbein (1991) states, after the initial population is created, "Each individual does local hill-climbing". Furthermore, after each off spring is created, "The off spring does local hill-climbing".

Experimental researchers and theoreticians are particularly divided on the issue of hybridization. By adding hill-climbing or hybridizing with some other optimization methods, learning is being added to the evolution process. Coding the learned information back onto the chromosome means that the search utilizes a form of Lamarckian evolution. The chromosomes improved by local hill-climbing or other methods are placed in the genetic population and allowed to compete for reproductive opportunities.

The main criticism is that if we wish to preserve the schema processing capabilities of the genetic algorithm, then Lamarckian learning should not be used. Changing information in the offspring inherited from the parents results in a loss of inherited schemata. This alters the statistical information about hyper-plane partitions that is implicitly contained in the population. Therefore using local optimization to improve each offspring undermines the genetic algorithm's ability to search via hyper-plane sampling.

Despite the theoretical objections, hybrid genetic algorithms typically do well at optimization tasks. There may be several reasons for this. First, the hybrid genetic algorithm is hill-climbing from multiple points in the search space. Unless the objective function is severely multimodal it may be likely that some strings (offspring) will be in the basin of attraction of the global solution, in which case hill-climbing is a fast and effective form of search. Secondly, a hybrid strategy impairs hyper-plane sampling, but does not disrupt it entirely. For example, using local optimization to improve the initial population of strings only biases the initial hyper-plane samples, but does not interfere with subsequent hyper-plane sampling. Thirdly, in general hill-climbing may find a small number of significant improvements, but may not dramatically change the offspring. In this case, the effects on schemata and hyper-plane sampling may be minimal.

In a gradient-based mathematical programming approach the optimization algorithm proceeds with the following steps: (i) Evaluation of displacements and stresses. (ii) Computation of sensitivities by perturbing each design variable by a small amount. (iii) Solution of the optimization problem and update the design of the structure. The most time-consuming part of this process is related to the sensitivity analysis phase, which is an important ingredient of all mathematical programming optimization methods and may consume a large part of the total computational effort (Deb, 2001) on the other hand, the application of evolutionary algorithm that are based on probabilistic searching, such as genetic algorithm and evolutionary strategies, do not need gradient information and therefore avoid performing the computationally expensive sensitivity analysis step.

Mathematical programming methods, such as the sequential quadratic programming (SQP) approach, make use of local curvature information derived from linearization of the original functions by using their derivatives with respect to the design variables. The linearization is performed at points obtained in the process of optimization to construct an approximate model of the initial problem. These methods present a satisfactory local rate convergence, but they cannot assure that the global optimum can be obtained. They do although assure if the problem is strictly convex. On the other hand, evolutionary algorithms are in general more robust, efficient and present a better global behavior than the mathematical programming approaches. They may suffer, however, from a slow rate of convergence towards the global optimum and do not guarantee convergence to the global optimum (Lagaros, Papadrakakis & Kokossalakis, 2002).

Production planning optimization problems are characterized by various objective and constraints function, which are generally non-linear functions of the decision variables. These functions are usually implicit, discontinuous and non-convex. The mathematical formulation of production planning optimization problems with respect to the decision variables, the objective and constraint functions depend on the type of the application. However, all optimization problems can be expressed in standard mathematical terms as a non-linear programming problem (NLP), which is general form can be stated as follows:

- Max $z(x)$
- Subject to $h_j(x) \leq 0$ $j=1,\ldots,m$
- With $x_i^l \leq x_i \leq x_i^u$ $i=1,\ldots,n$

Where, x is the vector of decision variables, z(x) is the objective function to be maximized, $h_i(x)$ are the behavioral constraints, x_i^l and x_i^u is the lower and the upper bounds of respective decision variables x_i. Equality constraints are rarely imposed in this type of problems except in some cases for decision variable linking. Whenever they are used they are treated for simplicity as a set of two inequality constraints.

In this research work the efficiency of various evolutionary algorithms is investigated in an industrial production planning optimization problems. Furthermore, in order to benefit from the advantages of both methodologies, combination of evolutionary algorithm with mathematical programming (Line Search (LS)) are strongly examined in an attempt to increase further the robustness as well as the intelligent computational efficiency of the optimization procedure. The numerical real life tests presented demonstrate the computational advantages of the discussed methods, which become more pronounced in large-scale and computationally intensive optimization problems.

EXPERIMENTAL RESULTS

In this section, the hybrid genetic algorithms with line search method been applied in solving industrial production planning problems. GA can do global search in entire space, but there is no way for exploring the search space within the convergence area of generated GA. Therefore, it is sometimes impossible or insufficient for GA to locate an optimal solution in the optimization problems with complex search spaces and constraints. To overcome this weakness, hybridization of GA with conventional search techniques of line search adopted in this section.

The proposed hybrid GA line search algorithms and the detailed procedure for implementation of HGA is as follows.

- **Step 1:** Initial population: Generate initial population randomly.
- **Step 2:** Genetic operators:
  ○ Selection: stochastic uniform
  ○ Crossover: arithmetic crossover operator
  ○ Mutation: Adaptive feasible mutation operator
- **Step 3:** Evaluation:
  ○ Best offspring and fitness function.
- **Step 4:** Stop condition:
  ○ If a pre-defined maximum generation number, time limit, fitness limit reached or an optimal solution is located during genetic search process, then stop; otherwise, go to Step 2.
- **Step 5:** Continue with line search techniques.
- **Step 6:** End

The following is the typical commands

- Parameter setting:
- Population: Double vector
- Population size: 100
- Fitness scaling: Rank

- Selection: Stochastic uniform
- Reproduction: Elite count 2 and Crossover fraction 0.8
- Mutation: Adaptive feasible
- Crossover: Arithmetic
- Migration: Forward
- Hybrid function: FMINCON (Code for LS method)

Stopping criteria: Generations 10,000; Time limit Inf; Fitness limit Inf and Function tolerance 1e-006.

Output function: Fitness value and Decision variables

Figure 2 depicts the fitness value for $\alpha = 13.813$ respect to level of satisfaction. Table 5 reports the feasible solution for the decision variables and the CPU computational time.

The best optimal fitness value is 200116.4. Total CPU time for running GA only is 18.83 seconds. Average CPU time for running GA is 1.71 seconds. Total CPU time for running GA and FMINCON is 60 seconds. The result for optimal fitness function for HGA is similar to the FMINCON result even though it is an improved from GA technique. Moreover the values for the decision variable x_8 still zero for $\gamma = 0.001$ to $\gamma = 0.9$.

Figure 3 depicts the performance of hybrid GA and LS for the best fitness value respect to eight decision variables. It's clearly observed that x_2 is the best decision variables from the result obtained in Figure 2. This feasible solutions are obtained for the $\alpha = 13.813509$ only. It's possible to carry out further experiment to investigate for other α values.

Figure 4 presents the outcome of the best feasible solutions obtained by the hybrid GA-LS techniques. Figure 3 clearly revealed that x_2 is the best feasible solution. This is one of the important contributions of this research work for the decision makers and implementers to select the best feasible decision variable in order to make a very highly productive production planning systems.

Figure 2. Fitness value versus level of satisfaction (γ)

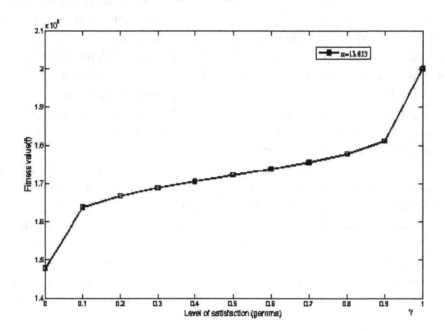

Table 5. Optimal value for objective function

γ	x_1	x_2	x_3	x_4	x_5	x_6	x_7	x_8	f	Time(s)
0.001	246.8	411.4	205.7	342.8	134.3	223.9	120.6	0.00	147712.9	1.48
0.1	284.8	474.7	239.2	398.7	148.8	248.0	150.4	0.00	163731.6	1.85
0.2	292.5	487.6	246.1	410.1	151.8	253.0	156.7	0.00	166763.3	1.69
0.3	297.9	496.5	250.8	418.0	153.8	256.4	161.2	0.00	168830.5	1.75
0.4	302.5	504.1	254.8	424.7	155.6	259.3	165.1	0.00	170548.7	1.69
0.5	306.8	511.7	258.6	431.0	157.2	262.1	168.8	0.00	172146.4	1.70
0.6	311.2	518.6	262.5	437.5	158.9	264.9	172.6	0.00	173763.9	1.69
0.7	316.1	526.9	266.9	444.8	160.8	268.1	176.9	0.00	175548.3	1.69
0.8	322.4	537.4	272.4	454.1	163.3	272.1	182.4	0.00	177754.9	1.70
0.9	332.3	553.9	281.2	468.6	167.1	278.5	191.3	0.00	181132.7	1.70
0.99	414.3	690.6	354.0	590.0	200.0	333.4	200.0	54.5	200116.4	1.89

Further investigation was carried out for various γ values from 1 to 37. Figure 5 depicts the simulation results for fitness function respect to various level of satisfaction.

The best optimal value for the fitness function is 200116 for all the α values from 1 to 37 at $\gamma = 0.99$.

A very through further investigation carried out for α values from 39 to 57. Figure 6 depicts this simulation result.

The above solution for $\alpha = 39$ to $\alpha = 57$ can be represented in the Figure 7.

Figure 8 describes the 3D mesh plot solution for the fitness function respect to vagueness factor and level of satisfaction.

Figure 3. Fitness value versus decision variables

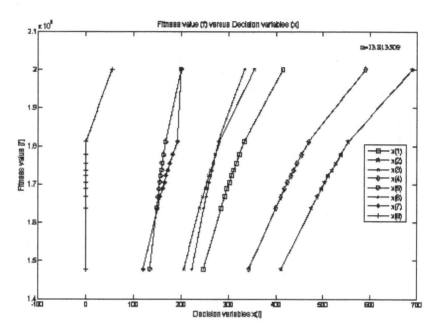

Figure 4. Values of decision variables respect to eight decision variables

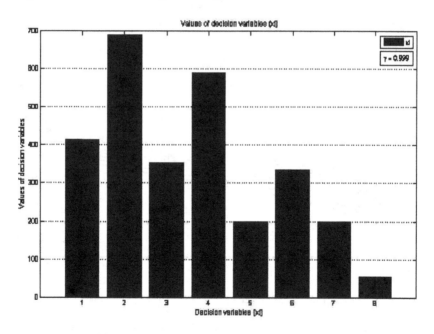

Figures 9, 10 and 11 presents the 2D view of the solutions obtained in the Figure 8. Figure 9 shows the performance of fitness values respect to vagueness factor α. Figure 10 depicts the performance of fitness values versus level of satisfaction. Figure 11 clearly indicates the removal of solutions that trapped or stuck by the GA techniques alone. This is one of the major contributions of this piece of

Figure 5. Fitness value versus level of satisfaction (γ)

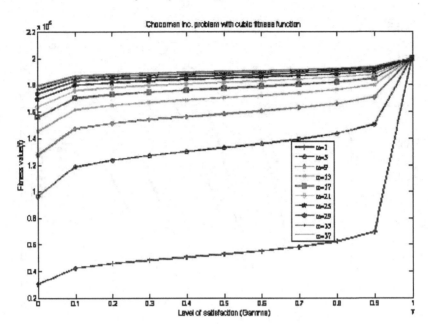

Figure 6. Fitness value versus level of satisfaction (γ)

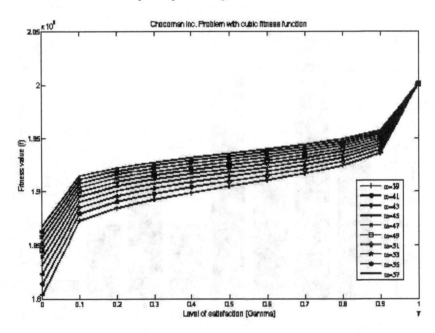

research work. The novelty and the originally of this hybrid GA-LS method is to provide the best near global optimal solution by escaping from the local optimal solution. In this research work the near global optimal solution for the feasible decision variables and fitness values are successfully obtained.

Figure 7. Fitness value versus level of satisfaction (γ)

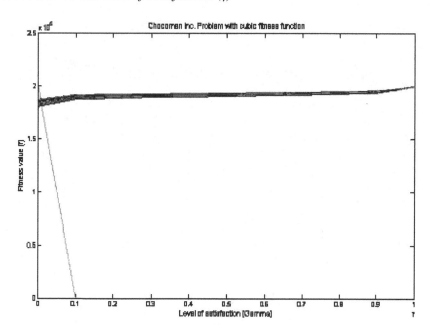

Figure 8. Fitness value versus vagueness factor and level of satisfaction (γ)

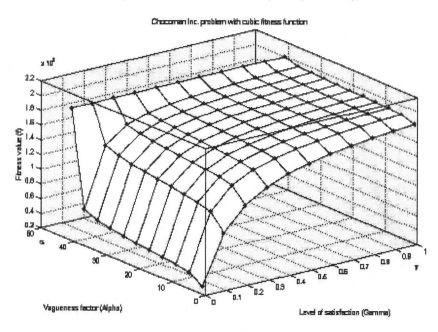

Figure 8 provides holistic solutions for the decision makers and implementers. This over all solutions will be very useful for the decision makers in order to make a refined and optimal best decision in an uncertain environment. A contour plot of 2D in Figures 9, 10 and 11 also will be an added value in the form of holistic solutions for the decision makers and implementers in order to

Figure 9. Fitness value versus vagueness factor (α)

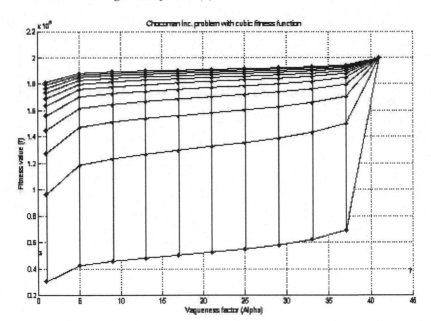

Figure 10. Fitness value versus level of satisfaction (γ)

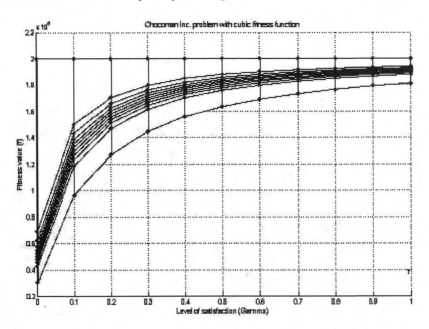

make an appropriate decision with some partial information in an uncertain situation. There is a very high flexibility and convenience in the decision making process due to alpha value factor in the optimization problems. The decision makers have to choose a very appropriate value as per the environment in an intelligent manner in order to obtain the best optimal solution with highest profit value.

Figure 11. Vagueness factor (α) versus level of satisfaction (γ)

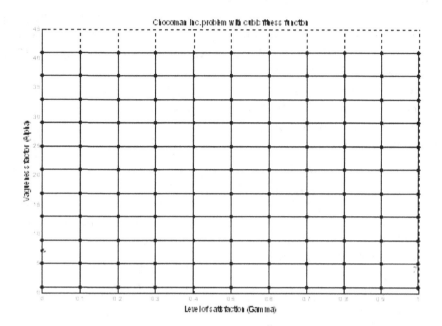

CONCLUSION AND FUTURE RESEARCH DIRECTIONS

The hybrid genetic algorithm with line search approach has improved the fitness value obtained by genetic algorithms alone. The proposed hybrid optimization approach proved to be extremely robust and excellent efficient method for non-linear industrial production planning problems. Both GA-LS manage to converge to better realistic solutions than those achieved by GA or LS alone at a reduced computational effort compared to the LS procedure. The combination of GA with LS is particularly promising in bad initial solutions due the speedy convergence of GA towards the neighborhood of the optimum and the property of LS to compute quickly the nearest optimum once in the neighborhood of the solution. However, the best optimal fitness function value obtained by hybrid genetic algorithms approach is similar to line search approach. There is no improvement on the value of the decision variables in the hybrid genetic algorithm approach compare to line search approach. Therefore, the author strongly believes that there should be another hybrid approach such as particle swarm optimization, ant colony optimization, artificial immune system, neural network, fuzzy logic, tabu search and evolutionary computation (Genetic programming, Evolutionary strategy & Genetic algorithms) to improve the solution for the decision variables in real world situation. The hybrid optimization techniques of meta-heuristic approaches with classical optimization approaches will be great added advantages for solving industrial production management problems in a fuzzy environment. Further research will investigate these real world solutions.

ACKNOWLEDGMENT

The author sincerely would like to thank the referees' for their valuable and constructive comments and suggestions for the improvement of the quality of this chapter.

REFERENCES

Abraham, A., Vasant, P., & Bhattacharya, A. (2008). Neuro-Fuzzy approximations of multi-criteria decision-making QFD methodology. In Kahraman, C. (Ed.), *Fuzzy multi-criteria decision making theory and applications with recent developments* (pp. 301–324). Berlin: Springer. doi:10.1007/978-0-387-76813-7_12

Ali, F. M. (1998). A differential equation approach to fuzzy non-linear programming problems. In Fuzzy Sets and Systems, (pp. 57-61).

Bellman, R. E., & Zadeh, L. A. (1970). Decision Making in a fuzzy environment. In Management Science, (pp. 141-164).

Bhattacharya, A., Abraham, A., & Vasant, P. (2008). FMS selection under disparate level-of-satisfaction of decision making using an intelligent Fuzzy-MCDM- Model. In Kahraman, C. (Ed.), *Fuzzy multi-criteria decision making theory and applications with recent developments* (pp. 263–280). Berlin: Springer. doi:10.1007/978-0-387-76813-7_10

Carlsson, C., & Korhonen, P. (1986). A parametric approach to fuzzy linear programming. *Fuzzy Sets and Systems*, *20*, 17–30. doi:10.1016/S0165-0114(86)80028-8

Davis, L. D. (1991). *Handbook of Genetic Algorithms*. New York: Van Nostrand Reinhold.

Deb, K. (2001). *Multi-objective Optimization Using Evolutionary Algorithms*. New York: John Wiley & Sons.

Ekel, P., Pedrycz, W., & Schinzinger, R. (1998). A general approach to solving a wide class of fuzzy optimization problems. In Fuzzy Sets and Systems, (pp. 49-66).

Elamvazuthi, I., Sinnadurai, R., Khan, M. A., & Vasant, P. (2009). Fruit sorting using fuzzy logic techniques. In N. Barsoum, A. H. Hakim & P. Vasant (Eds.), *Proceedings of the 2nd International Conference on Power Control and Optimization* (pp. 225-230). New York: American Institute of Physics.

Gen, M., & Cheng, R. (1996). *Genetic Algorithms and Engineering Design*. New York: Wiley. doi:10.1002/9780470172254

Goguen, J. A. (1969). The logic of inexact concepts. *Syntheses*, *19*, 325–373. doi:10.1007/BF00485654

Goldberg, D. E. (1989). *Genetic Algorithms in Search Optimization and Machine Learning*. Toronto: Addison Wesley.

Hannan, E. L. (1981). Linear programming with multiple fuzzy goals. *Fuzzy Sets and Systems*, *6*, 235–248. doi:10.1016/0165-0114(81)90002-6

Holland, J. H. (1975). *Adaptation in Natural and Artificial Systems*. Ann Arbor, MI: University of Michigan Press.

Hu, C. F., & Fang, S. C. (1999). Solving fuzzy inequalities with piecewise linear membership functions. *IEEE Transactions on Fuzzy Systems*, *7*, 230–235. doi:10.1109/91.755403

Inuiguchi, M., Ichihashi, H., & Kume, Y. (1990). A solution algorithm for fuzzy linear programming with piecewise linear membership functions. *Fuzzy Sets and Systems*, *34*, 15–31. doi:10.1016/0165-0114(90)90123-N

Jimenez, F. G'omez-Skarmeta, A. F., & S'anchez, G. (2004a). A Multiobjective Evolutionary approach for Nonlinear Constrained Optimization with Fuzzy Costs. *IEEE International Conference on Systems, Man & Cybernetics (SMC'04)*, The Hague, The Netherlands.

Jimenez, F., & Cadenas, J. M., S'anchez, G., Gmez-Skarmeta, A. F. & Verdegay, J. L. (2006). Multi-objective evolutionary computation and fuzzy optimization. *International Journal of Approximate Reasoning*, 59–75. doi:10.1016/j.ijar.2006.02.001

Jimenez, F., Gomez-Skarmeta, A. F., & Sanchez, G. (2004b). Nonlinear Optimization with Fuzzy Constraints by Multi-Objective Evolutionary Algorithms. In *Advances in Soft Computing* (pp. 713–722). Computational Intelligence, Theory and Applications.

Jimenez, F., Sanchez, G., & Vasant, P. (2008). Fuzzy optimization via multi-objective evolutionary computation for chocolate manufacturing. In Kahraman, C. (Ed.), *Fuzzy multi-criteria decision making theory and applications with recent developments* (pp. 523–538). Berlin: Springer. doi:10.1007/978-0-387-76813-7_20

Lagaros, N. D., Papadrakakis, M., & Kokossalakis, G. (2002). Structural optimization using evolutionary algorithms. *Computers & Structures, 80*, 571–589. doi:10.1016/S0045-7949(02)00027-5

Leberling, H. (1981). On finding compromise solutions in multicriteria problems using the fuzzy min-operator. *Fuzzy Sets and Systems, 6*, 105–118. doi:10.1016/0165-0114(81)90019-1

Michalewicz, Z. (1993). A hierarchy of evolution programs: An experimental study. *Evolutionary Computation, 1*(1), 51–76. doi:10.1162/evco.1993.1.1.51

Muhlenbein, H. (1991). Evolution in Time and Space. In Rawlins, G. (Ed.), *The Parallel Genetic Algorithm and Foundations of Genetic Algorithms* (pp. 316–337). San Francisco: Morgan Kaufmann.

Nowakowska, N. (1977). Methodological problems of measurement of fuzzy concepts in the social sciences. *Behavioral Science, 22*, 107–115. doi:10.1002/bs.3830220205

Peidro, D., & Vasant, P. (2009). Fuzzy multi-objective transportation planning with modified S-curve membership function. In N. Barsoum, A. H. Hakim & P. Vasant (Eds.), *Proceedings of the 2nd International Conference on Power Control and Optimization* (pp. 231-239). New York: American Institute of Physics.

Ramik, J., & Vlach, M. (2002). A unified Approach Based on Fuzzy Relations. In *Fuzzy Optimization and Decision Making* (pp. 335–346). Fuzzy Mathematical Programming.

Sakawa, M. (1983). Interactive computer program for fuzzy linear programming with multiple objectives. *J. Man-Machine Stud, 18*, 489–503. doi:10.1016/S0020-7373(83)80022-4

Sengupta, A., Vasant, P., & Andreeski, C. J. (2008). Fuzzy optimization with robust logistic membership function: A case study in home textile industry. In *Proceedings of the 17th World Congress, The International Federation of Automatic Control*, Seoul, Korea, (pp. 278-283).

Tabucanon, M. T. (1996). Multi objective programming for industrial engineers. In *Mathematical programming for industrial engineers* (pp. 487–542). New York: Marcel Dekker, Inc.

Tanaka, H., Okuda, T. & Asai, K. (1974). On fuzzy mathematical programming. *Journal of Cybernetics*, 37-46.

Tsoulos, I. G., & Vasant, P. (2009). Product mix selection using and evolutionary technique. In N. Barsoum, A. H. Hakim & P. Vasant (Eds.), *Proceedings of the 2nd International Conference on Power Control and Optimization,* (pp. 240-249). New York: American Institute of Physics.

Turabieh, H., Sheta, A., & Vasant, P. (2007). Hybrid optimization genetic algorithm (HOGA) with interactive evolution to solve constraint optimization problems for production systems. *International Journal of Computational Science, 1*(4), 395–406.

Vasant, P. (2003). Application of Fuzzy Linear Programming in Production Planning. *Fuzzy Optimization and Decision Making, 3*, 229–241. doi:10.1023/A:1025094504415

Vasant, P. (2004). Industrial production planning using interactive fuzzy linear programming. *International Journal of Computational Intelligence and Applications*, 13–26. doi:10.1142/S1469026804001173

Vasant, P. (2006). Fuzzy production planning and its application to decision making. *Journal of Intelligent Manufacturing*, 5–12. doi:10.1007/s10845-005-5509-x

Vasant, P. (2008). *Hybrid optimization techniques for industrial production planning*. Ph.D Thesis, University Putra Malaysia, Malaysia.

Vasant, P., & Barsoum, N. N. (2006). Fuzzy optimization of units products in mix-products selection problem using FLP approach. *Soft Computing Journal, 10*(2), 144–151. doi:10.1007/s00500-004-0437-9

Vasant, P., & Barsoum, N. N. (2008). Hybrid genetic algorithms and line search method for industrial production planning with non linear fitness function. In N. Barsoum, S. Uatrongjit & P. Vasant, (Eds.), *International Conference on Power Control and Optimization* (pp. 278-283). New York: American Institute of Physics.

Vasant, P., & Barsoum, N. N. (2009). Hybrid simulated annealing and genetic algorithms for industrial production management problems. In A. H. Hakim & P. Vasant (Eds.), *Proceedings of the 2nd International Conference on Power Control and Optimization* (pp. 254-261). New York: American Institute of Physics.

Vasant, P., Barsoum, N. N., Khatun, S., & Abbas, Z. (2008). Solving non linear optimization problems with adaptive genetic algorithms approach. In *Proceedings of the 9th Asia Pacific Industrial Engineering & Management Systems Conference (APIEMS)*, Bali- Indonesia (pp. 1549-1560).

Vasant, P., Bhattacharya, A., & Abraham, A. (2008). Measurement of level-of-satisfaction of decision maker in intelligent Fuzy-MCDM theory: A generalized approach. In Kahraman, C. (Ed.), *Fuzzy multi-criteria decision making theory and applications with recent developments* (pp. 235–262). Berlin: Springer. doi:10.1007/978-0-387-76813-7_9

Wang, H. F., & Wu, K. Y. (2004). Hybrid genetic algorithm for optimization problems with permutation property. *Computers & Operations Research, 31*(14), 2453–2471. doi:10.1016/S0305-0548(03)00198-9

Watada, J. (1997). Fuzzy portfolio selection and its applications to decision making. *Tatra Mountains Mathematics Publication, 13*, 219–248.

Zadeh, L. A. (1971). Similarity relations and fuzzy orderings. *Information Sciences, 3*, 177–206. doi:10.1016/S0020-0255(71)80005-1

Zimmermann, H. J. (1976). Description and optimization of fuzzy systems. *International Journal of General Systems, 2*, 209–215. doi:10.1080/03081077608547470

Zimmermann, H. J. (1978). Fuzzy programming and linear programming with several objective functions. *Fuzzy Sets and Systems, 1*, 45–55. doi:10.1016/0165-0114(78)90031-3

Chapter 9
Automatic Test Sequence Generation for State Transition Testing via Ant Colony Optimization

Praveen Ranjan Srivastava
Birla Institute of Technology and Science (BITS), India

Baby
Birla Institute of Technology and Science (BITS), India

ABSTRACT

Software testing is a key part of software development life cycle. Due to time, cost and other circumstances, exhaustive testing is not feasible, that's why there is need to automate the testing process. Generation of the automated and effective test suit is a very difficult task in the software testing process. Effective test suite can decrease the overall cost of testing as well as increase the probability of finding defects in software systems. Testing effectiveness can be achieved by the State Transition Testing which is commonly used in, real time, embedded and web-based kind of software system. State transition testing focuses upon the testing of transitions from one state of an object to other states. The tester's main job is to test all the possible transitions in the system. This chapter proposed an Ant Colony Optimization technique for automated and fully coverage state-transitions in the system. Through proposed algorithm all the transitions are easily traversed at least once in the test-sequence.

INTRODUCTION

Software development markets are highly competitive; therefore it is a critical task to provide the quality software product to the customer within the limited time period. Software testing is the key by using which tester/organization can gain the confidence of the customer. A primary purpose of testing is to detect software errors so that defects may be discovered and corrected (Aditya p Mathur, 2007). Due to the time and cost it is not possible to test the software manually and fix the defects (Somerville Ian, 2008). Thus the use of test automation plays very important role in the software testing proces (Pressman, 2005). Nowadays Artificial Intelligence

DOI: 10.4018/978-1-61520-809-8.ch009

(AI) methodologies are changing the nature of test automation process (Phil McMinn, 2004). Academicians and researchers are using AI approach in the area of software testing for better accuracy. The application of AI techniques in Software Engineering (SE) is an emerging area of research (Briand, L. C, 2002, and Pedrycz, W., &Peters, J. F, 1998). In AI approach, researchers are using Ant Colony Optimization (ACO), Genetic Algorithm (GA), Tabu search (TB) techniques etc (Phil McMinn, 2004, Mark Harman 2007). These terminologies are known as metaheuristic approach(Praveen Ranjan Srivastava,2008) and these approaches are being used in various processes of the software testing like test sequence generation, automation of testing etc. (Huaizhong LI and C. Peng LAM, 2005, & Mark Harman, 2007).

The quality of test data that we evaluate is based on the number of coverage for behavior of any software. The coverage of test data can be defined by many criteria. Testing of states is not sufficient (Offutt and Abdurazik, 1999 & Sabri A. Mahmoud, 2005), particularly for those systems which have large number of states (mainly real time system). Minimum acceptable strategy of software testing process for real time system is all-states, all-events, all-actions and all-transitions exercised at least once in the test suite (Offutt and Abdurazik, 1999 & Sabri A. Mahmoud, 2005, and Aditya P Mathur 2007). Literature survey reveals that under state transition testing process, tester focus upon the states, actions, events and transitions rather than states only (Sabri A. Mahmoud, 2005). UML State-transition diagrams are good tool to represent the state of the software under test (OMG, 2003). This chapter purposes an algorithm which uses an ACO optimization technique to generate the automatic state –transition test sequence, which is a strong level of software coverage.

An ACO algorithm (Yuan Zhan and John A. Clark, 2006) is a probabilistic technique for solving computational problems which can be used to find good paths through graph. It is inspired by the behavior of ants in finding paths from

their colony to food (Marco Dorigoa and Thomas Stutzle, 2005). Huaizhong LI and C. Peng Lam, 2005 uses ACO to generate test sequences for state-based software testing. They also tried to generate test data on the basis of state coverage. Because the present market is highly competitive, it is the need of software organizations to provide good quality software product to the customer within the estimated budget, here a strong level of coverage testing technique is essential.

This chapter uses UML State-transition diagrams (OMG, 2003) for generating test suite. An UML State-transition diagram describe all of the states that an object can have, the events under which an object changes state (transitions), the conditions that must be fulfilled before the transition will occur (guards), and the activities undertaken during the life of an object (actions). State-transition diagrams are very useful for describing the behavior of individual objects over the full set of use cases that affect those objects (Lee Copeland, 2004).

The benefits of the proposed approach are: (1) manual generated test data is not always reliable. On the other hand automatic test data is reliable, because human beings are the most dynamic and error introducing entity. (2) State-transition based testing provides all state coverage. (3) It provides all event coverage. (4) It provides all transition coverage and (5) UML state-transition diagram created, which shows the static behavior of the software.

BACKGROUND WORK

There are three main activities associated with software testing: (1) Optimal test data generation (Biswal, B. N, 2008), (2) Execution of those optimal set of test data and (3) Analysis of the of test results.(Huaizhong LI and C. Peng LAM, 2005), The key question addressed in the area of software testing is how to select optimal test cases with high degree of defects. Since we know exhaustive testing is not possible in terms of cost, time and other resources, that's why there is a key question is when and how do we determine whether testing has been conducted adequately or not. In order to achieve high quality of software with minimum cost and minimum time, any kind of extensive testing would require the automation of testing process. Of the above three activities mentioned above, test data generation and evaluation of test results are the most labour intensive and thus would benefit most from automation. (Huaizhong LI and C. Peng LAM, 2005)

The procedure of generation of test data involves activities for producing a set of input test data that satisfies a chosen testing criterion according to client need or specification. We can generate test case manually, but this process is too laborious and much time taking task.. A cost-effective approach is to automate the test data generation while ensuring that the given criterion is met. (Huaizhong LI and C. Peng LAM, 2005)

It has been identified that one of the SE areas with a more prolific use of AI techniques is software testing. The focus of these techniques involves the applications of genetic algorithms (GAs). (Raluca Lefticaru and Florentin Ipate, 2008) proposes coverage of state based testing using fitness function based on genetic algorithm, but the work suggested as a week level adequacy criteria.

P. McMinn and M. Holcomb, (2003) proposes, the chaining approach. In this approach, a sequence of statements, involving internal variables, which need to be executed prior to the test goal. By executing these statements, information previously unavailable to the search can be obtained, possibly used to guide it into potentially promising and unexplored areas of the test object's input domain. A GA-based test data generation technique has been proposed (Chartchai Doungsa-ard, Keshav Dahal, Alamgir Hossain, and Taratip Suwannasart, 2007) to generate test data from UML state diagram, so that test data can be generated before coding. They used fitness function regarding coverage for transition level, since they select only one best

solution, not all transitions can be reached in the diagrams with the final state. Due to performance of generating test data and a concern of size of test data set, heuristic techniques are applied for test data generation. GADGET (Michael, C., G. McGraw, and M.A. Schatz, 2001) and TGEN (Pargas, R., M. Harrold, and R. Peck, 1999) use genetic algorithm to improve quality of generating test data. Both GADGET and TGEN generate test data using white box method; therefore, test data can be generated only after software is finished.

Using Genetic algorithm to generate test data from software model is proposed (Cheon, Y., M.Y. Kim, and A. Perumandla, 2005), JML is a model for generating test data. Fitness function is calculated by coverage of paths and post condition defined by JML.

Praveen Ranjan Srivastava (2009) worked on test data generation using genetic algorithm. This work supported only test data generation didn't support any coverage level.

Recently, ACO is being used for software testing. (Doerner, K., Gutjahr, W. J., 2003) described an approach involving ACO and a Markov Software Usage model for deriving a set of test paths for a software system, and (McMinn and Holcombe, 2003) reported on the application of ACO as a supplementary optimization stage for finding sequences of transitional statements in generating test data for evolutionary testing.

The ACO is a probabilistic technique for solving computational problems which can be reduced to finding good paths through graphs.

Another approach for state based testing using an ACO represented by Huaizhong Li and C. Peng Lam (2005), in this research they consider only states not complete transitions.

One of the graph based algorithms that has already been proposed by D Jeya Mala and Dr. V Mohan (2007, 2008). This algorithm is based upon finding the shortest path between the starting node and the frontier nodes (nodes which are directly connected to the terminal node). This approach is thus able to cover all the nodes in the Execution

State Sequence Graph (ESSG) but still is not able to cover all the transitions (Edges in between the nodes) in the ESSG which is the recommended week level of coverage for software testing. Though this approach works better as compared to the other existing optimization techniques but still has a lot of scope for improvement.

P.K. Mahanti and S. Banerjee (2006) propose a new approach of software error trace and model checking, incorporating ant colony based agents and self regulated swarms.

Requirements are well defined using activity diagrams and this has lead to an increased interest on generating test scenarios using activity diagrams (OMG, 2003). Each path from the initial node to the final node in an activity diagram constitutes a test scenario. The problem encountered following the strategy is exponential when considering concurrent activities. (Sapna P.G., Hrushikesha Mohanty, 2008) investigates this problem and claims that the growth in test scenarios can be limited by considering domain dependency existing among concurrent activities. Presently there are many AI based techniques where have many disadvantages. In Neural Networks, the black-box data processing structure is very complex and it provides a slow convergence speed (Briand, L. C, 2002). Although the search in Genetic Algorithms is not exhaustive, the algorithm can get stuck in local extreme, thus fails to find a global optimum of the fitness (Pedrycz, W and Peters, J. F., 1998).

For locating the defects in software system and reducing the high cost, it's necessary to generate a proper test suite that automatically gives desired generated test sequence. However automatic test sequence generation remains a major problem in software testing. Praveen ranjan Srivastava and Vijay Kumar rai (2009) proposes an ACO approach to automatic test sequence generation for control flow based software testing. The proposed approach can directly use control flow graph to automatically generate test sequences to achieve required test coverage.

Test data generation using meta heuristic approaches was proposed by (Praveen ranjan Srivastava et al, 2008), this work is basically focus on data generation and path coverage, no consideration about transition coverage.

In this chapter, software testing and ACO concept are first introduced. ACO approach to test sequence generation discussed next. Another section illustrates suggested approach for test sequence generation, and next section describes analysis of the proposed algorithm and finally conclusions have been drawn in the last section.

SOFTWARE TESTING & ANT COLONY OPTIMIZATION

Automatic selection of test cases that are able to discover as many defects as possible in software under test decreases the overall cost and total testing time (K. Ayari, S. Bouktif and G. Antoniol, 2007).The most important part is how to select test cases that can increase the probability of finding defects, as no test case gives the guarantee for all defect detection. State transition testing is suitable approach for real time system, embedded system and web based system (Lionel C. Briand, Yvan Labiche and Marwa Shousha, 2005). These systems have a lot of transition between the pages, objects and states. Main problem with this type of software is a large or infinite number of test scenarios. In a finite time period, it is impossible to test all transitions. Possible solution to overcome above mentioned problem is to develop a software testing technique which can reduce the number of test cases and must provide a sufficient coverage of the system under test. Proposed approach provides solution in this regard.

An approach which traverses all states in a test sequence is basically providing weak level of coverage (Offutt and Abdurazik, 1999 & Sabri A. Mahmoud, 2005). By using an example as shown in Figure 1, try to explain the different test coverage criteria, which explain how to

Figure 1. Stopwatch behavior: state transition diagram

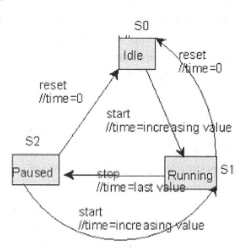

Figure 2. Stopwatch behavior: all state coverage

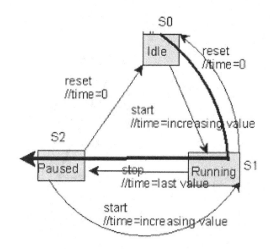

select the best test case in state transition testing for software under test. In this chapter we are using an example of stopwatch system (Louise Tamers, 2006) for understanding the adequacy criteria of software testing using state transition diagram. State transition diagram defines how a system interacts with the outside world, the events it processes, and the valid and invalid order of these events (Somerville Ian, 2008). It also an excellent tool to capture system behavior as well as certain special type of system requirements like document internal system design, outside event and the system's response. State shows the time state of the stopwatch system, and transition between the states shows the event/action criteria.

The selection of test cases under state based testing has a following criterion.

1. Create a set of test cases such that all states are visited at least once under test. A test case (S0→S1→S2) as shown below in Figure 2 which meets this requirement. Generally this is a weak level of test coverage (Sabri A. Mahmoud, 2005).

2. Create a set of test cases such that all events triggered at least once under test. Note that the test cases that cover each event can be

similar to those that cover each state. It shown in Figure 2 again, this is a weak level of coverage (Sabri A. Mahmoud, 2005).

3. Create a set of test cases such that all paths executed at least once under test. While this level is the most preferred, because of its level of coverage, are it may not be feasible. If the state-transition diagram has loops, then the number of possible paths may be infinite.

4. Create a set of test cases such that all transitions are exercised at least once under test. This level of testing provides a good level of coverage without generating large numbers of tests (Sabri A. Mahmoud, 2005). This level generally recommended to software testing world. In Figure 3 shows that there are two test cases (1, 2) that easily fulfill the requirement of at coverage of all transitions at least.

1: {S0→S1→S2→S1→S0}

2: {S0→S1→S2→S0}

Generally recommended level of testing uses state-transition diagram to create a set of test cases such that all transitions exercised at least once under test (Offutt and Abdurazik, 1999 &

Figure 3. Stopwatch behavior: all transition coverage

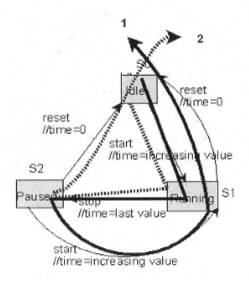

Sabri A. Mahmoud, 2005). High-risk systems may create even more test cases, approaching all paths if possible.

In this type of requirement, Ant's behavior is very useful. Blind Ants coordinate their activities via stigmergy (Marco Dorigoa, 2003). (Marco Dorigoa and Thomas Stutzle, 2005) proposed Ant Colony Optimization, which is inspired by foraging behaviors of ant colonies, and target discrete optimization problem. The main idea is that the self organizing principles which allow the highly coordinated behavior of real ants can be applied with the artificial agents which collaborate to solve the complex computational problems. Real ants coordinate with each other by dropping and sensing a chemical level known as pheromone on the paths. Selection of path by ants depends on stochastic or probability theory. In ACO ants generate pheromone level on the path and due to this level they remember the path in future, it is described by heuristic knowledge. Ants have the visibility of path as well as the destination by the sense of pheromone level and heuristic knowledge. Selection procedure for a path is based upon the

probability of path which has the highest pheromone level and heuristic knowledge.

In this chapter an ACO is proposed for finding the all transitions in UML State Transition Diagram of software under test. This algorithm is helpful to find out all the transitions between the states. Selection of transition depends on probability; higher probability means probability of selection of that transition increases. Probability of the transition depends upon the feasibility, pheromone value and heuristic information of the transition. By this approach tester can easily generate test sequence for software. ACO is an appropriate approach to select the path in a state transition graph as represented (Huaizhong Li and C. Peng Lam, 2005). Our approach is not only an extension of (Huaizhong Li and C. Peng Lam, 2005) work but also gives advantages over the work done in state transition testing by using Finite State Machine (FSM) (Abdelaziz Guerrouat, and Harald Richter, 2005).

This chapter proposed ACO concept in state transition based software testing. Next section, describes an ACO approach to generate test sequences automatically from UML state transition diagrams for state-transition software testing.

AUTOMATIC TEST SEQUENCE GENERATION BY APPLYING ACO

State-transition-based software testing is the most preferred testing (Sabri A. Mahmoud, 2005). It ensures that all transitions are coverage at least once. Though test sequences are generated on the basis of feasibility study of the various available transitions from the current state. Previous works have been done on State based testing by the help of ACO (Huaizhong Li and C. Peng Lam, 2005), they generate an automatic test sequence for state chart diagram, which has ability to cover all state at least once, but the main drawback of (Huaizhong Li and C. Peng Lam, 2005) approach is that the coverage of transition at least once is not considered and test sequence generated is a weak level of test coverage (Sabri A. Mahmoud, 2005). This is already described in previous section.

State-based testing does not work effectively for the software which has large number of states and transitions. Because small increment in the number of states may increase large number of transitions, for example: a system having n states and each state is connected to all other (n-1) states. These systems have large number of transitions in comparison to number of states and preferring to state based testing means testing the small part of the system and leaving major part (transitions). This is not desirable in software industry especially for real time and complex systems. Therefore tester's main job is to test all transitions at least once.

It is clear from above discussion an example of the stopwatch system which is explained in previous section that at least once all transition coverage gives all states and events coverage at least once. This chapter suggests the approach to generate the automatic test cases and provides a solution to above mentioned problem.

The given approach deals with the automatic test sequence generation from the UML state-transition artifact (OMG, 2003). The automatically generated test sequence has satisfied the criteria of (1) All state coverage at least once (2) All event coverage at least once (3) All transition coverage at least once (4) Feasibility- each test case has a feasible path in the state-transition diagram (4) Optimize test case - test suite has non redundant test cases, which has the shortest sequence of transitions.

UML state-transition artifact can be represented in the form of directed graph G = {V, E}, where vertices V are corresponding to states, throughout the chapter state and vertex used interchangeably. Edges E are corresponding to the transitions between the states (OMG, 2003). State means a condition during the life of an object in which it satisfies some condition, performs some action, or waits for some event. Event is an occurrence that may trigger a state transition. Event

types include an explicit signal from outside the system, an invocation from inside the system, the passage of a designated period of time, or a designated condition become true. Transition is the change of state of an object. One or more actions might be taken by an object in response to a state change.

The purpose of ACO algorithm is to cover the optimal transition at least once in UML State Transition Diagram of the Software under test. It provides optimal test sequence of transition in state transition diagram. Selection of transition is depends upon the probability of the transition. Higher probability values means chances to select the transition is also high. The probability value of transition is depends upon: feasibility of transition (F_{ij}), which shows direct connection between the vertices; pheromone value (τ_{ij}), which helps other ants to make decision in the future, and heuristic information (η_{ij}) of the transition, which indicates the visibility of a transition for an ant at the current vertex. In some cases if there are equal probabilities of feasible transition then by the following three steps the algorithm selects feasible transition (Marco Dorigo and Thomas Stutzle, 2004).

1. An ant will select Self-transition if it exist at current vertex otherwise ant will approach to rule second.
2. An ant will select the next state according to the value of visited status parameter (V_s). If current vertex V_1 is direct connected to the vertex say V_2 and it not visited yet by the ant, then ant will select V_2 as the next state that means the transition ($V_1 \rightarrow V_2$) traversed. This concept fulfills the criteria of all state coverage at least once.
3. After all the above consideration if selection is not possible then the ant will select any feasible transition randomly.

In proposed algorithm ant has ability to collect the knowledge of all feasible transitions from its current state. An approach for feasibility check of the transitions from current state is used. This approach is defined in feasibility set of transition (F_{ij}). The ant also has four other information about transition: pheromone level on transition (τ_{ij}), Heuristic information for the transitions (η_{ij}), visited states with the help of visited status (V_s) and last is probability parameter P. In after the selection of a particular transition ant will update the pheromone level as well as heuristic value. Pheromone level is increased according to last pheromone level and heuristic information but heuristic information, is update only on the basis of previous heuristic information.

An ant p at a vertex 'i' (here vertex means state of state transition diagram) and another vertex 'j' which is directly connected to "i", it means there is a transition between the vertices 'i' and 'j' i.e. (i→j). In the graph this transition associated with five tuple F_{ij} (p), τ_{ij} (p), η_{ij} (p), V_s(p) and P_{ij} (p) where (p) shows that values of tuple associated with ant p. All description about these attribute is given below:

1. **Feasible transition set:** F = {F_{ij} (p)} represents the direct connection with the current vertex 'i' to the neighboring vertices "j". Direct connection shows that the vertices are the adjacent to the current vertex 'i', i.e. a direct edge exist in between the current vertexes 'i' and the chosen vertex 'j'.
   ◦ F_{ij} =1 means that transition between the vertex 'i' and 'j' is feasible.
   ◦ F_{ij}=0 means the transition between the vertex 'i' and 'j' is not feasible.

2. **Pheromone trace set:** $\tau = \tau_{ij}$ (p) represents the pheromone level on the feasible transition (i→j) from current vertex 'i' to next vertex 'j'. The pheromone level is updated after the particular transition. This pheromone helps other ants to make decision in future.

3. **Heuristic set:** $\eta = \eta_{ij}$ (p) indicates the visibility of a transition for an ant at current vertex 'i' to vertex 'j'.

4. **Visited status set:** V_s shows information about all the states which are already traversed by the ant p. For any state 'i':
   ◦ V_s (i) =0 shows that vertex 'i' is not visited yet by the ant p.
   ◦ Whereas V_s (i) =1 indicates that state 'i' is already visited by the ant p.

5. **Probability set:** Selection of transition depends on probabilistic value of transition. Because it is inspired by the ant behavior. Probability value of the transition depends upon the feasibility of transition F_{ij} (p), pheromone value τ_{ij} (p) and heuristic information η_{ij} (p) of transition for ant p. There are α, β two more parameter which used to calculate the probability of a transition. These parameters α and β control the desirability versus visibility. α and β are associated with pheromone and heuristic value of the transitions respectively.

Proposed ant colony algorithm helps to get not only knowledge of present state but also all feasible transitions from current state to next state and historical knowledge of already traversed transitions and states by the ant.

PROPOSED APPROACH AND STTACO TOOL

An algorithm is purposed for easily traversing all the states and generating the test sequences which is the main purpose of the chapter of all the transition coverage at least once.

Algorithm for ant p:

1. Initialize all parameter
   1.1 **Set heuristic Value (η):** Choose a positive random number and initialize heuristic value for each transition in the state transition diagram, here we have chosen η =2.

1.2 **Set pheromone level (τ):** Choose a positive random number and initialize pheromone value for each transition in the State transition diagram, here we have chosen τ =1.

1.3 **Set visited status (V_s):** for every state V_s =0 (initially no state is visited by the ant)

1.4 **Set Probability (P):** for each transition initialize probability P=0.

1.5 α=1, β=1, here α and β are the parameter which controls the desirability versus visibility i.e. desirability means if an ant wants to traverse any particular transition on the basis of pheromone value and visibility means the solution which ant has on the basis of prior experience regarding the transition. These parameters are associated with pheromone and heuristic values of the transitions respectively.

1.6 **Set count:** count=maximum number of possible transitions. Number of vertices must be entered by the tester then tool automatically calculate the maximum number of possible transitions depending upon the value of number of states.

2. While (count>0)

Evaluation at current vertex 'i'

2.1 **Update the track:** Update the visited status of the current vertex 'i' i.e. V_s[i] =1.

2.2 **Evaluate connection:** Means determine F(p) for the current vertex 'i', this procedure evaluate all the possible transition from the current vertex 'i' to the all the neighboring vertices with the help of UML state transition diagram, and if there is not any feasible transition the it goes to step 6.

2.3 **Sense the trace:** To sense the trace, evaluate the probability from the current vertex 'i' to all non-zero connections in the F (p), as discussed earlier

ant's behavior is probabilistic. For every non-zero element belongs to feasible set F (p), we will calculate probability with the help of below formula.

$$(\tau_{ij})^{\alpha} * (\eta_{ij})^{-\beta}$$

$$P_{ij} = \sum_{l}^{k} ((\tau_{ik})^{\alpha} * (\eta_{ik})^{-\beta})$$

For every k belongs to feasible set F (p). Otherwise P_{ij} = 0 if state is not feasible from the current vertex. Probability may have the value as follow $0 \leq P_{ij} \leq 1$.

3. Move to next vertex:

3.1 **Select target vertex:** Ant follow the following rule to select the target vertex.

Select transitions (i→j) with maximum probability (P_{ij}) and if two or more transitions have equal probability from current vertex "i" i.e. ($P_{ij} = P_{ik}$) then select next vertex according to below rule:

3.1.1 If there is self transition i.e. (i→i) then select it.

3.1.2 Else Select the transition which have next state not visited yet i.e. Visited status V_s =0.

3.1.3 Else if two or more transitions have the same visited status i.e. V_s[j] =V_s[k] then select randomly.

4. Update the parameter:

4.1 **Update Pheromone:**

Pheromone is updated for transition (i→j) according to the following rule

$$(\tau_{ij}) = (\tau_{ij})^{\alpha} + (\eta_{ij})^{-\beta}$$

4.2 **Update Heuristic:**

$$\eta_{ij} = 2*(\eta_{ij})$$

Figure 4. Flow chart: proposed algorithm

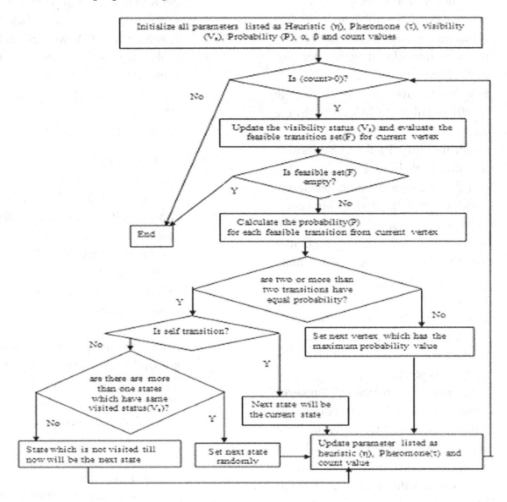

4.3 **Update count:** decrease count by one each time.

    Count=count-1.

5. **Go to the step 2.**

    // End of while loop

6. **End //end of algorithm.**

A flow chart is shown below for the clear understanding of the proposed algorithm.

In the proposed algorithm, count value depends on total number of feasible transition in state transition diagram. So if there are 'n' states then maximum total number of transitions can be (n*n). Count value is automatically calculated by the algorithm according to the feasible transitions in the optimal test sequence generation.

Algorithm will stop automatically in two condition, first if there is no feasible transition from the current state and second if the all feasible transitions are covered at least once.

An ant can start from any state and it can generate a sequence of test cases. Test sequence depends upon the feasibility of transition from the current vertex to other vertices and accordingly it will take decision for further proceeding and in the end it gives the optimal test sequence in state transition diagram of software under test. Here optimal means all states, events and transitions covered at least once. We have developed a pro-

Figure 5. Tape cassette player: state transition diagram

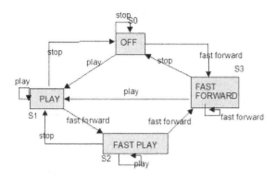

totype tool called STTACO using the proposed algorithm to generate automatically test sequence for given UML state transition diagram. This tool takes input as a state transition diagram. Tester will put the ant on any vertex and get optimal test sequence. The STTACO Tool also gives output analysis in file format. Tester can see internal values generated by an ant such as heuristic, pheromone values, probability calculation that describes selection of the transition according to the algorithm. At the end tool provides optimal test sequence generated by all test sequence. We have tested our proposed STTACO tool to real life example like the Tape Cassette player, for justification the result.

Tape cassette player state Transition diagram is shown in Figure 5. The State transition diagram is self-explanatory. There are four states (OFF, PLAY, FAST-PLAY and FAST-FORWARD) and three buttons (Stop, Play and Fast Forward) as input event in system. Total numbers of transitions are 12 between the states.

For testing of such type of system by STTACO tool, let assume state as

S0: STOP, S1: PLAY, S2: FAST-PLAY, S3:FAST-FORWARD

when any ant 'p' put at the vertex let S0 then below given automatic test sequence is generated:

In first trial:

S0→ S0→ S3→ S3→ S1→ S1→ S2→ S2→
S3→ S0→ S1→ S0→ S0→ S1→ S1→ S2→S1

In another case a second ant is also placed at vertex S0 the test sequence generation is given as

S0→ S0→ S1→ S1→ S2→ S2→ S3→ S3→
S1→ S0→ S3→ S0→ S0→ S1→ S1→ S0→
S3→ S3→ S1→ S2→S1

In third case again an ant is put at vertex S0

S0→ S0→ S3→ S3→ S1→ S1→ S0→ S0→
S3→ S0→ S1→ S2→ S3→ S3→ S1→ S2→
S2→ S3→S0

In fourth case when again ant is placed at state S0

S0→ S0→ S3→ S3→ S1→ S1→ S2→ S2→
S1→ S0→ S1→ S1→ S2→ S3→S0

A brief description about how this sequence and value of all parameters are generated is given in appendix. Figure 6 shows the representation of transitions which are chosen by the ant for first trial in, note that the numeric value which represents the sequence of transitions traversed by the ant and tabular representation is given in the appendix.

S0→ S0→ S3→ S3→ S1→ S1→ S2→ S2→
S3→ S0→ S1→ S0→ S0→ S1→ S1→ S2→S1

The STTACO tool requires in input the total number of states and start state where the particular ant is placed as input. The output snap shots are shown in Figure 7, Figure 8, Figure 9, and Figure 10.

The output is shown in Figure 9 of STTACO tool; this output has all transition coverage at least once.

Figure 6. Tape cassette player: under test

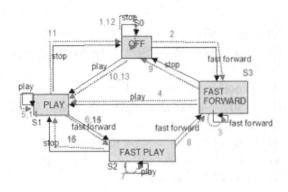

Figure 7. Enter of total state in state transition diagram

Figure 8. Enter the State where tester put the ant

Figure 9. Output of STTACO tool

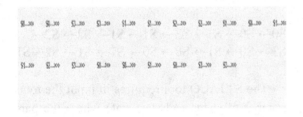

Put an ant at any particular vertex, algorithm can find the optimize path in state transition diagram because algorithm will stop automatically in two condition, first if there is no feasible transition from the current state and second if the

Figure 10. STTACO tool output as state transition diagram

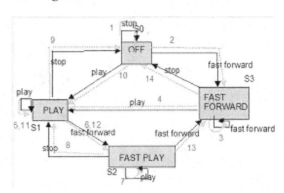

all feasible transitions are covered at least once. In the given example the four test sequence are generated with all transition coverage at least once. But fourth test sequence generated by ant is optimized also because in this sequence all transitions are covered with minimum repetition of the transitions as shown in Figure 10, light dotted transition between states with the sequence number shows the transitions chosen by the ant.

ANALYSIS OF PROPOSED ALGORITHM

In proposed algorithm comparison can be done in three areas: - (1) uses of this approach in real world, (2) advantages over previous work and (3) existing approach in this field of testing.

Software industry generally focuses on nowadays web-based, real time, embedded, scientific and objects oriented, agent based etc software system. In web based system there are transitions between one page to other, in system specification transitions are between ready to wait etc. We can say software field based on object behavior and its transitions. This showed need of testing approach to test transition from object or state or page etc. By using suggested approach tester easily get automated optimal test sequence generation in state transition diagram of software under test,

Figure 11. UML State chart diagram for CCVM

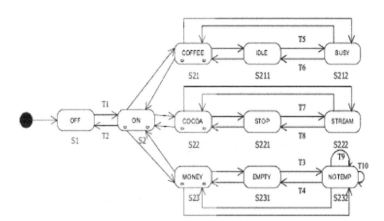

therefore resultant is increased the probability of finding error, with in specific constraints.

Previous work done in this field with FSM and other methods. The proposed algorithm is better than previous one in the following way (1) Use of Meta heuristic algorithms along with the artificial intelligence approach is the strength of the purposed algorithm. (2) FSMs are used to specify the control flow of a system however, they are less appropriate for modeling the data flow (Abdelaziz Guerrouat, and Harald Richter, 2005). To overcome this inconvenient, FSMs are extended by using additional state variables and interaction parameters but this introduced overhead, indeed. Such variables are used in programming languages specifying conditions on transitions and calculations are carried out during the execution. No additional overhead and transformations are required at the execution time in the purposed algorithm.

ACO approach has been already used in this field by Huaizhong LI and C. Peng LAM, 2005, but the main disadvantage of their work was the only focus on state, for clear understanding for proposed work in this chapter here we are trying to compare the previously done work by (Huaizhong LI and C. Peng LAM, 2005) with proposed algorithm. Figure 11 shows the state chart diagram of Coffee Vender Machine (CCVM)

used by Huaizhong LI and C. Peng LAM, 2005. It consists of twenty nine transitions all together.

Figure 12. shows the optimal test sequence generated by Huaizhong LI, C. Peng Lam, 2005 with the concept of state based testing criteria, which covered all the states at least once. According to C. Peng Lam work it is the acceptable criteria for a test sequence and the sequences for two different ants are shown below:

Ant 1: S1, S2, S23, S231, S232, S23, S2, S22, S221, S222

Ant 2: S1, S2, S23, S231, S232, S23, S2, S21, S211, S212

Above sequence fulfill the criteria for state coverage, but what will happen with the transitions which are not covered by the test sequences? From Figure 11 and Figure 12 it is clear that number of transitions covered by (Huaizhong LI and C. Peng Lam, 2005) is 15 out of 29 which may leave uncovered defects in the system. Therefore transition based testing is the preferable criteria (Offutt and Abdurazik, 1999 & Sabri A. Mahmoud, 2005) for real time, web based and complex systems.

The proposed STTACO tool, cover all transition rather than only state based coverage, this is

Figure 12. Optimal solution

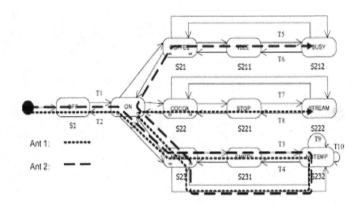

Figure 13. Optimal solution by STTACO tool

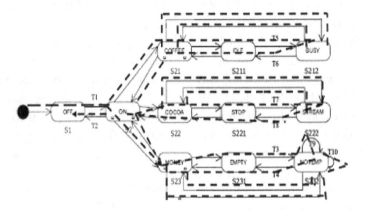

the prime beauty of STTACO Tool, all transition coverage shown in Figure 13 for CCVM.

Test sequence for transition covered are represented dotted lines as shown in Figure 13 and corresponding test sequence are generated by STTACO tool is

{S1, S2, S23, S231, S232,S232, S232, S231, S23, S232, S23, S2, S22, S221, S222, S221, S22, S222, S22, S2, S21, S211, S212, S211, S21, S212, S21, S2, S1}

Figure 14 represents the relative strength of transition coverage by proposed STTACO tool and the work done by Huaizhong LI and C. Peng LAM, 2005.

Time Complexity of the purposed algorithm is of O (n^2) in the worst case. This is another fruitful result of the proposed algorithm which gives advantages over previous work.

Though the proposed STTACO approach provide the good solution for state transition testing over the existing approaches but further improvement may also possible. The proposed approach have following limitation such as: The repetition of states which have the multiple transitions, proposed tool assumes that the tester has knowledge of the all transitions entered by the tester.

The advantage of proposed STTACO tool is easy to use for any software tester. The strength of STTACO tool is based upon high level of software

Figure 14. Relative transition coverage

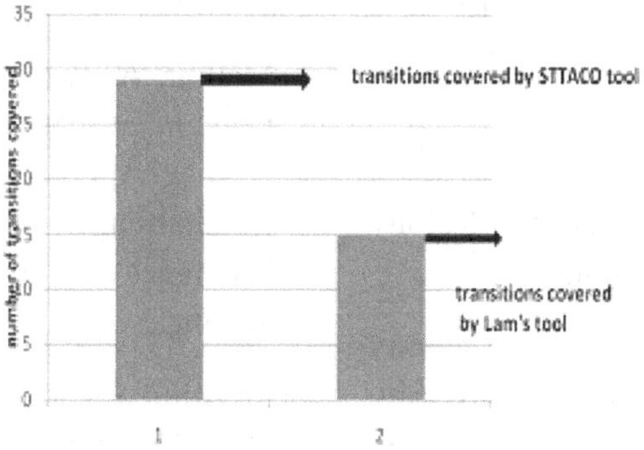

coverage because all state as well as transition coverage at least once during testing process.

CONCLUSION

The first part of this chapter describes the standard method of state based testing and its coverage level. Since existing method does not give, accurate results, there is a need to modified standard method. This chapter proposes a model for transition based coverage by using ant colony optimization. The result that we got by applying proposed method is very encouraging.

By using the strength of ACO approach, this chapter presents generation of the optimal test sequence for the state -transition based software testing. We have taken the directed graph which shows as a model of the system and shown the different state-transitions of the model during the execution. After successful execution of algorithm, it automatically selects a test sequence which covers the maximum transitions with at least once transition must be traversed i.e.: the result is an optimal test sequence in state transition testing.

Soft computing techniques can evaluate transition based testing which may ultimately help software industry to a greater extent. A number of extensions and applications of the model may be possible by using techniques like artificial neural networks, evolutionary computation and combination of neurons-fuzzy approach. These techniques can be used to model more complex nonlinear problems and in fact there is considerable need for applied research and strategy evaluation in this area using these techniques. This proposed model in this chapter is further extended for Future work is emphasizing the difference in between the ACO and other heuristic approach(TS, GA, SA etc) used to select a path, Also future work depends on stochastic property of transition by which we can judge which transition should be covered first.

ACKNOWLEDGMENT

I thank to my supervisor, Prof. G Raghurama, BITS Pilani, India for many insightful discussions during the development of the ideas in this chapter.

REFERENCES

Briand, L. C. (2002). On the many ways Software Engineering can benefit from Knowledge Engineering. *Proc. 14th SEKE,* Italy, (pp. 3-6).

Cheon, Y., Kim, M. Y., & Perumandla, A. (2005). A Complete Automation of Unit Testing for Java Programs. In SERP '05, Las Vegas, NV.

Doerner, K., & Gutjahr, W. J. (2003). *Extracting Test Sequences from a Markov Software Usage Model by ACO* (. *LNCS, 2724,* 2465–2476.

Dorigo, M. (2003). *The Ant Colony Optimization Metaheuristic: Algorithms, Applications, and Advances. International Series in Operations Research & Management Science* (*Vol. 57*, pp. 250–285). New York: Springer.

Dorigo, M., & Stutzle, T. (2004). Ant Colony Optimization. New York: Phi publishers.

Dorigoa, M., & Stutzle, T. (2005). Ant colony optimization. [New York: Cambridge University Press.]. *The Knowledge Engineering Review, 20,* 92–93.

Doungsa-ard, C., Dahal, K. P., Alamgir Hossain, M., & Suwannasart, T. (2007). Test Data Generation from UML State Machine Diagrams using Gas. IN ICSEA 2007, France, (p. 47).

Guerrouat, A., & Richter, H. (2005). Adaptation of State/Transition-Based Methods for Embedded System Testing. *World Academy of Science, Engineering and Technology, 10.*

Harman, M. (2007). The Current State and Future of Search Based Software Engineering. In *International Conference on Software Engineering: Future of Software Engineering,* (pp. 342-357). Washington, DC: IEEE Computer Society press.

http://ocw.kfupm.edu.sa/user/SWE41501/State-Transition%20Testing%20Example.ppt

Lefticaru, R., & Ipate, F. (2008). *Functional Search-based Testing from State Machines* (pp. 525–528). Denver, CO: ICST.

Li, H., & Lam, C. P. (2005). An Ant Colony Optimization Approach to Test Sequence Generation for State based Software Testing. In *Proceedings of the Fifth International Conference on Quality Software (QSIC'05),* (pp. 255 – 264).

Mahanti, P. K., & Banerjee, S. (2006). Automated testing in software engineering: using ant colony and self-regulated swarms. In *Proceedings of the 17th IASTED international conference on Modeling and simulation table of contents,* Montreal, Canada, (pp. 443 – 448).

Mahmoud, S. A. (2006). *State transition testing.* Retrieved from.

Mathur, A. P. (2007). New Delhi, India: India Pearson Education. Biswal, B. N., et al. (2008). A Novel Approach for Scenario-Based Test Case Generation. In *IEEE ICIT conference* (1st ed.). Bhubaneswar, India: Foundation of Software Testing.

McMinn, P. (2004). Search-Based Software Test Data Generation: A Survey. *Software Testing. Verification and Reliability, 14*(3), 212–223.

McMinn, P., & Holcomb, M. (2003), The State Problem for Evolutionary Testing, In *Proceedings of GECCO,* (LNCS vol. 2724, pp.2488-2500).

Michael, C., McGraw, G., & Schatz, M. A. (2001). Generating software test data by evolution. *IEEE Transactions on Software Engineering, 27*(12), 1085–1110. doi:10.1109/32.988709

Mohan, V., & Jeya, M. (2007). Intelligent ester – Software Test Sequence Optimization Using Graph Based Intelligent Search Agent. In *Proceedings of the International Conference on Computational Intelligence and Multimedia Applications (ICCIMA 2007),* (Vol. 01, pp. 22-27).

Mohan, V. & Jeya, M. (2008). Intelligent ester –Test Sequence Optimization framework using Multi-Agents. *Journal of computers, 3*(6).

Offutt, J., & Abdurazik, A. (1999). *Generating Tests from UML Specifications.* Presented at 2nd International Conference on the UML. Ayari, K., Bouktif, S. & Antoniol, G. (2007). Automatic Mutation Test Input Data Generation via Ant Colony. In *Genetic and Evolutionary Computation Conference,* London. Copeland, L. (2004). *A Practitioner's Guide to Software Test Design.* Boston: Artech House Publishers.

OMG. (2003). *OMG Unified Modeling Language Superstructure* (version 2.1).

Pargas, R., Harrold, M., & Peck, R. (1999). Test-data generation using genetic algorithms. *Software Testing. Verification and Reliability, 9*(4), 263–282. doi:10.1002/(SICI)1099-1689(199912)9:4<263::AID-STVR190>3.0.CO;2-Y

Pedrycz, W., & Peters, J. F. (1998). *Computational Intelligence in Software Engineering*. Singapore: World Scientific Publishers.

Pressman, R. S. (2005). *Software engineering: A Practitioner's Approach* (6th ed.). India: TMH.

Sapna, P. G., & Mohanty, H. (2008). Automated Scenario Generation based on UML Activity Diagrams. In *International Conference on Information Technology(ICIT),* Bhubaneswar, India, (pp 209-214).

Somerville, I. (2005). *Software Engineering* (7th ed.). New Delhi, India: Pearson Education.

Srivastava, P. R. & Kumar rai, V. (2009). An Ant Colony Optimization Approach to Test Sequence Generation for Control Flow based Software Testing. *Information System, Technology and Management, Communication in Computer and Information Science Series*(CCIS), (Vol 31,pp. 345-346). New York: Springer Verlag.

Srivastava, P. R. (2009)... *International Journal of Artificial Intelligence and Soft Computing, 1*(2-3), 363–375. doi:10.1504/IJAISC.2009.027301

Srivastava, P. R., et al. (2008). Generation of test data using Meta Heuristics Approach. IEEE TENCON 2008, India.

Srivastava, P. R., et al. (2009). Use of Genetic Algorithm in Generation of Feasible Test Data. *ACM SIGSOFT Software Engineering Notes, 34*(2).

Tamers, L. (2006). *Introducing Software Testing*. New Delhi, India: Pearson Education India.

Zhan, Y., & Clark, J. A. (2006). The State Problem for Test Generation in Simulink. In *Proceedings of the 8th annual conference on Genetic and evolutionary computation*, Seattle, WA, (pp. 1941 - 1948).

KEY TERMS AND DEFINITIONS

Ant Colony Optimization (ACO): A probabilistic technique for solving computational problems.

Automated Test Sequence Generation: Test data, which satisfy transition coverage level.

Software Testing: Verification and validation process for any software

State Transition Testing (STT): Testing all the sates in software.

Test Suite: Collection of test cases.

APPENDIX

How the algorithm works is describes here:-

Total State in state transition diagram N= 4

All transition is shown in Matrix M:-(if transition is feasible between state i and j than values M (i, j) = 1 otherwise 0)

$$
\begin{array}{cccc}
\text{Mij} = & 0\ 1\ 2\ 3 \\
 & 0\ 1\ 1\ 0\ 1 \\
 & 1\ 1\ 1\ 1\ 0 \\
 & 2\ 0\ 1\ 1\ 1 \\
 & 3\ 1\ 1\ 0\ 1
\end{array}
$$

In starting ant have equal knowledge about every transition

So every transition has equal values of

heuristic values (i, j) =2.0

Pheromone Value (i, j) =1.0 for all i, j

Starting state inputted by tester is (l) ==0

Yes there is feasible transition available:

So internal values easily calculate like:

heuristic values (0, 0) =2.0

Pheromone Value (0, 0) =1.0

Heuristic values (0, 1) =2.0

Pheromone Value (0, 1) =1.0

Heuristic values (0, 2) =2.0

Pheromone Value (0, 2) =1.0

Heuristic values (0, 3) =2.0

Pheromone Value (0, 3) =1.0

// here temp is needed in probability calculation

Probability Calculation done like:

Probability [0] [0] = 0.3333333333333333

Probability [0] [1] = 0.3333333333333333

Probability [0] [2] = 0.0

Probability [0] [3] = 0.3333333333333333

Selection of transition:

Max probability is= 0.3333333333333333 of transitions {(0, 0), (0, 1), (0, 3)}

// More than one transition with maximum values of probability

Automatically ant selects transition (0, 0)

j=0 // due to selection criteria given in algorithm select first self-transition

So now ant going to new state is S0

After updating heuristic and pheromone values for transition 0->0

New pheromone value (0, 0) =1.5

New heuristic value (0, 0) =4.0

l==0 (is there feasible transition from state S0)

Yes there is feasible transition available:

Internal values:

Heuristic values (0, 0) =4.0

Pheromone Value (0, 0) =1.5

Heuristic values (0, 1) =2.0

Pheromone Value (0, 1) =1.0

Heuristic values (0, 2) =2.0

Pheromone Value (0, 2) =1.0

Heuristic values (0, 3) =2.0

Pheromone Value (0, 3) =1.0

// here temp is needed in probability calculation

Probability Calculation done like:

Probability [0] [0] = 0.2727272727272727

Probability [0] [1] = 0.36363636363636365

Probability [0] [2] = 0.0

Probability [0] [3] = 0.36363636363636365

Selection of transition:

Max probability is: 0.36363636363636365 of transition {(0, 1), (0, 3)}

No self transition

Visited status of the V_s [1] = V_s [3] = 0

Automatic selecting randomly in between transition {(0, 1), (0, 3)} lets as (0, 3)

So now new next state is S3

Update heuristic and pheromone values for transition 0->3

New pheromone value (0, 3) =1.5

New heuristic value (0, 3) =4.0

This whole process is stored in file as per transition. Here is shown its tabular format for state where the ant calculating values for all parameter and check the feasibility and optimality of transition:

Table 1. At State S0

Start/next state	S0	S1	S2	S3
$F_{ij}(S0)$	1	1	0	1
V_s	1	0	0	0
$\tau_{ij}(S0)$	1	1	0	1
$\eta_{ij}(S0)$	2	2	0	2
$P_{ij}(S0)$	.33	.33	0	.33

Table 5. After S0→ S0→ S3→ S3→S1

Start/next state	S0	S1	S2	S3
$F_{ij}(S1)$	1	1	1	0
V_s	1	1	0	1
$\tau_{ij}(S1)$	1	1	1	0
$\eta_{ij}(S1)$	2	2	2	0
$P_{ij}(S1)$	.33	.33	.33	0

Table 2. After S0→S0

Start/next state	S0	S1	S2	S3
$F_{ij}(S0)$	1	1	0	1
V_s	1	0	0	0
$\tau_{ij}(S0)$	1.5	1	0	1
$\eta_{ij}(S0)$	4	2	0	2
$P_{ij}(S0)$	.27	.36	0	.36

Table 6. After S0→ S0→ S3→ S3→ S1→S1

Start/next state	S0	S1	S2	S3
$F_{ij}(S1)$	1	1	1	0
V_s	1	1	0	1
$\tau_{ij}(S1)$	1	1.5	1	0
$\eta_{ij}(S1)$	2	4	2	0
$P_{ij}(S1)$	.36	.27	.36	0

Table 3. After S0→ S0→S3

Start/next state	S0	S1	S2	S3
Fij(S3)	1	1	0	1
V_s	1	0	0	1
τij(S3)	1	1	0	1
ηij(S3)	2	2	0	2
Pij(S3)	.33	.33	0	.33

Table 7. After S0→ S0→ S3→ S3→ S1→ S1→S2

Start/next state	S0	S1	S2	S3
$F_{ij}(S2)$	0	1	1	1
Vs	1	1	1	1
$\tau_{ij}(S2)$	0	1	1	0
$\eta_{ij}(S2)$	0	2	2	0
$P_{ij}(S2)$	0	.33	.33	.33

Table 4. After S0→ S0→ S3→S3

Start/next state	S0	S1	S2	S3
$F_{ij}(S3)$	1	1	0	1
V_s	1	0	0	1
$\tau_{ij}(S3)$	1	1	0	1.5
$\eta_{ij}(S3)$	2	2	0	4
$P_{ij}(S3)$	.36	.36	0	.27

Table 8. After S0→ S0→ S3→ S3→ S1→ S1→ S2→S2

Start/next state	S0	S1	S2	S3
$F_{ij}(S2)$	0	1	1	1
V_s	1	1	1	1
$\tau_{ij}(S2)$	0	1	1.5	1
$\eta_{ij}(S2)$	0	2	4	2
$P_{ij}(S2)$	0	.36	.27	.36

Table 9. After S0→ S0→ S3→ S3→ S1→ S1→ S2→ S2→S3

Start/next state	S0	S1	S2	S3
$F_{ij}(S3)$	1	1	0	1
V_s	1	1	1	1
$\tau_{ij}(S3)$	1	1.5	0	1.5
$\eta_{ij}(S3)$	2	4	0	4
$P_{ij}(S3)$	.4	.3	0	.3

Table 10. After S0→ S0→ S3→ S3→ S1→ S1→ S2→ S2→ S3→S0

Start/next state	S0	S1	S2	S3
$F_{ij}(S0)$	1	1	0	1
V_s	1	1	1	1
$\tau_{ij}(S0)$	1.5	1	0	1.5
$\eta_{ij}(S0)$	4	2	0	4
$P_{ij}(S0)$	.3	.4	0	.3

Table 11. After S0→ S0→ S3→ S3→ S1→ S1→ S2→ S2→ S3→ S0→S1

Start/next state	S0	S1	S2	S3
$F_{ij}(S1)$	1	1	1	0
V_s	1	1	1	1
$\tau_{ij}(S1)$	1	1.5	1.5	0
$\eta_{ij}(S1)$	2	4	4	0
$P_{ij}(S1)$	.4	.3	.3	0

Table 12. After S0→ S0→ S3→ S3→ S1→ S1→ S2→ S2→ S3→ S0→ S1→S0

Start/next state	S0	S1	S2	S3
$F_{ij}(S0)$	1	1	0	1
V_s	1	1	1	1
$\tau_{ij}(S0)$	1.5	1.5	0	1.5
$\eta_{ij}(S0)$	4	4	0	4
$P_{ij}(S0)$	.33	.33	0	.33

Table 13. After S0→ S0→ S3→ S3→ S1→ S1→ S2→ S2→ S3→ S0→ S1→ S0→S0

Start/next state	S0	S1	S2	S3
$F_{ij}(S0)$	1	1	0	1
V_s	1	1	1	1
$\tau_{ij}(S0)$	1.75	1.5	0	1.5
$\eta_{ij}(S0)$	8	4	0	4
$P_{ij}(S0)$	.226	.387	0	.387

Table 14. After S0→ S0→ S3→ S3→ S1→ S1→ S2→ S2→ S3→ S0→ S1→ S0→ S0→S1

Start/next state	S0	S1	S2	S3
$F_{ij}(S1)$	1	1	1	0
V_s	1	1	1	1
$\tau_{ij}(S1)$	1.5	1.5	1.5	0
$\eta_{ij}(S1)$	4	4	4	0
$P_{ij}(S1)$	.33	.33	.33	0

Table 15. After S0→ S0→ S3→ S3→ S1→ S1→ S2→ S2→ S3→ S0→ S1→ S0→ S0→ S1→S1

Start/next state	S0	S1	S2	S3
$F_{ij}(S1)$	1	1	1	0
V_s	1	1	1	1
$\tau_{ij}(S1)$	1.5	1.75	1.5	0
$\eta_{ij}(S1)$	4	8	4	0
$P_{ij}(S1)$	.387	.226	.387	0

Table 16. After S0→ S0→ S3→ S3→ S1→ S1→ S2→ S2→ S3→ S0→ S1→ S0→ S0→ S1→ S1→S2

Start/next state	S0	S1	S2	S3
$F_{ij}(S2)$	0	1	1	1
V_s	1	1	1	1
$\tau_{ij}(S2)$	0	1	1.5	1.5
$\eta_{ij}(S2)$	0	2	4	4
$P_{ij}(S2)$	0	.4	.3	.3

Table 17. After S0→ S0→ S3→ S3→ S1→ S1→ S2→ S2→ S3→ S0→ S1→ S0→ S0→ S1→ S1→ S2→S1

Start/next state	S0	S1	S2	S3
$F_{ij}(S1)$	1	1	1	0
V_s	1	1	1	1
$\tau_{ij}(S1)$	1.5	1.75	1.75	0
$\eta_{ij}(S1)$	4	8	8	0
$P_{ij}(S1)$	.461	.269	.269	0

Now loop will stop.

Chapter 10
Object Oriented Software Testing with Genetic Programming and Program Analysis

Arjan Seesing
Enigmatry, Netherlands

Hans-Gerhard Gross
Delft University of Technology, Netherlands

ABSTRACT

Testing is a difficult and costly activity in the development of object-oriented programs. The challenge is to come up with a sufficient set of test scenarios, out of the typically huge volume of possible test cases, to demonstrate correct behavior and acceptable quality of the software. This can be reformulated as a search problem to be solved by sophisticated heuristic search techniques such as evolutionary algorithms. The goal is to find an optimal set of test cases to achieve a given test coverage criterion. This chapter introduces and evaluates genetic programming as a heuristic search algorithm which is suitable to evolve object-oriented test programs automatically to achieve high coverage of a class. It outlines why the object paradigm is different to the procedural paradigm with respect to testing, and why a genetic programming approach might be better suited than the genetic algorithms typically used for testing procedural code. The evaluation of our implementation of a genetic programming approach, augmented with program analysis techniques for better performance, indicates that object-oriented software testing with genetic programming is feasible in principle. However, having many adjustable parameters, evolutionary search heuristics have to be fined-tuned to the optimization problem at hand for optimal performance, and, therefore, represent a difficult optimization problem in their own right.

DOI: 10.4018/978-1-61520-809-8.ch010

INTRODUCTION

Testing is the most widely used and accepted technique for verification and validation of software systems. It is applied to measure to which extent a software system is conforming to its original requirements specification and to demonstrate its correct operation (IEEE, 1999). Testing is a search problem that involves the identification of a limited number of good tests out of a shear, nearly unlimited number of possible test scenarios. "Good tests" are those runtime scenarios that are likely to uncover failures, or demonstrate correctness of the system under test (SUT). Identifying good test cases typically follows predefined testing criteria, such as code coverage criteria (Beizer, 1990). This is based on the assumption that only the execution of a distinct feature, or its coverage, can reveal failures that are associated with this feature.

Because the primary activities of testing, test case identification and design, are typical search problems, they can be tackled by typical search heuristics. One of the most important search heuristics for software testing is known to be random testing. This is also one of the most commonly used testing strategies in industry today. Currently, also more advanced heuristic search techniques are applied to software testing. These are based on evolutionary algorithms, and they have also made their ways into industry (Baresel, 2003; Buehler & Wegener, 2003) since their performance in devising test cases was found to be at least as good as random testing, but usually much better (Gross, 2003; Tracey, Clarke & Mander, 1998). The group of these testing techniques is referred to as evolutionary testing (ET) according to Wegener and Grochtmann (1998).

ET is an automatic test case generation technique based on the application of evolution strategies (Schwefel & Männer, 1990), genetic algorithms (Goldberg, 1989; Holland, 1975), genetic programming (Koza, 1992), or simulated annealing (von Laarhoven & Aarts, 1987). ET searches for optimal test parameter combinations that satisfy a predefined test criterion. This test criterion is represented through a "cost function" that measures how well each of the automatically generated optimization parameters satisfies the given test criterion. For a test, various test criteria a perceivable, according to the goal of the test, such as how well a test case covers a piece of code, in the case of structural testing (Jones et al., 1996; Pargas et al, 1999), or how well a test case violates a (safety) requirement (Tracey et al, 1999), for example.

Evolutionary testing has initially only been applied to traditional procedural software. Here, ET is used to generate input parameter combinations for test cases automatically that achieve, i.e., high coverage, if the test target relates to some code coverage criterion. However, also object-oriented software testing with genetic algorithms has been tackled by researchers, e.g., Gross and Mayer (2002, 2003), Tonella (2004), and applying genetic programming approaches, e.g., Seesing and Gross (2006), Ribeiro, Zenha-Rela and de Vega (2008), and Gupta and Rohil (2008).

The main differences of object technology compared to the procedural paradigm are (1) that it is inherently based on states which are not readily visible outside of an object's encapsulating hull, and (2) that an object test, as the basic unit of testing, can incorporate an arbitrary number of operation invocations, or any arbitrary sequence or combination of method invocations.

An object's internal state depends on any previously performed operation invocations, the so called invocation history (Gross, 2005; Gross & Mayer, 2003), including input parameter settings. Hence, object testing involves not only the generation of suitable input parameter combinations for a single procedure under test, but, additionally, the generation of suitable test invocation sequences of various operations of an object, plus the generation of their respective input parameter combinations. As a consequence, in object testing, we have to deal with a number of test artifacts, such as the sequence or combination of operation invocations, the input parameter combinations for the tested operations, the sequence or combination of operation invocations that bring the object into an "interesting" initial testing state, including constructor invocation, and the input parameter combinations for the previously mentioned state setting operations.

When applied to objects, evolutionary testing must generate optimization-parameter values that correspond to a constructor, with input parameters, a number of operations, including input parameters, suitable to bring the test object into a distinct state, and a number of operations, including input parameter values, for the actual tested functionality. Object-oriented evolutionary testing can actually be regarded as search-based test software programming. In other words, the problem is suitable to be solved through genetic programming techniques. Genetic programming can be seen as a specialization of a genetic algorithm, and it is particularly aimed at evolving software programs according to the rules of simulated natural evolution. Genetic programming is well suited for test program generation for testing object-oriented code because the symbols used by GP are restricted only to operation invocations and input parameter types that are required and used by the SUT. This is quite in contrast to the generation of arbitrary functional code which is based on the full alphabet of the programming language under consideration. So, test code generation through genetic programming is much less complex.

This chapter introduces and explores an evolutionary testing approach for object oriented code that is based on the application of genetic programming. In the next section, Section 2, we will introduce evolutionary testing and explain briefly how it is typically applied under the procedural programming paradigm. Section 3 looks at related work, and it introduces two different approaches to apply genetic algorithms to the testing of object-oriented code. This indicates the issues of applying GA to test program generation,

and motivates the use of GP. Section 4 introduces our approach that applies genetic programming and code analysis to the generation of test software for object oriented code. Here, we explain the details of the algorithm used and show as a proof-of-concept with small examples on how to apply genetic programming for automated test case generation. Section 5 shows some results from experiments that we have carried out, and Section 6 presents our conclusions and gives an outlook on future research.

2 AUTOMATED SOFTWARE TESTING AND EVOLUTIONARY ALGORITHMS

Traditionally, a human tester develops the test scenarios and writes the test code for an SUT manually. Ideally, a testing tool should generate the entire test code automatically, but this is very difficult, so that only parts of the testing process can be automated. The process of test automation can be subdivided into three main activities, i.e.,

1. Generation of test scenarios according to testing criteria, also referred to as software test data generation,
2. Generation of a test oracle out of the SUT's specification,
3. Combination of both, test scenarios and oracle, into executable test cases.

The first activity can be automated with relative ease, and this is also what most commercial testing tools are capable to do, although, usually, existing tools apply crude heuristics to find test scenarios. The automation of the second activity is usually much more daunting in practice, due to poor quality, or low formality, of the SUT's requirements specification available. Without formalization of the specification, it is nearly impossible to automate the generation of the oracle. The last step simply involves the creation of an arbiter that compares the observation from the SUT's execution with the expected observation from the oracle, and decides whether the test passes or fails. This poses no particular difficulty on automation, once the oracle problem has been solved.

The work outlined in this chapter and the related work presented, concentrate on the first testing activity, the automated generation of the test scenarios. An efficient way to do this is with a random generator. Random testing can be used to create a volume of test scenarios, but it is not specifically obeying any test coverage criteria. Test tools based on random testing, generate test scenarios and simply measure and illustrate the coverage of the SUT. They cannot generate test scenarios that are "guided" by the coverage.

More advanced search heuristics such as evolutionary algorithms (EA) can be used to specifically look for test scenarios that cover certain branches of a program. This class of algorithms is loosely related to the mechanisms of natural evolution, and they are based on reproduction, evaluation and selection.

The following pseudo code represents a standard genetic algorithm that can be used for testing; P, P1, P2, and P3 represent populations of feasible test scenarios:

```
initialize_random (P);
fitness_function (P);
while not stopping_criterion do begin
    P1 = selection (P);
    P2 = recombination (P1);
    P3 = mutation (P2);
    fitness_function (P3);
    P = merge_populations (P3,P);
end-while
```

Each set of parameters, the so-called individual, is represented by a different binary string, the so-called chromosome, within a population. Each chromosome represents the input parameter values for the execution of the SUT.

The GA starts with a random initial population of chromosomes. Selection chooses the chromosomes out of this initial population to be recombined and mutated. Recombination reproduces the selected individuals and exchanges their information (pair-wise) in order to produce new individuals. This information exchange is called crossover. Mutation introduces a small change to each newly created individual. The resulting individuals (P3 in the pseudo-code) are then evaluated through the fitness function. This transfers the information encoded in the chromosome, the so-called genotype, into an execution of the SUT, the so-called phenotype. The fitness function measures how well the chromosome satisfies the test criterion. In this case it is the coverage of a program branch. The implementation of the fitness function follows earlier standards in evolutionary testing, described in other articles, i.e., by Jones, Sthamer and Eyres (1996), McMinn (2004), and Michael, McGraw and Schatz (2001). For the next generation, the old and the new populations are merged, thereby retaining the best individuals.

The process of selection, reproduction and evaluation is referred to as one generation, and these steps are repeated until the stopping criterion is satisfied, e.g., a predefined number of generations, or the satisfaction of the test criterion (branch covered). Fitter individuals, represented by their chromosomes that come closer to covering the current target are favored in the recombination and selection process, so that in subsequent generations, the population will comprise fitter individuals that are more likely to satisfy the test criterion. In order for such a search process to obtain full branch coverage, every branch must be successively selected as test target and solved through an individual search process. The application of evolutionary algorithms to such structural testing problems has been demonstrated in practice, i.e. by Baresel, Pohlheim, and Sadeghipour (2003), Jones, Sthamer, and Eyres (1996), Michael, McGraw and Schatz (2001), and Pargas, Harrold, and Peck (1999).

The previously described simple representation of input parameter values in a chromosome, is not sufficient in object-oriented software testing. Here, in addition to the input parameter values, the search process also needs to include any arbitrary number and sequence of operation invocations on the object, and any internal state settings, as described earlier. This turns the fixed-length, simple chromosome of the procedural evolutionary testing paradigm into an arbitrary-length, complex chromosome for the object-oriented evolutionary testing paradigm. Especially, the fact that initial state settings of an object are part of a test scenario (Gross, 2005), makes the implementation of the automatic test generation process more difficult.

Earlier publications on evolutionary testing of object-oriented systems have proposed encodings for dealing with this additional dimension. The first alternative is to encode the operation invocation sequences as chromosome and come up with new recombination and mutation strategies, as outlined by Tonella (2004). The second alternative is to use a standard binary encoding of the chromosome, so that standard GA tools can be used, and devise a specialized so-called *genotype–phenotype transfer function* that maps the chromosome representation to a test scenario, as described by Wappler and Lammermann (2005). How this can be done is briefly laid out in the following section, before we go on to propose a third way of organizing the chromosome as a tree structure, in Section 4, so that we can apply a standard genetic programming technique.

3 EVOLUTIONARY TESTING FOR OBJECT-ORIENTED PROGRAMS

Chromosome Encoding for Object-Oriented Evolutionary Testing

One way to deal with the enhanced complexity of objects in evolutionary testing is to enrich the chromosome with representations that are capable of dealing with these more complex entities (Tonella, 2005). This method adds structure to the chromosome during evolution, which can be mapped directly to an executing program. Tonella (2005) proposes the following grammar:

```
<chromosome>::=  <actions> @ <values>
<actions>::=       <action> {: <actions>}?
<action>::= $id = constructor({<parameters>}?)
           | $id = CLASS # NULL
           | $id. method({<parameters>}?)
<parameters>::=  <parameter> {, <parameters>}?
<parameter>::=      builtin-type {<generator>}?
                  | $id
<generator>::=    [ low ; up ]
                  | [ genclass ]
<values>::=        <value> {, <value>}?
<value>::=         integer
                  | real
                  | boolean
                  | string
```

The "@" separates the chromosome into two parts. The first part contains the sequence of operation invocations, including constructor and method invocations, each separated by ":", and the second part represents the input values that these operations take, each separated by ",".

Such a sequence of operation invocations plus parameter values represents a test scenario. An <action> can represent either a new object (indicated as $id), or a call to a method on an object identified by $id. Parameters of operation invocations (<parameters>) can represent built-in types such as int, real, boolean, and string, or chromosome variables ($id). The generation operator (<generator>) produces the values for the input parameters. It can generate random numbers in the range between "low" and "up", or it can use an external class to have a value produced.

The grammar proposed permits invalid chromosomes, so additional rules must be imposed for "well-formed-ness", i.e.,

- Chromosome variables cannot be used before they are assigned.
- Built-in types in the first part require a corresponding input value in the second part of the chromosome.
- Methods used in the chromosome must be visible for the used classes.

Because the genetic algorithm performs on chromosomes with this particular organization, the standard binary crossover and mutation operators may not be applied. Tonella (2005), therefore, proposes specific operators that lend their ideas from genetic programming.

Mutation can change values or operations (constructors and methods). A value can be mutated through change to a randomly generated value of the same type. A constructor can be mutated through random change to another constructor. Redundant input values are then dropped, missing ones generated. A new method may be inserted by a mutation including the respective input parameter values for the method. A method may also be removed through a mutation including all its input values.

Crossover between two chromosomes works in a similar way, although it usually involves various of the previously described measures at the same time. Two chromosomes are cut at a randomly determined location (at an <action>-delimiter), in the case of a simple one-point crossover, and their respective tails are swapped and rejoined. Redundant constructors must be removed, as well as needless input values. Finally, conflicting variable names must be changed.

Genotype—Phenotype Transfer for Object-Oriented Evolutionary Testing

A straight-forward way to apply evolutionary testing to the more complicated requirements of object technology, is to maintain a binary or numerical chromosome that can be handled by any standard genetic algorithm, and then provide rules, or a grammar, to map the binary representation into a test scenario. Each test program may be represented as a sequence of statements, and each statement consists of an object, an operation, constructor or method, and some parameters, following Wappler and Lammermann (2005).

The mapping of the chromosome to the test scenarios can be determined by sequentially reading the chromosome and turning it into operation invocations according to rules. Two genes can be assigned for operation invocations, one for the target object, and one that denotes the operation to be invoked on that object. Because operation invocations take varying numbers of input parameters, input values must be accommodated by a variable number of genes. The genes are then mapped into a real test scenario, a phenotype, according to the production rules of a grammar, i.e.:

```
test_program::=    {statement;}+
statement::=       [return_value]
                   {constr_call|method_call}
return_value::=    class_name instance_name =
constr_call::=     new class_name (parameters)
method_call::=     {class_name|instance_name}.
                   method_name(parameters)
parameters::=      [parameter {, parameter}*]
parameter::=       basic_type_value|instance_
                   name | NULL
```

In this grammar, [] represents an option, {|} alternatives, {}+ at least one repetition, and {}* arbitrary repetitions. Because these rules allow the generation of erroneous test scenarios, the fitness function assigns a degree of failure to the decoding. This failure is part of the fitness, so that such "defective genetic material" is eventually evading from the population.

The decoding from the chromosome into a real test scenario is performed through specific functions, fully described by Wappler and Lammerrmann (2005). Methods are numbered in a series, and each number of one gene in the chromosome corresponds to a specific number of a method.

Input parameters are represented by one gene in the chromosome, and they can map to concrete values and objects.

A disadvantage of applying genetic algorithms to the testing of object-oriented software is that, through the binary representation, the algorithm's operators destroy the natural structure of an evolving program. One solution is to devise a special representation of the genotype and come up with special operators suitable for this representation. A second alternative is to invent special genotype-phenotype transfer algorithms that generate the structure of a program encoded as binary chromosome. The two techniques described above are representatives of these approaches. A third alternative is the application of a genetic programming approach which is specifically crafted towards the evolution of program structures, and therefore, in our opinion much more suitable for the evolution of object-oriented testing code. This approach is described and evaluated in the remainder of this chapter.

4 SOFTWARE TEST CASE GENERATION WITH GENETIC PROGRAMMING

Genetic programming (GP) is a specialization of a genetic algorithm that is particularly aimed at evolving computer programs based on the principles of natural evolution (Koza, 1992). The chromosomes in genetic programming represent hierarchically structured computer programs made up of arithmetic operations mathematical functions, boolean and conditional operations, and terminal symbols, such as types, numbers, and strings. The genotype-phenotype mapping of GP is much more natural for the domain of test program generation compared with a standard genetic algorithm. The fact that GP is based on hierarchically organized trees requires specialized genetic operators for recombination and mutation (Koza, 1992).

Recombination takes sub-trees from previously selected parent individuals and swaps them in order to reorganize them into new individuals (trees). The chromosomes are always cut and reassembled at nodes, and not within nodes of the tree representing the computer program. The mutation operator introduces random changes in the tree by selecting a node of the tree randomly, deleting everything beyond that node, or adding a randomly generated sub-tree, or changing leaves of the tree randomly. These are all standard genetic programming operators following Koza (1992).

Chromosome Encoding for GP

Table 1 lists the basic classes of representations that are used in our proposed genetic programming approach. The types to be used by GP are arbitrary, because every single object created, represents a type. Every operation refers to an object, and thus a type, plus some input parameters, including their individual types. These must be created by the GP process and added as leaves to the node in the tree that represents the operation. Each operation maps to a sub-tree of the entire GP hierarchy, including constructors and input values for the required (sub)-objects.

There are two types of variables in programming languages, L(eft)-type and R(ight)-type variables. L-type variables define and initialize variables, and R-type variables reference them. The compiler will issue an error, when a variable is used as an R-type, before it has been used (initialized) as an L-type. R-types are terminal, and the L-types require one "child-node".

Apart from arbitrary object types, we also have to allow basic or primitive types, such as boolean, integer, real, char and the like. These are primarily used in order to denote input and return values. Because of the late binding principle in object technology, not all types are known to the GP system a-priori. The SUT is used as the starting point of the GP system. It indexes all its operations, that it has to test and which it can use

Table 1. Function set for the genetic programming approach to choose from

Node Name	Description	Can have Children	Can be Terminal
L-Variable	Variable definition	yes	no
R-Variable	Reference to an L-variable	no	yes
Constant	Primitive value (int, double, …)	no	yes
Constructor	Creates an object	yes	yes
Method	Calls an object's method	yes	no
Assignment	State change of an object	yes	no
SUT	Subject under test	yes	no
Array	Creates an array of objects	yes	no
NULL	Keyword (in the constructor)	no	yes

to change its state. All the classes to which it maintains references in the signatures of its operations are also indexed, plus all subsequent classes used by these. This indexing is performed recursively until all classes needed for the test case are loaded and known to the GP system. Abstract parameter types, or interfaces, and classes that extend or implement these must be added manually to the index of the GP system. That is, only if they are not referenced by some other already existing and indexed class. Figure 1 shows an example tree-shaped representation of a GP-chromosome that translates into the following Java testing code snippet (moving from left to right).

```
List var1 = new List ();
var1.add (new Object());
var1.add (null);
var.size();
```

Object Reflection

In order for GP to work properly and generate valid testing code, it needs rules, on the basis of which it can recombine existing nodes and generate new nodes. In traditional genetic programming, the grammar usually comprises all constructs of the programming language used (Koza, 1992). Test code is usually straight-forward, and all it needs to do is to invoke a certain sequence of operation invocations with parameter values, including the creation and initialization of the variables used.

The rules are restricted to the operations of the SUT plus the objects and return types that it uses in these operations. In Java, these can even be generated during runtime through Java's built-in reflection mechanism (Forman & Forman, 2004). This information is then stored in a repository of basic symbols representing the rules that the genetic programming algorithm can use to generate test programs, in other words, its instruction set. Earlier, we referred to this repository as the GP index.

The hierarchical structure of testing code is typically flat, like the one displayed in Figure 1. This flat hierarchy is due to the fact that testing has a more sequential nature, by calling one operation after another, leading to a single path through the test program. This is different from "normal functional code" that is usually made up of conditional executions, leading to various paths through the program. Every operation invoked is attached as sub-tree close to the root node of the entire chromosome tree. Extensive hierarchical structure is only exhibited if operation invocations

Figure 1. Example tree-shaped representation of a GP-chromosome

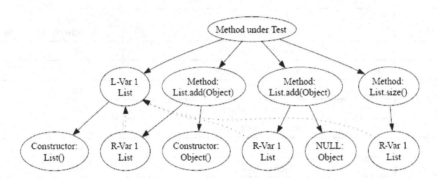

require objects as input parameters, although this can be circumvented by imposing flat hierarchies.

Operators for Genetic Programming

Initial Population

Two different methods are used in order to create the first population, i.e. a random population, or a population based on execution traces. The first method selects initial operation invocations including their input values randomly. The second method applies existing knowledge from executing the SUT. Here, we can form an initial population from already known typical usage scenarios of the SUT, or from unit tests. This leads to an initial population that can already cover many of the SUT's runtime paths for typical usage profiles. This method improves the performance of the test generation for the remaining coverage targets considerably.

Mutation

GP requires a separate mutation operator for each individual basic building block, each of which may be subject to mutation according to a predefined mutation rate. We can distinguish three types of mutation operators, a first one that creates a new

building block, a second one that changes an existing building block, and a third one that deletes a building block. Mutation operators have been devised for each of the functions summarized in Table 1.

A constructor can be created, deleted or changed to a different constructor. Creation or deletion implies that their respective sub-trees, comprising input parameters, are created or deleted. The same principles that apply to constructors apply also to other operations, the normal methods of an object. They can be added or removed, or their input values can be changed. Constructors and normal methods are different only in the way that we need at least one constructor in order to create the object, and the constructor must always be invoked before any other operation. An example of constructor mutation is shown in Figure 2.

Some methods take objects as arguments. These objects need to be created through a constructor and, maybe, also their operations need to be invoked. This principle may be applied recursively, depending on the operations required, thus potentially leading to constructor compositions of arbitrary depth. We have decided not to permit the generation of such hierarchies, and move the composite constructor sub-tree up towards the root node. The object constructor can then be moved to a position in the tree where it

Figure 2. Tree-based mutation of genetic programming

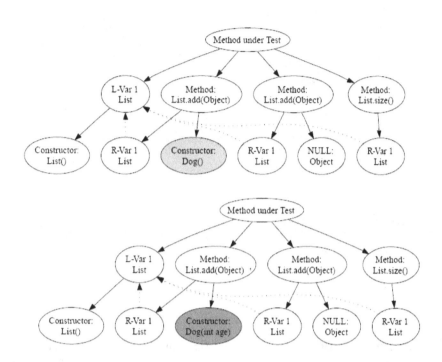

is executed before the object reference is used as input value. It is important to note that there is no reason for restricting the composition depth other than controllability of the experiments. It makes it easier to understand what the GP-algorithm is doing and to control and assess its behavior.

Crossover

In GP, unlike genetic algorithms, the crossover is only applied at nodes in the chromosome tree, and not at leaves. The nodes for crossover are determined randomly for each of the two partici-pating individuals, or through a search for distinct nodes. If the two crossover nodes are compatible, the crossover operator simply exchanges the en-tire sub-trees. Two sub-trees are compatible, if the types of the two root nodes of the candidate sub-trees are the same, and a search through the tree can actually determine feasible nodes of the

same type. Compatibility is always given at the root node level of the entire chromosome tree. The simplest crossover is performed at the method level, thus exchanging entire methods including input parameters. Input parameter nodes can also be exchanged, given that they have the same types, and constant values can be swapped between in-dividuals. Figure 3 illustrates an exchange at the root level, swapping entire sub-trees of methods.

Crossover and mutation can generate chro-mosomes of arbitrary length over time, simply by adding more and more sub-trees. This is not desirable, so overgrowth of the chromosome must be regulated through the introduction of a penalty on the overall fitness for larger individuals. This turns our approach into a multi-objective evolu-tionary algorithm, although, here, size of the test case is the second optimization objective, thus putting selective pressure on the generation of short test scenarios.

Figure 3. Tree-based crossover of genetic programming

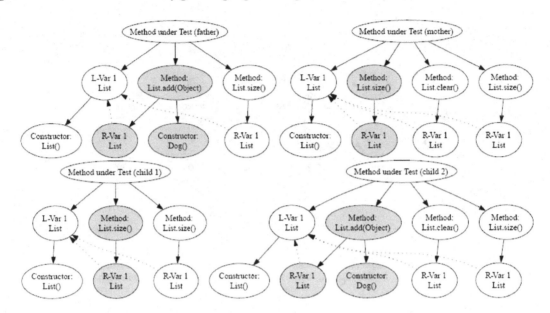

Optimization of the Genetic Programming Approach

Two-Stage Optimization

Every test case generated by the GP approach must be compiled, eventually, into an executable program. This creates a lot of overhead, considering the number of individuals (test cases) generated in order to cover a specific test target in the code. This can be optimized by separating the generation of the structure of the test case, i.e., its method invocations, represented as nodes in the tree of the generated program, from the generation of the parameter values applied in each of these method invocations. That way, a structure must only be generated and compiled once, and then executed with a large number of input values, generated separately by a standard genetic algorithm.

Program Analysis

The GP algorithm uses the complete instruction set of the SUT, although, some of the methods provided do not have any effect on the identi-fication of a suitable test case, because they do not alter the state of the SUT, e.g., typical get-information-type method invocations. They are useless for identifying a good method sequence for checking behavioral correctness, for example.

Methods not altering the internal state of the SUT are referred to as pure methods, according to Salcianu and Rinard (2004). Following their approach, we have implemented an analysis step in order to identify and mark pure methods, so that the GP approach omits them in the test case generation process. It is also possible to annotate methods with this purity information, in case the analysis fails to identify them automatically.

A further improvement in the GP-based test case generation process can be achieved if an operational profile of the SUT is available, i.e., in the form of unit tests, or real execution scenarios, and a tracing mechanism exists for the SUT. This is can be achieved through instrumentation of the code with coverage flags. The existing test cases can already provide coverage of a large extent of the SUT and be used as a starting point for the evolutionary search. They would be encoded as initial population, rather than creating a random population to start with. That way, GP can already build upon a number of standard individuals to be further recombined and mutated in order to drive the search process into other areas of interest.

Genotype-Phenotype Transfer and Program Execution

We are using coverage metrics to indicate an individual's fitness, following the work done by Jones, Sthamer and Eyres (1996), and by Pargas, Harrold, and Peck (1999). There are two approaches to execute an individual and obtain coverage information. The first one generates the test program code, for example as Java source or byte code, after which it will compile and execute it. The second one uses the reflection mechanism in Java. This allows us to skip the creation, compilation and class loading steps present in the first approach. For example, the method node has as its children a node which creates an object to call a method on (if it is not a static method), and nodes to create the arguments it might need. Although, reflection calls are much slower than the normal Java calls, using reflection compensates for the additional overhead of creation, compilation, and loading of a normal Java class.

5 EXPERIMENTS WITH TEST CASE GENERATION BASED ON GENETIC PROGRAMMING

In order to demonstrate the applicability of the proposed test case generation technique based on

GP, we have applied it to 5 test programs (SUT), XMLElement, an XML parsing package including a number of classes, and from the Java collection classes, HashMap, BitSet, TreeMap, and TreeTokenizer. All test runs were executed on a 2.1 GHz Athlon XP under Java 1.6. Mutation was set to 70% method introduction, 15% method removal, and 15% variable introduction.

The results displayed in Table 2 demonstrate the advantage of the GP approach over a traditional random testing strategy in terms of test coverage achieved. Only for the smallest SUT, StringTokenizer, the random testing technique could generate the same high coverage (100%) as the GP approach. For the other examples, the GP approach achieves much higher test coverage. The columns time in seconds, Time(s), give an indication of how much more processing time is required for the GP, which is a much more complex algorithm, compared to the random generator.

The outcome of the experiments displayed in Table 2 shows that the GP approach performs much better in terms of coverage that the random approach. The difference in coverage becomes larger with increasing complexity and size of the SUT, while the performance overhead of the much more complicated GP approach remains acceptable.

Although these results are promising, it is important to note that evolutionary algorithms employ a variety of parameters for their proper adjustment and tuning. Changing and adapting these parameters to the problem at hand can improve the results obtained significantly, or it can increase the speed of conversion drastically. Figures 4 and 5 demonstrate these effects.

The results shown in Table 2 are the best values obtained, after performing a number of experiments with a variety of GP parameter settings. Finding the settings leading to an optimal solution in terms of convergence and performance is an open research topic, and represents a multidimensional search problem in its own right. Future work should address this issue and come up with generally optimal parameter settings for evolutionary computation applied to software testing problems.

Table 2. Tested SUTs, comparison between GP-based testing and random testing; best results obtained

SUT Name	# of Branches	GP-testing		Random testing	
		Coverage(%)	Time(s)	Coverage(%)	Time(s)
BitSet	124	100	495	86	133
XML-Element	121	90	369	80	101
HashMap	50	94	180	72	43
TreeMap	39	92	13	46	29
StringTokenizer	5	100	5	100	2

Figure 4. Effects of the number of generations and static purity analysis on the coverage

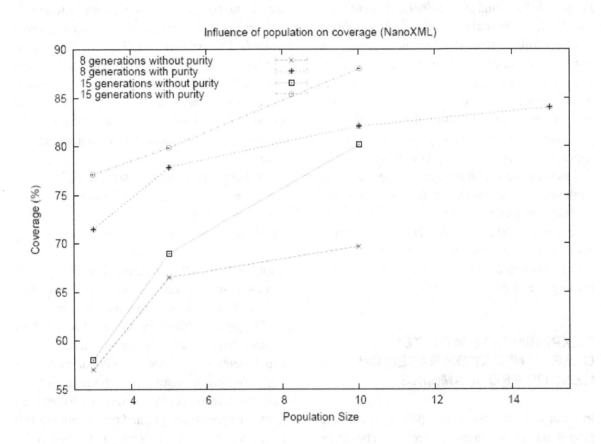

6 SUMMARY, CONCLUSION AND FUTURE WORK

This chapter introduced a method for generating test cases automatically according to a coverage criterion for object-oriented software, based on the application of genetic programming. We have argued in favor of genetic programming as a likely more suitable technique for the generation of test operation invocation sequences, in contrast to applying genetic algorithms. This is due to the more natural representation of the GP approach in terms of program trees, compared with the binary representation of a genetic algorithm.

Figure 5. Effects of the number of generations and static purity analysis on the performance

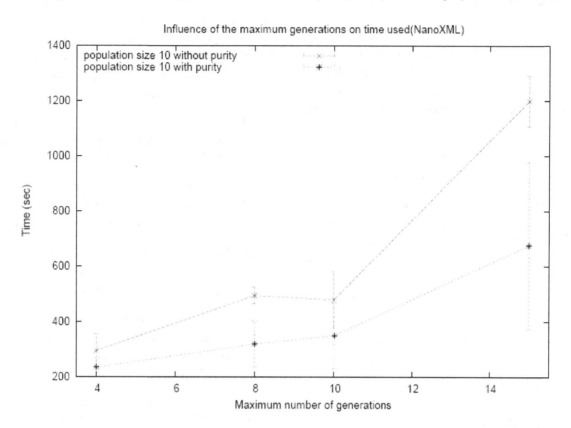

We have presented the principles of GP-based test case generation and shown how it can be improved with program analysis techniques and a two-stage execution. The outcome of our small proof-of-concept study and the experiments performed indicates that GP performs much better than random testing in terms of coverage, with an acceptable overhead in terms of performance.

The classical literature on genetic programming provides a large number of different genetic operators for recombination and mutation. We have only chosen a small subset of these and implemented them in our experimental approach. In general we can conclude that GP is well suitable to generate test scenarios for object-oriented programs. Many of the GP operators available have not been tried out, so there is still much room for improvement in the future.

Although, the range of operations used for our experiments is limited due to the small size of the test programs utilized for our experiments, larger classes with many more operations and, therefore, larger alphabets for the GP, are feasible in general. However, testing such large classes will lead to considerably larger hierarchical trees to be handled by the GP approach. These will expand the search space of the heuristic drastically with an expected considerable decrease in performance of the algorithm. Such scalability issues will have to be studied in the future and they are critical to the adoption of the technique in industrial contexts. Another issue to be addressed in the future is the selection of the right operators and their fine-tuning to the specific problem at hand. This can be seen as an optimization problem in its own right.

REFERENCES

Baresel, A., Pohlheim, H., & Sadeghipour, S. (2003). Structural and Functional Sequence Test of Dynamic and State-Based Software with Evolutionary Algorithms. In *Proc. of the Genetic and Evolutionary Computation Conference*, Chicago, IL.

Beizer, B. (1990). *Software Testing Techniques*. New York: Van Nostrand Reinhold.

Buehler, O., & Wegener, J. (2003). *Evolutionary Functional Testing of an Automated Parking System*. Intl. Conf. on Computer, Communication and Control Technologies (CCCT'03) and the 9th. Intl Conf. on Information Systems Analysis and Synthesis: ISAS '03, Orlando, Florida, July 31, August 1-2.

Forman, I. R., & Forman, N. (2004). *Java Reflection in Action*. Greenwich, CT: Manning.

Goldberg, D. E. (1989). *Genetic Algorithms in Search, Optimization and Machine Learning*. Reading, MA: Addison-Wesley.

Gross, H.-G. (2003). An *Evaluation of Dynamic, Optimization-based Worst-case Execution Time Analysis*. Proceedings of the International Conference on Information Technology: Prospects and Challenges in the 21st Century, Kathmandu, Nepal, May.

Gross, H.-G. (2005). *Component-Based Software Testing with UML. Springer, Heidelberg. Holland, J. (1975). Adaptation in Natural and Artificial Systems*. Cambridge, MA: MIT Press.

Gross, H.-G., & Mayer, N. (2002). *Evolutionary Testing in Component-Based Real-Time System Construction*. Proc. of the Genetic and Evolutionary Computation Conference, New York, July 8–14.

Gross, H.-G., & Mayer, N. (2003). *Search-Based Execution Time Verification in Object-Oriented and Component-Based Real-Time System Development*. Proc. of the 8th IEEE Intl. Workshop on Object-Oriented Real-Time Dependable Systems, Guadalajara, Mexico, January 15-17.

IEEE. (1999). *Standard Glossary of Software Engineering Terminology, (Volume IEEE Std. 610.12-1990)*. Washington, DC: Author.

Jones, B., Sthamer, H.-H., & Eyres, D. (1996). Automatic Structural Testing Using Genetic Algorithms. *Software Engineering Journal, 11*(5).

Koza, D. (1992). *Genetic Programming, On the Programming of Computers by Means of Natural Selection*. Cambridge, MA: MIT Press.

McMinn, P. (2004). Search-Based Software Test Data Generation: A Survey. *Software Testing. Verification and Reliability, 14*(2), 105–156. doi:10.1002/stvr.294

Michael, C., McGraw, G., & Schatz, M. (2001). Generating Software Test Data by Evolution. *IEEE Transactions on Software Engineering, 27*(12). doi:10.1109/32.988709

Pargas, R., Harrold, M., & Peck, R. (1999). Test data generation using genetic algorithms. *Software Testing, Verification & Reliability, 9*(4).

Ribeiro, J. C., Zenha-Rela, M., & de Vega, F. F. (2008). An Evolutionary Approach for Performing Structural Unit-Testing on Third-Party Object-Oriented Java Software. In *Studies in Computational Intelligence* (*Vol. 129*). Heidelberg, Germany: Springer.

Ribeiro, J.C., Zenha-Rela, M., de Vega, F.F. (2008). *A strategy for evaluating feasible and unfeasible test cases for the evolutionary testing of object-oriented software*.

Salcianu, A., & Rinard, M. (2004). *A combined pointer and purity analysis for java programs.* Technical Report MIT-CSAIL-TR-949, Massachusetts Institute of Technology.

Schwefel, H. P., & Männer, R. (1990). *Parallel Problem Solving from Nature.* Berlin: Springer.

Seesing, A. (2005, April). *An Overview of Automatic Object-Oriented Test Case Generation using Genetic Programming.* Internal Report, Research Assignment, EWI – Delft University of Technology.

Seesing, A., Gross, H.-G. (2006). A Genetic Programming Approach to Automated Test Generation of Object-Oriented Software. *Transactions on System Science and Applications, 1*(2).

Tonella, P. (2004, July 11–14). Evolutionary Testing of Classes. In *Proc. of the 2004 ACM SIGSOFT Intl. Symposium on Software Testing and Analysis*, Boston, (pp. 119–128).

Tracey, N., et al. (1999). Integrating Safety Analysis with Automatic Test-Data Generation for Software Safety Verification. In *Proc. of 17th International System Safety Conference*, August.

Tracey, N., Clarke, J., & Mander, K. (1998). The way forward in unifying dynamic test case generation: The optimisation-based approach. In *Proc. of the IFIP Intl Workshop of Dependable Computing,* South Africa, January.

von Laarhoven, P., & Aarts, E. (1987). Simmulatd Annealing: Theory and Applications. In *Mathematics and its Applications.* Dordrecht, The Netherlands: Kluwer.

Wappler, S., & Lammermann, F. (2005). Using Evolutionary Algorithms for the Unit Testing of Object-Oriented Software. In *Proc. of the Genetic and Evolutionary Computation Conference*, Washington, DC (June 25–29).

Wegener, J. & Grochtmann, M. (1998). Verifying timing constraints by means of evolutionary Testing. *Real-Time Systems, 3*(15).

Chapter 11
Assessment of Software Quality:
A Fuzzy Multi-Criteria Approach

Praveen Ranjan Srivastava
Birla Institute of Technology and Science (BITS), India

Ajit Pratap Singh
Civil Engineering Group, India

Vageesh K. V.
Indian Institute of Management (IIM), India

ABSTRACT

Software Quality Assurance consists of monitoring the software engineering processes and ensuring the highest quality. But, the software quality attributes that we deal with are not explicit in the outset and cannot be easily measured. The same attribute has multiple significance and importance in multiple contexts. The user, the developer and the manager of a software product may have different stands regarding the significance of a quality attribute. A software quality engineer, while measuring the total software quality should provide appropriate weight to each of the decision makers. This chapter proposes a fuzzy multi-criteria approach to measure the total software quality and to identify the best alternative from a set of software products.

INTRODUCTION

Software engineering is the application of a systematic, disciplined, quantifiable approach to the development, operation, and maintenance of software (Pierre Bourque and Robert Dupuis, 2004). Computerized systems now pervade every aspect of our daily life, increasing the importance on the quality of the software that run them. As the hardware systems became more sophisticated, the software became more complex and new programming paradigms were introduced. The development and use of software is becoming very important in today's life of rapid technological advancement. It becomes even more important when critical decisions are made by software driven systems (M. Lehman, 1996).

Therefore, as we become more dependent on software based systems, there is a need to produce high quality software which requires a systematic approach for quantification of quality of the software developed. Software quality is generally defined as "the degree to which a system or its components, or the processes involved in the system meets speci-

DOI: 10.4018/978-1-61520-809-8.ch011

fied requirements". It can also be expressed as "the degree to which a system, its components, or process meets customer or user based expectations." (Sivamuni Kalaimagal and Rengaramanujam Srinivasan, 2008). Quality, in general, is the totality of features and characteristics of a product or a service that bears on its ability to satisfy the given needs (Arun Sharma, Rajesh Kumar and P. S. Grover, 2008). According to Ljerka Beus Dukic and Jorgen Boegh (2003), software quality evaluation is defined as "the systematic examination of the software capability to fulfill specified quality requirements." A software quality model is defined as, "a set of characteristics and sub characteristics, as well as the relationships between them that provide the basis for specifying quality requirements and evaluating quality." To fulfill the expectations of user, good software should deal various quality attributes, the quantification of which is a challenging and complex prospect.

Many investigators have classified various software quality attributes depending on the important viewpoints of a software product (Luigi Buglione and Alian Abran, 1999) and (Praveen Ranjan Srivastava and Krishan Kumar, 2009) these can be as follows:

- Attributes with Manager's Perspective
- Attributes with User's Perspective
- Attributes with Developer's Perspective

These attributes can play important role while integrating the effect of each one of them to evaluate the best software quality among the given alternatives. All such important attributes for choosing the best alternative have to be considered which should not only deal with the uncertainty associated with specifying various attributes but also discuss different criteria. This can be dealt by applying the concept of fuzzy multi-criteria approach because the method is suitable for making decision under fuzzy environment. To deal with uncertainty in the form of fuzziness of the selection process of good software, the importance weights

of various criteria and the ratings of qualitative criteria are to be considered as linguistic variables. Fuzzy logic allows linguistic values such as good, poor and bad to take numerical values and thus enabling us to include such values in numerical calculations. In this chapter an application of fuzzy multi-criteria approach has been introduced to assess the software quality parameters by identifying the various types of software attributes.

BACKGROUND

The concept of software quality is more complex than what common people tend to believe. However, it is very important both for common user and IT professionals (Cote, M., A. Suryn and W. Georgiadou, 2006). If we look at the definition of quality in a dictionary, it is usual to find something like the following: set of characteristics that allows us to rank things as better as or worse than other similar ones. In many cases, dictionaries mention the idea of excellence together with this type of definitions.

Software Quality refers to the abilities related properties of software products which meet users' needs. According to its standards, the software quality evaluation is the software development process throughout the software quality and continuous measurement, revealing the current state, estimating the follow-up trend of software quality and providing precisely control of it (FuLi Jin, Guisheng Yin and Dekun Yang, 2008). Software quality can be evaluated quantitatively to assess precisely and efficiently so that it can provide an objective and impartial scientific basis (Souheil Khaddaj and G Horgan, 2004).

Software Quality Attributes are the benchmarks that describe system's expected behavior within the environment for which it was built. Software Quality Attributes provide visibility to management that the software products and processes in the project life cycle conform to the specified requirements and established plans (Sandra A. Slaughter, Donald E Harter and Mayuram S Krishnan,1998).Various quality metrics and factors are given by J. E. Gaffney (1981), but it is hard to evaluate total software quality.

Software quality can either refer to the software product quality or the software process quality. Examples used for product quality are the CMM (Capability Maturity Model) and CMM-I (Capability Maturity Model-Integrated) models (Pressman, 2005). The ISO standards have been set for both product as well as process quality. For example, ISO/IEC JTC1 ISO9126 (1-5), talks of software product quality while ISO/IEC JTC1, ISO-15504-5 talks about software process quality (Sivamuni Kalaimagal and Rengaramanujam Srinivasan 2008).

The discipline of software quality is a planned and systematic set of activities to ensure that quality is built into the software. It consists of software quality assurance, software quality control, and software quality engineering. According to the IEEE 610.12(IEEE, 1990) standard, software quality is a set of attributes of a software system and is defined as:

1. The degree to which a system, component, or process meets the specific requirements.
2. The degree to which a system, component, or process meets customer or user needs or expectations.
3. Quality comprises all characteristics and significant features of a product or an activity which related to the satisfaction of given requirements.

Measuring the quality of a software product is really a challenging task. One problem in making this determination is the absence of a widely accepted definition of software quality. This leads to confusion when trying to specify quality goals for software. A limited understanding of the relationships among the factors that comprise software quality is a further drawback to making quality specifications for software (Joseph P. Cavano and James A. McCall, 1978).

A second frequent problem in producing high quality software is that only at delivery and into operations and maintenance is one able to determine how good the software system is. At this point, modifications or enhancements are very expensive. The user is usually forced to accept systems that cannot perform their mission adequately because of funding, contractual, or schedule constraints (Joseph P. Cavano and James A. McCall, 1978).

In previous approach (Praveen Ranjan Srivastava and Krishan Kumar, 2009) proposed a model that took in to account the three perspectives of a manager, user and developer in calculating the total quality of a software product. Here, we extend the methodology and assign weights to each of the attributes and accommodate the three perspectives as three different decision makers. The quality attributes are considered as different criteria to select best alternative among the given software products using fuzzy based multi-criteria analysis.

The concept of Fuzzy Logic was conceived by Lotfi Zadeh, a professor currently at the University of California at Berkeley, and presented not as a control methodology, but as a way of processing data by allowing partial set membership rather than crisp set membership or non-membership. Fuzzy Logic is a problem-solving control system methodology that lends itself to implementation in systems ranging from simple, small, embedded micro-controllers to large, networked, multi-channel computers or workstation-based data acquisition and control systems. It can be implemented in hardware, software, or a combination of both. Fuzzy Logic provides a simple way to arrive at a definite conclusion based upon vague, ambiguous, imprecise, noisy, or missing input information. L.A. Zadeh (1976)

There are several other instances where researchers have used fuzzy logic, neural networks and other models to determine the quality of a software product. Previously Lily Lin and Huey-Ming Lee (2007) presented a new assessment method to obtain the integrated software quality for evaluating user satisfaction using fuzzy set theory based on the ISO 9126 Sample Quality Model with a single evaluator. Bo Yang, Lan Yao and Hong-Zhong Huang (2007) had proposed a software quality prediction model based on a fuzzy neural network which helps in identifying design errors in software products in the early stages of a software lifecycle.

The literature in multi-criteria ranking problems has considerably expanded over recent years. Some very old books, judged by today's criteria, are still relevant, (e.g. the books by Fishburn (1964). In most of the early books, the basic ranking problems have been considered when the values of criteria and the relative importance of criteria were taken as real numbers Fishburn (1964), Roy B (1971). Kahne (1975) proposed a ranking methodology to cope with the cases when criteria values and the relative importance of criteria were independent random variables with given distributions. In most of the widely used multi-criteria ranking methods it is assumed that the alternatives are evaluated by quantitative criteria. This seriously reduces the applicability of these methods to many real-world problems.

There is an enhanced interest in developing new approaches to multi-criteria decision making where the criteria of interest and their relative importance are expressed by qualitative terms (such as low, medium, high, etc.) The imprecision that is inherent in qualitative descriptions of criteria values and criteria weights can be formalized using fuzzy logic and fuzzy set theory (Klir and Folger, 1988). Bellman and Zadeh (1970) and Yager (1978) modeled objectives and attributes together to form the decision space which is represented by a fuzzy set whose membership function is the degree to which each alternative is a solution.

Baas and Kwakernak (1977) introduced fuzzy concepts in ranking, assuming that criteria values and the relative importance of criteria were fuzzy numbers. They extended the classical weighted average rating method to handle fuzzy numbers. The final evaluation of alternatives was given by their membership functions by Baas, S.M. and Kwakernaak, H (1977). Dong, W.M. and Wong, F.S (1987), employed algebraic operations of fuzzy numbers based on the extension principle.

Till the beginning of the nineties, the fuzzy integral was used as the aggregation tool for computing an average global score, taking into account the importance of criteria expressed by a fuzzy measure. Despite the somewhat empirical way fuzzy measures were used at the beginning, it was very early noticed that fuzzy measures can model in some sense a kind of interaction between criteria, but this issue was not formalized till M. Grabisch (1996) proposed a generalization of the index to any subset of criteria. Then, after the proposal of T. Murofushi and M. Sugeno (1989), to use the Choquet integral, which is an extension of classical Lebesgue integral, and thus of the well known weighted sum, it was quickly adopted among practitioners. If in decision under uncertainty, the use of the Choquet integral immediately received a firm theoretical basis through providing axiomatic characterizations D. Schmeidler (1989), the first works in MCDA remained on a rather intuitive and experimental level.

A reader who prefers contemporary texts can find interesting ideas for integration of knowledge based methods with multi-criteria decision making and fuzzy logic to deal with imprecision inherent in decision making. Carlsson C and Fuller R (1996) gave a survey of fuzzy multi-criteria decision making methods with emphasis on fuzzy relations between interdependent criteria (Singh Ajit Pratap and A. K. Vidarthi, 2008).

We use fuzzy multi-criteria approach to deal with the fuzziness that is known to exist in software quality attributes. The method is suitable for making decisions under fuzzy environment. To deal with uncertainty in the form of fuzziness of the total quality of a software product, the importance weights of various criteria and the ratings of qualitative criteria are considered as linguistic variables in this chapter. Fuzzy logic is then applied on each of the criteria and using the multi-criteria methodology the total software quality or the best software product out of a set of products can be found.

FUZZY LOGIC: AN OVERVIEW

In 1965, L.A. Zadeh laid the foundations of fuzzy set theory (Zadeh, L. A., 1965) to deal with the imprecision of practical Systems. Bellman and Zadeh have emphasized: "Much of the decision-making in the real world takes place in an environment in which the goals, the constraints and the consequences of possible actions are not known precisely" (R. E. Bellman and L. A. Zadeh,1970). The "impreciseness" or fuzziness is the core of fuzzy sets or fuzzy logic applications. These fuzzy sets were suggested as a generalization of conventional set theory (Pratap, S. A. and Vidarthi, A. K.,(2008)). Fuzzy logic is an extension of multivalued logics (Novák V and Perfilieva Močkoř; 1999) which offers the base for approximate reasoning with uncertain and vague propositions. Fuzzy logic allows qualitatively speaking the use of fuzzy predicates; e.g., instead of binary true and false propositions, we can use predicates such as" usual", or quantifiers like "all". In principle the binary valued logic can be extended to be multivalued logic [0, 1.(Petri Mähönen, 2000).More information about fuzzy set theory and fuzzy logic can be found from Klir and Folger (1988), Zadeh (1965), Driankov et al. (1994), and Pedrycz (1993). However, certain features of fuzzy approach to represent a system behavior are given as discussed below.

Fuzzy Logic is basically a multivalued logic that allows intermediate values to be defined between conventional evaluations like yes/no, true/false, black/white, etc. Notions like rather warm or pretty cold can be formulated mathematically using fuzzy logic and processed by computers (Peter B., Stephan N., Roman W, 1996). This type of formulation has the following advantages: 1) It is easy to implement since it uses "if-then" logic instead of sophisticated differential equations; 2) It is understandable by people who do not have process control backgrounds; and 3) Software and hardware tools are readily available for applying this technology.

Fuzzy Membership Function

Sometimes it is not necessary that the classification of the object is clear and precise in real life decision making process and no clear boundary exists among the objects; for instance, the boundary of the class of young people and old people. A kind of ambiguity appears in this case because of the absence of the clear defined boundary between these objects. The traditional Boolean logic of the classification, on the other hand, uses 0 and 1 to describe the membership relation between one specific object and the class of this kind of objects. When the specific object belongs to that class, the value of characteristic function that describes the membership relation between one specific object and classification is 1, whereas, the value is 0 when the specific object does not belong to the class completely.

However, Fuzzy Set Theory can describe the imprecisely defined 'classes' by introducing a degree of membership of an element with respect to some sets. The grade of membership can be achieved by adopting the concept of a membership function to assign a number ranging from zero (absolutely not belonging) to unit (fully belonging) according to the degree (grade) of belongingness to each element of a universe of discourse (Singh Ajit Pratap, 2008).

In fact the membership function is a graphical representation of the magnitude of participation of each input. It associates a weighting with each of the inputs that are processed, define functional overlap between inputs, and ultimately determines an output response. The rules use the input mem-

Figure 1. The characteristic function for the set of young people

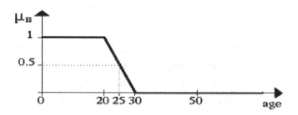

bership values as weighting factors to determine their influence on the fuzzy output sets of the final output conclusion. Once the functions are inferred, scaled, and combined, they are defuzzified into a crisp output which drives the system. There are different memberships functions exist which are associated with each input and output response. These membership functions could be triangular, trapezoidal, curved etc. which may be used depending upon the experience of the decision maker/project manager.

Let us consider an example in which it is required to describe the set of young people. More formally if it is denoted as B = {set of young people}. In this concept, $\mu G (B)$ is the membership function which represents the 'grade of membership' of B in G. The value of $\mu G (B)$ gives a way of giving a graded answer to the question "to what degree is object U a membership of set U?" For example, U is the set of the different assessment factors of the young people in a locality. The possible functional values of $\mu G (U)$ range from 0 to 1, and include the value between them.

To have better understanding, the set of young people can be explained by its characteristic function as shown in Figure 1. For example if it is required to determine the degree of membership of a 25 years old person, Figure 1 gives a value of membership function equal to 0.5 which still belongs to the set of young people with degree of 50 percent.

Linguistic Variables

In 1973, Professor Lotfi Zadeh proposed the concept of linguistic or "fuzzy" variables. Think of them as linguistic objects or words, rather than numbers. The sensor input is a noun, e.g. "experience", "software", "cost" etc. Since error is just the difference, it can be thought of the same way. The fuzzy variables themselves are adjectives that modify the variable (e.g. "large positive" error, "small positive" error, "zero" error, "small negative" error, and "large negative" error). As a minimum, one could simply have "positive", "zero", and "negative" variables for each of the parameters. Additional ranges such as "very large" and "very small" could also be added to extend the responsiveness to exceptional or very nonlinear conditions, but aren't necessary in a basic system.

Fuzzy Steps

Broadly, problems dealing with fuzzy logic concepts can divided into three steps:

1. Fuzzification of data: In this step, the fuzzification process is carried out by developing membership functions generated from different input sources.
2. Development of Fuzzy Rule Base: The fuzzy rule base is usually constructed from the experience of the decision maker. This phase comprises of applying the fuzzy rule base over the fuzzy input and arriving at the fuzzy output.
3. Defuzzification of Output Data: It converts the fuzzy output into crisp output. There are several ways of defuzzification. Some of them are mean-of-maxima method, center of gravity method, modified center of gravity method, height method etc. In this chapter, center of gravity technique has been used for defuzzification

Fuzzy Rule Based System

Fuzzy linguistic descriptions are formal representation of system made through fuzzy IF-THEN rules. They encode knowledge about a system in statement of the form-

IF (xi is X1, x2 is X2,……..xn is Xn) THEN (y1 is Y1, y2 is Y2,……..yn is Yn)

where linguistic variables xi, yj take the value of fuzzy sets Xi and Yj respectively. Examples are

If there is good software which has large application of it in real life problems then there must be high demand of the software. Here good, large are fuzzy sets qualifying the variables software, application and demand.

Fuzzy-to-Crisp Conversions (Defuzzification Methods)

In many situations, for a system whose output is fuzzy, it is easier to take a crisps decision if the output is represented as a single scalar quantity. This conversion of a fuzzy set to single crisp value is called defuzzififcation and is the reverse process of fuzzification. Defuzzification is necessary to alter its fuzzified value by a specific quantity. For example, we cannot instruct the voltage going into a machine to increase 'slightly', even if this instruction comes from fuzzy controller, we must alter its voltage by a specific amount. Several methods are available in the literature (Hellendoorn and Thomas,1993) of which we just mention a few of widely used methods, namely Max-membership principle, Centroid Method (Center of Gravity Method),Weighted average method, Mean –max Membership.(Padhy N.P, 2005)

METHODOLOGY

Generally software quality is assessed by considering various attributes which may be classified into three sub categories that are: internal, external, and managerial quality attributes Praveen Ranjan Srivastava and Krishan Kumar, 2009). These sub categories of attributes can be dealt with developer, user, and manager respectively. The internal quality factors such as maintainability, flexibility, portability, reusability, readability, testability, understandability, and industrial experience are used to be evaluated by the developer whereas the external quality factors such as correctness, usability, efficiency, integrity, adaptability, accuracy, robustness and reliability are used to be best evaluated by the software user. Similarly certain other attributes with regard to manager perspective can also be considered such as cost, time, and scheduling pressure of development of the software. These managerial attributes also play a very important role in the decision making process of the overall quality evaluation of the software. A pictorial representation of all these attributes is given in Figure 2.

The importance of any particular factor varies from application to application. The basic meaning of each software quality attributes are: software can be of a good quality if correctness is high i.e. the extent to which a program satisfies its specifications. Reliability is the property which defines how well the software meets its requirements. Usability is factor required to operate the software properly. Efficiency is a factor to relate execution of software. Integrity is a factor to relate nature of software as per need of customer. Adaptability is factor where user can easily adopt new software. Robustness reduces the impact of operational mistakes, erroneous input data, and hardware error. Maintainability is the effort required to locate and fix the proper error. Flexibility is the effort required to modify an operational program. Portability is the effort required to transfer the software from one hardware to another hardware. Reusability is the extent to which part of the software can be reused in other related application. Readability is a factor depends upon representation, programming style, consistency, structure of the system etc. Testability

Figure 2. Categorization of quality attributes

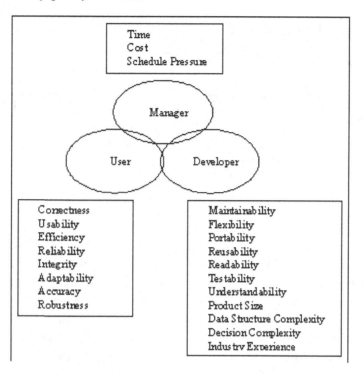

is the effort required to test to ensure that the system or a module performs its intended function. Understandability is a factor where developer can understand the structure of a system, when is there any problem. Product size represents total size of the software. Data structure complexity is a kind of algorithm representation for developer. Decision Complexity and Industry Experience is a factor for developer which represents capability and strength of a developer. Schedule pressure is defined as the relative compression of the development schedule mandated by management compared to the initial estimate provided by the development team based on project parameters. (Agrawal Manish and Chari Kaushal, 2007).

In this study we take in to account the 19 different quality attributes and 3 managerial factors that we defined. All the fuzzy criteria are denoted by the variable C with a numerical subscript i.e., as C1, C2 etc. Therefore we have a total of 22 such criteria. As discussed earlier, the three different perspectives are the three fuzzy decision makers

and are denoted by the variable D with a numerical subscript (D1, D2 and D3). However, there may be as many decision makers as can be included in the analysis. There are three different software products (A1, A2 and A3) have been considered to assess the superiority of the software among the three based on the opinion of all the decision makers and criteria mentioned above as shown in Figure 3.

The importance weights of each criterion and ratings of each product by the three decision makers are fuzzified and their means are calculated and tabulated. The normalized values of the ratings are used to calculate the vector corresponding to the value of final fuzzy evaluation of each alternative (P). The Fuzzy preference relation Matrix (E) is calculated from P vector accordingly. This matrix evaluation and its reduction is the last step to identify the best software among the three. Figure 4 explains step by step procedure to apply fuzzy logic concept for evaluation of software quality.

Figure 3. Selection of best software process

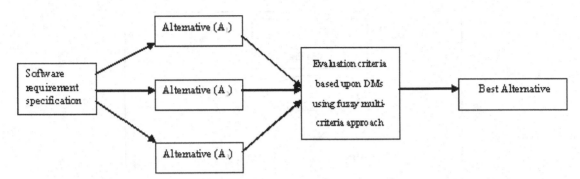

PROCEDURE

Step 1: As a first step, it is required to assign the attributes important to assess the software quality which may be collected from different decision makers. The attributes and the variables are tabulated in Table 1. We also assign variables for the decision makers as given in Table 2.

In Table 1, Criteria 1 to 8 are defined as external attributes and attributes 9 to 19 are defined as internal attributes. Criteria 20, 21 & 22 are Managerial quality attributes.

Step 2: After identifying appropriate attributes, it is required to develop membership function to incorporate fuzzy or linguistic behavior of each attribute. In this case the triangular fuzzy numbers for the different linguistic variables have been used to determine the importance of each criterion and in rating the software product. Each Decision maker allocates the weight of each criteria and thus giving rise to combined weight of the criteria which will be used in further calculations. The Decision maker only chooses one grade from the importance for each criteria, he/she ignores the decision maker's incomplete and uncertain thinking.

Therefore, if fuzzy numbers are used to assess the degree of feelings of a decision maker based on his own concepts, the computing results will be closer to the evaluator's real thought. The criteria ratings of importance are linguistic variables with

triangular fuzzy values which are very low (VL), low (L), medium (M), high (H) & very high (VH) as shown in Table 3. The triangular fuzzy number H.J. Zimmermann, 1991) representations of the linguistic values are:

Step 3: In addition to the importance of each criteria, triangular fuzzy numbers are also assigned to the ratings for each criteria. The quality ratings are very poor, poor, fair, good and very good for criteria 1 to 19.For the managerial Criteria we define the linguistic variables as very low (VL), low (L), middle (M), high (H) and very high (VH). The fuzzy numbers are similar to those assigned to the other ratings mentioned in Table 4.

To illustrate how the ratings and weights are added and multiplied we take up an example, compare the quality of three different software products A1, A2 & A3 from individual criteria importance and ratings given by the decision makers. In the following example we must remember that the values of importance and quality ratings are assumed because we know that the ratings and weight can vary across different types of software products The next step is to tabulate the weights of importance given by the decision makers for each of the criteria and mean weight is also calculated and tabulated

Step 4: Next we have to compute the fuzzy weight of each linguistic variable. The Fuzzy weight is calculated as follows: Consider criteria C2, the importance rating given by the decision

Figure 4. Various steps of fuzzy-based assessment of software quality

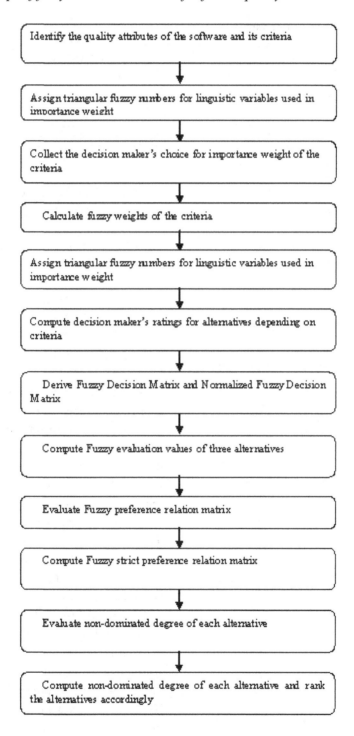

Table 1. Software quality attributes

Software Quality Attribute	Criteria Variable
Correctness	C_1
Usablity	C_2
Efficiency	C_3
Reliablity	C_4
Integrity	C_5
Adaptablity	C_6
Accuracy	C_7
Robustness	C_8
Maintainablity	C_9
Flexiblity	C_{10}
Portablity	C_{11}
Reusablity	C_{12}
Readablity	C_{13}
Testablity	C_{14}
Understandablity	C_{15}
Product Size	C_{16}
Data Structure Complexity	C_{17}
Decision Complexity	C_{18}
Industry Experience	C_{19}
Time	C_{20}
Cost	C_{21}
Schedule Pressure	C_{22}

Table 2. Different perspectives and corresponding decision makers

Perspectives	Decision Makers
Manager	D_1
User	D_2
Developer	D_3

Table 3. Linguistic values of the importance of criteria

Importance of Criteria	Triangular Fuzzy Number
Very low(VL)	(0.0,0.0,0.25)
Low(L)	(0.0,0.25,0.5)
Medium(M)	(0.25,0.5,0.75)
High(H)	(0.5,0.75,1.0)
Very high(VH)	(0.75,1.0,1.0)

makers D1, D2 and D3 are M, VH & M respectively. The importance weight of a criterion is calculated as the mean weight of the three decision makers.

Table 4. Linguistic values of the ratings

Ratings	Triangular Fuzzy Number
Very poor (VP)/ Very low(VL)	(0,1,3)
Poor(P)/ Low(L)	(1,3,5)
Fair(F)/ Medium(M)	(3,5,7)
Good(G)/ High(H)	(5,7,9)
Very good(VG)/ Very high(VH)	(7,9,10)

Fuzzy Mean Weight of C2 = Medium (M) + Very high (VH) + Medium (M) + / 3

= [(0.25, 0.5, 0.75) + (0.75, 1.0, 1.0) + (0.25, 0.5, 0.75)] / 3

= (0.25+0.75+0.25, 0.5+1.0+0.5, 0.75+1.0+0.75)/3

= (0.42, 0.67, 0.83)

Step 5: The next step is to tabulate the ratings given by the decision makers based on the definition of the quality attributes and the corresponding attributes of the three software products. Similarly, the ratings of the three different software products A1, A2 & A3 by the decision makers for each criterion is also assumed for ease of illustration.

The ratings given by the three different decision makers as mentioned above are then obtained and the normalized fuzzy rating for each criterion is calculated. Tables 6, 7 and 8 give the ratings and normalized fuzzy weights of the software products A1, A2 and A3 respectively.

Step 6: The next step is to calculate the normalized Fuzzy decision matrix for each criteria. Normalization is done by dividing each point by the maximum rating point of a criteria if the criteria is a benefit criteria and it is done by dividing the minimum rating point by the respective rating point if the criteria a cost criteria. Benefit Criteria contributes positively towards the over-all quality of the product and Cost Criteria have a negative

Table 5. Importance weight of each criterion

Criteria	D$_1$	D$_2$	D$_3$	Fuzzy Weight of the Criteria
C$_1$	H	VH	M	(0.50,0.75,0.92)
C$_2$	M	VH	M	(0.42,0.67,0.83)
C$_3$	H	VH	H	(0.58,0.83,1.0)
C$_4$	M	VH	H	(0.50,0.75,0.92)
C$_5$	H	VH	M	(0.50,0.75,0.92)
C$_6$	M	VH	M	(0.42,0.67,0.83)
C$_7$	H	VH	H	(0.58,0.83,1.0)
C$_8$	M	VH	H	(0.50,0.75,0.92)
C$_9$	H	H	VH	(0.58,0.83,1.0)
C$_{10}$	H	M	VH	(0.50,0.75,0.92)
C$_{11}$	H	H	VH	(0.58,0.83,1.0)
C$_{12}$	H	M	VH	(0.50,0.75,0.92)
C$_{13}$	H	H	VH	(0.58,0.83,1.0)
C$_{14}$	M	M	VH	(0.42,0.67,0.83)
C$_{15}$	M	H	VH	(0.50,0.75,0.92)
C$_{16}$	M	M	VH	(0.42,0.67,0.83)
C$_{17}$	M	H	VH	(0.50,0.75,0.92)
C$_{18}$	M	M	VH	(0.42,0.67,0.83)
C$_{19}$	M	H	VH	(0.50,0.75,0.92)
C$_{20}$	VH	L	H	(0.42,0.67,0.83)
C$_{21}$	VH	L	H	(0.42,0.67,0.83)
C$_{22}$	VH	VL	VH	(0.50,0.67,0.75)

impact on the same. In our quality attribute set, Criteria C20, C21 & C22 are cost criteria and other attributes benefit criteria.

Let Cij be the ratings matrix for Criteria A then the required normalized ratings is given by rij.

rij = (aij / cj*, bij / cj*, cij / cj*), if A is a benefit criteria and Cj* is max Cij

rij = (cj*/ aij, cj* /bij, cj*/ cij), if A is a cost criteria and Cj* is min Cij

For example, the fuzzy weights of criteria C1 for the products A1, A2 & A3 are taken as:

A1 (5.7, 7.7, 9.3)
A2 (5.0, 7.0, 6.7)
A3 (3.0, 5.0, 7.0)

The maximum rating for this criterion is 9.3 and by the above formulae the normalized fuzzy matrix for the criteria C1 is

A1 (0.61, 0.83, 1.0)
A2 (0.54, 0.75, 0.72)
A3 (0.32, 0.54, 0.75)

Step 7: After the above step, we calculate the fuzzy evaluation vector, The Fuzzy evaluation vector (P) for each software product by multiply-

Table 6. Ratings of software product A1 by D1, D2 and D3

Criteria	D_1	D_2	D_3	Fuzzy Ratings of the Criteria	Normalized Fuzzy Ratings
C_1	G	VG	G	(5.7,7.7,9.3)	(0.61,0.83,1.0)
C_2	G	VG	G	(5.7,7.7,9.3)	(0.61,0.83,1.0)
C_3	G	VG	G	(5.7,7.7,9.3)	(0.61,0.83,1.0)
C_4	G	VG	G	(5.7,7.7,9.3)	(0.61,0.83,1.0)
C_5	G	VG	G	(5.7,7.7,9.3)	(0.61,0.83,1.0)
C_6	G	VG	G	(5.7,7.7,9.3)	(0.61,0.83,1.0)
C_7	F	VG	F	(4.3,6.3,8.0)	(0.54,0.79,1.0)
C_8	G	VG	G	(5.7,7.7,9.3)	(0.61,0.83,1.0)
C_9	G	G	VG	(5.7,7.7,9.3)	(0.61,0.83,1.0)
C_{10}	G	P	VG	(4.3,6.7,8.0)	(0.54,0.84,1.0)
C_{11}	G	P	VG	(4.3,6.7,8.0)	(0.54,0.84,1.0)
C_{12}	VG	G	VG	(5.7,8.3,9.7)	(0.59,0.86,1.0)
C_{13}	F	G	VG	(5.0,7.0,6.7)	(0.65,0.90,0.87)
C_{14}	F	G	VG	(5.0,7.0,6.7)	(0.62,0.88,0.84)
C_{15}	F	G	VG	(5.0,7.0,6.7)	(0.65,0.90,0.87)
C_{16}	G	G	VG	(5.7,7.7,9.3)	(0.61,0.83,1.0)
C_{17}	G	G	VG	(5.7,7.7,9.3)	(0.61,0.83,1.0)
C_{18}	G	VG	VG	(5.7,8.3,9.7)	(0.59,0.86,1.0)
C_{19}	G	VG	VG	(5.7,8.3,9.7)	(0.59,0.86,1.0)
C_{20}	VH	M	H	(5.0,7.0,6.7)	(0.74,0.53,0.55)
C_{21}	VH	M	H	(5.0,7.0,6.7)	(0.74,0.53,0.55)
C_{22}	VH	M	VH	(5.7,7.7,9.0)	(0.65,0.48,0.41)

ing the respective ratings against their weights and adding it up.

$$P = \sum_{j=1}^{n} r_{ij} X w_j, \quad \text{where } i = 1,2,3, \& m$$

Where wj is normalized weights vector of each criteria.

The values of P1, P2 & P3 corresponding to the software products A1, A2 & A3 is evaluated using the above formulae and the total quality of the product can be obtained by adding the cumulative rating points.

For example, P1 is calculated by adding the products of the normalized ratings and weights of importance.

P1= (r1 x w1 + r2 x w2……..+r19 x w19)

= (0.50 x 0.61 + 0.42 x 0.61….. + 0.50 x 0.65, 0.75 x 0.83 + 0.67 x 0.83….+0.50 x 0.65, 0.92 x 1.0….+ 0.75 x 0.41)

= (6.94, 13.05, 18.27)

P1 (6.94, 13.05, 18.27)
P2 (6.60, 11.70, 17.19)
P3 (4.83, 10.10, 15.96)

Table 7.Ratings of software product A2 by D1, D2 and D3

Criteria	D_1	D_2	D_3	Fuzzy Weight of the Criteria	Normalized Fuzzy Ratings
C_1	F	VG	G	(5.0,7.0,6.7)	(0.54,0.75,0.72)
C_2	F	G	F	(3.7,5.7,7.7)	(0.40,0.58,0.83)
C_3	F	G	G	(4.3,6.3,8.3)	(0.46,0.68,0.89)
C_4	F	G	G	(4.3,6.3,8.3)	(0.46,0.68,0.89)
C_5	F	VG	F	(4.3,6.3,8.0)	(0.46,0.68,0.86)
C_6	F	VG	G	(5.0,7.0,6.7)	(0.54,0.75,0.72)
C_7	F	G	F	(3.7,5.7,7.7)	(0.46,0.71,0.96)
C_8	G	G	G	(5.0,7.0,9.0)	(0.54,0.75,0.97)
C_9	G	G	VG	(5.7,7.7,9.3)	(0.61,0.83,1.0)
C_{10}	G	VP	G	(3.3,5.0,7.0)	(0.41,0.62,0.88)
C_{11}	G	VP	G	(3.3,5.0,7.0)	(0.41,0.62,0.88)
C_{12}	VG	G	VG	(5.7,8.3,9.7)	(0.59,0.86,1.0)
C_{13}	P	G	G	(3.7,5.7,7.7)	(0.48,0.74,1.0)
C_{14}	P	G	VG	(4.3,6.3,8.0)	(0.54,0.79,1.0)
C_{15}	P	G	G	(3.7,5.7,7.7)	(0.48,0.74,1.0)
C_{16}	G	G	G	(5.0,7.0,9.0)	(0.54,0.75,0.97)
C_{17}	G	G	VG	(5.7,7.7,9.3)	(0.61,0.83,1.0)
C_{18}	G	G	VG	(5.7,7.7,9.3)	(0.59,0.79,0.96)
C_{19}	G	G	G	(5.0,7.0,9.0)	(0.51,0.72,0.93)
C_{20}	H	L	H	(3.7,5.7,7.7)	(1.0,0.65,0.48)
C_{21}	H	L	H	(3.7,5.7,7.7)	(1.0,0.65,0.48)
C_{22}	H	L	H	(3.7,5.7,7.7)	(1.0,0.65,0.48)

From P1, P2 & P3 values, the Z vector is obtained which is used in the construction of the matrix E.

$P1\alpha$ [P1l, P1u] = [6.94, 18.27]

$P2\alpha$ [P2l, P2u] = [6.60, 17.19]

$P3\alpha$ [P3l, P3u] = [4.83, 15.96]

Where Pil, Piu are the lower and upper limits of the vector Pi. From these values the vector corresponding to the fuzzy differences between upper and lower values (Z). The fuzzy differences between upper and lower values for all possibly occurring combinations have been calculated and presented below:

Z12l = P1l - P2u = 6.94 - 17.19 = -10.25

Z12u = P1u − P2l = 18.27 − 6.60 = 11.67

Z13l = P1l − P3u = 6.94 − 15.96 = -9.02

Z13u = P1u − P3l = 18.27 − 4.83 = 13.44

Z23l = P2l − P3u = 6.60 − 15.96 = -9.36

Z23u = P2u − P3l = 17.19 − 4.83= 12.36

Z12 = [-10.25, 11.67]

Z13 = [-9.02, 13.44]

Z23= [-9.36, 12.36]

Table 8. Ratings of software product A3 by D1, D2 and D3

Criteria	D_1	D_2	D_3	Fuzzy Weight of the Criteria	Normalized Fuzzy Ratings
C_1	F	F	F	(3.0,5.0,7.0)	(0.32,0.54,0.75)
C_2	F	F	F	(3.0,5.0,7.0)	(0.32,0.54,0.75)
C_3	F	F	F	(3.0,5.0,7.0)	(0.32,0.54,0.75)
C_4	F	F	F	(3.0,5.0,7.0)	(0.32,0.54,0.75)
C_5	F	F	F	(3.0,5.0,7.0)	(0.32,0.54,0.75)
C_6	F	F	F	(3.0,5.0,7.0)	(0.32,0.54,0.75)
C_7	F	G	F	(3.7,5.7,7.7)	(0.46,0.71,0.96)
C_8	G	G	G	(5.0,7.0,9.0)	(0.54,0.75,0.97)
C_9	G	G	G	(5.0,7.0,9.0)	(0.54,0.75,0.97)
C_{10}	P	P	P	(1.0,3.0,5.0)	(0.12,0.38,0.62)
C_{11}	P	P	P	(1.0,3.0,5.0)	(0.12,0.38,0.62)
C_{12}	G	G	G	(5.0,7.0,9.0)	(0.52,0.72,0.93)
C_{13}	P	G	G	(3.7,5.7,7.7)	(0.48,0.74,1.0)
C_{14}	P	G	G	(3.7,5.7,7.7)	(0.46,0.71,0.96)
C_{15}	P	G	G	(3.7,5.7,7.7)	(0.48,0.74,1.0)
C_{16}	G	G	G	(5.0,7.0,9.0)	(0.54,0.75,0.97)
C_{17}	G	G	G	(5.0,7.0,9.0)	(0.54,0.75,0.97)
C_{18}	G	G	G	(5.0,7.0,9.0)	(0.51,0.72,0.93)
C_{19}	G	G	G	(5.0,7.0,9.0)	(0.51,0.72,0.93)
C_{20}	H	H	H	(5.0,7.0,9.0)	(0.74,0.53,0.41)
C_{21}	H	H	H	(5.0,7.0,9.0)	(0.74,0.53,0.41)
C_{22}	H	H	H	(5.0,7.0,9.0)	(0.74,0.53,0.41)

Step 8: The next step is to compute the fuzzy preference relation matrix (E). The area covered under the triangular membership curve is to be found to evaluate the matrix. An equilateral triangle is constructed on the number line with the Z_{ij} values on the x-axis as one of the sides and the area under the other two sides is evaluated. The ratio of area under the positive side of x-axis (S1) and the total area gives the element e_{ij} of the Fuzzy Preference Relation Matrix E.

It is defined that,

$e_{ij} + e_{ji} = 1$; in Matrix E

In the following steps we solve for e_{ij} and e_{ji} using the Z12 vector,

Point(x1, y1) = (-10.25, 0)

Point(x2, y2) = (11.67, 0)

are the two vertices of the equilateral triangle (Figure 5). The third vertex is at height 1.0 and on the perpendicular bisector of line between (x1, y1) and (x2, y2). Therefore the third vertex (x3, y3) is of the form (x3, 1) and x3 = (x1+x2)/2 = (11.67-10.25)/2 = 0.71

The area under the positive side of the triangle (S1) and the negative side of the triangle (S2) are calculated and the ratios e12 and e21 are calculated. For calculating the above mentioned areas of the equilateral triangle we need to find

Figure 5. The fuzzy evaluation triangle for Z12

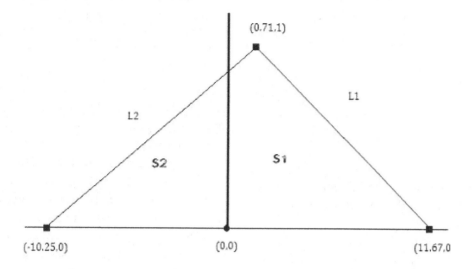

the equations of the lines L1 and L2 and integrate over proper limits.

We know that the equation of straight line in two point form is

$$y - y_1 = \frac{y_2 - y_1}{x_2 - x_1}(x - x_1)$$

And by using this formula we evaluate the equations of lines L1 and L2.

Equation of line L1: $y = -1/10.96(x-11.67)$

Equation of line L2: $y = 1/10.96(x+10.25)$

Now the total area of the equilateral triangle(S) = 0.5*base*height

= 0.5*(10.25+11.67)*1.0

= 10.96

The area under the negative side of the triangle is evaluated by using the area under the curve formula,

$$S2 = \int_{-10.25}^{0} \frac{x + 10.25}{10.96} = 4.793$$

As we know e12 = S1/S, e21 = S2/S and e12+ e21= 1,

We get e21= 4.793/10.96 = 0.44

and e12 = 0.56

Similarly from Z23 and Z13 we get the values of e23, e32, e13 and e31,

e23 = 0.63

e32 = 0.37

e13 = 0.68

e31 = 0.32

and from eij+eji = 1, we get e11=e22=e33 = 0.5 and hence from these values we construct the 3 X 3 Matrix E.

$$E = \begin{matrix} & A_1 & A_2 & A_3 \\ \begin{pmatrix} 0.5 & 0.56 & 0.68 \\ 0.44 & 0.5 & 0.63 \\ 0.32 & 0.37 & 0.5 \end{pmatrix} \end{matrix}$$

Step 9: Now, from E we construct strict preference matrix (ES) where,

$$eijs = \begin{cases} eij - eji, & \text{when } eij \geq \\ 0, & \text{otherwise} \end{cases}$$

$$E^S = \begin{matrix} & A_1 & A_2 & A_3 \\ & \begin{pmatrix} 0 & 0.12 & 0.36 \\ 0 & 0 & 0.26 \\ 0 & 0 & 0 \end{pmatrix} \end{matrix}$$

Step 10: From the the Strict preference matrix we compute the non-dominated degree of each alternative (μ)

μ (A1) = 1 – max ejis where j≠i = 1 – max (0, 0, 0)

μ (A2) = 1 – max ejis where j≠i = 1 – max (0.12, 0, 0)

μ (A3) = 1 – max ejis where j≠i = 1 – max (0.36, 0.26, 0)

μ(A1) = 1

μ (A2) = 0.88

μ (A3) = 0.64

the software product with highest μ-value is removed from the matrix therefore we delete software product A1 From the fuzzy strict relation matrix,

$$E^S = \begin{matrix} & A_2 & A_3 \\ & \begin{pmatrix} 0 & 0.26 \\ 0 & 0 \end{pmatrix} \end{matrix}$$

Now again by finding the μ-dominated degrees and we eliminate A2,

μ (A2) = 1, μ (A3) = 0.74

And the products are ranked in the order of elimination, thus we get

{A1} > {A2} > {A3}

Thus we can conclude that A1 is the product with highest total quality based on the weights of importance and ratings given by three different decision makers.

The fuzzy approach method presented here not only evaluates the ranking order of all possible company but also indicates the degree of preference of each alternative under fuzzy environment which is lacking otherwise. It also helps us to get the information about software quality factors characteristics which is more important than other for example functionality is most important attribute whereas maintainability is least important attribute among all of the characteristics.

DISCUSSION

In this study, the impreciseness or vagueness nature of different attributes have been considered to assess its qualitative value using fuzzy multi-criteria analysis and the final numerical rating of a specific software product has been analyzed. A step by step method is presented to determine the ranking order of fuzzy numbers which can help the user of the software to make a suitable decision under fuzzy environment. By using the degree of strict dominance and by deriving the fuzzy strict preference relation matrix, the suitable alternative among the given alternatives is determined. This methodology can be extended to select several software alternatives available in the market relative to each other. The given methodology is easier and more systematic in comparison with conventional methods in which the scores of each attributes are mainly assigned to get the final total score. The example clearly demonstrates that there will be significant impact on software product due to its efficiency, reliability, maintainability, Reusability and cost while selecting alternative 1. As far as the other attributes are concerned such as data structure complexity, industrial experience, usability etc., are not having so important role in this example. However, the importance of each attributes depends upon the decision maker choice and availability of data for a given product.

CONCLUSION AND FUTURE WORK

In this model, we have proposed a fuzzy multi-criteria approach to quantify the abstract software quality attributes. This approach gives a whole some method to identify the best software product from a set of products by accommodating the perspectives of a manager, user and developer involved with the product. This model can be further enhanced by increasing the number of quality attributes, and linguistic variables for example by increasing the degrees of importance to eleven linguistic values, we can arrive at more accurate results.

Further the example given above involves a single user, developer and manager who give the ratings for each criteria, in a practical scenario it usually involves more than one user, developer and manager involved with a product, in such a case the ratings can be averaged and used in evaluating the quality of the software. A number of extensions and applications of the model may be possible by incorporating the opinion of more number of decision makers and using other techniques like artificial neural networks, evolutionary computation and combination of neuro-fuzzy approach. These ideas and more enhancements would form the basis for subsequent study in this topic.

ACKNOWLEDGMENT

I thank to my supervisor, Prof. G Raghurama, BITS Pilani, Rajasthan Indiafor many insightful discussions during the development of the ideas in this chapter.

REFERENCES

Agrawal, M., & Kaushal, C. (2007). Software Effort, Quality, and Cycle Time: A Study of CMM Level 5 Projects. *IEEE Transactions on Software Engineering, 33*(3). doi:10.1109/TSE.2007.29

Baas, S. M., & Kwakernaak, H. (1977). Rating and Ranking of Multiple - Aspect Alternatives Using Fuzzy Sets. *Automatica, 13,* 47–58. doi:10.1016/0005-1098(77)90008-5

Bellman, R. E., & Zadeh, L. A. (1970). Decision-making in a fuzzy environment. *Management Science, 17,* 141–164. doi:10.1287/mnsc.17.4.B141

Bellman, R. E., & Zadeh, L. A. (1970). Decision-making in a fuzzy environment. *Management Science, 17,* 141–164. doi:10.1287/mnsc.17.4.B141

Bourque, P. & Dupuis, R. (2004). *Guide to the Software Engineering Body of Knowledge.*

Buglione, L., & Abran, A. (1999). A quality factor for software. In *Proceedings of QUALITA,* Paris, France, (pp. 335-44).

Carlsson, C., & Fuller, R. (1996). Fuzzy multiple criteria decision making: Recent developments. *Fuzzy Sets and Systems, 78,* 139–153. doi:10.1016/0165-0114(95)00165-4

Cavano, J. P., & McCall, J. A. (1978). A Framework for the Measurement of Software Quality, In *Proceedings of the software quality assurance workshop on Functional and performance,* (pp. 133 – 139).

Cote, M., Suryn, A., & Georgiadou, W. (2006). Software Quality Model Requirements for Software Quality Engineering. *Software Quality Management and inspire Conference (BSI),* (pp. 31-50).

Dong, W. M., & Wong, F. S. (1987). Fuzzy weighted averages and implementation of the extension principle. *Fuzzy Sets and Systems, 21*, 183–199. doi:10.1016/0165-0114(87)90163-1

Driankov, D., Hellendoor, H., & Reinfark, M. (1994). *An Introduction to Fuzzy Control*. New York: Springer.

Fishburn, P. C. (1964). Utility Theory for Decision Making. New York: Wiley publisher.

Gaffney, J. E. (1981). Metrics in Software Quality Assurance. In *ACM Annual Conference/Annual Meeting,* (pp. 126 – 130).

Grabisch, M. (1996). Order additive fuzzy measures. In *6th Int. Conf. on Information Processing and Management of Uncertainty in Knowledge-Based Systems (IPMU),* (pp. 1345-1350).

IEEE. (1990). *Standard Glossary of Software Engineering Terminology, IEEE Std 610.12*. Washington, DC: Author.

Information technologies.

Jin, F., Yin, G., & Yang, D. (2008). Fuzzy Integrated Evaluation for Measuring Quality of Feature Space-Based Component Model. In *ICICSE Proceedings of 2008 International Conference on Internet Computing in Science and Engineering,* (pp. 349-354).

Kalaimagal, S. & Srinivasan, R. (2008). A Retrospective on Software Component Quality Models. *SIGSOFT Software Engineering Notes, 33*(5).

Kanhe, S. (1975). A Contribution to Decision Making in Environmental Design. *Proceedings of the IEEE, 63,* 518–528. doi:10.1109/PROC.1975.9779

Khaddaj, S., & Horgan, G. (2004). The Evaluation of Software Quality Factors in Very Large Information Systems. *Electronic Journal of information system. Evaluation, 7*(1).

Klir, G., & Folger, T. (1988). *Fuzzy Sets, Uncertainty and Information*. Upper Saddle River, NJ: Prentice Hall.

Lehman, M. (1996). Laws of Software Evolution Revisited. In *Proc. 5th European Workshop on Software Process Technology*, (LNCS Vol. 1149, pp. 108–124).

Lin, L., & Lee, H.-M. (2007). A Fuzzy Software Quality Assessment Model to Evaluate User Satisfaction, ICNC, (vol. 1). Dukic, L.B. & Boegh, J. (2003). COTS Software Quality Evaluation. In proceedings of ICCBSS, Ottawa, Canada.

Mähönen, P. (2000). Fuzzy Classifier for Star-Galaxy Separation. *The Astrophysical Journal, 541,* 261–263. available at http://iopscience.iop.org/0004-637X/541/1/261/fulltext?ejredirect=migration. doi:10.1086/309424

Murofushi, T., & Sugeno, M. (1989). An interpretation of fuzzy measure and the Choquet integral as an integral with respect to a fuzzy measure. *Fuzzy Sets and Systems, 29,* 201–227. doi:10.1016/0165-0114(89)90194-2

Novák, V. Perfilieva, Močkoř, J. (1999). Mathematical principles of fuzzy logic. Dodrecht, The Netherlands: Kluwer Academic.

Padhy, N. P. (2005). *Artificial Intelligence and Intelligent System*. Oxford, UK: Oxford press.

Pedrycz, W. (1993). *Fuzzy Control and Fuzzy Systems*. New York: John Wiley & Sons.

Peneva, V., & Popchev, I. (2002). *Fuzzy Multicriteria Decision Making*. Cybernetics and.

Pratap, S. A. (2008). An Integrated Fuzzy Approach to Assess Water Resources' Potential in a Watershed. *Icfai Journal of Computational Fluid Mathematics, 1*(1), 7–23.

Pratap, S. A., & Vidarthi, A. K. (2008). Optimal allocation of landfill disposal site: A fuzzy multi-criteria approach. *Iranian Journal of Environmental Health Science & Engineering, 5*(1), 25–34.

Pressman. (2005). *Software Engineering: A Practitioner's Approach*, (6ht Ed.). New Delhi, India: Tata McGraw-Hill.

Roy, B. (1971). Problems and Methods with Multiple Objective Functions. *Mathematical Programming, 1*, 239–266. doi:10.1007/BF01584088

Schmeidler, D. (1989). Subjective probability and expected utility without additivity. *Econometrica, 57*(3), 571–587. doi:10.2307/1911053

Sharma, A., Kumar, R. & Grover, P. S. (2008). Estimation of Quality for Software Components – an Empirical Approach. *SIGSOFT Software Engineering, 33*(5).

Slaughter, S. A., Harter, D. E., & Krishnan, M. S. (1998)... *Communications of the ACM, 41*(8), 67–73. doi:10.1145/280324.280335

Srivastava, P. R. & Kumar, K. (2009). An approach towards software quality assessment. *Information System, Technology and Management, Communication in computer and Information Science(CCIS)*, (Vol. 31, pp. 150-160).

Yager, R. R. (1978). Fuzzy decision making including unequal objectives. *Fuzzy Sets and Systems, 1*, 87–95. doi:10.1016/0165-0114(78)90010-6

Yang, B., Yao, L., & Huang, H.-Z. (2007). Early Software Quality Prediction Based on a Fuzzy Neural Network Model. *ICNC, 1*, 760–764.

Zadeh, L. A. (1965). Fuzzy Sets. *Information and Control, 8*, 338–353. doi:10.1016/S0019-9958(65)90241-X

Zadeh, L. A. (1976). The Concept of a Linguistic Variable and its Application to Approximate Reasoning. *Information Sciences, 8*(I), 199–249. doi:10.1016/0020-0255(75)90036-5

Zimmermann, H. J. (1991). *Fuzzy Set Theory and Its Applications* (2nd Rev. Ed.). Boston: Kluwer Academic Publishers.

KEY TERMS AND DEFINITIONS

Fuzzy Logic: Is a power technique.

Software Quality Assurance: Is the procedure by software professionals to ensure software product level of excellence.

Software Quality Factors: Take care both product and process quality charteristics.

Software Quality Metrics: Software metrics are any measurement that relate to a software system.

Chapter 12
Verification of Attributes in Linked Lists Using Ant Colony Metaphor

Soumya Banerjee
Birla Institute of Technology, International Center, Mauritius

P. K. Mahanti
University of New Brunswick, Canada

ABSTRACT

The chapter describes the validation of the attributes of linked list using modified pheromone biased model (of Ant colony) under complex application environment mainly for kernel configuration and device driver operations. The proposed approach incorporates the idea of pheromone exploration strategy with small learning parameter associated while traversing a linked list. This process of local propagation on loop and learning on traversal is not available with the conventional validation mechanism of data structure using predicate logic. It has also been observed from simulation that the proposed ant colony algorithm with different pheromone value produces better convergence on linked list.

1. INTRODUCTION

Program verification has been a major area of research and development since last couple of years (Baresel, Binkley, Harman, & Korel, 2004; Manevich, Yahav, Ramalingam, & Sagiv, 2005; Lahiri & Qadeer, 2005). Different hybrid intelligent predicate and finite state machine based tools put a significant contribution to this progress. For a number of programs, the verification condition whose validity establishes the correctness of the program is expressible in a combination of first

order theories such as arithmetic, un-interrupted functions, and propositional logic. However the simple first order predicate logic fails to prove properties towards a crucial data structure e.g. linked list and its all variants. The main problem with reasoning about a data structure, such as a linked list, is that it is impossible to express an invariant about all members of a list using simple first-order logic. This requires a propagation and ripple loop in predicate logic to verify the attributes of linked list successfully.

It has been observed that kernel of operating systems and device drivers manipulate a variety of data structures, such as arrays, singly and doubly

DOI: 10.4018/978-1-61520-809-8.ch012

linked lists, and hash tables frequently. Current verification tools focus on control-dominated properties and are consequently unable to handle such programs in which the control flow interacts with the data in subtle ways and thus failed to create propagation and ripple loops as well.

Over the last two decades *Ant Colony Optimization (ACO)* has emerged as a leading nature-inspired metaheuristic method for the solution of *Combinatorial Optimization (CO)* problems (Yu & Zhang, 2009). The prime components of ACO are identified as the indirect communication between ants mediated by modifications of the environment and *differential path length which* signifies that the time spent on a path is proportional to the actual path length. The first property is called as *stigmergy.*

The chapter proposes an algorithm that relies on *differential path length* and *stigmergy*, incorporating a small learning component to improve the performance of the program verification. The property of learning and local propagation on loop is not possible using first order logic predicate.

We consider the following implementation of function Test_Cycle that iterates over an Acyclic list pointed to by the variable *Head* and sets *Data field* of each list element to 0.

```
void Test_Cycle() {
    iter = head;
    while (iter!=null){
    itr.data = 0;
    itr= itr.nxt;
    }
}
```

Here, the *linked list* acts as *set* and perform several iterations. In order to achieve a loop independent code, we need to establish a loop and propagation logic based on certain a mapping of cell for the next iteration until it encounters *Null field.*

In order to include the linked list traversal (to explore search path or reachability) under

defined conditions, the ant colony optimization with different pheromone bias has been presented in this work.

In classical ant colony, an artificial ant builds a solution by traversing the fully connected *construction graph GC (***V**, **E***)*, where **V** is a set of vertices and **E** is a set of edges (Neumann, Sudholt, & Witt, 2007). This graph can be obtained from the set of solution components **C** in two ways: components may be represented either by vertices or by edges. Artificial ants move from vertex to vertex along the edges of the graph, incrementally building a *partial solution.* Additionally, ants deposit a certain amount of pheromone on the components; that is, either on the vertices or on the edges that they traverse. The amount $\Delta\tau$ of pheromone deposited may depend on the quality of the solution found.

At each iteration, the pheromone values are updated by *all* the ants that have built a solution in the iteration itself. The pheromone τ_{ij}, associated with the edge joining two vertex i and j, is updated as follows:

$$\tau_{ij} \leftarrow (1-\rho)\cdot\tau_{ij} + \sum_{k=1}^{m}\Delta\tau_{ij}^{k} \qquad (1)$$

Hence the next iteration is decided by modifying the existing bias of ant colony pheromone deposition mechanism. Where ρ is the evaporation rate, m is the number of ants, and $\Delta\tau_{ij}$ is the quantity of pheromone laid on edge (i, j) by ant k.

Let M denote the total number of ant agents to be applied on the data structure of interest. At the initial time n = 0, all the agents are on the source node graph. Whenever ant k is at node S at time n, it probabilistically chooses an edge i to traverse at time n + 1. As mentioned earlier each agent traverses an edge one segment at a time. At every segment agent k decides to 'wait' with probability p or move ahead with probability 1−p, for some small p. Therefore the case code if modified like below:

```
void Test_Cycle() {
    head.data=0;      //modified
    iter = head.nxt; // modified
    while (iter!=head){
    itr.data = 0;
    itr= itr.nxt;
    }
}
```

The value of next *head* and next *itr* still remains constant and equal to the set of all elements in the list during the entire execution of the loop. As a result, we are able to write a simple loop invariant using simple *next* field without using predicate rather we can introduce the pheromone propagation and ripple to check both cyclic and acyclic linked list for predicting the next iteration.

We also introduce a modified pheromone update scheme with a simple recursive learning law given by the equation:

$X_i(n-1)=X_i(n)+a(n)X_i(n)T_i(n+1)$ for i= {1,2,...,d} and n ≥ 0   (2)

The a(n)'s are decreasing scalar step sizes that represent the learning rate of the multi-agent combinatorial problem and we assume that they satisfy the following:

$$\sum_n a(n) = \infty \ \ and \ \ \sum_n a(n)^2 < \infty \quad (3)$$

The $X_i(n)$'s denote the utility associated with edge *i* as learned by the agents after n time steps. They bias the choice of the agents. The probability of an agent choosing edge i at time n, denoted by $P_i(n)$, is given by the equation:

$$P_i(n) = \frac{X_i(n)}{\sum_{j=1}^{d} X_j(n)} \quad (4)$$

The proposed model is the modification of conventional ACO where heuristics, here we have not included the guided heuristics η. Thus the proposed algorithm will converge faster and this will facilitate to verify attribute all the similar data structures or data structure used as meta-form of data structure. For an example the sample linked data structure considered in the chapter is the *linked list* that has been quantified as set in the code.

Another feature of the proposed algorithm for data structure verification is the lack of external supervision. ACO algorithms and their convergence proofs usually rely on an elitist policy, i.e., the algorithm keeps track of the best-so-far or the iteration-best solution generated. It accordingly carries out the pheromone update. In our approach we do not require the ants to have any knowledge of the quality of solutions generated. They are simple autonomous agents and when applying them to the multi-stage shortest path problem or the traveling salesman problem, we just require them to have an internal memory that stores the sequence of nodes visited by them. This internal memory prevents the agents from getting trapped into sub-optimal loops and successfully predicts next *head* and *itr for* linked data structure.

The remaining part of the chapter is as follows:

Section 2 presents background of Ant colony and related suitable works in the context of program verification using ant colony or evolutionary approach. Section 3 describes the failure of predicate logic for linked data structure and introduces the idea of the proposed algorithm. Section 3.1 elaborates the proposed algorithm, its notation and implementation on sample linked list data structure. Section 4 gives a performance comparison of the new methodology over the contemporary research contributions followed by the conclusion in section 5.

2. BACKGROUND OF ANT COLONY OPTIMIZATION AND RELATED WORKS

Ant colony optimization (ACO) is a recently developed population-based approach. It has been successfully applied to several NP-hard combinatorial optimization problems (GamBardella, Tailard, & Dorigo, 1999; Dorigo & Stützle, 2004). As the name suggests, ACO was inspired by the observation of real ants' foraging behavior. Ants live in colonies. They use a cooperative method to search for food. While moving, ants initially explore the area surrounding their nest in a random manner. They initially leave a chemical pheromone trail on the ground. During the return trip, the quantity of pheromone that an ant leaves on the ground may depend on the quantity and quality of the food. This result in the amount of pheromone becomes larger on a shorter path. Then the probability that an ant selects this shorter path is higher. At last, the pheromone trails will guide other ants to the food source via the shortest path.

There are different close contributions pertaining to generate test data attribute generation in software testing paradigm. The recent work (Baresel et al., 2004) exposes and addresses the path problem for search-based test data generators. The path problem occurs when the input domain for the program is largely dominated by paths through the program which cannot lead to execution of the target, potentially suffocating the fitness function and preventing the search from receiving adequate guidance to the required test data.

The generation of test data by means of Evolutionary Algorithms, known as *Evolutionary Testing,* has been largely concentrated on the structural testing of individual program functions with input-output behavior (McMinn & Holcombe, 2005). Test data is generated for atomic function calls. However, functions and components at higher system levels can store internal data, and can exhibit different behaviors depending

on the state of that data. This presents additional challenges to the Evolutionary Testing method.

3. HOW AND WHEN THE PREDICATE LOGIC FAILS: POSSIBLE MEASURES

The first-order reasoning typically breaks down when we want to prove properties of programs that manipulate heap allocated linked data structures. The main problem with reasoning about a data structure, such as a linked list, is that it is impossible to express an invariant about all members of a list in first-order logic (Manevich et al., 2005). To achieve such a specification in general requires the use of the *reachability predicate* which cannot be expressed in first-order logic. Consequently, researchers have investigated richer logics such as combination of first order logic with transitive closure (Immerman, Rabinovich, Reps, Sagiv, & Yorsh, 2004) and monadic second-order logic. These approaches are typically unable to harness the advances made in automated theorem proving based on first-order logic.

To write the loop invariant for this program, we require the reachability function R_{next}, which maps each cell u to the set containing u and all cells reachable from by following next field and excluding null. Hence, about inked list we can write the following axiom (Lahiri & Qadeer, 2005):

$$\forall v \in R_{next}(head) : (iter \neq null \wedge v \in R_{next}(iter)) \vee v.data = 0$$

where R_{next} is the reachability function which maps each cell u to the set containing u and all cells reachable from u by following the *next* field. Here, there is one precondition added e.g. head != NULL.

The verification condition for this program is easily constructed using the weakest-precondition transformer (Dijkstra, 2005), and the verification condition can be proved from the axiom using purely first-order reasoning based on un-

Figure 1. Linked List Presentation from source to end

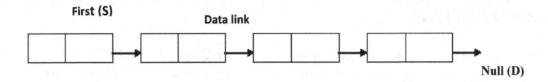

interpreted functions and quantifier instantiation. Thus, circularity of cyclic linked list breaks and verification also relinquishes at any point of time during the validation of the list using weaker precondition based predicate logic.

To illustrate the problem, we consider the following code segment under test of the first function that iterates over a cyclic list pointed to by *head* and sets the *data* fields of the list elements to 0. The complication, in this case, is that the *next* field of the last element of the list points to *head* rather than *Null*.

```
Void cyclic _Test() {
    head.data = 0;
    iter= head.nxt
    while(iter != head) {
    iter.data =0;
    iter= iter.next
    }
}
```

Therefore, to keep track the cyclic property, a bio-inspired agent based approach is solicited. Practically, the problem of cyclic property of linked list has been restored through pheromone deposition and evaporation mechanism on the list structure.

3.1 Proposed Algorithm: Mapping Linked List into Agent Based Traversal

Consider the two-node network Let i = {1.......d}, d≥2 be the edges between node S to D (analogous to *head* and *null* part of the list). The formation is similar to lined list. We assume L_i which denote the length of edge i. Each agent traverses edge i one segment at a time. To make Associated with each edge i are two parameters, the pheromone trail parameter T_i and an agent learning parameter X_i. The role of the agent learning parameter is to bias the probabilistic decision made by the agents. Each agent which is about to explore a new path on the list structure, chooses a new edge i with probability proportional to the associated agent learning parameter X_i. Let M denote the total number of agents in the system. At the initial time n = 0, all the agents are on the source node. Whenever agent k is at node S at time n, it probabilistically chooses an edge i to traverse at time n + 1.

As mentioned, each agent traverses an edge one segment at a time. At every segment agent k decides to 'wait' with probability p or move ahead with probability (1−p), for some small *p* (Dijkstra, 2005). With this device we introduce a random delay in the traversal of every agent. This is meant as a discrete approximation to the continuous valued random traversal time in real life. For purely algorithmic applications and improved performance, this could be dropped.

Once agent k has traversed all the mi segments on edge i, it reaches the destination node D, and invokes a procedure which increments the pheromone value Ti associated with edge i by a constant amount. It also instantaneously returns to the source node S and is ready to begin a new trip. To be faithful to real ant behavior, one may demand that agent k instead retrace edge i from D back to S. It also instantaneously returns to the source node S and is ready to begin a new trip. To be faithful to real ant behavior, one may demand that agent k instead retrace edge i from D back to S. The objective of the colony of agents is to iteratively discover the shortest edge between the source S and the destination D and thus mains the cyclic behavior of linked list. Hence, this work concentrates on the initial modified bias of validation strategy for linked list and it also indicates the point of failure of predicate logic for the validation process.

Let $\tau_{ij}^{k}(n)$ denote the pheromone trail associated with edge (i, j) of the list structure, The probability with which any agent chooses to move from node i to node j is given by:

$$P_{ij}^{k}(n) = \begin{cases} \dfrac{X_{ij}^{k}(n)}{\sum_{(i,l)\in N_i} X_{il}^{k}(n)}, & \text{if } (i, j) \in N_i; \\ 0, & \text{otherwise.} \end{cases}$$

(5)

N_i denotes the successors of i, i.e., the set of nodes $\{j\}$ such that there exists an edge (i, j). The pheromone update scheme is given by:

$$\tau_{ij}^{k}(n+1) = (1 - \rho)\tau_{ij}^{k}(n) + \rho Q R_{ij}^{k}(n)$$

(6)

for i = {1, 2,..., d} and n ≥ 0. Here:

- the magnitude of $\tau_i(n)$ denotes the pheromone strength on edge i at time n,
- $0 < \rho < 1$ is the constant pheromone decay rate,
- $R_i(n)$ is the number of agents who have finished traversing edge from head to data part i at time n, and,
- Q is the constant "quantum" of pheromone that each agent deposits once it has traversed any edge.
- $R_{ij}^{k}(n)$ denotes number of agents who have completed a trip between S and D at time n and have traversed the edge (i, j) in stage k.

3.1.1 Code Validation of Linked List Operations

Conventional linked list operation as insertion of new node is described initially with predicate axioms and then mapped through ant colony algorithm.

```
void insert(Cell 1, Cell p) {
Cell curr = 1;
Cell succ= 1.next;
While (succ !=null){
If (p.data> succ.data)
{
Curr =succ;
Succ = curr.nxt
}
else
break;
}
p.next=curr;
curr.nxt= p;
}
```

The function *insert* accepts an acyclic list 1 and a cell p as arguments. The cells in the list 1 are in sorted order based on the values of the field data of the cells. The predicate *sorted ()* is defined as: (u is defined as each cell in the linked list)

Sorted(1)=∀u∈R_{next}(1):u.next==null ‖ u.data<=u.next.data

The preconditions for coding are important for validating the list, but it is expected that the first element of 1 is a dummy whose data field is guaranteed to be less than any value that might be inserted in the list. The objective of *insert* is to insert the cell p in the appropriate place in 1 so that 1 remains sorted. According to precondition given, the cell p should not be in next search move. If p∈next search move then on return of the value it violates the post-condition p∈ next move.

The specification of *insert* uses a combination of facts about reachability via the next field of list, un-interpreted function, arithmetic and proportional logic.

The same instance of *insert* code segment can be described using pheromone model as follows:

The algorithm in contrast of predicate logic, sets the objective as Ω, which returns cyclic after execution. The pheromone updation and evaporation biased has been modified to explore best cyclic value of list at any point of traversal. Subsequently, the algorithm incorporates the learning parameter in traversal mechanism on *head* and *data part* of subjected linked list.

The generic expression for learning part is given by:

$$X_i(n+1)=X_i(n)+a(n)QR_i(n) \qquad (7)$$

As before, the probability of choosing any path is expressed as:

$$P_i(n) = \frac{X_i(n)}{\sum_{j=1}^{d} X_j(n)} \qquad (8)$$

The high level description is as follows:

```
f_best   ← ∞
objective ←Ω
tie ← false
Update pheromone trail param-
eters using Equation 5 and 6
 repeat for each head and Data
part of linked list
    fph ←average deposition of
pheromone in individual head and
tail of list (Equation 7)
    if  f_ph  ⟨ f_best fbest ← fph
    tie ←true
    if   tie = true
    objective ← breadth fast
search with fbest
    return Objective
```

The idea is to incorporate the optimization problem with the most promising population bias available at the moment of traversing the linked list. It should be noted that it is possible for a branch already treated to be candidate objective, once again, if during optimization phase a new individual is introduced in the set.

3.1.2 Implementation and Result

For the simulation[1], we consider a model with 10 cascaded blocks of lists between the *head point* S and the *destination or null point* D (insertion mode only). There is a unique shortest edge with length 50 and the remaining edges are assigned lengths in the interval. The time taken to traverse for traversing *head* to *null* is stochastic. It is implied, that edge i is considered to be the concatenation of m_i segments. Each agent decides to wait at a segment with probability $p = 0.1$ or move to the next head block of linked list with probability $(1 - p) = 0.9$. The algorithm was studied for various values of the modified evaporation rate $\rho = \{0.1, 0.3, 0.5, 0.7\}$, and different values for the total number of agents, $M = \{512, 1024, 2048\}$.

In Table 1, we report the simulation results. For every pair of values of ρ and M we executed 100 trials of proposed algorithm and report the number of trials on which the algorithm converged to the shortest edge. As will be seen from the table, for 2048 agents the algorithm in most of the instances converged to the shortest path. Also it will be noticed that for any particular value of ρ the performance of the algorithm improves with the increase in the number of agents. The best value for the pheromone evaporation rate was found.

For the two approaches, the graph shows the better result is obtained so far in the search for a particular cyclic consistent property of linked list (in case of insertion of item in the list), averaged over the ten repetitions of the experiment. This value is then normalized to allow for a direct comparison between the two methods. Due to the unidirectional landscape of the target under

Table 1. Simulation result for modified bias of pheromone value ρ

Modified Value of ρ	Number of Ant Agents(Only Insert Operation) 512 1024 2048		
0.1	74	98	100
0.3	64	94	99
0.5	62	92	100
0.7	54	82	97

Figure 2. Predicate logic in comparison with ant colony's modified ρ

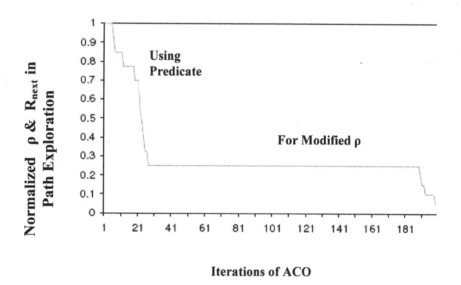

modified pheromone, the original method fails to make any progress at all; thus the horizontal line at the top of the figure (Refer Figure 2).

The success rates of each method are summarized in Table 2, along with the number of test data evaluations for successful and unsuccessful exploring of cyclic property convergence test. The normal predicate method performs average on every run, where as proposed modified pheromone bias value of ant colony outperforms in couple of instances.

Table 2. Comparison with predicate logic

	Rate of Convergence on List	Av. Number of Best Fit	
		Successful Explore	Failure
Using Predicate Modified ρ of ACO	4 45-50% 90%	Standard High	40% 0%

5. CONCLUSION

This chapter discusses a conceptual implementation to validate the cyclic attribute of linked list in case of insertion operation. The conventional predicate logic to perform validation on Linked list operation and finally the Ant Colony optimization algorithm with modified pheromone bias has been incorporated. Finally, convergence on the attribute of linked list has been compared to predicate logic.

REFERENCES

Baresel, A., Binkley, D., Harman, M., & Korel, B. (2004). Evolutionary testing in the presence of loop-assigned flags: A testability transformation approach. In *Proceedings International Symposium on Software Testing and Analysis, ISSTA 2004*, (pp. 43–52). Boston: ACM.

Dijkstra, E. W. (2005). *A Discipline of Programming*. Upper Saddle River, NJ: Prentice-Hall.

Dorigo, M., & Stützle, T. (2004). *Ant Colony Optimization*. Cambridge, MA: The MIT Press.

GamBardella, L., Tailard, E., & Dorigo, M. (1999). Ant colonies for the quadratic assignment problem. *The Journal of the Operational Research Society*, *50*, 167–176.

Immerman, N., Rabinovich, A. M., Reps, T. W., Sagiv, S., & Yorsh, G. (2004). The boundary between decidability and undecidability for transitive-closure logics. *CSL 04: 18th International Workshop on Computer Science Logic*, (LNCS 3210, pp. 160–174). Berlin: Springer-Verlag.

Lahiri, S. K., & Qadeer, S. (2005). *Verifying properties of well-founded linked lists*. Technical Report MSR-TR-2005-97. Redmond, WA: Microsoft Research.

Manevich, R., Yahav, E., Ramalingam, G., & Sagiv, M. (2005). Predicate abstraction and canonical abstraction for singly-linked lists. In VMCAI 05: Verification, Model Checking and Abstract Interpretation, (LNCS 3148, pp. 181–198). Berlin: Springer-Verlag.

McMinn, P., & Holcombe, M. (2005). Evolutionary testing of state-based programs. In [Washington, DC: ACM.]. *Proceedings of the Genetic and Evolutionary Computation Conference, GECCO, 2005*, 1013–1020.

Neumann, F., Sudholt, D., & Witt, C. (2007). Comparing variants of MMAS ACO algorithms on pseudo-Boolean functions. In T. Stützle, M. Birattari, & H.H. Hoos (Eds.) SLS 2007, (LNCS 4638, pp. 61–75). Berlin: Springer-Verlag.

Yu, X., & Zhang, T. (2009). Convergence and Run Time of an Ant Colony Optimization Model. *Information Technology Journal*, *8*(3), 354–359. doi:10.3923/itj.2009.354.359

ENDNOTE

[1]   Simulation is done through C compiler using 2.53 GHz Pentium 4 processor with 1 GB of RAM running the standard Windows XP Professional operating system with DOS shell.

Compilation of References

Abdel-Ghaly, A. A., Chan, P. Y., & Littlewood, B. (1986). Evaluation of competing software reliability predictions. *IEEE Transactions on Software Engineering, 12*(9), 950–967.

Abraham, A., Vasant, P., & Bhattacharya, A. (2008). Neuro-Fuzzy approximations of multi-criteria decision-making QFD methodology. In Kahraman, C. (Ed.), *Fuzzy multi-criteria decision making theory and applications with recent developments* (pp. 301–324). Berlin: Springer. doi:10.1007/978-0-387-76813-7_12

Abran, A., & Moore, J. W. (2004). Guide to the Software Engineering Body of Knowledge. Pierre Bourque and Robert Dupuis (Eds.). Washington, DC: IEEE Computer Society.

Abran, A., & Robillard, P. N. (1996). Function Points Analysis: An Empirical Study of its Measurement Processes. *IEEE Transactions on Software Engineering, 22*(12), 895–910. doi:10.1109/32.553638

Adnan, W. A., Yaakob, M., Anas, R., & Tamjis, M. R. (2000). *Artificial neural network for software reliability assessment.* Paper presented at the Proceedings of TENCON 2000.

Afzal, W., Torkar, R., & Feldt, R. (2008). *Prediction of fault count data using genetic programming.* Paper presented at the proceedings of INMIC 2008 IEEE International Multitopic Conference.

Agrawal, M., & Kaushal, C. (2007). Software Effort, Quality, and Cycle Time: A Study of CMM Level 5 Projects. *IEEE Transactions on Software Engineering, 33*(3). doi:10.1109/TSE.2007.29

Aguilar-Ruiz, J. S., Ramos, I., Riquelme, J. C., & Toro, M. (2001). An evolutionary approach to estimating software development projects. *Information and Software Technology, 14*(43), 875–882. doi:10.1016/S0950-5849(01)00193-8

Alander, J. T., & Lampinen, J. (1997). Cam shape optimization by genetic algorithm. In Poloni, C., & Quagliarella, D. (Eds.), *Genetic Algorithms and Evolution Strategies in Engineering and Computer Science, Trieste, Italy, Nov 1997* (pp. 153–174). New York: John Wiley & Sons.

Albrecht, S. J., & Gaffney, J. R. (1983). Software Function, Source Lines of Code, and Development Effort Prediction: A Software Science Validation. *IEEE Transactions on Software Engineering, 9*(6), 639–648. doi:10.1109/TSE.1983.235271

Ali, F. M. (1998). A differential equation approach to fuzzy non-linear programming problems. In Fuzzy Sets and Systems, (pp. 57-61).

Aljahdali, S. H., Sheta, A., & Rine, D. (2001). *Prediction of software reliability: A comparison between regression and neural network non-parametric models.* Paper presented at the proceedings of ACS/IEEE International Conference on Computer Systems and Applications.

Arcuri, A., & Yao, X. (2007). *Search based testing of containers for object-oriented software.* Technical Report CSR-07-3.

Ardissono, L., Furnari, R., Goy, A., Petrone, G., & Segnan, M. (2006). *Fault tolerant WS orchestraion by means of diagnosis* (pp. 2–16). Berlin: Springer verlag.

Ardissono, L., Furnari, R., Goy, R., Petrone, G., & Segnan, M. (2007). Monitoring choreographed services. In Sobth, S. V. T. (Ed.), *Innovations and advanced techniques in computer and information sciences and engineering* (pp. 283–288). doi:10.1007/978-1-4020-6268-1_51

Arthur Karl, K., Guido, F. S., & Mark, E. K. (2007). *Industrial evolutionary computing*. Paper presented at the Proceedings of the 2007 GECCO conference companion on Genetic and evolutionary computation.

Arthur, K. (2006). Evolutionary computation at Dow Chemical. *SIGEVOlution, 1*(3), 4–9. doi:10.1145/1181964.1181965

Austin, D., Barbir, A., Peters, E., & Ross-Talbot, S. (2004). *Web Services Choreography Requirements W3C Working Draft.* World Wide Web Consortium (W3C).

Baas, S. M., & Kwakernaak, H. (1977). Rating and Ranking of Multiple - Aspect Alternatives Using Fuzzy Sets. *Automatica, 13*, 47–58. doi:10.1016/0005-1098(77)90008-5

Bäck, T. (1996). *Evolutionary Algorithms in Theory and Practice*. Oxford, UK: Oxford University Press.

Bäck, T., Fogel, D. B., & Michalewicz, Z. (1997). *Handbook of Evolutionary Computation*. Philadelphia: IOP Publishing. doi:10.1887/0750308958

Bäck, T., Fogel, D. B., & Michalewicz, Z. (2000). [*Basic algorithms and operators*: San Francisco: Taylor & Francis Group.]. *Evolutionary Computation, 1*.

Baisch, E., & Liedtke, T. (1998). Automated knowledge acquisition and application for software development projects. In *Automated Software Engineering, Proceedings. 13th IEEE International Conference*, Honolulu, USA, (pp. 306–309).

Bansiya, J., & Davis, C. G. (2002). A Hierarchical Model for Object-Oriented Design Quality Assessment. *IEEE Transactions on Software Engineering, 28*(1), 4–17. doi:10.1109/32.979986

Baresel, A., Pohlheim, H., & Sadeghipour, S. (2003). Structural and Functional Sequence Test of Dynamic and State-Based Software with Evolutionary Algorithms. In *Proc. of the Genetic and Evolutionary Computation Conference*, Chicago, IL.

Barry, B., & Victor, R. B. (2001). Software Defect Reduction Top 10 List. *Computer, 34*(1), 135–137.

Becerra, L., Sagarna, R., & Yao, X. (2009). An evaluation of Differential Evolution in Software Test Data Generation. In *CEC'09, Proceedings of the Eleventh Conference on Congress on Evolutionary Computation*, (pp. 2850-2857).

Beizer, B. (1990). *Software Testing Techniques*. New York: Van Nostrand Reinhold.

Bellman, R. E., & Zadeh, L. A. (1970). Decision Making in a fuzzy environment. In Management Science, (pp. 141-164).

Benzhaf, W., Nordin, P., Keller, R. E., & Francone, F. D. (1998). *Genetic Programming: An Introduction*. San Francisco: Morgan Kaufmann.

Bernroider, E., & Koch, S. (2001). ERP Selection Process in Midsize and Large Organizations. *Business Process Management Journal, 7*(3), 251–257. doi:10.1108/14637150110392746

Bhattacharya, A., Abraham, A., & Vasant, P. (2008). FMS selection under disparate level-of-satisfaction of decision making using an intelligent Fuzzy-MCDM- Model. In Kahraman, C. (Ed.), *Fuzzy multi-criteria decision making theory and applications with recent developments* (pp. 263–280). Berlin: Springer. doi:10.1007/978-0-387-76813-7_10

Blickle, T. (1996). *Theory of Evolutionary Algorithms and Application to System Synthesis*. PhD Thesis, Swiss Federal Institute of Technology, Zurique, Switzerland.

Boehm, B. W. (1981). *Software Engineering Economics*. Englewood Cliffs, NJ: Prentice-Hall.

Bouktif, S., Kegl, B., & Sahraoui, H. (2002). Combining software quality predictive models: an evolutionary approach. *International Conference on Software Maintenance*, (pp. 1063–6773).

Bourque, P. & Dupuis, R. (2004). *Guide to the Software Engineering Body of Knowledge.*

Box, G. E. P., Hunter, W. G., & Hunter, J. S. (1978). *Statistics for experimenters: An introduction to design, data analysis, and model building.* Mahwah, NJ: Wiley-Interscience.

Braga, P. L. Oliveira, A. L. I. & Meira, S. R. L. (2008). A GA-based Feature Selection and Parameters Optimization for Support Vector Regression Applied to Software Effort Estimation. In *Proceedings of the 23rd ACM symposium on Applied computing*, Galé in Fortaleza, Ceará, Brazil, (pp. 1788-1792).

Braga, P. L., Oliveira, A. L. I., & Meira, S. R. L. (2007). Software Effort Estimation Using Machine Learning Techniques with Robust Confidence Intervals. In *Proceedings of the 19th IEEE International Conference on Tools with Artificial Intelligence*, Patras, Greece, (vol. 1, pp. 181-185).

Braga, P. L., Oliveira, A. L. I., Ribeiro, G. H. T., & Meira, S. R. L. (2007). Bagging Predictors for Estimation of Software Project Effort. In *Proceedings of the 20th IEEE International Joint Conference on Neural Networks*, Orlando, FL, (pp. 1595-1600).

Briand, L. C. (2002). On the many ways Software Engineering can benefit from Knowledge Engineering. *Proc. 14th SEKE,* Italy, (pp. 3-6).

Briand, L. C., & Wieczorek, I. (2002). *Software Resource Estimation* (pp. 1160–1196). Encyclopaedia of Software Engineering.

Briand, L., El Emam, K., Surmann, D., Wiekzorek, I., & Maxwell, K. (1999). An Assessment and Comparison of Common Software Cost Estimation Modeling Techniques. In *Proceedings of the 21st International Conference on Software Engineering*, Los Angeles, CA, (pp. 313–322).

Briand, L., Langley, T., & Wiekzorek, I. (2000). A Replicated Assessment and Comparison of Common Software Cost Modeling Techniques. In *Proceedings of the 22nd International Conference on Software Engineering*, Limerick, Ireland, (pp. 377–386).

Brooks, W., & Motley, R. (1980). *Analysis of discrete software reliability models.* IBM Federal Systems.

Brownlee, J. (2005). *Artificial immune recognition system: A review and analysis* (Report No. 1-02). Melbourne, Australia: Swinburne University of Technology.

Bruce, W. S. (1995). *The Application of Genetic Programming to the Automatic Generation of Object-Oriented Programs.* Ph.D. Dissertation, School of Computer and Information Sciences, Nova Southeastern University, Fort Lauderdale.

Buehler, O., & Wegener, J. (2003). *Evolutionary Functional Testing of an Automated Parking System.* Intl. Conf. on Computer, Communication and Control Technologies (CCCT'03) and the 9th. Intl Conf. on Information Systems Analysis and Synthesis: ISAS '03, Orlando, Florida, July 31, August 1-2.

Buglione, L., & Abran, A. (1999). A quality factor for software. In *Proceedings of QUALITA,* Paris, France, (pp. 335-44).

Bugzilla homepage. (Last checked: October 2008). from http://www.bugzilla.org

Burgess, C. J., & Lefley, M. (2001). Can genetic programming improve software effort estimation? A comparative evaluation. *Information and Software Technology, 43*(14), 863–873. doi:10.1016/S0950-5849(01)00192-6

Burke, E. K., & Kendall, G. (2005). *Search methodologies–Introductory tutorials in optimization and decision support techniques.* Berlin: Springer Science and Business Media.

Cai, K.-Y. (1996). Fuzzy methods in software reliability modeling. In *Introduction to fuzzy reliability.* Amsterdam: Kluwer International Series in Engineering and Computer Science, Kluwer Academic Publishers.

Cai, K.-Y., Wen, C., & Zhang, M. (1991). A critical review on software reliability modeling. *Reliability Engineering & System Safety, 32*(3), 357–371. doi:10.1016/0951-8320(91)90009-V

Cai, K.-Y., Wen, C., & Zhang, M. (1993). A novel approach to software reliability modeling. *Microelectronics and Reliability, 33*(15), 2265–2267. doi:10.1016/0026-2714(93)90066-8

Carlsson, C., & Fuller, R. (1996). Fuzzy multiple criteria decision making: Recent developments. *Fuzzy Sets and Systems, 78*, 139–153. doi:10.1016/0165-0114(95)00165-4

Carlsson, C., & Korhonen, P. (1986). A parametric approach to fuzzy linear programming. *Fuzzy Sets and Systems, 20*, 17–30. doi:10.1016/S0165-0114(86)80028-8

Carolyn, M., Gada, K., Martin, L., Keith, P., Chris, S., & Martin, S. (2000). An investigation of machine learning based prediction systems. *Journal of Systems and Software, 53*(1), 23–29. doi:10.1016/S0164-1212(00)00005-4

Carter, J. H. (2000). The immune system as a model for pattern recognition and classification. *Journal of the American Medical Informatics Association, 7*(1), 28–41.

Catal, C., & Diri, B. (2007). Software defect prediction using artificial immune recognition system. In *Proceedings of 25th IASTED International Multi-Conference on Software Engineering, Innsbruck, Austria*, (pp. 285-290).

Catal, C., & Diri, B. (2007). Software fault prediction with object-oriented metrics based artificial immune recognition system. In *Proceedings of Product-Focused Software Process Improvement Conference (PROFES 2007), Riga, Latvia*, (pp. 300-314).

Catal, C., & Diri, B. (2008). A fault prediction model with limited fault data to improve test process. *Proceedings of Product Focused Software Process Improvement Conference (PROFES 2008)*, Frascati, Italy, (pp. 244-257).

Catal, C., & Diri, B. (2009). A systematic review of software fault prediction studies. *Expert Systems with Applications, 36*(4), 7346–7354. doi:10.1016/j.eswa.2008.10.027

Catal, C., & Diri, B. (2009). Investigating the effect of dataset size, metrics sets, and feature selection techniques on software fault prediction problem. *Information Sciences, 179*(8), 1040–1058. doi:10.1016/j.ins.2008.12.001

Cavano, J. P., & McCall, J. A. (1978). A Framework for the Measurement of Software Quality, In *Proceedings of the software quality assurance workshop on Functional and performance*, (pp. 133 – 139).

Cheon, Y., Kim, M., & Perumendla, A. (2005). A complete automation of unit testing for Java programs. In *International Conference on Software Engineering Research and Practice*, Las Vegas, Nevada, (pp. 290–295).

Chidanber, S. R., & Kemerer, C. F. (1994). A Metrics Suite For Objected-Oriented Design. *IEEE Transactions on Software Engineering, 20*(6), 476–493. doi:10.1109/32.295895

Chiu, N. H., & Huang, S. (2007). The Adjusted Analogy-based Software Effort Estimation based on Similarity Distances. *Journal of Systems and Software, 80*(4), 628–640. doi:10.1016/j.jss.2006.06.006

Claes, W., Per, R., Martin, H., Magnus, C. O., Björn, R., & Wesslén, A. (2000). *Experimentation in software engineering: An introduction*. Amsterdam: Kluwer Academic Publishers.

Coello, C. (2001). *Theoretical and Numerical Constraint-Handling Techniques used with Evolutionary Algorithms: A Survey of the State of the Art*. Computer Methods in Applied Mechanics and Engineering.

Coello, C. A. C. (1999). A comprehensive survey of evolutionary-based multiobjective optimization techniques. *Knowledge and Information Systems, 1*(3), 269–308.

Conte, D., Dunsmore, H., & Shen, V. (1986). *Software Engineering Metrics and Models*. San Francisco, CA: The Benjamin/Cummings Publishing Company, Inc.

Cortes, C., & Vapnik, V. (1995). Support-vector networks. *Machine Learning, 20*(3), 273–297. doi:10.1007/BF00994018

Costa, E. O., de Souza, G. A., Pozo, A. T. R., & Vergilio, S. R. (2007). Exploring Genetic Programming and Boosting Techniques to Model Software Reliability. *Reliability. IEEE Transactions on, 56*(3), 422–434.

Cote, M., Suryn, A., & Georgiadou, W. (2006). Software Quality Model Requirements for Software Quality Engineering. *Software Quality Management and inspire Conference (BSI),* (pp. 31-50).

Dandashi, F. (1998). *A Method for Assessing the Reusability of Object-oriented Code Using a Validated Set of Automated Measurements.* Ph.D. Dissertation, SITE, George Mason University, Fairfax, VA.

Davis, L. (1996). *Handbook of Genetic Algorithms.* New York: Van Nostrand Reinhold.

Davis, L. D. (1991). *Handbook of Genetic Algorithms.* New York: Van Nostrand Reinhold.

De Castro, L. N., & Von Zubben, F. J. (2000). The clonal selection algorithm with engineering applications. In *Proceedings of Genetic and Evolutionary Computation Conference, Las Vegas, Nevada,* (pp. 36–37).

Deb, K. (2001). *Multi-objective Optimization Using Evolutionary Algorithms.* New York: John Wiley & Sons.

Deng, J. (1989). Introduction to Grey System Theory. *Journal of Grey System, 1*, 1–24.

Department of Defense (1994). Military Standard Software Development and Documentation. MIL-STD-498.

Desharnais, J. M. (1989). *Analyse Statistique de la Productivitie des Projets Informatique a Partie de la Technique des Point des Function.* Unpublished Masters Thesis, University of Montreal, Montreal, Canada.

Doerner, K., & Gutjahr, W. J. (2003). *Extracting Test Sequences from a Markov Software Usage Model by ACO. LNCS 2724* (pp. 2465–2476). Berlin: Springer Verlag.

Dolado, J. J. (1999). Limits to the methods in software cost estimation. In Ryan C. and Buckley J. (Eds.), *Proceedings of the 1st International Workshop on Soft Computing Applied to Software Engineering,* University of Limerick, Ireland, 12-14 April 1999, (pp. 63–68). Limerick, Ireland: Limerick University Press.

Dolado, J. J. (2000). A validation of the component-based method for software size estimation. *IEEE Transactions on Software Engineering, 26*(10), 1006–1021. doi:10.1109/32.879821

Dolado, J. J. (2001). On the problem of the software cost function. *Information and Software Technology, 43*(1), 61–72. doi:10.1016/S0950-5849(00)00137-3

Dolado, J. J., Fernandez, L., Otero, M. C., & Urkola, L. (1999). *Software effort estimation: The elusive goal in project management.* Paper presented at the Proceedings of the International Conference on Enterprise Information Systems.

Donald, E. N. (2002). An Enhanced Neural Network Technique for Software Risk Analysis. *IEEE Transactions on Software Engineering, 28*(9), 904–912. doi:10.1109/TSE.2002.1033229

Dong, W. M., & Wong, F. S. (1987). Fuzzy weighted averages and implementation of the extension principle. *Fuzzy Sets and Systems, 21*, 183–199. doi:10.1016/0165-0114(87)90163-1

Dorigo, M. (2003). *The Ant Colony Optimization Metaheuristic: Algorithms, Applications, and Advances. International Series in Operations Research & Management Science (Vol. 57*, pp. 250–285). New York: Springer.

Dorigo, M., & Stutzle, T. (2004). Ant Colony Optimization. New York: Phi publishers.

Dorigo, M., Maniezzo, V., & Colorni, A. (1996). *The Ant System: Optimization by a colony of cooperating agents.* IEEE Transactions on Systems, Man and Cybernetics - Part B.

Dorigoa, M., & Stutzle, T. (2005). Ant colony optimization. [New York: Cambridge University Press.]. *The Knowledge Engineering Review, 20*, 92–93.

Doungsa-ard, C., Dahal, K. P., Alamgir Hossain, M., & Suwannasart, T. (2007). Test Data Generation from UML State Machine Diagrams using Gas. IN ICSEA 2007, France, (p. 47).

Driankov, D., Hellendoor, H., & Reinfark, M. (1994). *An Introduction to Fuzzy Control*. New York: Springer.

Eduardo Oliveira, C., Silvia, R. V., Aurora, P., & Gustavo, S. (2005). *Modeling Software Reliability Growth with Genetic Programming*. Paper presented at the Proceedings of the 16th IEEE International Symposium on Software Reliability Engineering.

Eduardo, O., Aurora, P., & Silvia Regina, V. (2006). *Using Boosting Techniques to Improve Software Reliability Models Based on Genetic Programming*. Paper presented at the Proceedings of the 18th IEEE International Conference on Tools with Artificial Intelligence.

Eiben, A. E., & Bäck, T. (1997). Empirical investigation of multiparent recombination operators in evolution strategies. *Computational Intelligence, 5*(3), 347–365.

Ekel, P., Pedrycz, W., & Schinzinger, R. (1998). A general approach to solving a wide class of fuzzy optimization problems. In Fuzzy Sets and Systems, (pp. 49-66).

Elaine, J. W., & Thomas, J. Ostrand & Robert, M. B. (2005). Predicting the Location and Number of Faults in Large Software Systems. *IEEE Transactions on Software Engineering, 31*(4), 340–355. doi:10.1109/TSE.2005.49

Elamvazuthi, I., Sinnadurai, R., Khan, M. A., & Vasant, P. (2009). Fruit sorting using fuzzy logic techniques. In N. Barsoum, A. H. Hakim & P. Vasant (Eds.), *Proceedings of the 2nd International Conference on Power Control and Optimization* (pp. 225-230). New York: American Institute of Physics.

Erradi, A., Maheshwari, P., & Tosic, V. (2006). Recovery policies for enhancing web services reliability. In *IEEE International Conference on Web Services, ICWS*, (pp. 189-196).

Evett, M., Khoshgoftar, T., Chien, P., & Allen, E. (1998). GP-based software quality prediction. In J. R. Koza, W. Banzhaf, K. Chellapilla, K. Deb, M. Dorigo, D. B. Fogel, et al (eds.), *Genetic Programming 1998: Proceedings of the Third Annual Conference*, University of Wisconsin, Madison, WI, (pp. 60–65). San Francisco: Morgan Kaufmann.

Evett, P., Khoshgoftaar, T., & Allen, E. (1999). Using genetic programming to determine software quality. In A. N. Kumar, & I. Russell, (Eds.), *Proceedings of the Twelfth International Florida Artificial Intelligence Research Society Conference*, Orlando, USA, May 1999, (pp. 113–117). Cambridge, MA: AAAI Press.

Fagerholt, K., & Christiansen, M. (2000). A Travelling Salesman Problem with Allocation, Time Window, and Precedence Constraints – an Application to Ship Scheduling. Intl. Trans. In Op. Res., 7, 231-244.

Far, B. H. (2005). Course Notes. *SENG 635: Software Reliability and Testing*. Date Accessed February 2005 from http://www.enel.ucalgary.ca/People/far/Lectures/SENG635/p1/02_files/v3_document.html

Farr, W. (Last checked March 2009). SMERFS3 homepage. Retrieved from http://www.slingcode.com/smerfs/downloads/

Feldt, R. (1999). Genetic programming as an explorative tool in early software development phases. In C. Ryan & J. Buckley, (Eds.), *Proceedings of the 1st International Workshop on Soft Computing Applied to Software Engineering*, University of Limerick, Ireland, April 12-14, 1999, (pp. 11–20). Limerick, Ireland: Limerick University Press.

Finnie, G. R., Wittig, G. E., & Desharnais, J. M. (1997). A Comparison of Software Effort Estimation Techniques: Using Function Points with Neural Networks, Case-based Reasoning and Regression Models. *Journal of Systems and Software, 39*(3), 281–289. doi:10.1016/S0164-1212(97)00055-1

Fishburn, P. C. (1964). Utility Theory for Decision Making. New York: Wiley publisher.

Fonseca, C. M., & Fleming, P. J. (1993). Genetic Algorithms for Multiobjective Optimization: Formulation, Discussion and Generalization. Genetic Algorithms. In S. Forrest, (ed.), *Proceedings of the Fifth International Conference*. San Mateo, CA: Morgan Kaufmann.

Fonseca, C. M., & Fleming, P. J. (1995). An overview of evolutionary algorithms in multiobjective optimization. *Evolutionary Computation, 3*(1), 1–16. doi:10.1162/evco.1995.3.1.1

Forman, I. R., & Forman, N. (2004). *Java Reflection in Action*. Greenwich, CT: Manning.

Gaffney, J. E. (1981). Metrics in Software Quality Assurance. In *ACM Annual Conference/Annual Meeting,* (pp. 126 – 130).

Gen, M., & Cheng, R. (1996). *Genetic Algorithms and Engineering Design*. New York: Wiley. doi:10.1002/9780470172254

Genero, M., Piattini, M., Manso, E., & Cantone, G. (2003). Building UML Class Diagram Maintainability Prediction Models Based on Early Metrics. In *IEEE Proceedings of the Ninth International Software Metrics Symposium.*

Gillies, A. C. (1992). *Software Quality, Theory and management*. London: Chapman Hall Computing Series.

Giovanni, D., & Mauro, P. (2002). *An empirical evaluation of fault-proneness models*. Paper presented at the Proceedings of the 24th International Conference on Software Engineering.

Glover, F., & Laguna, M. (1997). *Tabu Search*. Boston: Kluwer Academic Publishers.

Goel, A. L. (1985). Software Reliability Models: Assumptions, Limitations, and Applicability. *Software Engineering. IEEE Transactions on, SE-11*(12), 1411–1423.

Goel, A. L., & Okumoto, K. (1979). Time dependent error detection rate model for software reliability and other performance measures. *IEEE Transactions on Reliability, R-28*(3), 206–211. doi:10.1109/TR.1979.5220566

Goguen, J. A. (1969). The logic of inexact concepts. *Syntheses, 19*, 325–373. doi:10.1007/BF00485654

Goldberg, D. (1989). *Genetic Algorithms in Search, Optimization and Machine Learning*. Boston: Addison-Wesley.

Gonzalez, F. (2005). Comprendre l'approche orientée service. Saint Maurice, France: BG informatique.

Grabisch, M. (1996). Order additive fuzzy measures. In *6th Int. Conf. on Information Processing and Management of Uncertainty in Knowledge-Based Systems (IPMU),* (pp. 1345-1350).

Gray, A. R., & MacDonell, S. G. (1997). A comparison of techniques for developing predictive models of software metrics. *Information and Software Technology, 39*(6), 425–437. doi:10.1016/S0950-5849(96)00006-7

Gross, H.-G. (2003). An *Evaluation of Dynamic, Optimization-based Worst-case Execution Time Analysis*. Proceedings of the International Conference on Information Technology: Prospects and Challenges in the 21st Century, Kathmandu, Nepal, May.

Gross, H.-G. (2005). *Component-Based Software Testing with UML. Springer, Heidelberg. Holland, J. (1975). Adaptation in Natural and Artificial Systems.* Cambridge, MA: MIT Press.

Gross, H.-G., & Mayer, N. (2002). *Evolutionary Testing in Component-Based Real-Time System Construction*. Proc. of the Genetic and Evolutionary Computation Conference, New York, July 8–14.

Gross, H.-G., & Mayer, N. (2003). *Search-Based Execution Time Verification in Object-Oriented and Component-Based Real-Time System Development*. Proc. of the 8th IEEE Intl. Workshop on Object-Oriented Real-Time Dependable Systems, Guadalajara, Mexico, January 15-17.

Guerrouat, A., & Richter, H. (2005). Adaptation of State/Transition-Based Methods for Embedded System Testing. *World Academy of Science, Engineering and Technology, 10.*

Gunn, S. R. (1998). *Support vector machines for classification and regression. School of electronics and computer science*. UK: University of Southampton.

Guo, P., & Lyu, M. R. (2004). A pseudoinverse learning algorithm for feedforward neural networks with stacked generalization applications to software reliability growth data. *Neurocomputing, 56*, 101–121. doi:10.1016/S0925-2312(03)00385-0

Hammer, T., Rosenberg, L., Huffman, L., & Hyatt, L. (1997). Measuring Requirements Testing. In *Proc. International Conference on Software Engineering.* Boston: IEEE Computer Society Press.

Hannan, E. L. (1981). Linear programming with multiple fuzzy goals. *Fuzzy Sets and Systems, 6*, 235–248. doi:10.1016/0165-0114(81)90002-6

Harman, M. (2007). The Current State and Future of Search Based Software Engineering. In *International Conference on Software Engineering: Future of Software Engineering,* (pp. 342-357). Washington, DC: IEEE Computer Society press.

Harman, M., & Jones, B. F. (2001). Search based software engineering. *Information and Software Technology, 43*(14), 833–839. doi:10.1016/S0950-5849(01)00189-6

Haykin, S. (1999). *Neural Networks: A Comprehensive Foundation* (2nd ed.). Upper Saddle River, NJ: Prentice-Hall.

Heylighen, F. (2003). The science of self organization and Adaptativity. In *Knowledge Management, organizational intelligence and learning and complexity.* Boca Raton, FL: E. P. Ltd.

Hitz, M., & Montazeri, B. (1996). Chidamber and Kemerer's Metrics Suite: A Measurement Theory Perspective. *IEEE Transactions on Software Engineering, 22*(4), 267–271. doi:10.1109/32.491650

Ho, S. L., Xie, M., & Goh, T. N. (2003). A study of the connectionist models for software reliability prediction. *Computers & Mathematics with Applications (Oxford, England), 46*(7), 1037–1045. doi:10.1016/S0898-1221(03)90117-9

Hochmann, R., Khoshgoftaar, T., Allen, E., & Hudepohl, J. (1996). Using the genetic algorithm to build optimal neural networks for fault-prone module detection. In *Proceedings of the Seventh International Symposium on Software Reliability Engineering,* White Plains, Nov 1996, (pp. 152–162). Washington, DC: IEEE Computer Society Press.

Hochmann, R., Khoshgoftaar, T., Allen, E., & Hudepohl, J. (1997). Evolutionary neural networks: a robust approach to software reliability problems. In *Proceedings of the Eight International Symposium on Software Reliability Engineering,* Albuquerque, NM, (pp. 13–26). Washington, DC: IEEE Computer Society Press.

Holland, J. (1975). *Adaptation in Natural and Artificial Systems.* Ann Arbor, MI: University of Michigan Press.

Hollander, M., & Wolfe, D. A. (1999). *Non-parametric statistical methods.* New York: John Wiley and Sons, Inc.

Hu, C. F., & Fang, S. C. (1999). Solving fuzzy inequalities with piecewise linear membership functions. *IEEE Transactions on Fuzzy Systems, 7*, 230–235. doi:10.1109/91.755403

Huang, C. L., & Wang, C. J. (2006). A GA-based Feature Selection and Parameters Optimization for Support Vector Machines. *Expert Systems with Applications, 31*(2), 231–240. doi:10.1016/j.eswa.2005.09.024

Huang, S. J., Chiu, N. H., & Chen, L. W. (2008). Integration of the Grey Relational Analysis with Genetic Algorithm for Software Effort Estimation. *European Journal of Operational Research, 188*(3), 898–909. doi:10.1016/j.ejor.2007.07.002

IEEE Standard 982.2 (1987). Guide for the Use of Standard Dictionary of Measures to Produce Reliable Software.

IEEE. (1990). *IEEE standard glossary of software engineering terminology.* Technical Report 610.12-1990, IEEE, New York.

Inuiguchi, M., Ichihashi, H., & Kume, Y. (1990). A solution algorithm for fuzzy linear programming with piecewise linear membership functions. *Fuzzy Sets and Systems, 34*, 15–31. doi:10.1016/0165-0114(90)90123-N

Ioannidis, J. P. A. (2005). Why most published research findings are false. *PLoS Medicine*, *2*(8), 696–701. doi:10.1371/journal.pmed.0020124

Iseminger, D. (2000). *Com+ Developer's Reference Library*. Redmond, WA: Microsoft Press.

Jeff, T. (1996). An integrated approach to test tracking and analysis. *Journal of Systems and Software*, *35*(2), 127–140. doi:10.1016/0164-1212(95)00092-5

Jeremy, G., & Art, F. (2007). Data mining static code attributes to learn defect predictors. *IEEE Transactions on Software Engineering*, *33*(1), 2–13. doi:10.1109/TSE.2007.256941

Jimenez, F. G'omez-Skarmeta, A. F., & S'anchez, G. (2004). A Multiobjective Evolutionary approach for Nonlinear Constrained Optimization with Fuzzy Costs. *IEEE International Conference on Systems, Man & Cybernetics (SMC'04)*, The Hague, The Netherlands.

Jimenez, F., & Cadenas, J. M., S'anchez, G., Gmez-Skarmeta, A. F. & Verdegay, J. L. (2006). Multi-objective evolutionary computation and fuzzy optimization. *International Journal of Approximate Reasoning*, 59–75. doi:10.1016/j.ijar.2006.02.001

Jimenez, F., Gomez-Skarmeta, A. F., & Sanchez, G. (2004). Nonlinear Optimization with Fuzzy Constraints by Multi-Objective Evolutionary Algorithms. In *Advances in Soft Computing* (pp. 713–722). Computational Intelligence, Theory and Applications.

Jimenez, F., Sanchez, G., & Vasant, P. (2008). Fuzzy optimization via multi-objective evolutionary computation for chocolate manufacturing. In Kahraman, C. (Ed.), *Fuzzy multi-criteria decision making theory and applications with recent developments* (pp. 523–538). Berlin: Springer. doi:10.1007/978-0-387-76813-7_20

Jin, F., Yin, G., & Yang, D. (2008). Fuzzy Integrated Evaluation for Measuring Quality of Feature Space-Based Component Model. In *ICICSE Proceedings of 2008 International Conference on Internet Computing in Science and Engineering*, (pp. 349-354).

Jones, B., Sthamer, H.-H., & Eyres, D. (1996). Automatic Structural Testing Using Genetic Algorithms. *Software Engineering Journal*, *11*(5).

Jos, & Javier, D. (2000). A validation of the component-based method for software size estimation. *IEEE Trans. Softw. Eng.*, *26*(10), 1006-1021.

Juristo, N., & Moreno, A. M. (2001). *Basics of software engineering experimentation*. Amsterdam: Kluwer Academic Publishers.

Kachigan, S. K. (1982). *Statistical analysis - An inter-disciplinary introduction to univariate and multivariate methods*. New York: Radius Press.

Kai-Yuan, C., Lin, C., Wei-Dong, W., Zhou-Yi, Y., & David, Z. (2001). On the neural network approach in software reliability modeling. *Journal of Systems and Software*, *58*(1), 47–62. doi:10.1016/S0164-1212(01)00027-9

Kalaimagal, S. & Srinivasan, R. (2008). A Retrospective on Software Component Quality Models. *SIGSOFT Software Engineering Notes*, *33*(5).

Kanhe, S. (1975). A Contribution to Decision Making in Environmental Design. *Proceedings of the IEEE*, *63*, 518–528. doi:10.1109/PROC.1975.9779

Karunanithi, N. (1993). *A neural network approach for software reliability growth modeling in the presence of code churn*. Paper presented at the Proceedings of Fourth International Symposium on Software Reliability Engineering.

Karunanithi, N., & Malaiya, Y. K. (1996). Neural networks for software reliability engineering. In *Handbook of software reliability and system reliability*. Hightstown, NJ: McGraw-Hill Inc.

Karunanithi, N., Malaiya, Y. K., & Whitley, D. (1991). *Prediction of software reliability using neural networks*. Paper presented at the proceedings of the 1991 International Symposium on Software Reliability Engineering.

Kehan, G., & Khoshgoftaar, T. M. (2007). A Comprehensive Empirical Study of Count Models for Software Fault Prediction. *IEEE Transactions on Reliability*, *56*(2), 223–236. doi:10.1109/TR.2007.896761

Kemerer, C. F. (1987). An Empirical Validation of Software Cost Estimation Models. *Communications of the ACM, 30*(5), 416–429. doi:10.1145/22899.22906

Kennedy, J., & Eberhart, R. C. (1995). Particle Swarm Optimization. In *Proceedings of IEEE International Conference on Neural Networks,* Beijing, China, (pp. 1942–1948).

Khaddaj, S., & Horgan, G. (2004). The Evaluation of Software Quality Factors in Very Large Information Systems. *Electronic Journal of information system. Evaluation, 7*(1).

Khoshgoftaar, T. M., & Allen, E. B. (1999). Logistic regression modeling of software quality. *International Journal of Reliability Quality and Safety Engineering, 6*(4), 303–317. doi:10.1142/S0218539399000292

Khoshgoftaar, T. M., & Seliya, N. (2003). Fault Prediction Modeling for Software Quality Estimation: Comparing Commonly Used Techniques. *Empirical Software Engineering, 8*(3), 255–283. doi:10.1023/A:1024424811345

Khoshgoftaar, T. M., & Szabo, R. M. (1996). Using neural networks to predict software faults during testing. *IEEE Transactions on Reliability, 45*(3), 456–462. doi:10.1109/24.537016

Khoshgoftaar, T. M., & Yi, L. (2007). A Multi-Objective Software Quality Classification Model Using Genetic Programming. *IEEE Transactions on Reliability, 56*(2), 237–245. doi:10.1109/TR.2007.896763

Khoshgoftaar, T. M., Pandya, A. S., & More, H. B. (1992). *A neural network approach for predicting software development faults.* Paper presented at the Proceedings of the Third International Symposium on Software Reliability Engineering.

Khoshgoftaar, T., Allen, E., Hudepohl, J., & Aud, S. (1997). Application of neural networks to software quality modeling of a very large telecommunications system. *IEEE Transactions on Neural Networks, 8*(4). doi:10.1109/72.595888

Kitchenham, B. A., Pickard, L. M., MacDonell, S. G., & Shepperd, M. J. (2001). What accuracy statistics really measure? *Software. IEE Proceedings, 148*(3), 81–85. doi:10.1049/ip-sen:20010506

Kitchenham, B., & Pfleeger, S. (1996). Software Quality: The Elusive Target. *IEEE Software, 13*(1), 12–21. doi:10.1109/52.476281

Klir, G., & Folger, T. (1988). *Fuzzy Sets, Uncertainty and Information.* Upper Saddle River, NJ: Prentice Hall.

Koch, S., & Mitlöhner, J. (2009). Software Project Effort Estimation with Voting Rules. *Decision Support Systems, 46*(4), 895–901. doi:10.1016/j.dss.2008.12.002

Kordon, A., Smits, G., Jordaan, E., & Rightor, E. (2002). *Robust soft sensors based on integration of genetic programming, analytical neural networks, and support vector machines.* Paper presented at the Proceedings of the CEC '02 Proceedings of the 2002 Congress on Evolutionary Computation, 2002.

Kotanchek, M., Smits, G., & Kordon, A. (2003). Industrial strength genetic programming. In *Genetic programming theory and practice* (pp. 239–256). Amsterdam: Kluwer.

Koza, J. (1992). *Genetic programming: on the programming of computers by means of natural selection.* Cambridge, MA: MIT Press.

Koza, J. R. (1994). *Genetic Programming II: Automatic Discovery of Reusable Programs.* Cambridge, MA: MIT Press.

Kunal, V., & Amit, S. (2007). Semantically Annotating a Web Service. *IEEE Internet Computing, 11*(2), 83–85. doi:10.1109/MIC.2007.48

Kuri, A. (1998). An Alternative Model of Genetic Algorithms as Learning Machines. In *Expert Systems with Applications* (pp. 173–184). New York: Elsevier Science.

Kuri, A. (2002). In Coello, C., Albornoz, A., Sucar, E., & Cairó, O. (Eds.), *A Methodology for the Statistical Characterization of Genetic Algorithms, (LNAI 2313* (pp. 79–88). Berlin: Springer-Verlag.

Kuri, A., & Gutiérrez, J. (2002). In Coello, C., Albornoz, A., Sucar, E., & Cairó, O. (Eds.), *Penalty Function Methods for Constrained Optimization with Genetic Algorithms: a Statistical Analysis, (LNAI 2313* (pp. 79–88). Berlin: Springer-Verlag.

Lagaros, N. D., Papadrakakis, M., & Kokossalakis, G. (2002). Structural optimization using evolutionary algorithms. *Computers & Structures, 80*, 571–589. doi:10.1016/S0045-7949(02)00027-5

Langdon, W. B. (2008). *A Field Guide to Genetic Programing.* Published via http://lulu.com and freely available at http://www.gp-field-guide.org.uk

Laura Ignizio, B. (1991). Introduction to artificial neural systems for pattern recognition. *Computers & Operations Research, 18*(2), 211–220. doi:10.1016/0305-0548(91)90091-5

Leberling, H. (1981). On finding compromise solutions in multicriteria problems using the fuzzy min-operator. *Fuzzy Sets and Systems, 6*, 105–118. doi:10.1016/0165-0114(81)90019-1

Lefley, M., & Shepperd, M. J. (2003). Using Genetic Programming to Improve Software Effort Estimation Based on General Data Sets. In Cantú Paz, E. (Eds.), *GECCO 2003, LNCS 2724* (pp. 2477–2487).

Lefticaru, R., & Ipate, F. (2007). Automatic State-Based Test Generation Using Genetic Algorithms. In V. Negru, T. Jebeleanu, D. Petcu, & D. Zaharaie (Eds.), *Proceedings of the Ninth International Symposium on Symbolic and Numeric Algorithms for Scientific Computing*, SYNASC 2007, Timisoara, Romania, September 26-29, 2007, (pp. 188-195). Washington, DC: IEEE Computer Society.

Lefticaru, R., & Ipate, F. (2008). Functional Search-based Testing from State Machines. In *First International Conference on Software Testing, Verification, and Validation, ICST 2008*, Lillehammer, Norway, April 9-11, (pp. 525-528). Washington, DC: IEEE Computer Society.

Lehman, M. (1996). Laws of Software Evolution Revisited. In *Proc. 5th European Workshop on Software Process Technology*, (LNCS Vol. 1149, pp. 108–124).

Lesley, P., Barbara, K., & Susan, L. (1999). *An Investigation of Analysis Techniques for Software Datasets.* Paper presented at the Proceedings of the 6th International Symposium on Software Metrics.

Leung, H., & Varadan, V. (2002). *System modeling and design using genetic programming.* Paper presented at the Proceedings of First IEEE International Conference on Cognitive Informatics.

Li, H., & Lam, C. (2005). Software Test Data Generation using Ant Colony Optimization. In Proceedings of World Academy of Science, Engineering and Technology, (1), 1-4.

Li, H., & Lam, C. P. (2005). An Ant Colony Optimization Approach to Test Sequence Generation for State based Software Testing. In *Proceedings of the Fifth International Conference on Quality Software (QSIC'05)*, (pp. 255 – 264).

Li, P. L., Shaw, M., & Herbsleb, J. (2003). *Selecting a defect prediction model for maintenance resource planning and software insurance.* Paper presented at the proceedings of the Fifth Workshop on Economics-Driven Software Research.

Li, W., & Henry, S. (1993). Object-Oriented Metrics That Predict Maintainability. *Journal of Systems and Software, 23*, 111–122. doi:10.1016/0164-1212(93)90077-B

Li, Y. F., Xie, M., & Goh, T. N. (2009). A Study of Project Selection and Feature Weighting for Analogy based Software Cost Estimation. *Journal of Systems and Software, 82*(2), 241–252. doi:10.1016/j.jss.2008.06.001

Lionel, C. B., Victor, R. B., & Christopher, J. H. (1993). Developing Interpretable Models with Optimized set Reduction for Identifying High-Risk Software Components. *IEEE Transactions on Software Engineering, 19*(11), 1028–1044. doi:10.1109/32.256851

Lionel, C. B., Victor, R. B., & William, M. T. (1992). A Pattern Recognition Approach for Software Engineering Data Analysis. *IEEE Transactions on Software Engineering, 18*(11), 931–942. doi:10.1109/32.177363

Lionel, C. B., Walcelio, L. M., & Wust, J. (2002). Assessing the applicability of fault-proneness models across object-oriented software projects. *IEEE Transactions on Software Engineering, 28*(7), 706–720. doi:10.1109/TSE.2002.1019484

Liu, Y., & Khoshgoftaar, T. (2001). Genetic programming model for software quality classification. In *Sixth IEEE International Symposium on High Assurance Systems Engineering,* (pp. 127–136).

Lorenz, M., & Kidd, J. (1994). *Object-Oriented Software Metrics.* Upper Saddle River, NJ: Prentice Hall.

Lucas, S. M. (2004). Exploiting Reflection in Object Oriented Genetic Programming. In *European Conference on Genetic Programming.*

Lyu, M. R. (1995). *Handbook of Software Reliability Engineering.* New York: McGraw-Hill.

Magnus, C. O., & Per, R. (2002). *Experience from Replicating Empirical Studies on Prediction Models.* Paper presented at the Proceedings of the 8th International Symposium on Software Metrics.

Mahanti, P. K., & Banerjee, S. (2006). Automated testing in software engineering: using ant colony and self-regulated swarms. In *Proceedings of the 17th IASTED international conference on Modeling and simulation table of contents,* Montreal, Canada, (pp. 443 – 448).

Mahmoud, S. A. (2006). *State transition testing.* Retrieved from.

Mähönen, P. (2000). Fuzzy Classifier for Star-Galaxy Separation. *The Astrophysical Journal, 541,* 261–263. available at http://iopscience.iop.org/0004-637X/541/1/261/fulltext?ejredirect=migration. doi:10.1086/309424

Malaiya, Y. K., Karunanithi, N., & Verma, P. (1990). *Predictability measures for software reliability models.* Paper presented at the Proceedings of COMPSAC 90 Fourteenth Annual International Computer Software and Applications Conference.

Mantere, T., & Alander, J. T. (2005). Evolutionary software engineering, a review. *Applied Soft Computing, 5*(3), 315–331. doi:10.1016/j.asoc.2004.08.004

Markov, A. A. (1971). *Extension of the limit theorems of probability theory to a sum of variables connected in a chain.* Chichester, UK: John Wiley and Sons.

Martin, D. (2006). Putting web services in context. In *Electronic notes in theoretical Computer Science* (pp. 3–16). New York: Elsevier.

Martin, S., & Gada, K. (2001). Comparing Software Prediction Techniques Using Simulation. *IEEE Transactions on Software Engineering, 27*(11), 1014–1022. doi:10.1109/32.965341

Mathur, A. P. (2007). New Delhi, India: India Pearson Education. Biswal, B. N., et al. (2008). A Novel Approach for Scenario-Based Test Case Generation. In *IEEE ICIT conference* (1st ed.). Bhubaneswar, India: Foundation of Software Testing.

Matson, J. E., Barrett, B. E., & Mellichamp, J. M. (1994). Software Development Cost Estimation using Function Points. *IEEE Transactions on Software Engineering, 20*(4), 275–287. doi:10.1109/32.277575

Matsumoto, K., Inoue, K., Kikuno, T., & Torii, K. (1988). *Experimental evaluation of software reliability growth models.* Paper presented at FTCS-18, Digest of Papers, the proceedings of Eighteenth International Symposium on Fault-Tolerant Computing.

McCabe, T. J., & Butler, C. W. (1994). Software complexity. *Crosstalk. Journal of Defense Software Engineering, 7*(12), 5–9.

McMinn, P. (2004). Search-Based Software Test Data Generation: A Survey. Software Testing. *Verification and Reliability, 14*(2), 105–156. doi:10.1002/stvr.294

McMinn, P., & Holcombe, M. (2003). The State Problem for Evolutionary Testing. In GECCO 2003, (LNCS Vol. 2724, pp. 2488-2500). Berlin: Springer Verlag.

Mellah, H., Hassas, S., & Drias, H. (2006). A communication model of distributed information sources bacteria colonies inspired. In *10th IEEE International Conference on Intelligent Engineering Systems, INES'06,* London.

Mellah, H., Hassas, S., & Drias, H. (2006). Information systems self organization: Problematic, principles and methodologies. In *2nd International conference on Advanced Database Conference-IADC*, (pp. 170-175), USA.

Mellah, H., Hassas, S., & Drias, H. (2007). Towards a self organizing protocol for a Multi Agents System. In Proceeding IEEE of the sixth international conference on Networking ICN 07, (pp. 60-66), France.

Menzies, T., Greenwald, J., & Frank, A. (2007). Data mining static code attributes to learn defect predictors. *IEEE Transactions on Software Engineering, 33*(1), 2–13. doi:10.1109/TSE.2007.256941

Metropolis, N., Rosenbluth, A., Rosenbluth, M., Teller, A., & Teller, E. (1953). Equation of State Calculations by Fast Computing Machines. *The Journal of Chemical Physics, 21*(6), 1087–1092. doi:10.1063/1.1699114

Michael, C., McGraw, G., & Schatz, M. A. (2001). Generating software test data by evolution. *IEEE Transactions on Software Engineering, 27*(12), 1085–1110. doi:10.1109/32.988709

Michael, R. L., & Allen, N. (1992). Applying Reliability Models More Effectively. *IEEE Software, 9*(4), 43–52. doi:10.1109/52.143104

Michalewicz, Z. (1993). A hierarchy of evolution programs: An experimental study. *Evolutionary Computation, 1*(1), 51–76. doi:10.1162/evco.1993.1.1.51

Michalewicz, Z. (1996). *Genetic Algorithms + data structures = evolution programs.* Berlin: Springer-Verlag.

Mitchell, M. (1996). *Introduction to Genetic Algorithms.* Cambridge, MA: MIT Press.

Mitchell, M., Forrest, S., & Holland, J. (1992). The Royal Road for genetic algorithms: Fitness Landscapes and GA Performance. In F.J. Varela & P. Bourgine, (eds.), *Toward a practice of autonomous Systems: Proceedings of the First European Conference on Artificial Life.* Cambridge, MA: MIT Press.

Mohan, V. & Jeya, M. (2008). Intelligent ester –Test Sequence Optimization framework using Multi-Agents. *Journal of computers, 3*(6).

Mohan, V., & Jeya, M. (2007). Intelligent ester – Software Test Sequence Optimization Using Graph Based Intelligent Search Agent. In *Proceedings of the International Conference on Computational Intelligence and Multimedia Applications (ICCIMA 2007),* (Vol. 01, pp. 22-27).

Montana, D. J. (1993). Strongly typed genetic programming. Technical Report #7866, Cambridge, MA, 02138.

Moon, C., Kim, J., Choi, G., & Seo, Y. (2002). An Efficient Genetic Algorithm for the Traveling Salesman Problem with Precedence Constraints. *European Journal of Operational Research, 140,* 606–617. doi:10.1016/S0377-2217(01)00227-2

Müller, R., Lembeck, C., & Kuchen, H. (2004). A symbolic Java virtual machine for test-case generation. In *Proceedings IASTED Conference on Software Engineering,* (pp. 365—371).

Muhlenbein, H. (1991). Evolution in Time and Space. In Rawlins, G. (Ed.), *The Parallel Genetic Algorithm and Foundations of Genetic Algorithms* (pp. 316–337). San Francisco: Morgan Kaufmann.

Munson, J. C., & Khoshgoftaar, T. M. (1992). The detection of fault-prone programs. *IEEE Transactions on Software Engineering, 18*(5), 423–433. doi:10.1109/32.135775

Murofushi, T., & Sugeno, M. (1989). An interpretation of fuzzy measure and the Choquet integral as an integral with respect to a fuzzy measure. *Fuzzy Sets and Systems, 29,* 201–227. doi:10.1016/0165-0114(89)90194-2

Musa, J. (1998). *Software Reliability Engineering.* New York: McGraw-Hill.

Musa, J. D., Iannino, A., & Okumoto, K. (1987). *Software Reliability: Measurement, Prediction, Applications.* New York: McGraw-Hill.

Nachimuthu, K., Darrell, W., & Yashwant, K. M. (1992). Prediction of Software Reliability Using Connectionist Models. *IEEE Transactions on Software Engineering, 18*(7), 563–574. doi:10.1109/32.148475

Nachimuthu, K., Darrell, W., & Yashwant, K. M. (1992). Using Neural Networks in Reliability Prediction. *IEEE Software, 9*(4), 53–59. doi:10.1109/52.143107

NASA Software Assurance guidebook (1989). *NASA GSFC MD, Office of Safety and Mission Assurance.*

Niclas, O., & Hans, A. (1996). Predicting Fault-Prone Software Modules in Telephone Switches. *IEEE Transactions on Software Engineering, 22*(12), 886–894. doi:10.1109/32.553637

Niclas, O., Ann Christin, E., & Mary, H. (1997). Early Risk-Management by Identification of Fault-prone Modules. *Empirical Software Engineering, 2*(2), 166–173. doi:10.1023/A:1009757419320

Niclas, O., Ming, Z., & Mary, H. (1998). Application of multivariate analysis for software fault prediction. *Software Quality Control, 7*(1), 51–66. doi:10.1023/A:1008844909795

Nidhi, G., & Manu Pratap, S. (2005). Estimation of software reliability with execution time model using the pattern mapping technique of artificial neural network. *Computers & Operations Research, 32*(1), 187–199. doi:10.1016/S0305-0548(03)00212-0

Nikora, A. P. (2009). *CASRE homepage.* Retrieved from http://www.openchannelfoundation.org/projects/CASRE_3.0

Nikora, A. P., & Lyu, M. R. (1995). *An experiment in determining software reliability model applicability.* Paper presented at the Proceedings of the Sixth International Symposium on Software Reliability Engineering.

Novák, V. Perfilieva, Močkoř, J. (1999). Mathematical principles of fuzzy logic. Dodrecht, The Netherlands: Kluwer Academic.

Nowakowska, N. (1977). Methodological problems of measurement of fuzzy concepts in the social sciences. *Behavioral Science, 22*, 107–115. doi:10.1002/bs.3830220205

Offutt, J., & Abdurazik, A. (1999). *Generating Tests from UML Specifications.* Presented at 2nd International Conference on the UML. Ayari, K., Bouktif, S. & Antoniol, G. (2007). Automatic Mutation Test Input Data Generation via Ant Colony. In *Genetic and Evolutionary Computation Conference*, London. Copeland, L. (2004). *A Practitioner's Guide to Software Test Design.* Boston: Artech House Publishers.

Oliveira, A. L. I. (2006). Estimation of Software Project Effort with Support Vector Regression. *Neurocomputing, 69*(13-15), 1749–1753. doi:10.1016/j.neucom.2005.12.119

OMG. (2003). *OMG Unified Modeling Language Superstructure* (version 2.1).

Padhy, N. P. (2005). *Artificial Intelligence and Intelligent System.* Oxford, UK: Oxford press.

Palathingal, P., & Chandra, S. (2004). Agent Approach for Service Discovery and Utilization. In *Proceedings of the 37th Hawaii International Conference on System Sciences,* Hawaii.

Palu, S. (Last checked November 2008). *Instance-based learning: A Java implementation.* Retrieved from http://www.developer.com/java/other/article.php/10936_1491651_1

Pargas, R., Harrold, M., & Peck, R. (1999). Test-data generation using genetic algorithms. *Software Testing. Verification and Reliability, 9*(4), 263–282. doi:10.1002/(SICI)1099-1689(199912)9:4<263::AID-STVR190>3.0.CO;2-Y

Parlos, A. G., Fernandez, B., Atyla, A., Muthusami, J., & Tsai, W. (1994). An Accelerated Algorithm for Multilayer Preceptor Networks. *IEEE Transactions on Neural Networks, 5*(3), 493–497. doi:10.1109/72.286921

Pat, P., Lyu, M., & Malek, M. (2006). Making services fault tolerant. In Penkler, D., Reitenspiess, M., & Tam, F. (Eds.), *ISAS 2006* (pp. 43–61). Berlin: Springer Verlag.

Paul Luo, L., Mary, S., Jim, H., Bonnie, R., & Santhanam, P. (2004). *Empirical evaluation of defect projection models for widely-deployed production software systems*. Paper presented at the Proceedings of the 12th ACM SIGSOFT twelfth international symposium on Foundations of software engineering.

Pedrycz, W. (1993). *Fuzzy Control and Fuzzy Systems*. New York: John Wiley & Sons.

Pedrycz, W., & Peters, J. F. (1998). *Computational Intelligence in Software Engineering*. Singapore: World Scientific Publishers.

Peidro, D., & Vasant, P. (2009). Fuzzy multi-objective transportation planning with modified S-curve membership function. In N. Barsoum, A. H. Hakim & P. Vasant (Eds.), *Proceedings of the 2nd International Conference on Power Control and Optimization* (pp. 231-239). New York: American Institute of Physics.

Peltz, C. (2003). Web Services Orchestration and Choreography. *Computer, 26*(10), 46–52. doi:10.1109/MC.2003.1236471

Peneva, V., & Popchev, I. (2002). *Fuzzy Multicriteria Decision Making*. Cybernetics and.

Pratap, S. A. (2008). An Integrated Fuzzy Approach to Assess Water Resources' Potential in a Watershed. *Icfai Journal of Computational Fluid Mathematics, 1*(1), 7–23.

Pratap, S. A., & Vidarthi, A. K. (2008). Optimal allocation of landfill disposal site: A fuzzy multi-criteria approach. *Iranian Journal of Environmental Health Science & Engineering, 5*(1), 25–34.

Pressman, R. S. (2005). *Software engineering: A Practitioner's Approach* (6th ed.). India: TMH.

Raj Kiran, N., & Ravi, V. (2008). Software reliability prediction by soft computing techniques. *Journal of Systems and Software, 81*(4), 576–583. doi:10.1016/j.jss.2007.05.005

Ramanna, S., Peters, J., & Ahn, T. (2002). Software quality knowledge discovery: a rough set approach. In *Proceedings 26th Annual International Computer Software and Applications*, (pp. 1140–1145). Los Alamitos, CA: IEEE Computer Soc.

Ramik, J., & Vlach, M. (2002). A unified Approach Based on Fuzzy Relations. In *Fuzzy Optimization and Decision Making* (pp. 335–346). Fuzzy Mathematical Programming.

Raymond, E. S. (1999). Cathedral and the bazaar. Sebastopol, CA: O'Reily & Associates.

Reformat, M., Pedrycz, W., & Pizzi, N. J. (2003). Software quality analysis with the use of computational intelligence. *Information and Software Technology, 45*(7), 405–417. doi:10.1016/S0950-5849(03)00012-0

Rennard, J.-P. (2002). *Vie Artificielle où la biologie rencontre l'informatique*. Vuibert.

Ribeiro, J. C. B., Rela, M. Z., & de Vega, F. F. (2007). *An Evolutionary Approach for Performing Structural Unit-Testing on Third-Party Object-Oriented Java Software* (pp. 379–388). NICSO.

Ribeiro, J. C., Zenha-Rela, M., & de Vega, F. F. (2008). An Evolutionary Approach for Performing Structural Unit-Testing on Third-Party Object-Oriented Java Software. In *Studies in Computational Intelligence (Vol. 129)*. Heidelberg, Germany: Springer.

Rosenberg, L., & Hammer, T. (1998). Metrics for Quality Assurance and Risk Assessment. In *Proc. Eleventh International Software Quality Week*, San Francisco, CA.

Rosenberg, L., Hammer, T., & Shaw, J. (1998). Software Metrics and Reliability (ISSRE 1998 Best Paper). *IEEE International Symposium on Software Reliability Engineering*.

Roy, B. (1971). Problems and Methods with Multiple Objective Functions. *Mathematical Programming, 1*, 239–266. doi:10.1007/BF01584088

Rudolph, G., Convergence Analysis of Canonical Genetic Algorithms, (1994). *IEEE Transactions on Neural Networks, 5*(1), 96-101. doi:10.1109/72.265964

Rumelhart, D. E., Hinton, G. E., & Williams, R. J. (1988). Learning representations by back-propagating errors. In *Neurocomputing: foundations of research,* (pp. 696-699).

Russell, S., & Norvig, P. (2003). *Artificial intelligence-A modern approach.* New York: Prentice Hall Series in Artificial Intelligence.

Ruszczynski, A. (2006). *Nonlinear Optimization.* Princeton, NJ: Princeton University Press.

Sakawa, M. (1983). Interactive computer program for fuzzy linear programming with multiple objectives. *J. Man-Machine Stud, 18,* 489–503. doi:10.1016/S0020-7373(83)80022-4

Salcianu, A., & Rinard, M. (2004). *A combined pointer and purity analysis for java programs.* Technical Report MIT-CSAIL-TR-949, Massachusetts Institute of Technology.

Sapna, P. G., & Mohanty, H. (2008). Automated Scenario Generation based on UML Activity Diagrams. In *International Conference on Information Technology(ICIT),* Bhubaneswar, India, (pp 209-214).

Sarah, B., & Bev, L. (1996). Techniques for prediction analysis and recalibration. In *Handbook of software reliability engineering* (pp. 119–166). New York: McGraw-Hill, Inc.

Satyananda Reddy, C., & Raju, K. V. S. V. N. (2009). An Improved Fuzzy Approach for COCOMO's Effort Estimation Using Gaussian Membership Function. *Journal of Software, 4*(5), 452–459.

Schach, S. R. (2002). *Object-Oriented and Classical Software Engineering* (5th ed.). New York: McGraw-Hill.

Schmeidler, D. (1989). Subjective probability and expected utility without additivity. *Econometrica, 57*(3), 571–587. doi:10.2307/1911053

Schwefel, H. P., & Männer, R. (1990). *Parallel Problem Solving from Nature.* Berlin: Springer.

Sean, L., & Liviu, P. (2006). A comparison of bloat control methods for genetic programming. *Evolutionary Computation, 14*(3), 309–344. doi:10.1162/evco.2006.14.3.309

Seesing, A. (2005, April). *An Overview of Automatic Object-Oriented Test Case Generation using Genetic Programming.* Internal Report, Research Assignment, EWI – Delft University of Technology.

Seesing, A., & Gross, H. G. (2006). A genetic programming approach to automated test generation for object-oriented software. *ITSSA, 1*(2), 127–134.

Seliya, N., Khoshgoftaar, T. M., & Zhong, S. (2004). Semi-supervised learning for software quality estimation. In *Proceedings of the 16th International Conference on Tools with Artificial Intelligence,* Boca Raton, FL, (pp. 183-190).

Sengupta, A., Vasant, P., & Andreeski, C. J. (2008). Fuzzy optimization with robust logistic membership function: A case study in home textile industry. In *Proceedings of the 17th World Congress, The International Federation of Automatic Control,* Seoul, Korea, (pp. 278-283).

Shan, Y., Mckay, R. I., Lokan, C. J., & Essam, D. L. (2002). Software Project Effort Estimation using Genetic Programming. In *Proceedings of International Conference on Communications Circuits and Systems,* Chengdu, China, (Vol. 2, pp. 1108–1112).

Sharma, A., Kumar, R. & Grover, P. S. (2008). Estimation of Quality for Software Components – an Empirical Approach. *SIGSOFT Software Engineering, 33*(5).

Shepperd, M., & Schofield, C. (2000). Estimating Software Project Effort using Analogies. *IEEE Transactions on Software Engineering, 23*(11), 736–743. doi:10.1109/32.637387

Shepperd, M., Cartwright, M., & Kadoda, G. (2000). On Building Prediction Systems for Software Engineers. *Empirical Software Engineering, 5*(3), 175–182. doi:10.1023/A:1026582314146

Sheta, A. F. (2006). Estimation of the COCOMO Model Parameters Using Genetic Algorithms for NASA Software Project. *Journal of Computer Science, 2*(2), 118–123. doi:10.3844/jcssp.2006.118.123

Shin, M., & Goel, A. L. (2000). Empirical Data Modeling in Software Engineering using Radical Basis Functions. *IEEE Transactions on Software Engineering, 26*(6), 567–576. doi:10.1109/32.852743

Shukla, K. K. (2000). Neuro-Genetic Prediction of Software Development Effort. *Information and Software Technology, 42*(10), 701–713. doi:10.1016/S0950-5849(00)00114-2

Silva, S. (2007). *GPLAB - A Genetic Programming Toolbox for MATLAB*. Retrieved from http://gplab.sourceforge.net (Last checked 27 February 2009)

Sitte, R. (1999). Comparison of software-reliability-growth predictions: neural networks vs parametric-recalibration. *IEEE Transactions on Reliability, 48*(3), 285–291. doi:10.1109/24.799900

Slaughter, S. A., Harter, D. E., & Krishnan, M. S. (1998)... *Communications of the ACM, 41*(8), 67–73. doi:10.1145/280324.280335

Smola, A. J., & Schölkopf, B. (2004). A tutorial on support vector regression. *Statistics and Computing, 14*(3), 199–222. doi:10.1023/B:STCO.0000035301.49549.88

So, S. S., Cha, S. D., & Kwon, Y. R. (2002). Empirical evaluation of a fuzzy logic-based software quality prediction model. *Fuzzy Sets and Systems, 127*(2), 199–208. doi:10.1016/S0165-0114(01)00128-2

Somerville, I. (2005). *Software Engineering* (7th ed.). New Delhi, India: Pearson Education.

Srinivasan, K., & Fisher, D. (1995). Machine Learning Approaches to Estimating Software Development Effort. *IEEE Transactions on Software Engineering, 21*(2), 126–137. doi:10.1109/32.345828

Srivastava, P. R. & Kumar rai, V. (2009). An Ant Colony Optimization Approach to Test Sequence Generation for Control Flow based Software Testing. *Information System, Technology and Management, Communication in Computer and Information Science Series*(CCIS), (Vol 31,pp. 345-346). New York: Springer Verlag.

Srivastava, P. R. & Kumar, K. (2009). An approach towards software quality assessment. *Information System, Technology and Management, Communication in computer and Information Science(CCIS)*, (Vol. 31, pp. 150-160).

Srivastava, P. R. (2009). *International Journal of Artificial Intelligence and Soft Computing, 1*(2-3), 363–375. doi:10.1504/IJAISC.2009.027301

Srivastava, P. R., et al. (2008). Generation of test data using Meta Heuristics Approach. IEEE TENCON 2008, India.

Srivastava, P. R., et al. (2009). Use of Genetic Algorithm in Generation of Feasible Test Data. *ACM SIGSOFT Software Engineering Notes, 34*(2).

Stefan, L., Bart, B., Christophe, M., & Swantje, P. (2008). Benchmarking Classification Models for Software Defect Prediction: A Proposed Framework and Novel Findings. *IEEE Transactions on Software Engineering, 34*(4), 485–496. doi:10.1109/TSE.2008.35

Storn, R., & Price, K. (1995). *Differential evolution - a simple and efficient adaptive scheme for global optimization over continuous spaces. Technical report*. Berkley, CA: International Computer Science Institute.

Storn, R., & Price, K. (1997). Differential evolution a simple and efficient heuristic for global optimisation over continuous spaces. *Journal of Global Optimization, 11*, 341–359. doi:10.1023/A:1008202821328

Stringfellow, C., & Andrews, A. A. (2002). An Empirical Method for Selecting Software Reliability Growth Models. *Empirical Software Engineering, 7*(4), 319–343. doi:10.1023/A:1020515105175

Susan Elliott, S., Steve, E., & Richard, C. H. (2003). *Using benchmarking to advance research: a challenge to software engineering*. Paper presented at the Proceedings of the 25th International Conference on Software Engineering.

Tabucanon, M. T. (1996). Multi objective programming for industrial engineers. In *Mathematical programming for industrial engineers* (pp. 487–542). New York: Marcel Dekker, Inc.

Tadashi, D., Yasuhiko, N., & Shunji, O. (1999). Optimal software release scheduling based on artificial neural networks. *Annals of Software Engineering, 8*(1-4), 167–185.

Taghi, M. K., & Naeem, S. (2002). *Tree-Based Software Quality Estimation Models For Fault Prediction*. Paper presented at the Proceedings of the 8th International Symposium on Software Metrics.

Taghi, M. K., Edward, B. A., Wendell, D. J., & John, P. H. (1999). *Classification Tree Models of Software Quality Over Multiple Releases*. Paper presented at the Proceedings of the 10th International Symposium on Software Reliability Engineering.

Taghi, M. K., John, C. M., Bibhuti, B. B., & Gary, D. R. (1992). Predictive Modeling Techniques of Software Quality from Software Measures. *IEEE Transactions on Software Engineering, 18*(11), 979–987. doi:10.1109/32.177367

Taghi, M. K., Naeem, S., & Nandini, S. (2006). An empirical study of predicting software faults with case-based reasoning. *Software Quality Control, 14*(2), 85–111.

Taghi, M. K., Yi, L., & Naeem, S. (2004). *Module-Order Modeling using an Evolutionary Multi-Objective Optimization Approach*. Paper presented at the Proceedings of the 10th International Symposium on Software Metrics.

Tamers, L. (2006). *Introducing Software Testing*. New Delhi, India: Pearson Education India.

Tanaka, H., Okuda, T. & Asai, K. (1974). On fuzzy mathematical programming. *Journal of Cybernetics,* 37-46.

Thomas, J. O., & Elaine, J. W. (2002). *The distribution of faults in a large industrial software system*. Paper presented at the Proceedings of the 2002 ACM SIGSOFT international symposium on software testing and analysis.

Tian, L., & Noore, A. (2004). Software reliability prediction using recurrent neural network with Bayesian regularization. *International Journal of Neural Systems, 14*(3), 165–174. doi:10.1142/S0129065704001966

Tian, L., & Noore, A. (2005). Dynamic software reliability prediction: An approach based on Support Vector Machines. *International Journal of Reliability Quality and Safety Engineering, 12*(4), 309–321. doi:10.1142/S0218539305001847

Tian, L., & Noore, A. (2005). Evolutionary neural network modeling for software cumulative failure time prediction. *International Journal of Reliability Quality and Safety Engineering, 87*(1), 45–51.

Tian, L., & Noore, A. (2005). On-line prediction of software reliability using an evolutionary connectionist model. *Journal of Systems and Software, 77*(22), 173–180.

Tian, L., & Noore, A. (2007). Computational intelligence methods in software reliability prediction. *Computational Intelligence in Reliability Engineering, 39*, 375–398. doi:10.1007/978-3-540-37368-1_12

Tibor, G., Rudolf, F., & Istvan, S. (2005). Empirical Validation of Object-Oriented Metrics on Open Source Software for Fault Prediction. *IEEE Transactions on Software Engineering, 31*(10), 897–910. doi:10.1109/TSE.2005.112

Timmis, J. (2008). *Collaborative bio-inspired algorithms.* Retrieved August 13, 2009, from www.artificial-immune-systems.org/courses/Lectures/lecture6.pdf

Timmis, J., & Neal, M. (2000). Investigating the evolution and stability of a resource limited artificial immune systems. In *Proceedings of Genetic and Evolutionary Computation Conference, Las Vegas, Nevada*, (pp. 40-41).

Tonella, P. (2004). Evolutionary testing of classes. In *International Symposium on Software Testing and Analysis (ISSTA)*, (pp. 119–128).

Tonella, P. (2004, July 11–14). Evolutionary Testing of Classes. In *Proc. of the 2004 ACM SIGSOFT Intl. Symposium on Software Testing and Analysis*, Boston, (pp. 119–128).

Tracey, N., Clarke, J., & Mander, K. (1998). The way forward in unifying dynamic test case generation: The optimisation-based approach. In *Proc. of the IFIP Intl Workshop of Dependable Computing,* South Africa, January.

Tracey, N., et al. (1999). Integrating Safety Analysis with Automatic Test-Data Generation for Software Safety Verification. In *Proc. of 17th International System Safety Conference*, August.

Triantafyllos, G., Vassiliadis, S., & Kobrosly, W. (1995, February). On the Prediction of Computer Implementation Faults Via Static Error Prediction Models. *Journal of Systems and Software, 28*(2), 129–142. doi:10.1016/0164-1212(94)00050-W

Tsoulos, I. G., & Vasant, P. (2009). Product mix selection using and evolutionary technique. In N. Barsoum, A. H. Hakim & P. Vasant (Eds.), *Proceedings of the 2nd International Conference on Power Control and Optimization,* (pp. 240-249). New York: American Institute of Physics.

Turabieh, H., Sheta, A., & Vasant, P. (2007). Hybrid optimization genetic algorithm (HOGA) with interactive evolution to solve constraint optimization problems for production systems. *International Journal of Computational Science, 1*(4), 395–406.

Turing, A. (1936). On Computable Numbers, with an Application to the Entscheidungsproblem. *Proceedings of the London Mathematical Society, 42*, 230–265. doi:10.1112/plms/s2-42.1.230

Utkin, L., Gurov, S., & Shubinsky, M. (2002). A fuzzy software reliability model with multiple-error introduction and removal. *International Journal of Reliability Quality and Safety Engineering, 9*(3). doi:10.1142/S0218539302000780

Uysal, M. (2008). Estimation of the Effort Component of the Software Projects Using Simulated Annealing Algorithm. In *Proceedings of World Academy of Science* (pp. 258–261). Buenos Aires, Argentina: Engineering and Technology.

Uysal, M. (2008). Estimation of the Effort Component of the Software Projects Using Simulated Annealing Algorithm. In *Proceedings of World Academy of Science* (pp. 258–261). Buenos Aires, Argentina: Engineering and Technology.

Van Veldhuizen, D. A., & Lamont, G. B. (2000). Multi-objective Evolutionary Algorithms: Analyzing the State-of-the-Art. *Evolutionary Computation, 8*(2), 125–147. doi:10.1162/106365600568158

Vasant, P. (2003). Application of Fuzzy Linear Programming in Production Planning. *Fuzzy Optimization and Decision Making, 3*, 229–241. doi:10.1023/A:1025094504415

Vasant, P. (2004). Industrial production planning using interactive fuzzy linear programming. *International Journal of Computational Intelligence and Applications*, 13–26. doi:10.1142/S1469026804001173

Vasant, P. (2006). Fuzzy production planning and its application to decision making. *Journal of Intelligent Manufacturing*, 5–12. doi:10.1007/s10845-005-5509-x

Vasant, P. (2008). *Hybrid optimization techniques for industrial production planning*. Ph.D Thesis, University Putra Malaysia, Malaysia.

Vasant, P., & Barsoum, N. N. (2006). Fuzzy optimization of units products in mix-products selection problem using FLP approach. *Soft Computing Journal, 10*(2), 144–151. doi:10.1007/s00500-004-0437-9

Vasant, P., & Barsoum, N. N. (2008). Hybrid genetic algorithms and line search method for industrial production planning with non linear fitness function. In N. Barsoum, S. Uatrongjit & P. Vasant, (Eds.), *International Conference on Power Control and Optimization* (pp. 278-283). New York: American Institute of Physics.

Vasant, P., & Barsoum, N. N. (2009). Hybrid simulated annealing and genetic algorithms for industrial production management problems. In A. H. Hakim & P. Vasant (Eds.), *Proceedings of the 2nd International Conference on Power Control and Optimization* (pp. 254-261). New York: American Institute of Physics.

Vasant, P., Barsoum, N. N., Khatun, S., & Abbas, Z. (2008). Solving non linear optimization problems with adaptive genetic algorithms approach. In *Proceedings of the 9th Asia Pacific Industrial Engineering & Management Systems Conference (APIEMS),* Bali- Indonesia (pp. 1549-1560).

Vasant, P., Bhattacharya, A., & Abraham, A. (2008). Measurement of level-of-satisfaction of decision maker in intelligent Fuzy-MCDM theory: A generalized approach. In Kahraman, C. (Ed.), *Fuzzy multi-criteria decision making theory and applications with recent developments* (pp. 235–262). Berlin: Springer. doi:10.1007/978-0-387-76813-7_9

Venkata, U. B. C., Farokh, B. B., Yen, I. L., & Raymond, A. P. (2005). *Empirical Assessment of Machine Learning based Software Defect Prediction Techniques.* Paper presented at the Proceedings of the 10th IEEE International Workshop on Object-Oriented Real-Time Dependable Systems.

Victor, R. B., & Lionel, C. B., Walc, & lio, L. M. (1996). A Validation of Object-Oriented Design Metrics as Quality Indicators. *IEEE Transactions on Software Engineering, 22*(10), 751–761. doi:10.1109/32.544352

von Laarhoven, P., & Aarts, E. (1987). Simmulatd Annealing: Theory and Applications. In *Mathematics and its Applications.* Dordrecht, The Netherlands: Kluwer.

Wang, H. F., & Wu, K. Y. (2004). Hybrid genetic algorithm for optimization problems with permutation property. *Computers & Operations Research, 31*(14), 2453–2471. doi:10.1016/S0305-0548(03)00198-9

Wappler, S., & Lammermman, F. (2005). Using evolutionary algorithms for the unit testing of object-oriented software. In *Proceedings of the 2005 Conference on Genetic and Evolutionary Computation,* (pp. 1053-1060).

Wappler, S., & Schieferdecker, I. (2007). *Improving evolutionary class testing in the presence of non-public methods* (pp. 381–384). ASE.

Wappler, S., & Wegener, J. (2006). Evolutionary unit testing of object-oriented software using strongly-typed genetic programming. In *GECCO '06: Proceedings of the 8th annual conference on Genetic and evolutionary computation,* (pp. 1925–1932). New York: ACM Press.

Wasif, A., & Richard, T. (2008). *A Comparative Evaluation of Using Genetic Programming for Predicting Fault Count Data.* Paper presented at the Proceedings of The Third International Conference on Software Engineering Advances.

Wasif, A., & Richard, T. (2008). *Suitability of Genetic Programming for Software Reliability Growth Modeling.* Paper presented at the Proceedings of the International Symposium on Computer Science and its Applications.

Watada, J. (1997). Fuzzy portfolio selection and its applications to decision making. *Tatra Mountains Mathematics Publication, 13,* 219–248.

Watkins, A. (2001). *AIRS: A resource limited artificial immune classifier.* Master Thesis, Mississippi State University. Retrieved from http://www.cse.msstate.edu/~andrew/research/publications/watkins_thesis.pdf

Watkins, A. (2005). *Exploiting immunological metaphors in the development of serial, parallel, and distributed learning algorithms.* Doctoral Dissertation, Mississippi State University. Retrieved from http://www.cse.msstate.edu/~andrew/research/publications/watkins_phd_dissertation.pdf

Windisch, A., Wappler, S., & Wegener, J. (2007). *Applying particle swarm optimization to software testing* (pp. 1121–1128). GECCO.

Witten, I. H., & Frank, E. (2005). *Data mining-Practical machine learning tools and techniques.* San Francisco: Morgan Kaufmann Publishers.

Wood, A. (1996). Predicting software reliability. *Computers, 29*(11), 69–77. doi:10.1109/2.544240

ISBSG. (2009). *International Software Benchmarking Standards Group.* Retrieved from www.isbsg.org

Koza, J. R. (1992). *Genetic Programming: On the Programming of Computers by Means of Natural Selection.* Cambridge, MA: MIT Press.

Lin, L., & Lee, H.-M. (2007). A Fuzzy Software Quality Assessment Model to Evaluate User Satisfaction, ICNC, (vol. 1). Dukic, L.B. & Boegh, J. (2003). COTS Software Quality Evaluation. In proceedings of ICCBSS, Ottawa, Canada.

OMG Unified Modeling Language Specification. (2003). Version 1.5, formal/03-03-01.

Yang, B., Yao, L., & Huang, H.-Z. (2007). Early Software Quality Prediction Based on a Fuzzy Neural Network Model. *ICNC, 1,* 760–764.

Zadeh, L. A. (1965). Fuzzy Sets. *Information and Control, 8,* 338–353. doi:10.1016/S0019-9958(65)90241-X

Zadeh, L. A. (1976). The Concept of a Linguistic Variable and its Application to Approximate Reasoning. *Information Sciences, 8*(I), 199–249. doi:10.1016/0020-0255(75)90036-5

Yager, R. R. (1978). Fuzzy decision making including unequal objectives. *Fuzzy Sets and Systems, 1,* 87–95. doi:10.1016/0165-0114(78)90010-6

Yamada, S., Ohba, M., & Osaki, S. (1983). S-shaped reliability growth modeling for software error detection. *IEEE Transactions on Reliability, R-32*(5), 475–478. doi:10.1109/TR.1983.5221735

Yongqiang, Z., & Huashan, C. (2006). *Predicting for MTBF Failure Data Series of Software Reliability by Genetic Programming Algorithm.* Paper presented at the Proceedings of the Sixth International Conference on Intelligent Systems Design and Applications - Volume 01.

Yu, T. J., Shen, V. Y., & Dunsmore, H. E. (1988). An Analysis of Several Software Defect Models. *IEEE Transactions on Software Engineering, 14*(9), 1261–1270. doi:10.1109/32.6170

Yu-Shen, S., & Chin-Yu, H. (2007). Neural-network-based approaches for software reliability estimation using dynamic weighted combinational models. *Journal of Systems and Software, 80*(4), 606–615. doi:10.1016/j.jss.2006.06.017

Zadeh, L. A. (1971). Similarity relations and fuzzy orderings. *Information Sciences, 3,* 177–206. doi:10.1016/S0020-0255(71)80005-1

Zebulum, R. S., Pacheco, M. A. C., & Vellasco, M. M. B. R. (2001). *Evolutionary Electronics: Automatic Design of Electronic Circuits and Systems by Genetic Algorithms.* Boca Raton, FL: CRC Press.

Zhan, Y., & Clark, J. A. (2006). The State Problem for Test Generation in Simulink. In *Proceedings of the 8th annual conference on Genetic and evolutionary computation*, Seattle, WA, (pp. 1941 - 1948).

Zhang, D., & Tsai, J. (2003). Machine Learning and Software Engineering. *Software Quality Journal, 11*(2), 87–119. doi:10.1023/A:1023760326768

Zhong, S., Khoshgoftaar, T. M., & Seliya, N. (2004). Unsupervised learning for expert-based software quality estimation. In *Proceedings of the 8th International Symposium on High Assurance Systems Engineering*, Tampa, FL, (pp. 149-155).

Zimmermann, H. J. (1976). Description and optimization of fuzzy systems. *International Journal of General Systems, 2,* 209–215. doi:10.1080/03081077608547470

Zimmermann, H. J. (1978). Fuzzy programming and linear programming with several objective functions. *Fuzzy Sets and Systems, 1,* 45–55. doi:10.1016/0165-0114(78)90031-3

Zimmermann, H. J. (1991). *Fuzzy Set Theory and Its Applications* (2nd Rev. Ed.). Boston: Kluwer Academic Publishers.

About the Contributors

Monica Chiş received her BS degree in Computer Science from Babes-Bolyai University, Cluj-Napoca, Romania in 1995. She is currently Project Manager at SIEMENS IT Solutions and Services, Romania. She was working in a private University in Cluj-Napoca, Romania as Senior Lecturer. Her research activities focuses on data mining, computational intelligence and swarm intelligence, applications of evolutionary computation in data mining, software engineering, software engineering and evolutionary computation, e-learning, time series data mining, social networks. She has published research articles in book chapters and conference proceedings. She served on the program committee for international conferences and she is additional reviewer for international conferences and journals. She has some important collaboration with foreign companies in the field of project management, research and data analysis.

***

Wasif Afzal is a PhD student in software engineering at Blekinge Institute of Technology (BTH), Sweden. He received his Licentiate (2009) and MSc (2007) degrees in software engineering from BTH. His current research focuses on empirical evaluation of different techniques for software fault prediction. In particular, He is interested in evolutionary computation approaches for software fault prediction. He has over two years of industrial experience in software quality and Software testing. He is a member of IEEE.

Baby is doing M.E. in Software Systems at BITS, Pilani.

Soumya Banerjee obtained his bachelor in engineering (B.E. (Hones)) degree in Computer Science from Regional Engineering College Maharastra, India and Ph.D. in Computer Science and Engineering from Birla Institute of Technology, Mesra, India. He has accomplished large-scale and medium software projects in different capacities in ISRO (Indian Space Research Organization), TTTI, ISI and Microsoft as participant, trainee and served as project leader in Cognizant Technology Solution, ICICI InfoTech both in India, south East Asia and Europe. Dr. Banerjee has 36 international journal and conference publications (peer reviewed) and 5 book chapters published from Springer, Germany, IEEE and IGI Global, USA to his credit covering bio-inspired intelligence, soft computing and optimization and Hybrid Scheduling. Dr. Banerjee is also developed a new bio-agent called as emotional ant for modeling and waiting for the patent and participating in Entrepreneurship development program at IIM Bangalore, India and Stanford tie up. He had recently developed 2 monographs from VDM-Verlag, Germany on knowledge sharing and E-Guided tourism on live projects and in the process of developing textbook on *Engineering C++ from Thomson learning International*. Dr. Banerjee has nominated and trained at prestigious Sun Guru Program, a specialized Solaris internal program conducted by Sun Microsystem, Bangalore, India in 2008. He is also a project participant and consultant in IRIDIA (*The National Lab of Computational Intelligence*), *Belgium, and Simula lab*. Norway. He was acting as head of the department of computer science at Birla Institute of Technology, International Center Mauritius. Dr. Banerjee is also leading several Govt. of India projects in opinion mining and sentiment analysis. He is also principal investigator for a recent DST (Department of Science and Technology, Govt. of India) based project of *Cognitive Modeling and Crowd Dynamics* worth of Rs/-10,000,000(INR) in Birla Institute of Technology, Jaipur, India. He is also in the process of getting different projects grants on sentiment analysis and opinion mining paradigm from Govt. of India.

Cagatay Catal received his BS and MSc degree in Computer Engineering from Istanbul Technical University in 2002 and 2004 respectively, and PhD degree in Computer Engineering in 2008 from Yildiz Technical University, Istanbul, TURKEY. He's been working for The Scientific and Technological Research Council of TURKEY (TUBITAK) since 2002 and currently he's project manager of a project which focuses on practical software fault prediction problems. He worked on several large-scale military and commercial software projects at TUBITAK since 2002. His research interests are Software Quality Engineering, Software Metrics, Software Architecture Design, Machine Learning, and Software Product Line Engineering. He served on the program committee for UYMS 2009, ISCIS 2009, ICSEA 2009, ISDE 2009, COGNITIVE 2009, ICCE 2006 conferences. He is a member of IEEE. Contact him at TUBITAK, Marmara Research Center, Information Technologies Institute, Gebze, Kocaeli, Turkey, 41470; cagatay.catal@bte.mam.gov.tr; +902626772634, www.cagataycatal.com

André Vargas Abs da Cruz got a BSc in Computer Engineering at the Pontifical Catholic University of Rio de Janeiro (1998), MSc in Electrical Enginnering at the Pontifical Catholic University of Rio de Janeiro (2003) and a DSc in Electrical Engineering at the Pontifical Catholic University of Rio de Janeiro (2007). Works as a researcher at the Pontifical Catholic University of Rio de Janeiro and has experience in Computer Science, with emphasis in genetic algorithms, computational biology and neural networks.

Habiba Drias has received the master degree in computer science from Case Western Reserve University, Cleveland OHIO USA in 1984 and the doctorate degree from Algiers USTHB University in 1993. She has directed the computer science institute of USTHB and the Algerian national institute of computer science –INI- for many years. She has over a hundred published papers in the domain of artificial intelligence, e-commerce, computational complexity and the satisifiability problem.

Robert Feldt is an associate professor of software engineering at Blekinge Institute of Technology in Sweden. He received an MSc degree from Chalmers University of Technology in 1997 and a PhD degree from the same university in 2002. His main research interests include software testing and verification and validation, automated and biomimetic software engineering, psychology of programming, user experience and human-centered software engineering. The research is conducted mainly through empirical methods such as controlled experiments, surveys and case studies, but also through technical and theory development.

Filomena Ferrucci received the Laurea degree in Computer Science (cum laude) from the University of Salerno (Italy) in 1990 and the PhD degree in Applied Mathematics and Computer Science from the University of Naples in 1995. She is an Associate Professor in Computer Science at the University of Salerno where teaches courses on Software Engineering. Her main research interests include software metrics and effort estimation, software-development environments, human-computer interaction, and e-learning. She has served as Program Committee member for several international conferences and she has been program co-chair of the International Schools on Software Engineering (2005-2009). She is co-author of more than 100 papers published in international journals, books, and proceedings of international conferences.

Tony Gorschek is an associate professor of software engineering at Blekinge Institute of Technology (BTH). He holds a PhD in software engineering and a Bachelor in Economics from BTH. Prior to, and in parallel with, his academic career Dr. Gorschek has worked as a consultant in industry and has also held the positions of CTO, chief architect, and project manager in a number of companies doing development of software intensive systems, totalling over ten years industrial experience.

Carmine Gravino received the Laurea degree in Computer Science (cum laude) in 1999, and his PhD in Computer Science from the University of Salerno (Italy) in 2003. Since march 2006 he is assistant professor in the Department of Mathematics and Informatics at the University of Salerno. His research interests include software metrics to estimate software development effort, software-development environments, and design pattern recovery from object-oriented code.

Thiago S. M. Guimarães got a BSc in Computer Engineering at the Pontifical Catholic University of Rio de Janeiro (…) and an MSc in Electrical Engineering at the Pontifical Catholic University of Rio de Janeiro (...). Has experience in Computer Science, with emphasis in genetic algorithms and software engineering.

Salima Hassas is a full professor at University of Lyon, where she leads a research group on multi-agents for complex systems modeling. She has supervised more that 15 PhD thesis and published more than 50 papers in the domain of Multi-Agents Systems and Self-Organisation. She is vey involved in many international conferences related to her domain of research (ACM AAMAS, IEEE SASO, SSS, JFSMA, ECCS, etc.) , where chez served as PC member, PC vice chair or co-chair of associated workshops.

Angel Fernando Kuri-Morales is an Engineer in Electronics by the Universidad Anáhuac in Mexico City. He got a M.Sc. degree from the University of Illinois and a Ph.D. from Kennedy-Western University. He is the author of five text books and more than 80 articles published in international magazines and conferences. He is a member of the National System of Researchers (SNI). He won an international prize for the best solution to the "Iterated Prisoner's Dilemma" during the International Congress on Evolutionary Computation in 2000. He has been included in "Who is Who in the World" in 1988, 1998, 2000, 2002, 2003 and 2007. He received the best paper award during the 7th Industrial Conference in Data Mining, Leipzig, Germany. He has been president of several International Congresses, and invited speaker in many national and international scientific events. He belongs to the Evaluating Committee in the Area of Computer Science of CONACYT (the National Council for Science and Technology in Mexico). He was founding partner of Micromex, Inc. and IDET, Inc. and Director of Applied Research in the Center for Research in Computation of the National Polytechnic Institute. He was member of the Board of IBERAMIA, and President of the Mexican Society for Artificial Intelligence. He is a Distinguished Lecturer of the Association for Computing Machinery (ACM) and member of the Scientific Committee of the World Scientific and Engineering Academy and Society (WSEAS). Currently he is Professor in the Autonomous Technological Institute of Mexico (ITAM) and Consultant for Grupo Nacional Provincial.

Prabhat Mahanti is a Professor in Computer Science at the University of New Brunswick, Saint John, Canada. He received Ph.D. (Indian Institute of Technology, Bombay, India), 1976, M.Sc. (Indian Institute of Technology, Kharagpur, India), 1971 B.Sc. (Calcutta University, India), 1968. Prof. Mahanti's research interests include: software engineering, software metrics, reliability modeling, modeling and simulation, numerical algorithms, finite elements, mobile and soft computing, and verification of embedded software, neural computing, data mining, and multi-agent systems. He has authored over 70 technical research papers and authors of 10 books including chapters. He has been the supervisor and thesis committee member of many Ph.D. and M.S. graduate students. Prof. Mahanti actively participates in numerous technical conferences as well served as conference chairs. Currently, he is on the editorial boards of the Computer and Informatics, Slovak Academy of Sciences, Slovakia, International Journal of Computing and ICT Research, Uganda, Africa, International Journal of Network and Distributed Systems, Inderscience Publication, Switzerland and, Journal of Computing and Information Technology, Croatia. He is as well editor-in-Chief of journal of Computers,Finland.

Hakima Mellah Charged of research at Research Center in Scientific and Technical Information(CERIST)_ information system and multimedia system department. She is preparing a Doctorat thesis at computing high school (ESI). Her researches concern interacting distributed and agile information system based on Multi-Agents Systems. Taking inspiration from natural phenomena information system, networks are more robust and agile especially by co_evolution and adaptation.

Rocco Oliveto received (cum laude) the Laurea in Computer Science from the University of Salerno (Italy) in 2004. From October 2006 to February 2007 he has been a visiting student at the University College London, UK, under the supervisor of prof. Anthony Finkelstein. He received the PhD in Computer Science from the University of Salerno (Italy) in 2008. He is currently a research fellow at the Department of Mathematics and Informatics of the University of Salerno. Moreover, since 2005 he is also contract lecturer at the Faculty of Science of the University of Molise. His research interests include traceability management, information retrieval, software maintenance, program comprehension, and empirical software engineering.

Marco Aurélio Pacheco got a BSc in Eletrical Engineering at the Pontifical Catholic University of Rio de Janeiro (1976), a MSc in Eletrical Engineering at the Pontifical Catholic University of Rio de Janeiro (1980) and a PhD in Computer Science at the University of London (1991). Has experience in Computer Science, focusing on Information Systems, acting on the following subjects: genetic algorithms, neural networks and neuro-fuzzy.

Federica Sarro received (cum laude) the Laurea in Computer Science from the University of Salerno (Italy) in 2009. She is currently a research fellow at the Department of Mathematics and Informatics of the University of Salerno. Her research area is Metrics and Estimations Methods for Software Development Effort Estimation, with particular interest in applying Computational Intelligence and Search-Based Techniques to build novel estimation model.

Ajit Pratap Singh is an Assistant Professor and Assistant Dean in Civil Engineering Group of Birla Institute of Technology and Science, Pilani, Rajasthan, India. He has more than 14 years of teaching and research experience in field of mathematical modeling, simulation and soft computing with its special emphasis on the application in Environmental Engineering and Sustainable Water Resources Management Groundwater Contaminant Transport prediction, assessment and management. He has published more than 26 research papers in different Journals and International conference proceedings of his area of interest. He has been actively involved in reviewing various research papers submitted in his field to Journals of International and National repute such as Journal of Water Resources Management, Springer, Journal of Environment Management, Elsevier, International Journal of Environmental Engineering Science (IJEES), and World Scientific and Engineering Academy and Society (WSEAS) conferences etc.

Praveen Ranjan Srivastava is working in computer science and information systems group at Birla Institute of Technology and Science (BITS) Pilani India. He is currently doing research in the area of Software Testing. His research areas are software testing, quality assurance, testing effort, software release, test data generation, agent oriented software testing, soft computing techniques. He has a number of publications in the area of software testing. He has been actively involved in reviewing various research papers submitted in his field to different leading Journals and various International and National level conferences.

Dilza Szwarcman got a BSc in Eletrical Engineering at the Pontifical Catholic University of Rio de Janeiro (1982), a MSc in Eletrical Engineering at the Pontifical Catholic University of Rio de Janeiro (1986) and a DSc in Informatics at the Pontifical Catholic University of Rio de Janeiro (2001). Works as a researcher at the Applied Computational Intelligence Lab at the Pontifical Catholic University of Rio de Janeiro. Her main fields of research are Computer Science, with emphasis in Graphic Processing, Distributed Systems and Computational Intelligence.

Richard Torkar received his BSc in computer science from University West, Sweden, and later the PhD degree in software engineering from Blekinge Institute of Technology, Sweden. He is currently an associate professor in software engineering at Blekinge Institute of Technology. He performs empirical research in software engineering in general, and software testing and software reliability in particular. His research focuses on applying different combinations of search-based strategies to software engineering activities.

Vageesh K. V. is doing PGP from IIM Calcutta; previously he received B.tech (computer science) at BITS, Pilani.

Pandian Vasant was born in Sungai Petani, Malaysia in 1961. Currently, he is a Lecturer of Engineering Mathematics for Electrical & Electronics Engineering Program and Fundamental & Applied Sciences Department at University Teknologi Petornas in Tronoh, Perak, Malaysia. He has graduated in 1986 from University of Malaya (MY) in Kuala Lumpur, obtaining his BSc Degree with Honors (II

Class Upper) in Mathematics, and in 1988 also obtained a Diploma in English for Business from Cambridge Tutorial College, Cambridge, England. In the year 2002 he has obtained his MSc (By Research) in Engineering Mathematics from the School of Engineering & Information Technology of University of Malaysia Sabah, Malaysia, and has a Doctoral Degree (2008) from University Putra Malaysia in Malaysia. After graduation, during 1987-88 he was Tutor in operational research at University Science Malaysia in Alor Setar, Kedah and during 1989-95 he was teacher of Engineering Mathematics at the same university but with Engineering Campus at Tronoh, Perak. There after during 1996-2003 he became a lecturer in Advanced Calculus and Engineering Mathematics at Mara University of Technology, in Kota Kinabalu. He became Senior Lecturer of Engineering Mathematics in American Degree Program at Nilai International College, Nilai (MY), during 2003-2004 before taking his present position at University Teknologi Petronas in Tronoh. His main research interests are in the areas of Optimization Methods and Applications to Decision Making and Industrial Engineering, Fuzzy Optimization, Computational Intelligence, and Hybrid Soft Computing. Vasant has published seven articles in national journals and another fifty in international journals and book chapters, and more than eighty in international and national conference proceedings. He has been serving on TC-9.3 (Developing Countries) as a group initiator and Vice Chair for Asia from September 2004 - July 2011. Currently he's a reviewer for some reputed international journals and conference proceedings.

Index